WRITING THE CLASSROOM

D1616098

WRITING THE CLASSROOM

Pedagogical Documents as Rhetorical Genres

EDITED BY
STEPHEN E. NEADERHISER

UTAH STATE UNIVERSITY PRESS
Logan

Published by Utah State University Press
An imprint of University Press of Colorado
245 Century Circle, Suite 202
Louisville, Colorado 80027

The University Press of Colorado is a proud member of
the Association of University Presses.

The University Press of Colorado is a cooperative publishing enterprise supported, in part, by Adams State University, Colorado State University, Fort Lewis College, Metropolitan State University of Denver, University of Alaska Fairbanks, University of Colorado, University of Denver, University of Northern Colorado, University of Wyoming, Utah State University, and Western Colorado University.

∞ This paper meets the requirements of the ANSI/NISO Z39.48-1992 (Permanence of Paper).

ISBN: 978-1-64642-291-3 (paperback)
ISBN: 978-1-64642-292-0 (ebook)
https://doi.org/10.7330/9781646422920

Library of Congress Cataloging-in-Publication Data

Names: Neaderhiser, Stephen E. (Stephen Edwin), 1978– editor.
Title: Writing the classroom : pedagogical documents as rhetorical genres / edited by
    Stephen E. Neaderhiser.
Description: Logan : Utah State University Press, [2022] | Includes bibliographical refer-
    ences and index.
Identifiers: LCCN 2022032109 (print) | LCCN 2022032110 (ebook) | ISBN 9781646422913
    (paperback) | ISBN 9781646422920 (epub)
Subjects: LCSH: Education, Higher—Curricula. | College teaching. | English language—
    Rhetoric—Study and teaching (Higher) | Literary form—Study and teaching (Higher)
Classification: LCC LB2361 .W75 2022 (print) | LCC LB2361 (ebook) | DDC
    378.1/99—dc23/eng/20220718
LC record available at https://lccn.loc.gov/2022032109
LC ebook record available at https://lccn.loc.gov/2022032110

CONTENTS

ACKNOWLEDGMENTS

Much like the genres explored within, this book does not exist in isolation. It is the result of conversations, collaborations, and inspirations from long before I ever sent out the initial CFP. I am extremely grateful to everyone who helped make *Writing the Classroom* a reality.

Most importantly, I want to acknowledge and thank the contributors in this collection, all of whom have affirmed and demonstrated how the genres of teaching deserve critical attention—for both pedagogical and scholarly merits. I valued all our conversations on the rhetorical complexity of pedagogical genres, carried out in the margins of manuscript drafts, through phone calls, and over video chats. I appreciated their commitment throughout the course of developing this collection, but I became even more appreciative when, in the middle of the process, the world seemed to grind to a halt with the advent of a pandemic. I am grateful for their dedication to ensuring this collection would be a success.

I also want to thank the team at Utah State University Press, especially Rachael Levay, acquisitions editor, whose early interest in the book and continued feedback gave me encouragement and guidance throughout the process. My most sincere thanks go out to our external reviewers as well, who gave constructive and supportive criticism through multiple iterations of the chapters, all to the betterment and strengthening of the collection as a whole.

I am also grateful to my academic colleagues, who acted as readers not of the collection itself but of the many genres that contributed to its formation—calls for proposals, acceptance emails, prospectuses, memos, and so many others. Special thanks go to Jayne Moneysmith, Katrina Bloch, Jen Cunningham, Aaron Toscano, and Angela Holzmeister, all of whose time, patience, and support were invaluable in making this edited collection possible.

WRITING THE CLASSROOM

Introduction
SHEDDING LIGHT ON GENRES
IN THE SERVICE OF PEDAGOGY

Stephen E. Neaderhiser

At first glance, a syllabus is just a syllabus. Many (if not most) of us in academia have created course syllabi, and we all certainly received our fair share as students ourselves. The syllabus's purpose seems fairly straightforward: to give an overview of a class's topic, expectations, policies, and activities. It is one of the first documents that students come into contact with at the outset of a new class, and it provides necessary information for how that class will operate. However, as a genre, the syllabus is far from simple. It doesn't just describe a class that already exists; it gives shape and definition to the classroom itself, articulating the teacher's vision of the dynamic that will emerge over the duration of the course. It becomes a constitutional document, outlining subjectivities and relationships for the shared classroom participants, and it gives students their first view of their teacher's identity as a professional, as an academic, and—perhaps most importantly—as a *teacher*.

Even outside of the classroom, that same syllabus represents potential engagement in other academic contexts where a teacher's professional identity and pedagogical activity are expressed, assessed, or influenced. The syllabus might, in fact, be operative in the course's very formation, as a university curriculum board may review it along with a course proposal before the class is approved. Alternatively, hiring committees may request sample syllabi as evidence of job applicants' past teaching experience and pedagogical approach, and reappointment/tenure review boards may ask for teaching observations to include commentary on an instructor's syllabi and other classroom documents as a way to ensure faculty are holding to departmental or university teaching standards. Separate from the students and classrooms for which a syllabus might be written, there are multiple other scenarios with different audiences

https://doi.org/10.7330/9781646422920.c000

interested in that syllabus—each with its own expectations, ways of reading, and intended outcomes.

What an example like the syllabus shows is that when faculty create
pedagogical documents, they are not only writing for the classroom—for
students—but also *about* the classroom for other academic scenarios and
audiences. They are composing the reality of that classroom, complete
with subjectivities associated with student learning and teacherly identity
while also being influenced by external factors ranging from disciplinary values to administrative mandates. It is this dynamic of pedagogical
genres, including classroom genres like the syllabus but also the many
other genres composed within academia for pedagogical purposes, that
is explored in the chapters collected within *Writing the Classroom.*

As the collection's subtitle indicates, pedagogical documents represent rhetorically complex actions, genres operating within a network
of academic contexts. This has implications beyond any single genre:
if we understand genres as shaping a discourse community, then
understanding the rhetorical nature of pedagogical genres can give
us insight into the academic pedagogical community. Furthermore,
by recognizing the rhetorical complexity of pedagogical genres, we
in turn support the practitioners whose academic and professional
identities are intimately tied to the writing they do in the service of
teaching: faculty instructors, departmental administrators, and even
graduate students in the process of developing their academic identities. When faculty create new courses and curricula, their ability
to promote that pedagogical work as a valued contribution to their
department and school can either be supported or constrained by
whether the documents reflecting that activity—such as course proposals or syllabi of record—are recognized as professional academic
activity, with implications for reappointment, tenure, and promotion.
When departments establish shared teaching practices, their ability to
give guidance can either be clarified or obscured by the documents
faculty members are expected to consult—such as policy statements or
teaching handbooks—when crafting their own classroom genres, with
implications for how faculty negotiate their membership within the
shared community identity while also asserting their own individual
agency. For graduate students, their ability to enter and engage the
academic community can either be endorsed or undermined by how
the documents showcasing their ability to teach—such as statements
of teaching philosophy or sample teaching materials—are understood
as representing not only their current experience but also their capacity to build their teacherly identity further, with implications for their

success at getting a job within academia. Clearly, pedagogical genres are more than just two-dimensional documents exclusively defined by static, functional purposes.

RHETORICAL GENRE STUDIES AND THE SITUATIONS OF PEDAGOGY

The contributors to *Writing the Classroom* explore how documents written for pedagogical purposes represent complex rhetorical genres that construct, reflect, and endorse teachers' professional activities and identities—within the classroom, but also outside of it. Such an exploration is made possible, in large part, by scholarship from rhetorical genre studies (RGS), inspired by Carolyn Miller's seminal 1984 essay, "Genre as a Social Action." In the decades since Miller established her titular thesis, asserting that genres are "typified rhetorical actions based on recurrent situations" (159), RGS scholars have contributed to how we understand genres as rhetorical, social, and situated actions that both shape and reflect the discourse communities within which they are used. Anne Freadman (1994, 2002) has identified the rhetorical and social interaction represented in a genre's "uptake," which she describes as demonstrating the ongoing call-and-response within a continuum of genres, with each genre anticipating—and prompting—potential responses that can be taken up and made real in the actions of subsequent or corresponding genres. Janet Giltrow (2002) has similarly provided insight into the dialogic nature of genres with her classification of "meta-genres," genres themselves that also coordinate—and regulate—the interactive potential between other genres within the same situated context. Further, scholars such as Amy Devitt (1991), Charles Bazerman (1994b), and Anis Bawarshi (2001) have presented genre case studies to investigate how systems and sets of interrelated genres inform and facilitate a variety of professional and public processes. As Bawarshi notes, recognizing the situated nature of genre isn't just a matter of identifying a static backdrop upon which a genre operates, but rather a way to understand "the sociorhetorical ecosystems within which communication and communicators take place and are made possible—the conditions that prompt us to write and that our writing makes possible" (2001, 78). Whether by showing how courtroom instructions construct—and complicate—the subsequent uptake of a jury's verdict statement (Devitt et al. 2003) or how the genre of the scientific article has evolved since the seventeenth century (Bazerman 1988), RGS scholars have shown that genres should not be underestimated or dismissed as static documents, neutral in transmission, with interchangeable scenarios or passive audiences.

Writing the Classroom draws on RGS as the prevailing theoretical framework for studying pedagogical genres, but the collection also responds to calls arguing that increased critical genre awareness is itself a pedagogical imperative. In fact, the intersection of genre and pedagogy frequently plays a part in RGS scholarship. Bawarshi (2001), Devitt (2004), and Mary Jo Reiff (2004) have each advocated for teaching genre awareness in the classroom, arguing it not only helps students learn to write specific genres but also enhances their critical awareness of the ideological frameworks that enable or restrict their ability to take ownership of the genres they are asked to write—now or in the future. Likewise, Elizabeth Wardle's (2009) proposal to shift the focus of first-year composition courses to "writing about writing" stresses the importance of providing students with critical awareness that will aid them in writing "the genres of the academy" (778), and subsequent scholarship on knowledge transfer has employed the concept of uptake as a way to consider how to teach transferable genre awareness (Rice 2015; Rounsaville 2012). Students have even been encouraged to examine pedagogical genres specifically, as a pathway toward genre awareness. Devitt, for example, describes having her first-year-writing students collect and analyze course syllabi, noting that such activities can "reveal [to students] much about expected language, tone, and content and show more clearly the ideology underlying the syllabus genre as well as the range of choices teachers can already make" (2004, 200).

In addition to considering how genre analysis can help students understand the choices involved with the act of writing, however, I and the many contributors to this collection believe it is vital to understand how genre shapes pedagogy itself—not just in considering how students take up genres as part of their education, but also in recognizing how teachers engage and negotiate with the genres of their teaching experience. As Devitt (2009) explains, it's essential that we practice what we preach—that the critical genre awareness we seek to foster in our students must be reflected in our own genred experience as teachers: "The first and most important genre pedagogy, then, is the teacher's genre awareness: the teacher being conscious of the genre decisions he or she makes and what those decision will teach students" (339). And even outside of genre studies scholarship, calls for the critical recognition of pedagogical genres commonly appear in the background of books and essays on topics ranging from faculty development to writing program administration (Alsup 2006; Desmet 2005; Franke 2010). Pedagogical genres may not always be at the forefront of such conversations, but they are often noted as playing instrumental (yet underacknowledged) roles in providing insight and agency within the academic experience.

Examining and understanding the genres used in and by a community can, as Carol Berkenkotter and Thomas Huckin (1995) assert, "reveal much about a discourse community's norms, epistemology, ideology, and social ontology" (25). This is certainly the case for academic institutions, as Bazerman (1994a) demonstrates in his illustration of the complex network of genres underpinning the classroom:

> There are genres that flow from the surrounding institutions into the classroom to regulate it; there are genres within the classroom that carry out the mandate of the regulation; and there are genres that flow out from the classroom that represent the work and competence of teacher and student, thereby holding them accountable to institutional expectations. It is our choice whether those definitions of the classroom and the genres that act out these definitions are wholeheartedly accepted, wholeheartedly resisted, compromised with, or sublated into some fuller understanding of our tasks. Whichever choice we make, we must consider the prices and responsibilities of our institutional places. (60)

Bazerman's description of the "flow" between genres presages Giltrow's characterization of meta-genres as the "atmospheres surrounding genres" (Giltrow 2002, 195). Furthermore, he highlights the implications associated with the pedagogical genres to which this collection seeks to draw further attention—both the genres located within specific academic settings (including the classroom) and the meta-genres regulating the flow of genres between those settings. By investigating the interrelated and rhetorical nature of pedagogical genres, not only can we identify and define the choices dictating our academic pedagogical practices, but we can also recognize and navigate the tensions existing within those decisions.

OCCLUSION IN (AND OF) PEDAGOGICAL GENRES

Even though RGS scholars often highlight the classroom as a nexus of genre and pedagogy, there is otherwise a noticeable lack of sustained discussion regarding the pedagogical genres that are regularly part of academic life. For example, in his book *Genre and the Invention of the Writer*, Bawarshi describes the syllabus's dominance in shaping and enforcing relationships between a teacher and students, alongside other classroom genres. He notes, however, that "it is curious that, as significant a genre as it is, the syllabus has received so little critical attention" (2003, 120). There is, of course, an abundance of literature on the syllabus, but the large majority of that literature qualifies as guides and advice texts describing the *form* of the syllabus, with only superficial attention to its rhetorical, situated context. They do not interrogate how the syllabus "frames the discursive and ideological site of action in which teacher and students engage in coordinated commitments, relations, subjectivities, and practices" (120). The rhetorical qualities of pedagogical genres have largely been glossed over in the literature of teaching, meaning we have at best a partial view of how those genres "flow" between situations and subjectivities (to recall Bazerman). We are also less capable of ensuring that the best practices of pedagogy are endorsed and perpetuated when new instructors or administrators are faced with the need to compose those genres for the first time.

When Carolyn Miller first presented her argument for genres being social actions, one implication she addressed was how this new approach broadens the range of genres that merit critical study—not just traditional or "classic" genres, like the apologia or public address, but also more quotidian de facto genres, like "the letter of recommendation, the user manual, the progress report, the ransom note, the lecture, and the white paper" (1984, 155). Miller's call to acknowledge the critical merit of genres otherwise overlooked is particularly relevant to the study of pedagogical genres. A parallel focus that recognizes the value of studying academic genres can be found in English for academic purposes (EAP) scholarship. Similarly inspired by Miller's formative essay but within the field of applied linguistics, EAP scholars have used genre study to investigate activity within academic discourse communities. Citing Miller's advocacy for de facto genres, John Swales (1990) argued that analyzing academic genres could potentially reveal valuable insights:

> As students and struggling scholars, we may learn that we may create a research space for ourselves, we may promote the interests of our discourse community, we may fight either for or against its expansion, we may uncouple the chronological order of research action from the spatial order of its description and justification, we may approach unexpected sources for funding, or we may negotiate academic or editorial decisions. (1990, 44)

EAP's impetus for genre study was further solidified by Swales's (1996) classification of the occluded genres of the academy that work behind the scenes to support scholarly activity, like the manuscript submission letter or book proposal.

> On one hand, they are typically formal documents which remain on file; on the other, they are rarely part of the public record. They are written for specific individual or small-group audiences, and yet may also be seriously

invested with demonstrated scholarship and seriously concerned with representing their authors in a favourable professional light. (1996, 46)

These genres are not public scholarship in and of themselves but are often instrumental in enabling someone to navigate the academic community, advance their professional identity, and produce scholarly work. EAP scholars have argued that occluded genres are vital components of the academic community and have applied Swales's analytical framework to the study of several such genres, including those supporting the publishing process, like manuscript submission letters (Shaw et al. 2014), reader review comments (Hewings 2004), and editor decisions (Flowerdew and Dudley-Evans 2002). Additionally, EAP scholars have analyzed how occluded genres operate as gatekeepers for new members within academia, in cases like graduate school application statements (Wang and Flowerdew 2016), letters of recommendation (Vidali 2009), and dissertation proposals (Cheng 2014).

However, despite the apparent level of interest in studying genres that underwrite the academic community, EAP scholarship has focused almost exclusively on academic *research* genres. In fact, this collection represents an effort to draw a parallel between the study of genres supporting academic *research* identities and the study of the genres supporting academic *pedagogical* identities. As I have argued elsewhere, many academic professionals embody both roles—scholar and teacher—yet the writing they do in the service of pedagogy is often occluded, much in the same way Swales describes occlusion in academic research genres (Neaderhiser 2016b). Genres of teaching often occupy a space between public and private: written for small groups or limited readers (perhaps only a classroom of students or a curriculum committee) but meant to enable a teacher to conduct the more visible work of pedagogy. While the classroom is often considered the face of teaching, as the primary location where teaching can be visibly witnessed, the pedagogical enterprise is much more expansive, spanning the many academic arenas wherein faculty represent their teacherly identities, promote and advocate for pedagogical values, and participate in decisions influencing policy and practice. In order to do these things, multiple genres are employed—some meant for direct classroom use, but others that occur before a class is formed or even afterward, as reflections of classroom activity for entirely external purposes. And, like the example of the syllabus I described at the start of this introduction, even genres recognized as primarily classroom-based may play a part in other academic venues extending beyond a single classroom. In recognizing these diverse scenarios and purposes, pedagogical genres can be "un-occluded" (as

EAP scholars have done for occluded research genres) and studied as academic genres that both facilitate and endorse teachers' pedagogical activity and, consequently, their professional academic identities. Acknowledging and prioritizing the value of analyzing occluded pedagogical genres is not just a theoretical matter. There are material concerns that directly impact teachers when the genres and context of pedagogy are occluded, especially when that occlusion potentially leads to pedagogical genres working at cross-purposes—a reality addressed by many of the chapters in this collection.

Select scholarship has already set the stage for a concerted inquiry into the occluded nature of pedagogical genres. Irene Clark's (2005) examination of assignment prompts highlights how teachers can use the genre to negotiate their identities as participant readers in student writing, and David Thomas Sumner's (2001) study of the syllabus shows how it offers instructors the opportunity to construct a sustainable pedagogical and disciplinary identity. Similarly, I have analyzed the statement of teaching philosophy as a pedagogical genre—external of the classroom—wherein both novice and experienced teachers negotiate tensions between the genre's value as a reflective document and its common use as an evaluative document in job searches and faculty reviews (Neaderhiser 2016a). Dylan Dryer (2012) has also explored how graduate teaching assistants might struggle with genres meant to reflect their identities as teachers while they themselves still identify as students. Dryer notes that these genres extend beyond "obvious" classroom teaching genres, like syllabi or assignment prompts, to include the many "smaller" genres teaching assistants must compose, like office announcements, student rosters, and grade feedback, all of which "help produce the identities of novice graduate students/novice composition teachers by operationalizing the routines and subject positions through which these students and teachers *become* learners and teachers" (442). Dryer argues for a critical understanding of pedagogical genres that "deroutinize[s] the practices such genres make commonsensical, transparent, or otherwise beneath notice" (442). It is this sort of critical genre awareness that *Writing the Classroom* endorses and promotes, with a purview encompassing not only classroom-centric genres such as assignment prompts, syllabi, or evaluative feedback, but also pedagogical genres that operate in the academic contexts of department or program administration, such as course proposals, departmental teaching handbooks, or policy statements.

This collection stands as a model of how pedagogical genres can be analyzed and recognized as rhetorical actions that (a) construct and endorse individual teacherly identity, (b) shape and reflect academic discourse communities, and (c) function within dynamic genre systems in multiple rhetorical scenarios. However, the contributors to *Writing the Classroom* are not content with simply proving that pedagogical genres warrant serious scholarly study. In addition to interrogating how the subjectivities of the teaching experience are constructed by and through genre, these chapters explore how those genres evolve, change shape, and even take on new dimensions as they come into contact with new voices and purposes. How, for example, are intentions of uptake complicated when institutional policy statements or administrative outcomes are applied not only to student audiences but also to the faculty expected to fold those statements into their pedagogical material? How do instances of a genre like the course proposal expand to address not only the pedagogical goals of a single department but also the interdisciplinary relationships within an institution? What happens when writers push the boundaries of genres meant to be guides or reflections of individual teacher development, like handbooks or teaching statements? Equally, what happens when pedagogical genres push *back* against efforts to add new intentionality or subjectivities to their purpose? These are but a few of the questions taken up within *Writing the Classroom* as a critical study of pedagogical genres, meant to benefit both experienced and beginning teachers while also contributing new insights to the broader theoretical frameworks of genre study.

CHAPTER OVERVIEW

The sixteen essays in this book explore a diverse set of genres that influence and reflect the pedagogical decisions, experiences, and identities of teachers both within the classroom and beyond its boundaries. By employing a variety of methodological frameworks, including corpus analysis, reflective narrative, and ethnographic study, the contributors show how our critical awareness of pedagogical genres is enhanced by different analytical approaches. Readers will recognize the influences of both RGS and EAP as the contributors investigate the influence of pedagogical meta-genres, questions of both student and faculty uptake, and issues of pedagogical occlusion. These essays, however, are not just an application of prior genre theory; in their analyses, the contributors draw on social and cultural theories, psychological and legal concepts, organizational studies, and professional writing scholarship to add new ways to understand the social and rhetorical nature of genres. In bringing these voices together, *Writing the Classroom* generates a critical dialogue that not only sheds much-needed light on the wide range of pedagogical genres within academia but also shows how the lessons learned by analyzing those genres can reciprocally enhance further genre theory and studies—both in the realm of pedagogy and beyond to the other academic and professional communities within which genres play fundamental roles.

Part 1 opens the collection with what might be considered the most traditional location of pedagogical genres: the classroom, a site where the construction of documents like syllabi or assignment prompts highlights the complex rhetorical work teachers often do to foster a space of learning. Michael Albright interrogates how the standardized or "common" syllabus transforms the syllabus genre into a "protected, read-only" document that withholds "layers of context" from the instructors required to use it—who are often themselves contingent faculty. Such a transformation, he argues, not only undermines those instructors' individual professional authority and pedagogical values within the classroom, but also alienates them from the broader teaching community with serious implications for their ability to showcase their pedagogical identity and activity in other academic contexts, such as in full-time faculty applications or teaching evaluations. Kate Navickas further reinforces the notion that pedagogical genres operate as a direct endorsement of a teacher's identity in her analysis of writing assignment prompts written by self-identified feminist teachers. Through her investigation of how those assignments assert subjectivities and arguments associated with feminist theory, Navickas shows the assignment prompt genre to be a crucial locus connecting teachers and students to "a particular academic genealogy and history," and argues that it is incumbent upon faculty to ensure the pedagogical values of their personal academic genealogy are visibly endorsed within the genres they intend to be taken up by students. Even though Navickas and Albright examine different genres, their analyses show how classroom genres like the syllabus or assignment prompt can either occlude or enable a teacher's ability to create pedagogical connections to both their students and the broader academic communities within which they seek to participate.

Critical genre analysis can also show how classroom genres act as a conduit for disciplinary values to manifest within a teacher's practice, as Virginia M. Schwarz demonstrates in her comparative analysis of the grading contract genre as it has emerged from assessment scholarship. Schwarz shows how rhetorical variations in the different models of grading contracts correlate with ideological frameworks that cast both students and teachers in significantly different types of roles, thus exposing a contested situational context that calls into question the genre's supposed stability. As she argues, the grading contract genre must be strategically negotiated in order to ensure pedagogical values and practices align with the genre's activity—by individual teachers as well as administrators and assessment scholars advocating for contract grading as a socially just practice. Jessica Rivera-Mueller explores a similar dynamic in evaluative feedback genres, using practitioner self-study to analyze grade feedback letters she wrote for students in her own teacher education courses. Through her reflective study, Rivera-Mueller considers how the feedback genre allows her to model a teacherly identity while also enabling her to inhabit a position of situated expertise and authority. However, she also observes how the genre can push back against individual pedagogical goals, when tensions arise between the genred expectation of authoritative evaluation and her individual desire to communicate a more intimate sense of supportive encouragement. Both Schwarz and Rivera-Mueller's insights demonstrate not only how teachers can utilize classroom genres to connect to broader disciplinary values, but also how those genres might resist efforts to negotiate new subjectivities beyond those imposed by external academic contexts.

Dustin Morris and Lindsay Clark return to the assignment prompt as a base of study, analyzing its activity in conjunction with grading rubrics, thus demonstrating how pedagogical genres don't operate in isolation but rather as part of a genre system that both supports teachers' pedagogical goals and generates student uptake. While the two genres' rhetorical moves are contextually situated at different stages of the writing process, with the assignment prompt initiating student uptake and the rubric dictating the subsequent assessment of the completed assignment, Morris and Clark show how the two genres work in concert to construct more complex subjectivities taken up by teachers and students mutually engaged in the holistic process of writing. In addition to exploring the interconnected nature of pedagogical genres within the classroom setting, their study highlights the risk of occlusion and its implications when that genred interactivity is left unacknowledged.

Part 2 continues to explore genres traditionally attributed to the classroom, but it also considers the scope of those genres *outside* of the classroom, where they often operate as meta-genres influencing the rhetorical contexts of other academic scenarios, such as curriculum review, faculty development, or administrative oversight. Amy Ferdinandt Stolley and Christopher Toth bring our attention back to the syllabus, but with a specific focus on the syllabus of record (SOR): a course's initial blueprint when added to the curriculum, often kept as an institutional record but rarely used within actual classroom settings. Through an account of their department's collaborative overhaul of SORs for accreditation review, Stolley and Toth show how the genre not only contributes to a course's continued pedagogical relevance but also can become a dialogic action representing the shared pedagogical values of a departmental faculty community. Similarly, Dana Comi explores how departmental teaching handbooks function as a meta-generic resource for new teachers in a graduate program. Comi combines genre analysis with discourse-based interviews to examine how the teaching handbook regulates graduate teaching assistants' relationships with the genres they use in the classroom, and how their uptake represents efforts to negotiate a balance between their developing pedagogical identities and their graduate program's community identity. As she demonstrates, an analysis of meta-genres like the teaching handbook reveals both the productive and limiting forces shaping initiate teachers' perceptions of such genres as generative resources, consulted guidelines, or the final word on what they are allowed to do (and *be*) as teachers.

Mark Hannah and Christina Saidy continue the focus on the meta-generic movement of pedagogical genres between institutional settings and individual classrooms, but from the perspective of program administration. Through a content analysis of policy documents, they explore how departmental policies broadly articulate shared pedagogical values, but also how such policies can become coercive pedagogical imperatives that inhibit individual teachers' agency and complicate students' uptake. Their findings also contribute to the broader study of rhetorical genre, with their identification of the "rhetorical bleed" that can occur within genre systems and the tensions that can result from that bleed. As a counterpart to Hannah and Saidy's chapter, Matt Dowell narrows the focus to examine policy statements specifically addressing disability accommodation and classroom accessibility through a purposeful analysis of accessibility policy statements—as well as the framing language that accompanies those statements within faculty teaching resources. He uses this analysis to examine how instructors are sanctioned for particular uptake options and how that sanction expresses itself in both senses of the term, with faculty constrained to specific social actions articulated within the policy statements while also being granted authorized allowances by the language describing how they are expected to include the policy within their own classroom genres like the syllabus. Additionally, Dowell draws on disability studies scholarship to show how these statements are not ideologically isolated but rather rhetorical social actions with ableist implications for students, instructors, and faculty administrators. These two chapters provide valuable insight and increased visibility for broader policy documents and individual policy statements, both of which are too often occluded not only in pedagogical contexts but also in the authorship by which they come into being.

Megan Schoen, Jim Nugent, Cindy Mooty, and Lori Ostergaard further demonstrate how pedagogical genres act as conduits between classroom and institutional contexts. Taking up both Carolyn Miller's notion of "homely discourse" and John Swales's concept of occluded genres, the authors study the genres used by instructors within a single writing program over the course of seven years—an important historical timeframe after the program transitioned into an independent department. Through a comparative analysis of syllabi and assignment descriptions, they show how those documents are more than artifacts of institutional history; they are genred agents of social action that forged a new academic identity for faculty within the program-turned-department. Alternatively, Lesley Bartlett explores the restricting impact of institutionalized assessment standards on genred uptakes, pedagogical practice, and culture. Drawing on her experience at a university that instituted curriculum-wide reflective writing requirements in response to state educational mandates, Bartlett examines how such mandates influence a system of genres broadly dictating the pedagogical practices endorsed by programs, taught by teachers, and taken up by students. Her investigation highlights tensions that can arise within a genre system that intersects multiple academic contexts, as well as how those tensions may be occluded to some stakeholders—and glaringly visible to others.

Last, part 3 maintains focus on the broader ecosystem of genres in academic contexts, but with attention to the genres that facilitate pedagogical activity and identity entirely outside of the classroom. Laura Micciche and Lora Arduser analyze the genred activity of curriculum development, based on their experience proposing a new certificate program within their department. They argue that even though the curricular proposal might seem a purely functional and stable "workhorse genre" with straightforward outcomes and uptakes, it is actually a "living document" exposing emotional tensions and pedagogical assumptions as it circulates through various academic communities involved in curricular review. Micciche and Arduser's analysis shows how the proposal genre can act as a destabilizing force, activating departmental anxieties about shared faculty identity while also stimulating administrative interest in pedagogical innovation. Similarly, Cynthia Pengilly focuses on the individual course proposal genre in her reflective account of developing a course that, during the process of curricular review, was challenged by another department. Pengilly recounts the ensuing process of collaborative revision, highlighting the genre's capacity as a negotiative site of interdisciplinary communication. Like Micciche and Arduser, she argues that the proposal genre, often occluded due to its routinized nature within isolated departments, holds destabilizing potential not only for the identity of an academic community but also for that of an individual teacher, when that teacher feels compelled to defend their pedagogical integrity as represented within the genre.

Megan Knight and Kate Nesbit continue exploring how occlusion impacts genres at the intersection of pedagogy and identity, in their study of the statement of teaching philosophy. Drawing on their respective experiences as faculty mentor and graduate mentee, they argue the teaching statement is a genre troubled by duality: it is meant to be both an experience of self-reflective discovery and an opportunity to prove pedagogical merit; it is expected to demonstrate teaching experience yet is often written by graduate students still learning to teach; it is an occluded genre rarely seen by more than a small group of readers, while also itself occluding the ongoing development of a teacher's identity. Rather than questioning the teaching statement's value (as some critics have), Knight and Nesbit instead recast the genre as a "learning to teach statement" that highlights the mutable and continuous process of evolution inherent to a teacher's pedagogical identity. Zack De Piero conducts a similar inquiry into how teachers' embodied pedagogies are reflected—and evaluated—in contexts outside of the classroom through the classroom teaching observation. By analyzing a diverse set of rubrics, forms, and guides meant to give direction for conducting classroom observations, De Piero constructs a layered, multidimensional portrait of the classroom observation genre, along with apparent tensions in its dual purposes of offering productive feedback to teachers and providing evaluative commentary to administrators. He also identifies the influence of what he calls perigenres: other pedagogical genres, ranging from syllabi to student course evaluations, that orbit the classroom observation genre, directly or indirectly determining perceptions of a teacher's pedagogical performance.

In a final return to curricular genres contributing to pedagogical identity, Logan Bearden argues that department or program outcomes statements function as a meta-genre whose uptake joins faculty, administrators, and students in a collective academic culture. Bearden traces the history of a single writing program as revealed in the successive stages of revision to its outcome statements, which led to productive changes in how teachers and students connected to institutional and disciplinary pedagogical imperatives. Furthermore, his analysis shows how faculty and administrators may redefine outcomes statements less as a genre that sanctions acceptable uptakes and more as one that acts as a transformative catalyst for cultural shifts in shared pedagogical and academic values.

* * *

The majority of contributors to *Writing the Classroom* come from backgrounds in rhetoric and composition, and many of them use the teaching of writing—in courses ranging from first-year composition to graduate teaching practica—as entry points for discussions of pedagogical genre. However, the insights provided by their analyses are not bound to the writing classroom or writing teacher: new and experienced faculty and administrators across disciplines can use these insights to gain perspective on how they craft the genres of their own pedagogical activity, professional experience, and academic identities. These are the genres that we all, as teachers, employ in our pursuit of pedagogy, and it is through analyzing these genres that we can better understand our goals as individual teachers, the values of our academic communities, and our collective efforts as advocates for both the manufacture and sharing of knowledge.

Moreover, these studies offer inspiration for further explorations of the genres that impact and embody teachers' pedagogical experience and identity, in ways that pursue new insights. The analysis of genres like the shared syllabus, policy statement, teaching handbook, and grading contract demonstrate how the study of pedagogical genres is relevant both to theories of genre study and to material practices that intersect with concerns of social justice, labor issues, and disability studies. While this collection opens that conversation, there is so much more that remains to be explored. It is our hope, then, that this collection serves as a resource not only for those who study writing and genre but also for the broader pedagogical community within academia, provoking conversations in graduate classrooms, departments, and institutions that recognize the writing that teachers and administrators do as being rhetorically and contextually integral to the pedagogical experience.

As a closing note, the title of this collection, *Writing the Classroom*, was initially intended to include a preposition. However, I couldn't settle on a single preposition that would satisfactorily capture the full scope of what it means to write genres for pedagogical purposes. In the following chapters, readers will find a wide range of prepositions linking the act of writing genres and the scenarios of pedagogy. Teachers write *for* the classroom, with genres like assignment prompts or rubrics, but they also write *about* the classroom, with genres like course proposals or teaching handbooks. Pedagogical genres are written *before, during,* and *after* teaching occurs in a classroom, like syllabi, evaluative feedback, or classroom observations, and they are written *within* or *outside* the boundaries of a single classroom, like grading contracts or outcomes statements. Bawarshi and Reiff (2010) argue that pedagogical genres aid in "transforming the physical space of a classroom into a socially bounded, ideological space" (2010, 80). This collection shows not only how the many pedagogical genres aid in that transformation of a physical (or online) classroom space, but also how those genres support, enable, and endorse the activity and identities of teachers in the enactment of pedagogy, wherever it is invoked—and whatever preposition is used.

REFERENCES

Alsup, Janet. 2006. *Teacher Identity Discourses: Negotiating Personal and Professional Spaces.* Mahwah, NJ: Lawrence Erlbaum.

Bawarshi, Anis. 2001. "The Ecology of Genre." In *Ecocomposition: Theoretical and Pedagogical Approaches,* edited by Christian R. Weisser and Sidney I. Dobrin, 69–80. Albany: State University of New York Press.

Bawarshi, Anis. 2003. *Genre and the Invention of the Writer: Reconsidering the Place of Invention in Composition.* Logan: Utah State University Press.

Bawarshi, Anis, and Mary Jo Reiff. 2010. *Genre: An Introduction to History, Theory, Research, and Pedagogy.* West Lafayette, IN: Parlor Press.

Bazerman, Charles. 1988. *Shaping Written Knowledge: The Genre and Activity of the Experimental Article in Science.* Madison: University of Wisconsin Press.

Bazerman, Charles. 1994a. *Constructing Experience.* Carbondale: Southern Illinois University Press.

Bazerman, Charles. 1994b. "Systems of Genres and the Enactment of Social Intentions." In *Genre and the New Rhetoric,* edited by Aviva Freedman and Peter Medway, 67–85. Bristol, PA: Taylor & Francis.

Berkenkotter, Carol, and Thomas N. Huckin. 1995. *Genre Knowledge in Disciplinary Communication: Cognition/Culture/Power.* Hillsdale, NJ: Lawrence Erlbaum.

Cheng, Ying-Hsueh. 2014. "Dissertation Grant Proposals as 'Writing Games': An Exploratory Study of Two L2 Graduate Students' Experiences." *English for Specific Purposes* 36 (October): 74–84.

Clark, Irene. 2005. "A Genre Approach to Writing Assignments." *Composition Forum* 14 (2). http://compositionforum.com/issue/14.2/clark-genre-writing.php.

Desmet, Christy. 2005. "Beyond Accommodation: Individual and Collective in a Large Writing Program." In *Discord and Direction: The Postmodern Writing Program Administrator,* edited by Sharon James McGee and Carolyn Handa, 40–58. Logan: Utah State University Press.

Devitt, Amy J. 1991. "Intertextuality in Tax Accounting." In *Textual Dynamics of the Professions: Historical and Contemporary Studies of Writing in Professional Communities,* edited by Charles Bazerman and James G. Paradis, 22. Madison: University of Wisconsin Press.

Devitt, Amy J. 2004. *Writing Genres.* Carbondale: Southern Illinois University Press.

Devitt, Amy J. 2009. "Teaching Critical Genre Awareness." In *Genre in a Changing World*, edited by Charles Bazerman, Adair Bonini, and Débora Figueiredo, 337–51. Fort Collins, CO: WAC Clearinghouse.

Devitt, Amy J., Anis Bawarshi, and Mary Jo Reiff. 2003. "Materiality and Genre in the Study of Discourse Communities." *College English* 65 (5): 541–58.

Dryer, Dylan B. 2012. "At a Mirror, Darkly: The Imagined Undergraduate Writers of Ten Novice Composition Instructors." *College Composition and Communication* 63 (3): 420–52.

Flowerdew, John, and Tony Dudley-Evans. 2002. "Genre Analysis of Editorial Letters to International Journal Contributors." *Applied Linguistics* 23 (4): 463–89.

Franke, David. 2010. "Curriculum, Genre and Resistance: Revising Identity in a Professional Writing Community." In *Design Discourse: Composing and Revising Programs in Professional and Technical Writing*, edited by David Franke, Alex Reid, and Anthony DiRenzo, 113–30. Fort Collins, CO: WAC Clearinghouse.

Freadman, Anne. 1994. "Anyone for Tennis?" In *Genre and the New Rhetoric*, edited by Aviva Freedman and Peter Medway, 37–56. Bristol, PA: Taylor & Francis.

Freadman, Anne. 2002. "Uptake." In *The Rhetoric and Ideology of Genre: Strategies for Stability and Change*, edited by Richard M. Coe, Lorelei Lingard, and Tatiana Teslenko, 39–53. Cresskill, NJ: Hampton Press.

Giltrow, Janet. 2002. "Meta-Genre." In *The Rhetoric and Ideology of Genre: Strategies for Stability and Change*, edited by Richard M. Coe, Lorelei Lingard, and Tatiana Teslenko, 187–205. Cresskill, NJ: Hampton Press.

Hewings, Martin. 2004. "An 'Important Contribution' or 'Tiresome Reading'?: A Study of Evaluation in Peer Reviews of Journal Article Submissions." *Journal of Applied Linguistics* 1 (3): 247–74.

Miller, Carolyn R. 1984. "Genre as Social Action." *Quarterly Journal of Speech* 70 (2): 151–67.

Neaderhiser, Stephen. 2016a. "Conceiving of a Teacherly Identity: Metaphors of Composition in Teaching Statements." *Pedagogy* 16 (3): 413–43.

Neaderhiser, Stephen. 2016b. "Hidden in Plain Sight: Occlusion in Pedagogical Genres." *Composition Forum* 33. http://www.compositionforum.com/issue/33/hidden.php.

Reiff, Mary Jo. 2004. "Mediating Materiality and Discursivity: Critical Ethnography as Metageneric Learning." In *Ethnography Unbound: From Theory Shock to Critical Praxis*, edited by Stephen Gilbert Brown and Sidney I. Dobrin, 35–51. Albany: State University of New York Press.

Rice, Mary Frances. 2015. "Finding Space for Transfer of Writing in Common Core Curricular Standards." *Journal of Teaching Writing* 30 (2): 47–72.

Rounsaville, Angela. 2012. "Selecting Genres for Transfer: The Role of Uptake in Students' Antecedent Genre Knowledge." *Composition Forum* 26. http://compositionforum.com/issue/26/selecting-genres-uptake.php.

Shaw, Philip, Maria Kuteeva, and Akiko Okamura. 2014. "Submission Letters for Academic Publication: Disciplinary Differences and Promotional Language." *Journal of English for Academic Purposes* 14 (June): 106–17.

Sumner, David Thomas. 2001. "Don't Forget to Argue: Problems, Possibilities, and Ecocomposition." In *Ecocomposition: Theoretical and Pedagogical Approaches*, edited by Christian R. Weisser and Sidney I. Dobrin, 265–80. Albany: State University of New York Press.

Swales, John M. 1990. *Genre Analysis: English in Academic and Research Settings*. Cambridge: Cambridge University Press.

Swales, John M. 1996. "Occluded Genres in the Academy: The Case of the Submission Letter." In *Academic Writing: Intercultural and Textual Issues*, edited by Eija Ventola and Anna Mauranen, 45–58. Philadelphia, PA: John Benjamins.

Vidali, Amy. 2009. "Rhetorical Hiccups: Disability Disclosure in Letters of Recommendation." *Rhetoric Review* 28 (2): 185–204.

Wang, Simon Ho, and John Flowerdew. 2016. "Participatory Genre Analysis of Statements of Purpose: An Identity-Focused Study." *Writing & Pedagogy* 8 (1): 65–89.

Wardle, Elizabeth. 2009. "'Mutt Genres' and the Goal of FYC: Can We Help Students Write the Genres of the University?" *College Composition and Communication* 60 (4): 765–89.

PART 1

Genres in the Classroom

1

THE SYLLABUS
A Gateway to or Gatekeeper of the Profession

Michael Albright

Whether freshly printed from the department copier or posted online in a learning management system, a syllabus exists as a touchstone for any course, acting as a channel of communication between instructor and student to convey key philosophies, plans, and objectives. A fair degree of researched guidance has been devoted to the pedagogical possibilities, designs, and rewards of the course syllabus for instructors and students (Slattery and Carlson 2005; Habanek 2005; Grunert O'Brien et al. 2008). Notably less scholarship exists examining the syllabus as a means of professionalization vital to an instructor's development and identity as a professional academic. As Cheryl Albers (2003) indicates, "A soundly-crafted syllabus, based in curricular, subject matter, and pedagogical knowledge, demonstrates the research and reflection put into the course's construction. It reveals both the instructor's mastery of the subject matter and the ability to make this subject matter accessible to the students" (70). In this way, the syllabus serves an important function in terms of demonstrating the quality of instruction or one's pedagogical abilities—criteria that are prized among search committees or departments looking to hire or vet the advancement of colleagues. The professionalizing potential of the syllabus genre, however, hinges on the openness or flexibility of the document itself. If access to this document is limited or completely restricted by a department, institution, or, in some cases, corporation, instructors may find themselves occupying a dislocated subject position that prevents them from enacting key personal, pedagogical, and professional moves that are intrinsic to any classroom environment—as well as an instructor's individual academic identity. While it may seem that such restrictions on an instructor's pedagogical activity would be draconian and unlikely, such instances are readily available for consideration in the form of the standardized, shared, or "common" syllabus.

https://doi.org/10.7330/9781646422920.c001

In this chapter, I confront the ramifications associated with course syllabi that obfuscate or erase the instructor by virtue of generic design, especially as it occurs through the enforcement of a "common syllabus." Particularly, contingent faculty or early-career scholars often find themselves at the mercy of common syllabi—usually as part of lower-level, high-yield courses taught by multiple and different instructors. And these are often the same instructors who are actively pursuing more secure or stable teaching-focused opportunities that require evidence of original pedagogy as part of an application packet. When the syllabus becomes a premade script, these instructors must perform and conceive of their labor differently, thus becoming alienated from their work and pedagogical identity in the process.

By framing the syllabus not only as a pedagogical genre of the classroom but also as an artifact of professional development, I would like to complicate pervading assumptions that syllabi are created equally by single authors, thereby exposing the rhetorical implications of the common or shared syllabus for instructors (both faculty and graduate students) as they seek to embody their identities as professionals. In addition to analyzing the rhetorical purposes and allowances of the syllabus as a genre (as well as the subgenre of the common syllabus), I draw upon my own professional development and localized experiences as a former adjunct instructor at multiple institutions in order to argue that standardized syllabi place vulnerable career-focused instructors at a distinct disadvantage, as they are less able to claim the same professional benefits that would typically be associated with original or individually authored pedagogical materials. I also consider how faculty might circumvent or mitigate this not infrequent arrangement in their own professional pursuits.

THE SYLLABUS: GENRE PURPOSES AND AFFORDANCES

In the twenty-first-century academy, the typical course syllabus serves a range of functions and capacities depending on the course, the instructor, and the institution. Gone are the days of single-page lists of texts and pertinent contact details. Instead, today's syllabi act as veritable storehouses of information, philosophies, and policies. Broadly, researchers have noted the course syllabus's versatility as a document that serves distinctly pedagogical and procedural ends. Maria Shine Stewart (2016) describes the syllabus using the language of heavy construction, arguing that it acts "like scaffolding that supports an emerging building [and] requires a sound structure and ballast. And it needs a quality of resilience." Jay Parkes and Mary Harris (2002) note that syllabi "seem to vary in two fundamental areas: (a) the apparent reasons for writing the syllabus and (b) the material that it contains," while further assigning labels like "contract," "permanent record," and "learning tool" to the document's designs (55).[1] For their part, Charles Fornaciari and Kathy Lund Dean (2014) look beyond the syllabus as a strictly "operational tool" and call attention to its potential as a "class culture-building and collaboration opportunity" (702). The syllabus's functions and efficacy as an educational tool are complemented by its design and intended use within a classroom context.

Conventional syllabi that lay out policies, procedures, and contingencies naturally differ in scope and appeal from other more student-centered syllabus models, which are likely less familiar to present and past generations of students and teachers. Christine Courtade Hirsch (2010) chronicles the use of what she dubs a "promising syllabus" within her communications classroom. As its name suggests, this syllabus design relies on "learner-centered process and evaluation" to declare transparently what a course will offer to students and their learning—not what students will sacrifice to the course (79). In their examination of the syllabus's largescale evolution in higher education, Michael Palmer et al. (2016) extol the virtues of what they label a "learning-focused syllabus" and insist that "instructors have very little to lose" and "much to gain" in the process of creating one (37). Yet these sorts of gains are less possible for instructors who lack the authority or latitude to create or shape their own syllabi. If bound to common, standardized, or corporate documents in their teaching, these instructors are more apt to be restricted to syllabi of the traditional sort, thus lacking the ability to promise anything on their own terms.

In fact, the only terms that seem to matter according to the language of some syllabi are those set forth by the institution or corporation. In my period of instruction of four different courses across two different departments at an online, for-profit university with a national reach, I had no presence as an instructor in the foundational course documents, including the syllabus. Students were referred to as a plural collective, and they were tasked to explore, use, apply, or demonstrate various course outcomes. Other course activities, such as online class discussions, were designed to "facilitate the process for college-level writing." My role in any sort of facilitation, although required by the

---

1. To this list, Ken Matejka and Lance Kurke (1994) add "communication device," "plan," and "cognitive map," while corroborating the syllabus's resemblance to a contract (115).

institution, was absent from the syllabus, as was information pertaining to my identity or presence within the framework of the course. In these courses, I lacked a name, identity, and role—at least, according to the syllabus as it was structured by the institution. In fact, when conducting a keyword search within an introductory writing course's syllabus at that institution, the only hits for the words *instruction, instruct,* or *instructor,* corresponded to mentions of Instructure, the trademark of the course's online learning management system vendor.

Without opportunities to craft inclusive and accessible learning-focused or promising syllabi, instructors who must rely on common syllabi may further miss out on infusing this course document with any vestiges of their personality as individuals or professors. Not only does a syllabus provide a valuable first impression of the course and its overall designs for students, but it also conveys the persona of its creator. Ken Matejka and Lance Kurke (1994) frame the syllabus as a cornerstone for capturing and sharing one's identity, directly imploring the instructor to be mindful of this capacity: "At the very least, the syllabus sends a symbolic message to the students regarding your personality as a teacher and the amount of investment you have made in the course" (115). To this presence of personality, Parkes and Harris (2002) add that an instructor's pedagogical philosophies "will shape the course and consequently the syllabus both implicitly and explicitly" (58). If instructors must displace their philosophies and personality to demur to a standard syllabus, the shaping of critical course components along with any accompanying symbolic values fail to materialize. Even further obscured in such situations is an instructor's sense of professional authority as a thinking, creating autonomous being.

Authority, for the purposes of this discussion, refers to the capacity of an instructor to occupy his or her position in the classroom with credibility and legitimacy. In fact, as Baecker (1998) notes, for teaching assistants the syllabus is "one of the first places we assert our authority as teachers" (59). Nevertheless, it is only fair to acknowledge that any ideal or innocuous constructions of professional authority can quickly devolve and give way to more sinister displays of tyranny over students. And, when construed as an extension of this sort of power, an instructor's syllabus can easily lay waste to any semblance of the democratic, egalitarian classroom that theorists like Paulo Freire (1970) situate as an antidote to totalitarian regimes outside the classroom. For this reason, many are quick to caution instructors from creating or implementing "the controlling syllabus," or, "the club we teachers use" to enforce order in the classroom (Singham 2007). Fornaciari and Dean (2014) argue that student learning ultimately suffers when "power resides within the instructor role and is operationalized with syllabus design" (707). Yet, when another entity entirely wields and operationalizes the syllabus according to its desires, not only do instructors lose an element of their teaching authority within the classroom, but they also lack an important pathway toward professional development offered by the syllabus's polyvalence as a genre as well as its prominence in today's academy.

Anis Bawarshi (2003) captures the syllabus's massive potential by calling it a "master classroom genre" that is simultaneously generative and "coercive" for both students and instructors (120). For Bawarshi, the syllabus shapes subjectivities, enacts ideologies, and enforces authorities among various stakeholders of institution, student, and instructor. The syllabus, in this view, transcends its ostensibly passive role as a repository of policies and course information to emerge as a powerful site of action in which "teachers invent their classes, themselves, as well as their students by locating themselves within the situated topoi of the syllabus" (126). Yet this prospect of invention only materializes when an instructor has a self to locate within the syllabus. While it is probably safe to venture a guess that most rational and invested instructors are not dissociated from their selfhood by nature, it is less of a guarantee that instructors will be able to meaningfully enact their subjectivity through a syllabus that they had no hand in composing—even if their students assume that they are solely behind its creation.

Bawarshi adopts this common vantage point when addressing an instructor's agency and argues that the syllabus "constructs its writer, the teacher, as an abstract nominalization" (2003, 124). What happens, though, when an instructor's agency is eliminated or absent by virtue of the generic constructs of the syllabus as document? What if the syllabus is already designed, structured, or distributed by another entity, which ends up supplanting the course instructor's agency entirely? How do instructors tasked with adopting or implementing these sorts of restricted syllabi—particularly instructors in more contingent or precarious positions (such as nontenured faculty, adjuncts, and graduate teaching assistants) or those in concurrent enrollment positions—demonstrate their pedagogy, evince their subjectivity as teachers, and engage in the work of professionalization?

These were the sorts of questions and dilemmas that I confronted when encountering various iterations of common, corporate, or standardized syllabi in my own developing career as an adjunct and instructor of dual-enrollment college courses. The more that I took on new courses and joined other institutions—online and on-the-ground, for- and not-for-profit—I found myself affixing little more than my name and new dates to syllabi. I became acutely aware that I had very little to show in terms of planning and creating a vital cornerstone of my pedagogy.

THE SYLLABUS AS PROFESSIONAL ARTIFACT

To appreciate the implications of the absence of professional authority to create course syllabi is to understand how the syllabus naturally supports professional development in ali stages of career growth—from the job search to promotion or tenure opportunities. Beyond its function as a channel of communication, a course syllabus can be implemented as an artifact of professionalization, that is, the trajectory of one's effort to claim and maintain status in the field (Fink 2012, 4). For Cheryl Albers (2003), the potential for capturing this area of an instructor's presence is enormous, as the "syllabus is one of the few tools available for documenting the scholarship required for integrating isolated learning activities into a coherent and meaningful whole" (63). In addition to this documentary quality, the syllabus also possesses an enormous "evidentiary value" that results in its reflection and revelation of essential markers of pedagogical and professional growth (Leduc 2011, 2). Parkes and Harris (2002) cite additional forms of evidence within the syllabus, including the author's "clarity of writing, attitudes toward students, knowledge of pedagogy, and fairness of education" (57). However, if an instructor lacks the input to craft the syllabus, these revelations end up bypassing a key driver of the learning process—the teacher, thus reflecting for students a set of principles and ideas whose origins may be unknown or, at best, imprecise.

The course syllabus offers instructors key evaluative opportunities from their peers and, by extension, programs or departments as a whole (Parkes and Harris 2002, 57). One of the appeals of including the syllabus as part of a faculty review process, for instance, is that it concretizes and supplements data that might not be as readily or objectively available. Michael Woolcock (2006) states that the burdens of "relying on student evaluations alone as the measure of effective teaching can be at least partially obviated by including course outlines as a major component of one's overall teaching portfolio" (9). Laurent Leduc (2011) deems a syllabus "suitable to attest to the *quality* of teaching" because it forms "proper evidence of a faculty's effectiveness both in terms of teaching abilities . . . and of scientific skills or attitude toward learners" (1–2). Leduc's use of the qualifier "proper" to describe the evidentiary value of the syllabus is notable. With this label in consideration, the syllabus not only emerges as an appropriate form of evidence but also comes across as an authentic, legitimate metric to assess one's professional work, status, or ability in ways that other measures cannot do as well or as transparently.

Lacking an original creation—one that increasingly serves as proper evidence of quality, ability, or growth—these instructors find themselves beholden to a static document whose closed design prevents them from representing their active, ongoing professionalization as professors with academic and pedagogical freedom. It is no wonder that instructors are openly encouraged to consider their syllabi as documents that work for them in the service of their professional development. Susan Fink (2012) also assigns a reflexive value to the syllabus, stating that "instructors might want to keep copies to observe their own growth and changes over the years as well as for documentation on application portfolios" (4). As an enduring document that can and does follow an instructor after any given course's conclusion, the syllabus emerges as an ideal evaluative artifact that provides a point of reference and ground of truth regarding key classroom decisions, approaches, and philosophies used at the time. While it is only fair to acknowledge that not all instructors automatically recognize or buy into the notion that their course syllabi yield such insights,[2] the fact remains that instructors expected to employ a standardized syllabus are forestalled entirely from the prospect of introducing their syllabus as a product of their professionalization since they had no input or stake in its generation.

THE COMMON SYLLABUS: ORIGINS, USES, AND ALIENATION

While it is virtually impossible to provide a precise ratio of common course syllabi that exist to individually authored (or original) syllabi, it is safe to characterize the standardized form according to its most typical uses, applications, and forms. Ranging from requisite core elements to complete documents, common syllabi run the gamut in terms of their designs and origins. Usually, the implementation of a common syllabus (or common required elements) occurs at the program or department level, sometimes only reaching certain courses based on various factors such as student population, course content, and instructor availability

---

2. Fink notes in her study of instructor perceptions of syllabi that its purpose "as *Artifact for Teacher Evaluation/Permanent Record/Evidence for Accreditation, Assessment of Curriculum Planning* . . . was neither high nor low on being considered essential or useful by instructors" (2012, 9).

or experience. But in other cases, common syllabi can be implemented rather widely across universities—particularly within programs that attract high volumes of learners while relying on a wide, revolving instructor pool. Perhaps the most conventional sites of common syllabi are those courses in which the "regular teaching faculty is routinely supplanted by graduate assistants or part-time or temporary instructors" (Brosman 1998, 60). Classes that fill large lecture halls, cover subjects steeped in foundational scientific or general concepts, or rely on objective assessment techniques tend to fit the common syllabus mold equally well—especially since the labor pool for these courses often contains the types of instructors Brosman identifies.

The wisdom behind drafting and distributing a common syllabus across the ranks in these situations is, ostensibly, to mitigate against perceived (or, in some cases, actual) inexperience in terms of creating such a central component of the course (Brosman 1998, 61). Yet, with the possible exception of first-year teaching assistants, many contingent or novice instructors possess more experience than their positions would suggest. And if they do not, they more than likely would crave the opportunity to expand their portfolios and repertoires as instructors by having the license to create such content. In my experiences as an adjunct instructor of online composition courses at two very different for- and not-for-profit universities, I was never involved in the creation of a course syllabus. In fact, these documents were always preloaded within an equally standardized course shell with prepopulated modules and content. My only contribution to the course beyond discussion posts, announcements, and grading was to provide an updated instructor profile, which would serve as the only stable locus of my professional identity.

Logistics aside, common syllabi have the capacity to project powerful messages to all stakeholders—instructors, students, administrators, accreditors. As Matejka and Kurke (1994) argue, "Common formats convey to students that the faculty are organized and hold similar high standards" (116). These same standards, however, can also undercut the integrity of the course when they overshadow the presence of the instructor. For Brosman (1998), the syllabus can become a "false front" that obscures critical quality issues, limits authority, and even projects dubious political aims or agendas (63). Even those course syllabi that require common components, such as university or department boilerplate, suffer from cases of "syllabus creep," eroding the presence and authority of the instructor in the process (Gannon 2016). When a disembodied "they" become the author of part or all of any course, instructors must defer by default to a body of content that might or might not reflect their own pedagogical instincts, values, or philosophies.

It may seem tempting for instructors to disregard or even "hack" common syllabi to circumvent these hurdles, but the consequences of such decisions can be steep. Scott Jaschik (2008) tells the story of Pejman Norasteh, a former adjunct instructor who was terminated from his position for having deviated from the syllabus. In an effort to respond to students' complaints regarding course content and the perceived difficulty of the prescribed textbook, Norasteh created and distributed supplementary materials. When the division chair learned that students were being tasked with extra work, based on another round of complaints, the adjunct was released from his position. The chair offered the following explanation to Norasteh, reinforcing just how immutable the course's common syllabus was: "Individual instructors do not have the option of straying from the syllabus and/or textbook" (Jaschik 2008). Although Norasteh refuted the allegations by insisting that he never required any extra work, his case and position lost to the power of the common syllabus in place, and he was forced to move on.

It is for this reason that instructors are often cautioned from willingly adopting even degrees of standardization as part of their syllabus design—much less an entirely prepared document. Brosman (1998) advises: "The departmental syllabus would seem appropriate as a guide—but not as a yoke" (65), and Kevin Gannon (2016) categorically states that an abundance of "institutional syllabus statements" are "not good pedagogy." Writing as the associate vice chancellor for adjunct faculty and curriculum, CharMaine Hines (2013) offers her adjunct pool the following counsel on syllabus design:

> Finally, the syllabus serves as a professional development opportunity for faculty. Effective practitioners do not use "boiler plate" templates but continuously update and review the syllabus each semester allowing them to remain current on concepts, research and teaching tools for the course. Writing and revising provides the reoccurring opportunity to reflect on both the form and purpose of your approach to teaching. (1)

This messaging, which appears in a column of the Wayne County Community College District's inaugural adjunct faculty newsletter, is heartening, as it affirms the innate value of the syllabus as a key element of one's professional arsenal—even for those contingent faculty members. However, not every faculty member receives such open encouragement to create and invest in original content—most typically those faculty who are not bound to contingent roles in which common syllabi are commonplace. The instructors thus encounter a set of distinct disadvantages and liabilities relative to peers whose autonomy is greater in this respect.

The reality of teaching with an "imposed syllabus," as Brosman (1998) calls it, is that the pedagogical and professional presence is partly obscured or obfuscated completely by the document's (oftentimes mandated) existence (61). Because of its fixed—almost scripted—design, the common syllabus encourages an element of performance on the part of the faculty beholden to it, which ultimately results in various degrees of damaging alienation from the course, the students, oneself, and the profession as a whole.

The performance or performer analogy is not uncommon when discussing the broad strokes of the profession of teachers or professors. A range of handbooks, guides, and critical articles advise prospective and practicing educators on the best ways to incorporate elements of theatrical performance into their practice.[3] However, these techniques and strategies can collapse upon themselves if instructors fail to consider or appreciate how their performative brand of pedagogy translates into tangible results. In fact, this lack of understanding can cause teachers to "stop being professionals," as "teaching stops being a profession" (Tauber and Mester 2007, 25). Beyond compromising the integrity of the profession, performance can cause the instructor to resemble less of a knowledgeable, capable authority and more of a passive pawn ready to follow the same script that any number of colleagues have performed in the past or are seemingly waiting in the wings to perform if only given the scheduled opportunity to do so. When a common syllabus elicits the sorts of scripted or rigid performance on the part of students and faculty that are devoid of such reflective opportunities altogether, the "academic community is lost in the process" (Agger and Shelton 2017, 358). For instructors who are unable to claim or derive authority in their classrooms as a result of a common syllabus, this sense of loss leads to a ripple effect of alienation for instructors.

Alienation that stems from a common syllabus (or a predominance of common components) is pervasive and affects both instructors and students at various stages of the course—before, during, and after. The syllabus is only one impetus of alienation, as it "plays out everywhere," according to Agger and Shelton (2017), who look to sites beyond the classroom to identify "vita building" and "administrative priorities" as additional targets (367). Most immediately, the "professor's authority over how materials should be presented, in what doses and when, and

3. See also Jyl Lynn Felman's *Never a Dull Moment: Teaching and the Art of Performance* (2001).

how competence should be tested, can produce alienation in the strict sense of the term" (Brosman 1998, 65). To receive a completed syllabus with weeks' worth of instruction meticulously planned, texts selected, and assessments decided, is to receive an accompanying, albeit implicit, message that one's intellectual and professional presence is secondary to what has already been established by that document.

CONFRONTING THE COMMON SYLLABUS: A CASE IN POINT

In my work as an adjunct instructor for an on-the-ground, for-profit career college (whose parent company recently folded due to accreditation issues), I found myself on the receiving end of this message with the start of every new term. As an instructor of speech, literature, and composition courses, I taught a range of students over multiple terms twice a week. Despite my active and familiar presence on campus, my existence was all but erased within my course syllabi. While this institution allowed me to input my name and email address into a protected field on a document, I did not have any freedom to craft my own framing language or content. Unlike the corporate online university for which I also taught, the career college did acknowledge vestiges of instruction in phrases such as "instructional materials" and "instructional methods." However, instructors were still largely hidden within this on-the-ground institution's syllabus genre, as the syllabus for a contemporary literature course stipulated: "Daily tasks will be assigned which are due by the end of the class meeting each day." Rendered in the passive voice, the assignment, or officially phrased as "delivery method," of these tasks fell upon the syllabus as document, effectively erasing me as the instructor from such tasks, their assignment, or, for that matter, the meeting itself.

Students at this institution were most frequently referred to by the plural collective of "students"—just as in the online university's documents. Yet there were occasions in which a more familiar instance of "you" or "we" was introduced to advise students on library use or technology support. As the syllabus laid out, "Reference materials are available in our college library," while "the help desk is available to help you 24 hours a day, 7 days per week, including holidays." The section further adds that at the help desk, "they can assist you with issues" that ran the gamut from technological to institutional matters. Curiously, as a body referred to as "them," the help desk staff was endowed with more subjectivity than the course instructor, who instead appeared on the margins somewhere outside the encompassing "we" of the college while bound to the syllabus and its mandates.

Files would appear in my inbox weeks, days, or even hours before the beginning of a new term, and I had to print, copy, click, or link depending on the course environment and setup. Steeped in policies, objectives, and assignments that were not my own, these syllabi were as foreign to me as they were to my students on their first day in the classroom. I lacked important layers of context necessary to respond to legitimate questions about courses and content. Deferring to the syllabus as it had been written and, by extension, the institutional or corporate structure of the entity that devised the content became my default and best strategy at the time. Incidentally, the questions I had seemed to mount from one week to the next. Why, for example, did a class billed as Contemporary Literature only use a text containing thirty recent short stories from American authors? Why did extensive sections on dress code and professionalism seem to crowd out other pages on the syllabus? Why in subsequent terms did I receive my syllabus premade with dates and my name already attached? Was this document not something that I as an instructor—a professor—was supposed to create and present as my own? After all, my training as a secondary education teacher and my work as a graduate student required my direct input as the instructor. Ultimately, my students and I found ourselves satisfying objectives and wading through material that had been decided by unnamed authorities at an unknown time for unexplained reasons.

While I dutifully passed along these documents to my students, I intuitively knew that having such a distance from the creation of a course syllabus would not do me any favors as a fledgling faculty member who sought to advance in the academic marketplace. What I had not fully internalized at the time was that my ambitions to broaden my classroom experience, while developing course content and syllabi along the way, were increasingly incompatible, as I experienced this literal erasure from the courses I taught each Tuesday and Thursday via my course syllabi's phrasing and structure. How could I take ownership of my pedagogy and professional development if I lacked a place in the language of the course?

CONCLUSIONS: WHERE DO WE GO FROM HERE?

The advice that Shine Stewart (2016) offers faculty to be "your best self" in the creation of a syllabus seems all but impossible if the self is lost in another entity's words, dictates, or designs. Despite the enforced absence or effective erasure of the self within the common syllabus, the fact remains that instructors must still lay claim to some sort of professional authority if they expect to deliver the course effectively or seamlessly. When a course's "activities become substitutes for the agents who perform them," (Bawarshi 2003, 125), instructors who inherit common syllabi must strike a balance between appropriating something that is not of their own making and assuming a position of authority in front of students who may be none the wiser. Even if students are unaware of the prep work (or lack thereof, as the case may be), instructors are by force alienated from their learners whenever syllabi are structured to erase instances of instruction through vague, passive, or catch-all statements. Unless their course syllabus is crafted as a learning-focused or student-centered document, instructors will lack a crucial opportunity to offer their students a document that opens and establishes a lasting dialogue with them. During the class, instructors may find themselves having to become spokespeople for a program, course, department, or university as a whole if a student asks about or calls attention to some confusing or perhaps even controversial aspect of the syllabus—and, by extension, the course.

Even if the instructor manages to study up on the syllabus before the course and imbues its spirit as an ideal ambassador of its creators, the legacy of alienation threatens to follow an instructor's professionalization in a course's aftermath. Because syllabi are regarded as artifacts of professional development and serve as data points of evaluation and accreditation, it is often desirable for instructors to possess a portfolio or collection that can attest, in part, to their quality and abilities as an educator. When on the job market or vying for an advancement in rank or position, these materials become all the more prized by candidates and committees alike. To have a collection of common syllabi is to lack crucial sections of one's pedagogical and professional journeys. The printouts of others' content, of institutional or corporate philosophies, of departmental dictates seem to encourage parroting or endorsement from candidates regarding their syllabi. The origin story of a syllabus's creation, how it captures the essence of an individual's values, and the ways that it supports the fundamentals of a discipline are essentially spoken for by other agents when common syllabi are subjects of review or interpretation. To lay claim to these features as original products of the instructor would be unethical, yet such claims are often gateways to advancing one's position.

The traditional (personally crafted) syllabus may act as a gateway to professional development and advancement, but the common syllabus can instead emerge as a stalwart gatekeeper, preventing professionalization from occurring as a result of the alienation that tends to result

from such arrangements. It is also worth noting that the recent proliferation of open educational resources that amenably pair with common
syllabi—especially in early-sequence, high-volume courses—would seem
to exacerbate even further the dissolution of an instructor's identity and
professionalization efforts. Longstanding debates and controversies concerning academic freedom are also further complicated when the common syllabus emerges as an effective barrier to the creation of a document
that is very much at the center of a course and the person who delivers it.

Although this case is disheartening for instructors who are already
often vulnerable in experience or job stability, it is possible to reconcile
one's professionalization with the imposition of a common syllabus.
More progressive or attentive common syllabi may already account for
the act of instruction or an instructor's presence without erasing that
presence rhetorically. For example, as part of the syllabus for an English
composition class at one not-for-profit, online university, a dedicated
section entitled "Instructor Availability and Response Time" advises
students on what to expect from the course instructor:

> Your class interaction with the instructor and your classmates will take
> place on a regular, ongoing basis. Your instructor will be actively engaged
> within the course throughout the week. You will normally communicate
> with your instructor in the weekly discussions or the General Questions
> discussion topic so that your questions and the instructor's answers benefit
> the entire class. You should feel free, however, to communicate with your
> instructor via [university] email at any time, particularly when you want
> to discuss something of a personal or sensitive nature. Your instructor will
> generally provide a response within 24 hours.

This language is notable for the way it emphasizes the visibility and inclusion of the instructor as part of the course as a whole. Instructors are
placed alongside the reader and fellow classmates to form a cohesive
unit. The instructor's availability and role are made clear to the students
for whom the instructor is humanized as an entity capable of discussing "personal or sensitive" content. The above clause makes up part of
a larger syllabus that is standardized across hundreds of sections, but
it makes significant strides to endow instructors with crucial degrees of
presence and agency, something that many other common syllabi fail to
validate or privilege.

* * *

Whenever I taught from common syllabi, I tried to play a version of
Peter Elbow's "believing game" in which I worked to locate the value
of the documents "imposed" on me by other entities.[4] In doing so, I

---

4. See Elbow's *Writing without Teachers* (1973) for an appendix devoted to this methodology of critical thinking.

modeled what being a generous critic looked like if students confronted policies or tasks that were undesirable to them. If students had questions, I used the opportunity to mine the syllabus for data and answers, or I made sure to track down what we were missing. Transparency—not performance—was the key to my survival in such situations. When on the job market, I used the common syllabi I had received to emphasize my versatility as a candidate. I explained that I had experience teaching composition courses that were modes-based, courses that used handbooks, and courses that relied on several essays or one sustained project. I also took the opportunity in cover letters or interviews to juxtapose these common syllabi with my own ideas, making sure to demonstrate how I had situated myself as part of a larger critical and pedagogical landscape. As a more established professor today, I am mindful of how initiatives to create content, standardize objectives, or frame course syllabi can work against the very stakeholders we care most about: our students, colleagues, and professional selves. No matter the task or constraints of genre, I have endeavored to maintain my visibility and authority as a thinking, active professional—even if it ostensibly appears that I am only tasked with deferring to photocopies or protected files.

REFERENCES

Agger, Ben, and Beth Anne Shelton. 2017. "Time, Motion, Discipline: The Authoritarian Syllabus on American College Campuses." *Critical Sociology* 43 (3): 355–69.

Albers, Cheryl. 2003. "Using the Syllabus to Document the Scholarship of Teaching." *Teaching Sociology* 31 (1): 60–72.

Baecker, Diann L. 1998. "Uncovering the Rhetoric of the Syllabus: The Case of the Missing I." *College Teaching* 46 (2): 58–62.

Bawarshi, Anis. 2003. *Genre and the Invention of the Writer: Reconsidering the Place of Invention in Composition.* Logan: Utah State University Press.

Brosman, Catharine Savage. 1998. "The Case for (and against) Departmental Syllabi." *Academic Questions* 11 (4): 58–65.

Elbow, Peter. 1973. *Writing without Teachers.* New York: Oxford University Press.

Felman, Jyl Lynn. 2001. *Never a Dull Moment: Teaching and the Art of Performance.* New York: Routledge.

Fink, Susan B. 2012. "The Many Purposes of Course Syllabi: Which Are Essential and Useful?" *Syllabus* 1 (1): 1–12.

Fornaciari, Charles J., and Kathy Lund Dean. 2014. "The 21st-Century Syllabus: From Pedagogy to Andragogy." *Journal of Management Education* 38 (5): 701–23.

Freire, Paulo. 1970. *Pedagogy of the Oppressed.* New York: Seabury Press.

Gannon, Kevin. 2016. "DIY Syllabus: What Is a Syllabus Really for, Anyway?" ChronicleVitae. September 15, 2016. Accessed October 11, 2018. https://chroniclevitae.com/news/1545-diy-syllabus-what-is-a-syllabus-really-for-anyway. Archived at https://web.archive.org/web/20181011191821/https://chroniclevitae.com/news/1545-diy-syllabus-what-is-a-syllabus-really-for-anyway.

Grunert O'Brien, Judith, Barbara J. Millis, and Margaret W. Cohen. 2008. *The Course Syllabus: A Learning-Centered Approach.* 2nd ed. San Francisco, CA: John Wiley & Sons.

Habanek, Darlene V. 2005. "An Examination of the Integrity of the Syllabus." *College Teaching* 53 (2): 62–64.

Hines, CharMaine. 2013. "Success from Day One: An Effective Syllabus." *Adjunct Faculty* 1 (1): 1.

Hirsch, Christine Courtade. 2010. "The Promising Syllabus Enacted: One Teacher's Experience." *Communication Teacher* 24 (2): 78–90.

Jaschik, Scott. 2008. "Out of Work for Doing Extra Work?" Inside Higher Ed. July 23, 2008. https://www.insidehighered.com/news/2008/07/23/out-work-doing-extra-work.

Leduc, Laurent. 2011. "Using the Course Syllabus to Document the Quality of Teaching and Identifying Its Most Useful Items According to the Students." In *Sixth European Quality Assurance Forum.* Anvers, Belgium. http://hdl.handle.net/2268/112328.

Matejka, Ken, and Lance B. Kurke. 1994. "Designing a Great Syllabus." *College Teaching* 42 (3): 115–17.

Palmer, Michael S., Lindsay B. Wheeler, and Itiya Aneece. 2016. "Does the Document Matter? The Evolving Role of Syllabi in Higher Education." *Change: The Magazine of Higher Learning* 48 (4): 36–47.

Parkes, Jay, and Mary B. Harris. 2002. "The Purposes of a Syllabus." *College Teaching* 50 (2): 55–61.

Shine Stewart, Maria. 2016. "Ensuring That Your Course Syllabus Does Its Job." Inside Higher Ed. April 26, 2016. https://www.insidehighered.com/advice/2016/04/26/ensuring-your-course-syllabus-does-its-job-essay.

Singham, Mano. 2007. "Death to the Syllabus!" *Association of American Colleges & Universities* 93 (4). https://aacu.org/publications-research/periodicals/death-syllabus.

Slattery, Jeanne M., and Janet F. Carlson. 2005. "Preparing an Effective Syllabus." *College Teaching* 53 (4): 159–64.

Tauber, Robert T., and Cathy Sargent Mester. 2007. *Acting Lessons for Teachers: Using Performance Skills in the Classroom.* Westport, CT: Praeger.

Woolcock, Michael J. V. 2006. *Constructing a Syllabus: A Handbook for Faculty, Teaching Assistants and Teaching Fellows.* 3rd ed. Providence, RI: The Harriet W. Sheridan Center for Teaching and Learning.

2

FEMINIST WRITING ASSIGNMENTS
Enacting Pedagogy through Classroom Genres

Kate Navickas

Ever since James Berlin's early analysis of pedagogical rhetorics that argues teaching is never neutral,[1] numerous cases have been made in composition research and pedagogy scholarship for how pedagogical values can be enacted through particular strategies for teaching, assignment sequences, writing feedback, course content and curricula, and assessment practices. Indeed, teachers embed pedagogical values, hopes, and desires in their courses—even larger epistemological, ideological, and perhaps political objectives. While scholarship and teachers tend to put a great deal of thought into their pedagogical values, how can we assess such aspirations in practice? Isolating the writing assignment prompt as one site of pedagogy, in this chapter I use rhetorical genre studies (RGS) as a framework to locate and reflect on the values that are visible in feminist writing assignment prompts.

Within the classroom, the assignment is a central textual artifact that invites students to write—in specific genres and for specific purposes and audiences. Whether in pedagogical scholarship or teacher-talk, teachers often explain writing courses by describing the specific genres taught or the sequence of assignments; assignments are thus the movement of the classroom. Carefully crafted and designed, writing assignments help teachers define a course and plan day-to-day classroom activities. And then, as scholars like Jennie Nelson (1990) have found, when students take on the task of interpreting writing assignment prompts, something entirely new is created in response (391)—a process Anne Freadman has subsequently called "uptake" (Freadman 2002). Further, the writing assignment is a classroom genre with the power to influence students' thinking, writing, and understanding of what is possible. That is, the directions and text of an assignment can influence the

---

1. A point made especially clear in his often-reprinted 1988 essay, "Rhetoric and Ideology in the Classroom."

https://doi.org/10.7330/9781646422920.c002

topics students pursue in their writing, what they think of those topics (as positive, negative, complicated, etc.), and how they understand their own role as students, writers, and people engaged with the world around them. Considering these various roles for both teachers and students, I've come to understand the writing assignment as the link between a teacher's pedagogical desires and students' writing. I argue that because writing assignments connect pedagogy to student writing, there is a pedagogical imperative to be more conscious of how the values we are committed to are signaled in assignment texts.

For me, the question of translating pedagogical values into practice emerged when designing my first upper-division research-writing course. The course, an archival investigation of university student histories, grew out of a pedagogical desire to recover stories of student struggles and help students see their histories as relevant to the contemporary present. During the course development, a mentor noted that concluding with a traditional research paper seemed counter to my stated pedagogical goal of making student histories matter. She was right. This moment pushed me to think more critically not just about assignment genres, but also about how assignment texts signal pedagogical aims. Thus, in response, I started to ask: *How do writing assignments allow feminist teachers to signal their pedagogical values textually?*

In this chapter, I share findings from a study of a corpus of feminist-oriented writing assignments that seeks to answer the above question. Through analyzing the assignments with an RGS framework, I have found two things: First, that feminist values were signaled in moments that named positions or subjectivities for students to inhabit and in moments that made arguments or assumptions about the subject being studied. And second, students were most often positioned in ways that attempted to empower them through valuing their experiences and knowledges, and the assignments most often posed epistemological arguments about how knowledge on different topics (including gender, women's memorials, literacy, etc.) is constructed through particular rhetorical choices, contexts, histories, and discourses. Through this work, I have come to believe that regardless of pedagogical orientation (feminist or otherwise), the values and theory underlying an instructor's pedagogy should be visible in assignment texts and that an attention to how assignments position students and their arguments can provide one set of textual cues that make that pedagogy visible. Although these are small textual moments, I argue that such attention is a form of self-reflection that guards against unknowingly upholding hegemonic oppressive discourses and ideologies—work that is especially essential for teachers invested in pedagogies aiming for social justice.

WRITING ASSIGNMENTS IN SCHOLARSHIP

Precisely because writing assignments—feminist or not—are so central to the teaching of writing, they come up in a vast array of composition scholarship. There is a wealth of practical advice guides for teachers designing assignments (Lindemann 2001; Gardner 2008; White 2007). In writing across the curriculum and genre studies, scholars have analyzed collections of writing assignments in order to consider the various assigned genres and their disciplinary purposes (Graves et al. 2010; Hilgers et al. 1999; Melzer 2009). Pedagogical scholarship often highlights one assignment and its strengths or weaknesses in particular institutional, curricular, or pedagogical contexts (Shipka 2007; Strasma 2007) or makes pedagogical arguments for a larger sequence of assignments (Bartholomae and Petrosky 1986). Additionally, writing assignments appear in specific areas of composition pedagogy, like teaching research practices (Allan 2018; Davis and Shadle 2000) or the variety of discussions regarding digital composing practices (Molloy 2016; Shipka 2013).

Several scholars have offered theoretical frameworks for studying and analyzing specific writing assignments. For instance, in an early *fforum* essay, David Bartholomae (1982) presents four principles of writing assignments that are mostly practical advice (e.g., scaffold assignments); however, his last principle, interference, suggests a more ideological aim—that assignments should interfere with students' previous thinking and ways of knowing (44). Other frameworks include Susan Peck MacDonald's (1987) analysis of how problems are defined in discipline-specific journals, Kip Strasma's (2007) rhetorical concepts that act as "terministic screens" (via Burke), and Carmen Manning and Heather Hanewell's (2007) use of Fred Newmann's explanation of "authentic intellectual engagement." While these examples suggest promising approaches, they are less suited to understanding more generally how assignments function as texts themselves.

Anis Bawarshi (2003) offers an intervention by theorizing how the first-year writing classroom functions as a system of genres facilitating student and teacher subjectivities, relationships, and writing. Interested in how classroom genres like the syllabus, writing prompt, and student essay organize and construct the ideological and discursive means used in the invention process, Bawarshi argues that writing prompts create subjectivities that students must inhabit and exigencies they must see themselves responding to in order to follow the premises of the prompt. As he explains, "The prompt situates student writers within a genred site of action in which students acquire and negotiate desires, subjectivities, commitments, and relations before they begin to write. The writing prompt not only moves the student writer to action; it also cues the student writer to enact a certain kind of action" (127). Using literacy narratives as an example, Bawarshi explains that even when a more complex and dynamic approach to the assignment is given, the ideological notion that literacy is empowering is often part of the prompt, eventually becoming part of the "successful" student essay (128). In this way, writing assignments cue not only a position for students to inhabit but also the ideological assumptions students must incorporate into their writing in order to produce "successful" writing.

Like Bawarshi, I believe writing assignments carry significant pedagogical power. If writing assignments do indeed cue students to how they should think and feel toward a particular subject, then they should be treated more consciously as a direct extension of pedagogy that carries epistemological power. Treating writing assignments as pedagogical extensions means understanding them as texts that signal the epistemologies and ideologies informing a particular pedagogy and, thus, a teacher's desires and hopes for how an assignment invites students into a particular subjective framework.

METHODS

Corpus of Writing Assignments

This study relies on a corpus of feminist-oriented writing assignments collected from the 2013 Feminisms and Rhetorics Conference.[2] I emphasized self-identified feminist assignments when recruiting participants because my research has not sought to determine or validate whether assignments are or are not feminist, but rather how these assignments point back to the teachers' feminist pedagogy. Of course, pedagogical self-identifications are complex, individual, numerous, and not as easily generalizable as the term *feminist pedagogy* might imply. Thus, I use the term *feminist-oriented* as a way to capture the complexity of naming and identifying a diverse array of feminist pedagogies, many of which are also informed by critical pedagogy, composition pedagogies and writing center studies, and other theoretical areas like cultural studies, Black feminist thought, women and gender studies, and queer studies.

---

2. Additional participants were recruited from the feminist workshop at the 2014 Conference on College Composition and Communication.

The corpus includes seventy-three writing assignments from twenty-six participating teachers and thirty different courses,[3] including: ten 100-level courses with twenty-eight assignments; five 200-level courses with thirteen assignments; ten upper-division courses with eighteen assignments; one professional writing course with four assignments; and four graduate-level courses with ten assignments. The corpus represents twenty different schools, all of which are public and private four-year liberal arts colleges and universities. The represented course topics range from first-year inquiries into literacy to upper-division courses on feminist theory to graduate seminars on rhetoric and composition. Only thirteen of the courses' titles explicitly emphasize feminist content. Perhaps surprisingly, given that many participants expressed concerns over whether their course was "feminist enough" to contribute, only twenty-seven of the assignments (37%) have explicit feminist content. Such content includes subject matter focused on women's lives (example course titles: Women Rhetors, Global Women's Lives, and Women of Color Across the African Diaspora), or feminism and gender as a central framework (example course titles: Romance, Gender, Identity, Gender and Writing, or Feminist Narratives: Theory and Practice). The courses not on feminist content are oriented instead to particular writing genres or skill sets, like classes on grant writing or composing with sound.

Identification of Feminist Pedagogy

By including both feminist content courses and courses on other topics, I hope to establish feminist pedagogy more broadly within the realm of a "conscious attention to worldview and goals" (Rupiper-Taggart et al. 2014, 4). That is, feminist pedagogy is not the same as teaching feminist *content* (e.g., reading feminist texts), but rather the enactment of feminist values in classroom practices, including but not limited to using feminist texts. In *Composing Feminisms*, Kay Siebler (2008) traces feminist pedagogical practices as emerging alongside critical and liberatory pedagogies in early women's studies courses (14). Siebler identifies sixteen themes from the history of feminist pedagogical scholarship, such as "confronting sex biases," "teaching with the whole self," "being overt with one's political and social location," and "working toward student critical consciousness" (38–39). Teaching texts speaking to these values is only one way that feminist pedagogy is enacted; other ways she describes include the physical arrangement of classrooms, allowing

---

3. Four participants submitted assignments for two different courses.

conflict in class discussion, and opening up one's syllabus for student critique and response. Of course, Siebler's feminist teaching themes are not the only version of feminism; however, they offer an example of how feminist pedagogy functions in complex ways that can be adapted to different classrooms, students, and purposes.

Throughout my analysis, I made efforts to connect what I see as feminist about the assignment texts to feminist scholarship; however, I also wanted to acknowledge that these identifications belie a complexity of overlapping feminist pedagogies as well as other critical pedagogies. Some might argue that feminist teaching values are simply good composition pedagogy. Indeed, feminist writing pedagogy's early emergence in composition occurred alongside process theories (Flynn 1988; Caywood and Overing 1987). Over time, feminism in composition evolved not only through composition theory and research but also through influences from women and gender studies theorists and feminists in outside fields. Each feminist teacher's pedagogy, thus, is an amalgamation of the historical and disciplinary versions of feminist pedagogy they have learned and the connections to scholarship they have engaged with. This co-emergence and development, coupled with the often-simultaneous learning of composition and feminist principles in graduate school, means there may be a natural overlap between feminist pedagogy and "good composition pedagogy." However, beyond my own identification of feminist values, these assignments are feminist because each teacher willingly submitted them to this study and self-identified as being influenced by feminism in their teaching.

Grounded Theory Analysis

I conducted an adapted grounded theory coding, drawing on sociology scholar Kathy Charmaz's (2006) heuristics to establish an approach wherein "data form the foundation of our theory and our analysis of these data generates the concepts we construct" (2). The corpus of writing assignments was coded in two rounds: the initial round involved line-by-line descriptions of the texts, and the second round of coding created focused categories that emerged from the descriptive codes (46).

My use of grounded theory was adapted to address my specific research question. Instead of coding with gerunds, as is done in sociology (Glaser and Strauss 1967), my coding emphasized detailed descriptions of each line, often relying on the actual language of the assignments. The coding was generally directed by my larger research question, specifically: How are feminist pedagogical values signaled in writing assignment texts? What assumptions, ideologies, epistemologies, and subjectivities are potentially embedded in feminist-oriented writing assignments? Although this theoretical RGS framework is in tension with the aim of traditional grounded theory, the methodological foundation of grounded theory—that categories and findings emerge from the data—was the primary motivation of the coding.

FEMINIST-ORIENTED WRITING ASSIGNMENTS: FINDINGS

Overview

Across the seventy-three feminist-oriented writing assignments, I coded thirty-eight (52%) as signaling feminist pedagogy through subjectivities and forty-five (62%) through arguments. In terms of subjectivities, the assignments most commonly position students as empowered or having valuable knowledge, ideas, experiences, and contributions. The most common arguments signaling feminist pedagogy are epistemological—about the construction of knowledge (often a specific type of knowledge, like gender or literacy). While most of the assignments uniquely position students and make specific arguments, they nonetheless share connections to a variety of feminist pedagogical values, offering students new ways of understanding their roles as students in the classroom, multiple ways of approaching a project in terms of methods or genres, and invitations for students to critically consider how knowledge and identity are constructed in particular spaces, discourses, or images.

Although Bawarshi's (2003) work suggests potential dangers in how assignments identify student subjectivities and values, I did not find any writing assignment texts to be problematic or even the slightest bit risky in terms of how they position students or the arguments they make. Bawarshi establishes the potential risk of assignments, claiming "the assumption seems to be that the student exists a priori as a writer who has only to follow the instructions of the teacher's prompt rather than as a reader who is first invoked or interpellated into the position of writer by the teacher's prompt" (130). His point and quick examples hint that interpellating students into particular subjectivities through assignment prompts is problematic because students may not want to identify with the subjectivities and arguments that assignments require them to identify with in order to write the successful essay. Theoretically, Bawarshi is right to caution about the dangers of subjectivities: not all students feel comfortable with the positions offered to them. However, through studying a larger collection of assignments, I found most of the assignment texts attempted to empower students, for instance by referencing their previous knowledge and life experiences, highlighting their expertise on a particular subject, or giving them more control and choices.

There does seem to be some risk in how the assignment genre might shape desires, thinking, and even worldviews; this risk relates to whether an assignment text—through its arguments, ideologies, and assumptions—aligns and forwards feminist pedagogy. Assignments not consciously connected to pedagogy both represent a lost opportunity and potentially shape students in ways that are less in line with feminist pedagogical values. Assignments signaling a feminist ideology offer particular frameworks from which students can reimagine the subject at hand, their understanding of knowledge construction, or their own roles as writers and people. Indeed, feminist subjectivities and arguments, as shown below, invite students to acknowledge and value their own knowledges, experiences, and contributions. Such textual cues are sometimes political, sometimes ethical, and certainly always value-based reorientations offered by the feminist pedagogy signaled within assignment prompts.

Student Subjectivities

Writing assignment prompts can provide particular subjectivities for students—expected writing class subjectivities like "writer," "researcher," or "critical thinker," but also more complex positions like "museum curator" or "sympathetic listener." Within this corpus of feminist-oriented assignments, there are six categories of explicit subjectivities[4] offered to students: empowering subjectivities, writer and/or researcher subjectivities, responsible to other subjectivities, novice subjectivities, developing subjectivities, and a final category of specific or otherwise unrelated subjectivities. Through studying these subjectivities, I found that the way we talk about who students are in assignments offers small but powerful moments that legitimize students—naming their agency, explicitly valuing them as whole beings, and empowering them to have confidence in their own knowledges and perspectives.

To further exemplify how these subjectivities work, I look at two sample assignments—one that includes both empowering and

---

4. Only thirty-six out of seventy-three assignments gave explicit subjectivities for students: moments describing or naming who students are, who they should be, or what the assignment asked them to be. By contrast, assignments with implicit subjectivities solely emphasized the writing task (e.g., "Select three of the readings and write a response").

Table 2.1. Subjectivities coded as feminist pedagogy

Categories (# of coded instances) Definition of Category	Selected Examples of Subjectivity Codes "Students are positioned as . . ."
Empowering Subjectivities (14) Positioning students as having valuable knowledge and experiences.	Individuals prepared for college [emotionally, socially, academically, experientially]
	Rhetorical critics [capable of analyzing rhetorical artifacts]
	Grant writers [having expert knowledge of their clients]
	Museum curators [having expert knowledge of texts]
	Students with agency [capable of thoughtful decisions about assignment objects and criteria]
	Valued experts [having valuable perspectives on course content, discussions, assignments, writing, or even the books used]
	Members of a discipline [that they are passionate about]
	Instruction-writers about love [romantic teachers, but with an eye toward cultural critique]
	Manifesto writers [with visions for the future and making positive change]
Writer & Researcher Subjectivities (10) Positioning students in terms of their roles as writers or researchers.	Social activists [enacting social change through writing and research]
	Researchers [with academic genealogies and theoretical family trees]
	Observers of place [researching their locations of city and buildings]
	Writers with audiences invested in writing [having readers interested in their literacy and writing processes]
	Motivated investigators [having a "burning question" to answer]
	Participants in a conversation [engaging in an intellectual conversation of research, writing, and thinking]
	Reflective writers [using a journal]
Specific & Random Subjectivities (7) Positioning students in roles outside of other categorical subjectivities.	Sympathetic listeners [with and to songs they hate]
	Product designers, inventors, and advertisers
	Curators of experiences with failure
	Correspondents [writing about college experiences to family, friends, and the college president]
Subjectivities Responsible to Others (3) Positioning students as responsible to other people.	Citizens/community partners with a social responsibility [engaging in social action]
	Grant writers [with obligations to clients after the end of the semester]

continued on next page

Table 2.1—*continued*

Categories (# of coded instances) Definition of Category	Selected Examples of Subjectivity Codes "Students are positioned as . . ."
Novice Subjectivities (2) Positioning students as new to an idea or activity.	Novices in the disciplinary conversations [learning how to participate in those conversations]
	Novices seeking to experience failure [with difficult tasks]
Developing Subjectivities (2) Positioning students as changing, growing or developing over time.	Changed/developed writers [through the course's reading, writing, and reflection activities]
	Changed/evolved thinkers [through exposure to different positions, new evidence, possibilities]

writer/researcher subjectivities and one that includes novice subjectivities. The assignment prompt containing empowering and writer/researcher subjectivities comes from a final project for a graduate-level course called Feminist Narratives: Theory and Practice. The syllabus explains that for the final project, course participants will: "complete . . . a substantial and significant piece of writing that integrates the theory and practice of feminist narratives in the context of her/his/hir ongoing scholarly work." To elaborate, a final page attached to the end of the syllabus says:

> **By class consensus, we decided** that the end-of-semester project would be a piece of text or digital writing that:
> 1. used narrative and narrative techniques in some significant way
> 2. addressed issues of gender in some significant way
> 3. consciously engaged with gender and narrative in the context of hegemonic power relations, either through the content of the writing and/or through its form and language
> 4. consciously wrestled with narrative and gender as existing and overlapping with some multiple realities and intersectional identities—which could include but are not limited to sexuality, class, race/nation/ethnicity, religion, dis/ability, language of origin, colonization, imperialism, capitalism, etc.
>
> This end-of-semester writing must be work that grows out of the semester of writing done for [this course], and can certainly be woven from writing exercises accomplished for the class. **There is no required length. Do the work you need to do to be serious and questioning.**
>
> Whatever semester writings are used, in this end-of-semester project these should also be consciously arranged, elaborated upon, and revised into a coherent (but necessarily in-process) whole. **All of this work should be done with an eye and ear to exploration of one or more of the "burning question(s)" that have occupied you during the semester.**

The opening line, which establishes that the assignment text was developed as a result of a classroom discussion, positions students and the professor as a collective body with the power to make decisions not only about individual writing goals, but also the purpose, context, direction, and requirements of classroom assignments. This first line is categorized as an empowering subjectivity because students are positioned alongside the professor as having control over major classroom decisions; students are given power and agency in the classroom. The last two paragraphs' concluding sentences (in bold) are each categorized as writing-based subjectivities, though they also overlap with the empowering category. In those, students are positioned as serious, questioning thinkers and writers in control of their writing enough to know how long a successful final project needs to be. Similarly, the final sentence positions students as intellectually motivated by a "burning question" throughout the entire semester. While these three moments might suggest overlapped subjectivities, the main subjectivity offered to students is one of being in control over their writing and as part of a larger collective in control of classroom assignments; students are empowered to understand themselves as both thoughtful writers and thoughtful classroom decision makers. These textual moments naming students' agency are informed by feminist pedagogical scholarship (and likely critical pedagogies) encouraging students to democratically make curriculum decisions.

Reviewing some of the "empowering" subjectivities in table 2.1—theorizers, contributors to women's rhetorics, manifesto writers, experts on their own writing—we might question whether these are actually empowering or if, perhaps more likely, students may understand these positions as difficult, more work, or simply academic jargon. Contributing to women's rhetorics, for instance, may feel empowering to *me* as a feminist teacher, while just sounding like an academic request that students see no value or interest in. However, I would argue that the ways a prompt situates students in relation to knowledge and expertise can help those students understand their position within the classroom and what is possible with each writing task. Prompts asking them to inhabit a position of knowledge and insight invite them to reconsider their sense of their own capabilities.

Even though many of the empowering subjectivities position students as experts or knowledgeable, this points to the fact that critical thinking—indeed, many of the writing skills or tasks we ask students to perform in assignments—might actually be new for students. Therefore, how do we position students in writing assignments that tackle new topics and skills? Two of the coded assignments position students as novices.[5] The role of a novice might seem a disempowered position, since novices lack experience and knowledge by definition; however, both of the prompts contextualize and explain the novice subjectivity in empowering terms. In one example, from the course Rhetorics of Failure, students are asked to become novices of anything they choose for the purposes of failing, trying again, and then writing a critical narrative of their experiences. In this example, students are literally novices for the purpose of failing; we might rightly ask, what could be more disempowering? The full text of the assignment (from the syllabus) reads as follows:

> For this project, you will embark on a weeks-long adventure to learn or achieve something you've always wanted to do but have never attempted: juggling, riding a unicycle, playing a song on an instrument, translating a passage of writing from one language to another, making a short film, writing a play, or something else. Whatever you choose to attempt, it should be significantly difficult that you will expect to experience failure in the process. In other words, the object here is not to succeed, but to try, fail, and try again. You should meticulously document your process with a journal, blog, vlog, or other record of progress, recording not only your strategies for learning, but also your feelings and thoughts about difficulty and failure. Your final submission should also include a reflection on the process as a whole, drawing on course discussions and readings, so that the final submission demonstrates creative, personal, and critical engagement with important course concepts.

While being a novice who fails doesn't sound very empowering, the scope of the listed activities casts failure as part of the process of learning new and challenging activities, a vast array of life experiences we might expect people to encounter at some point in their lives. The assignment suggests part of this process is "feelings and thoughts about difficulty and failure." In other words, students can expect that failing involves an emotional response and thinking about the struggle itself. The assignment positions students as having to tackle a "new-to-them" activity and fail, not because of any "inherent-to-them" reason, but because failure is simply a necessary part of trying new things. This basic assumption assignment suggests that rather than disempowering students (by asking them to fail), this experience will allow students to understand failure in more complex and different ways than they might have previously.

While this assignment may not seem explicitly feminist-oriented, it enacts Siebler's (2008) feminist pedagogical value of "working towards

5. Although these two assignments could also be counted as empowering subjectivities, they were only counted once (as novice subjectivities). While my analysis explores connections and trends across categories, none of the subjectivity codes were double-counted, primarily for clarity's sake.

student critical consciousness" (56–59). Siebler describes part of critical consciousness as "shun[ning] easy binary models of pro/con, right/ wrong, and good/bad and instead replace them with models that integrate multiple viewpoints and opinions" (57). Additionally, through the assignment's explicit references to emotions and learning as a form of doing, students are positioned as whole beings. Feminist teachers (like hooks 1994; Siebler 2008) have long discussed that teaching as a whole being—emotional, physical, intellectual, and spiritual—is central to feminist pedagogy. Furthermore, in the full text of the final project (the "novice narrative"), students are allowed to choose between this option and two other options, providing choice for less adventurous students more comfortable with other subjectivities they can embody when completing the final project.

This example illustrates how the subjectivities offered to students in writing prompts are understood within the context of the assumptions and arguments each assignment makes. For instance, the "novice who fails" subjectivity can only be understood within the assignment's larger arguments about failure—that failing is natural, necessary, part of the learning process, and something everyone experiences differently. The connection between subjectivities and arguments of each assignment is also clear in the subjectivities charted in table 2.1—more context is almost always necessary to understand, for instance, what a "writer and critic" subjectivity means. While I am separating subjectivities and arguments into two sections, I hope the analysis reflects the direct relationship between the two.

Arguments and Assumptions

Four broad trends emerge in regard to the implied arguments signaling feminist pedagogy within the analyzed assignments: epistemological arguments, identity-based arguments, arguments connecting theory to personal experiences, and arguments promoting social action. The two largest trends are arguments about epistemology, which make or imply claims about how knowledge is constructed (socially, culturally, and materially) and situated (historically and contextually), and arguments about identity, which define or contextualize identity in general or in specific situations. There is quite a lot of coherence across the epistemological codes, in that many of the assignments used similar language to describe how a subject is constructed; however, there are fewer similarities in the identity-based codes, as the instances tend to be more assignment-specific and address a variety of aspects about identity in specific contexts. For instance, in the eight assignments that make arguments about gender, each one explains or contextualizes gender in different ways. For example, one assignment builds on the argument of how women are constrained by men's ideas and expectations, another assignment argues how women rhetors' historical and rhetorical context is important for understanding their rhetorical choices, and a third makes the argument that students' previous classes and textbooks make implicit claims about gender, sex, and the gender spectrum. The emphasis on and overlap between identity and epistemology arguments is not surprising, as both are central interests within feminist scholarship, coming from a desire to understand how a particular identity is constructed in specific contexts, or how identities are affected by historic, economic, social, material, and cultural issues (see Hesford 1999; Lu 1998; Ronald and Ritchie 2006; Wilson Logan 1998; Pough 2006; Jung 2005).

Through studying the arguments in these feminist-oriented assignments, I found one strand running through all four categories, which may explain many of the overlaps between the categories. This strand is an echo of the early feminist political motto, *the personal is political.* While not every code directly invokes this feminist mantra, the selected examples in table 2.2 show how feminist teachers demonstrate students' identities, experiences, knowledges, and reflections as being central to the knowledge-making work of the classroom—and to consciousness-raising efforts to foster students' critical understanding of the world and their own lives.

Arguments about Identity and Epistemology in a First-Year Writing Assignment Sequence

In order to provide a more in-depth view of how assignments signal feminist pedagogy through arguments, in this section I analyze a sequence from a first-year writing course on identity, literacy, and representations. The inferred course inquiry[6] and assignments for this course are a useful example of how a feminist teacher might bring feminist theories and arguments into a course without an explicitly feminist theme. The sequence begins with a "representations" assignment, followed by a literacy-focused autobiography, a literacy biography, and a final writing process reflection and course portfolio.

The first assignment, called the "Representations Assignment Sequence," makes arguments about epistemology and identity. The assignment is a set of smaller writing tasks requiring students to consider

---

6. This teacher did not submit a full syllabus, only the assignment sequence.

Table 2.2. Arguments coded as feminist pedagogy

Category (# of coded instances)	Selected Examples of Argument Codes (# of instances) "Arguments about how . . ."
Epistemological Arguments (27)	Failure is socially constructed (2)
	Memorials reflect social constructions of race, class, gender, and sexuality (1)
	Gender is constructed through textbooks, educational classes, and cultural texts that represent courtship (2)
	WOC (women of color) writers employ themes of location to advance themselves and their communities (1)
	The meaning of the veil/burka is historically situated and determined based on context and emphasis (1)
	Globalization is an academic object of study with its own set of questions, parameters, definitions, arguments, and key players (1)
	Taste is constructed [in terms of songs we love and hate] (1)
	Sounds construct our environments and carry meaning (2)
Identity Arguments (25)	Arguments about gender (8)
	Arguments about gender and sexuality (2)
	Arguments about student identity (1)
	Arguments about women rhetors (2)
	Arguments about intersectional identities (4)
	Arguments about bodies and embodiment (2)
	Arguments about women of color (2)
Arguments Connecting Theory to Personal Experiences (8)	Theory/readings can better help us understand our experiences (7)
	Theory/readings might conflict with or complicate our experiences (1)
Arguments Tied to Social Action (5)	Students participate in social action [contributing to society by doing something to make change] (3)
	Students understand social action (2)

how they represent themselves through various means. The assignment's excerpted overview says:

> Identity is a process of construction. Identity is a process of communication in which we write ourselves (figuratively) and literally (using words and writing technologies). Identity as a process of communication and writing almost always involves the entwined modes of visual and verbal. In

this assignment sequence, writers focus on the interplay of the visual and the verbal in the communicative act by constructing and communicating a representation of themselves to their classmates. How do we choose the details that communicate our meaning? How do those details represent meaning? How do visual and verbal work together to communicate meaning?

This framing paragraph connects identity to how we construct meaning and represent ourselves, verbally and visually. The emphasis on how both communicating and understanding communications are processes of constructing meaning is explicit. The concept of identity is more vague; however, the actual writing tasks suggest that identity is meant to be understood as the complexity of who students understand themselves to be as individuals. The tasks ask students to: first, "select three objects which communicate something about you as a person and as a writer"; second, "select a piece of music that communicates something about yourself"; and finally, "write a 1000 word reflection on the process of representing yourself without words." With each task, students are prompted to write about how their identity is uniquely communicated.

These tasks make an argument that, while the construction of self and meaning is complex and difficult, individuals do have some control over that construction through the choices they make. In the assignment, students have control over their literal choices of objects and music; however, the assignment also asserts that students choose their self-representation on a daily basis through the clothing they wear, the objects they carry, the music they listen to, the things they read. The assignment invokes a feminist investment in the materiality of how identities are constructed—a move echoing Marguerite Helmers' (2006) similar assignment that calls on feminist rhetoricians to use everyday objects in the classroom as "an opportunity to exercise a certain kind of mindfulness in which things are brought out of habitual use to explain their use in daily ritual and identity formation" (126). Similarly, the "representations" assignment asks students to be self-reflexive, using their object and music selection as sites to critically reflect on how their values and identities are constructed and represented through those choices. While perhaps a stretch, I also see this assignment as making a suggestion to students regarding how they interpret other students' choices of objects and music—that is, in the process of encouraging students to understand the complexity of their own self-representations, they are invited to interpret and understand the self-representations of others more kindly.

The second and third assignments in this course sequence, the autobiography and biography, contain epistemological arguments about how students' understandings of literacy develop. The following excerpt from the Literacy Autobiography assignment gives an overview:

> Writing is always an act of interpretation, construction, and meaning making. Even when writers appear to be making statements of fact no one would disagree with, the written words the writer constructs into sentences are ones which are filtered through her own unique way of putting things. No two people see everything exactly the same; no two people write exactly the same thing even when they are writing about the same event or theme.
>
> This assignment asks that you pause to think about where and when and how literacy enters into your life. What early or significant memories do you have about literacy? Why do those memories remain? What was significant about them, or how do you carry the lessons you learned in those instances with you today? This assignment asks that you contemplate and sift back through your memories to think carefully (as in "with care," slowly and deliberately) about the ways your early interactions with literacy might have affected your later (current) relationships with literacies.

The opening paragraph starts by explicitly explaining that writing itself is a construction. The writer is positioned as having a unique perspective on the world as well as a specifically individual way of writing—this individualism is explained as the reason that "writing is always an act of interpretation, construction, and meaning making." The assignment, thus, argues that students' own understanding of literacy is constructed by their personal set of experiences *with* literacy.

For Bawarshi (2003), one of the risks of an assignment's assumptions and arguments is that for students to write a successful essay, they often have to adopt the same perspectives endorsed by the assignment. He notes, in regard to literacy assignments in particular, that often "the transformative power of literacy as a necessary tool for success and achievement" is "embedded" within the assignment, and thus encouraged in the uptake (128). This particular literacy narrative assignment, however, seems to almost consciously not define or position literacy exclusively as empowering. For instance, the following excerpted heuristic questions (from the end of the assignment) makes the same argument—that specific literate experiences are constructed and situated by the places, people, technologies, and affordances of literacies:

> Recall your earliest experiences with literacy, literate activities, literate behaviors.
>
> - where do you remember seeing people reading and writing?
> - what did your parents and older siblings read? write?
> - what do you remember about learning how to read and write? who taught you? what feelings did you have about it?

- was reading and writing different for you in school than it was outside school?
- what role has visual communication played in your life?
- how do the visual and verbal work together to communicate meaning?
- do you think there are social consequences or potential impacts on your lifestyle that depend on your literate capabilities?
- how do you expect to deal with new literacies in the future?
- what advantages and problems do you see with the way you approach technology?

In these invention-based questions, there are no qualifying adjectives; students are not prompted to consider both positive and negative literacy experiences, rather they are simply directed to specific contexts in which they may have experiences with literacy. The argument is that literacy is individually defined, and each person's definition is constructed by their personal history. While the first sentence offers the theoretical explanation, most of the assignment focuses on more concrete language situating literacy in relation to specific contexts—an underlying argument that orients individual experiences and histories as intrinsic to the construction of knowledge.

This assignment sequence successfully draws on feminist theories of identity construction and makes them visible in ways that enact feminist pedagogical values. While the corpus includes many assignments with textual arguments that likewise signal feminist pedagogy, this sequence suggests that understanding an assignment's arguments and assumptions is important precisely because they orient students in particular ways toward specific subjects—including literacy, feminism, writing, and their role as students and people in the world. In other words, an assignment's arguments have the power to influence how students approach and engage with a writing assignment, how they understand the topic, and what they think is possible.

CONCLUSION

Although I'm working within a feminist framework here, I would argue that whatever a teacher's pedagogical orientation might be, their pedagogy should inform what writing assignment texts look like—specifically in how they position students, make assumptions and arguments, and construct different orientations toward subjects. These textual cues make pedagogical values visible. Indeed, how we align ourselves pedagogically and academically matters because it connects us to a particular academic genealogy and history, thus helping us understand how and why our individual (feminist) genealogy is important for assignments and praxis. Alexander and Mohanty (1997) argue that academic genealogies and legacies matter precisely because we sometimes inherit and continue to uphold (sometimes unknowingly) hegemonic oppressive discourses, ideologies, and actions. I would extend their argument to encourage teachers to be aware of their pedagogical rationales and disciplinary genealogies for assignments and to clearly signal them in assignment texts. Assignment design is often informed by departmental learning objectives, course descriptions, and new trends or ideas from scholarship and colleagues; however, building academic values like empowered subjectivities, critical consciousness, and new perspectives into genres like the assignment prompt fosters a finely tuned pedagogically conscious academic genealogy that is essential for feminist teachers and those invested in transformative teaching. The goal is alignment between the pedagogical values we claim to have and the classroom genres that enact those values.

REFERENCES

Alexander, M. Jacqui, and Chandra Talpade Mohanty. 1997. "Genealogies, Legacies, Movements." In *Feminist Genealogies, Colonial Legacies, Democratic Futures*, edited by M. Jacqui Alexander and Chandra Talpade Mohanty, xii–xlii. New York: Routledge.

Allan, Elizabeth G. 2018. " 'Real Research' or 'Just for a Grade'?: Ethnography, Ethics, and Engagement in the Undergraduate Writing Studies Classroom." *Pedagogy* 18 (2): 247–77.

Bartholomae, David. 1982. "Writing Assignments: Where Writing Begins." *fforum* 4 (1): 35–45.

Bartholomae, David, and Anthony Petrosky. 1986. *Facts, Artifacts, and Counterfacts: Theory and Method for a Reading and Writing Course.* Portsmouth, NH: Boynton/Cook.

Bawarshi, Anis. 2003. *Genre and the Invention of the Writer: Reconsidering the Place of Invention in Composition.* Logan: Utah State University Press.

Berlin, James. 1988. "Rhetoric and Ideology in the Writing Class." *College English* 50 (5): 477–94.

Caywood, Cynthia L., and Gillian R. Overing, eds. 1987. *Teaching Writing: Pedagogy, Gender, and Equity.* Albany: State University of New York Press.

Charmaz, Kathy. 2006. *Constructing Grounded Theory: A Practical Guide through Qualitative Analysis.* Thousand Oaks, CA: SAGE.

Davis, Robert, and Mark Shadle. 2000. " 'Building a Mystery': Alternative Research Writing and the Academic Act of Seeking." *College Composition and Communication* 51 (3): 417–46.

Flynn, Elizabeth A. 1988. "Composing as a Woman." *College Composition and Communication* 39 (4): 423–35.

Freadman, Anne. 2002. "Uptake." In *The Rhetoric and Ideology of Genre: Strategies for Stability and Change*, edited by Richard M. Coe, Lorelei Lingard, and Tatiana Teslenko, 39–53. Cresskill, NJ: Hampton Press.

Gardner, Traci. 2008. *Designing Writing Assignments.* Urbana, IL: NCTE.

Glaser, Barney G., and Anselm L. Strauss. 1967. *The Discovery of Grounded Theory: Strategies for Qualitative Research.* Chicago, IL: Aldine.

Graves, Roger, Theresa Hyland, and Boba M. Samuels. 2010. "Undergraduate Writing Assignments: An Analysis of Syllabi at One Canadian College." *Written Communication* 27 (3): 293–317.

Helmers, Marguerite. 2006. "Objects, Memory, and Narrative: New Notes toward Materialist Rhetoric." In *Teaching Rhetorica: Theory, Pedagogy, Practice,* edited by Kate Ronald and Joy S. Ritchie, 114–30. Portsmouth, NH: Boynton/Cook.

Hesford, Wendy S. 1999. *Framing Identities: Autobiography and the Politics of Pedagogy.* Minneapolis: University of Minnesota Press.

Hilgers, Thomas L., Edna Lardizabal Hussey, and Monica Stitt-Bergh. 1999. " 'As You're Writing, You Have These Epiphanies': What College Students Say about Writing and Learning in Their Majors." *Written Communication* 16 (3): 317–53.

hooks, bell. 1994. *Teaching to Transgress: Education as the Practice of Freedom.* New York: Routledge.

Jung, Julie. 2005. *Revisionary Rhetoric, Feminist Pedagogy, and Multigenre Texts.* Carbondale: Southern Illinois University Press.

Lindemann, Erika. 2001. "Making and Evaluating Writing Assignments." In *A Rhetoric for Writing Teachers,* 4th ed., 213–21. New York: Oxford University Press.

Lu, Min-Zhan. 1998. "Reading and Writing Differences: The Problematic of Experience." In *Feminism and Composition Studies: In Other Words,* edited by Susan C. Jarratt and Lynn Worsham, 239–51. New York: MLA.

MacDonald, Susan Peck. 1987. "Problem Definition in Academic Writing." *College Writing* 49 (3): 315–31.

Manning, Carmen, and Heather Hanewell. 2007. "Creating More Effective Assignments: The Challenge of Authentic Intellectual Engagement." *Journal of Teaching Writing* 23 (2): 35–54.

Melzer, Dan. 2009. "Writing Assignments across the Curriculum: A National Study of College Writing." *College Composition and Communication* 61 (2): 240–61.

Molloy, Cathryn. 2016. "Multimodal Composing as Healing: Toward a New Model for Writing as Healing Courses." *Composition Studies* 44 (2): 134–52.

Nelson, Jennie. 1990. "This Was an Easy Assignment: Examining How Students Interpret Academic Writing Tasks." *Research in the Teaching of English* 24 (4): 362–96.

Pough, Gwendolyn. 2006. " 'Each One, Pull One': Womanist Rhetoric and Black Feminist Pedagogy in the Writing Classroom." In *Teaching Rhetorica: Theory, Pedagogy, Practice,* edited by Kate Ronald and Joy S. Ritchie, 66–81. Portsmouth, NH: Boynton/Cook.

Ronald, Kate, and Joy S. Ritchie, eds. 2006. *Teaching Rhetorica: Theory, Pedagogy, Practice.* Portsmouth, NH: Boynton/Cook.

Rupiper-Taggart, Amy, Brooke Hessler, and Kurt Schick. 2014. "What Is Composition Pedagogy? An Introduction." In *A Guide to Composition Pedagogies,* edited by Gary Tate, Amy Rupiper-Taggart, Kurt Schick, and Brooke Hessler, 2nd ed., 1–19. New York: Oxford University Press.

Shipka, Jody. 2007. "This Was (NOT!) an Easy Assignment: Negotiating an Activity-Based Multimodal Framework for Composing." *Computers and Composition Online.* http://cconlinejournal.org/not_easy.

Shipka, Jody. 2013. "Including, but Not Limited to, the Digital: Composing Multimodal Texts." In *Multimodal Literacies and Emerging Genres,* edited by Tracey Bowen and Carl Whithaus, 73–89. Pittsburgh, PA: University of Pittsburgh Press.

Siebler, Kay. 2008. *Composing Feminism(s): How Feminists Have Shaped Composition Theories and Practices.* Cresskill, NJ: Hampton Press.

Strasma, Kip. 2007. "Assignments by Design." *Teaching English in the Two-Year College* 34 (3): 248–63.

White, Edward M. 2007. *Assigning, Responding, Evaluating: A Writing Teacher's Guide.* 4th ed. New York: Bedford/St. Martin's.

Wilson Logan, Shirley. 1998. "'When and Where I Enter': Race, Gender, and Composition Studies." In *Feminism and Composition Studies: In Other Words,* edited by Susan C. Jarratt and Lynn Worsham, 45–57. New York: MLA.

3
PATTERNS, NEGOTIATIONS, AND IDEOLOGIES
Contract Grading as Genre

Virginia M. Schwarz

There are many reasons why teachers in higher education resist or eschew traditional grading practices or, as Jesse Stommel (2018) puts it, "ungrade." Asao Inoue (2012) has identified several problems that grades pose: they replace authentic, formative feedback; they create false hierarchies that work against building a collaborative learning environment; and they serve as extrinsic motivators that do not necessarily develop into intrinsic motivation or support learning. Additionally, in writing courses in particular, grades are often calculated through dominant cultural linguistic and behavioral norms that disproportionally privilege affluent white students and those who have the most access to academic resources and support. This desire to move away from grades to create better learning environments has resulted in a range of assessment methods, including portfolios, peer evaluations, process and reflection letters, and grading contracts (Stommel 2018).

Contract grading serves as an alternative to points, percentages, and other grade-based forms of evaluation that accumulate throughout a term and derive from teachers' definitions and perceptions of quality. Thus, the factors that determine a required end-of-course grade shift so that individual assignments become pass/no pass or acceptable/unacceptable rather than traditionally graded. The process a teacher chooses for calculating end grades may depend on their reason for this shift to begin with, but most of the time the course grade signifies the number of assignments a student completes—i.e., labor (Inoue 2015). This labor is articulated through a "grading contract," a written agreement between teachers and students that outlines specific pathway(s) for each possible end-of-course grade—for example, the requirements for earning grades such as A, B, or C. Furthermore, grading contracts might include opportunities for students to co-design

https://doi.org/10.7330/9781646422920.c003

those course requirements or develop rubrics for individual assignments. In these classrooms, contract grading is often situated in critical or justice-centered pedagogies (Inoue 2015; Shor 1996). As a writing teacher in higher education committed to anti-oppressive approaches to teaching and learning, I have remained curious about the ways this method of assessment has been or could be taken up—in other words, the ways contract grading lives in practice and mediates our educational experiences.

Grading contracts have been present in higher education literature and writing courses since at least the 1960s (Farber 1990; Villanueva 2014). Despite its longevity in the classroom, however, research on contract grading remains limited in scope: namely, it has yet to be theorized and studied as a pedagogically diverse body of work. This is due in part to a lack of scholarship: that is, the publications available to us do not accurately capture the many practitioners in the field working with grading contracts and the improvements and innovations they likely implement at the close of each term. Additionally, most research does not offer empirically based studies, instead consisting mainly of classroom narratives (e.g., Farber 1990; Shor 1996) or intellectual debates (e.g., Danielewicz and Elbow 2009; Shor 2009). In these works, authors primarily justify and argue for their own version of the contract over another. Furthermore, published studies that are empirical in nature tend to focus on examining student outcomes and behaviors in relation to a contract's perceived impact (Inman and Powell 2018; Inoue 2012; Spidell and Thelin 2006). While this research is crucial to the field's understanding of contract grading, the specific features of the grading contracts used in those studies and the decision-making processes of the teachers composing them remain "occluded" and unexplored in scholarship (Neaderhiser 2016). A genre approach would bring these pedagogical components to the surface by expanding the unit of analysis from an individual text to a collection of texts and their situated contexts. This would allow more robust comparison across practitioners. Currently, we have examples of grading contracts but very few ways of talking about them.

Rhetorical genre studies (RGS) is capable of addressing these gaps by defining and conceptualizing contract grading through its many "uptakes" (Freadman 2002) or "principles of variation" (Danielewicz and Elbow 2009, 257). Seeing these variations as an area worthy of study allows the field to recognize individual typified features and distinguish between multiple existing models. Furthermore, as educators become more aware of the differences between and nuances within grading contracts, we should be able to design better methods and arrive at more specific conclusions when evaluating their effectiveness. Finally, with a deeper understanding of grading contracts' variations, teachers might also be able to identify and defamiliarize the genre's conventions that have been adopted uncritically and could be harmful to students. The goal, then, becomes not to advocate for one version of a contract over another, but rather to develop a heuristic so that all teachers continually revise their assessment practices to create more accessible, inclusive, and socially just classroom environments.

This chapter is intended for current and future practitioners of contract grading, especially for those who teach in writing and writing-intensive courses. However, those in other disciplines might be asking similar questions posed here about the design of grading contracts (e.g., what should count toward the end of the course grade and how each of those components are weighted). This chapter may also be relevant for those wanting to think more deeply about classroom assessment generally. Additionally, as a part of this particular collection, contract grading serves as an example of a classroom genre that would benefit from more theoretical development as a body of work and as differentiated iterations, or subgenres. This discussion begins by articulating the concept of assessment genres and argues that contract grading, as an assessment genre, is an expression of ideology that comes into being through many choice points. Then several approaches to grading contracts are brought into conversation, prompting readers to explore their affordances and constraints and theorize potential innovations. Throughout this chapter, I seek to accumulate an inventory of typified features within contract grading so that readers may critically engage with the many moving components of its design, each representing a negotiation and decision on the part of its author.

CONTRACT GRADING AS AN ASSESSMENT GENRE

Genres are not simply categories of texts; they are socially constructed patterns that mediate texts and actions (Miller 1984, 1994). In a classroom, sets of genres—documents and their situations or enactments—operationalize teaching and learning, such as syllabi, assignment prompts, and end comments (Bawarshi and Reiff 2010). Within this interconnected system or "ecology" (Inoue 2015), assessment constitutes a series of social actions that are ideologically and rhetorically complex—that is, they are formed by and respond to people, spaces, and relationships (Miller 1984; Bawarshi and Reiff 2010).

Assessment genres might entail a variety of classroom activities, such as peer review, marginal comments, student-teacher conferences, or grades on individual assignments. They might also constitute others within the institution: admissions, hiring, and tenure and promotion. These types of assessment—or "assessment genres"—communicate beliefs about performance, often relying on habituated appraisals of standards.

Contract grading, as a classroom assessment genre, intervenes in the very specific activity of determining students' end-of-course grade. This methodological shift does not happen in isolation; removing grades throughout the term, either fully or partially, impacts interconnected processes around assignments, rubrics, and feedback. Furthermore, as a class unfolds, a series of ongoing, emergent contexts and responses will continuously shape the ways the grading contract is actualized and performed. Assessment genres are also shaped by the assumptions and values of teachers, students, and—to some extent—administrators and other outside constituents. Whether teachers employ contract grading or grade-based processes, these patterns of assigning end-of-course grades should always be seen as ideological.

Assessment genres mediate relationships by communicating or emphasizing specific values; therefore, choices about grading can either further or undermine a teacher's vision for the course. For example, in student-centered classes, teachers might tell students to take risks. However, their course policies may not allow revision and rewrites. As Farber (1990) notes, "You can tell students anything you want about 'taking responsibility' and 'thinking for yourself.' The grading system you employ—a middle finger extended before them—is more eloquent still" (136). Similarly, Inoue (2015) emphasizes the centrality of classroom writing assessment in course design, arguing that it is "more important than pedagogy because it always trumps what you say or what you attempt to do with your students. And students know this. They feel it." (9).

Because of assessment's critical mediating role in the classroom, Shor (2009) argues that "grading is a social practice in a public space, the classroom" and "forms us into the people we become" (21). Assessment genres function as mechanisms for eliciting certain classroom and writing behaviors; thus, they produce and maintain ideal writing and ideal students compliant with particular standards. Grading contracts are no different. Some grading contracts do aim to interrupt, even momentarily, dominant cultural assumptions about quality or merit; however, they still, in part, come into being through an imagined student audience with specific characteristics and needs. In her analysis of syllabi, Bailey (2010) theorizes that teachers, consciously and unconsciously, "orient their syllabi and their teaching practices to the image of 'who they think they are teaching' (knowledgeable competent students who want to learn? Irresponsible students who party too much?)" (152). Teachers often begin conceptualizing courses and their corresponding grading practices by thinking about what students lack and what they will need to be successful. These approximations are typically made before the course begins and policies are given to students or presented to students for negotiation. Although the methods and calculations may be different from traditional grades, grading contracts still reward certain students, behaviors, or learning tasks over others. They are always designed with a socially constructed and inherently problematic "other" in mind: the student. The goal of contract grading may be to resist or reject meritocratic assessment, but without critical attention to genre, merit is simply reconfigured, never fully problematized.

Student agreement is an additional, sometimes unpredictable factor that determines how grades will function. When students enter a college classroom, their assumptions and values play a role in creating the environment. As researchers have noted, grading contracts cannot supplant years of prior socialization; students' prior experiences have reified the symbolic meaning of grades and are attached to grades as a sign of progress (Inman and Powell 2018). In fact, in cases where grading contracts have "failed," students and teachers have voiced concerns about grading contracts failing to meet their needs and expectations going into the course that were no doubt formed through years of schooling (Inman and Powell 2018). This makes sense. Students are regularly expected to assess and negotiate various classroom documents, including syllabi, assignment prompts, and feedback. From a student perspective, successfully completing a class often requires accurately appraising a series of teacher-authored texts. Any interruption in routine and normalized practices might cause discomfort and anxiety; contracts are, in fact, a new assessment genre that students need to learn in a high-stakes situation.

As Afros and Schryer (2009) point out in their study of syllabi, students are not the only audience for institutional documents. This is also true for assessment genres. Typically, these genres are articulated through documents that have readers outside the classroom and, depending on the institution, are bound up in processes of accountability. Because systems like contract grading, which push back on traditional grading practices, occur within this larger context, designing classroom practices that may be perceived as weird or radical could pose a risk for teachers in precarious or contingent positions, such as non-tenure-track or adjunct faculty. As an institutional policy document, assessment genres also have multiple audiences and purposes. For example, many believe that grades introduce students into the rituals of the campus community and its specific discourses. Grades might communicate to students that they need to try harder or try again. Department colleagues and administrators hold their own opinions and expectations of what course grading should look like. In fact, just as many institutions have common syllabi, required language, or templates to assist teaching staff in design, they often present rubrics and offer opportunities for "grade norming." Because institutions need to ensure students are meeting learning outcomes, the burden is usually on individual teachers authoring an intervention to explain their reasoning rather than on the group(s) upholding current, accepted policy. This explaining can mean significant energy and labor. Grading contracts are formed by and within the values of their institutions, and teachers must be aware of campus grading structures, exit exams, and placement tests.

Assessment genres are bound to a multitude of stakeholders. When grading alternatives are utilized, they still must fulfill an evaluative role and emerge from corresponding sets of expectations. By providing a framework for theorizing assessment as social practice, RGS affords educators and researchers promising ways to move beyond what is traditionally functional, handbook-style knowledge to understand contract grading—and assessment genres more broadly—as an enactment of values that expands and restricts classroom possibilities. The genre is regulated, in part, through material pressures, such as grading templates circulating within the department or proficiency exams required by the institution. Pressures might also linger in the lore or assumptions we have about students and perceptions of what they need. Given this focus on the socio-rhetorical aspects of assessment, RGS makes possible certain important (and often neglected) questions like, what is contract grading and what does/can contract grading *do*?

CONTRACT GRADING: A WORKING DEFINITION

As an assessment genre, grading contracts exist as a constellation of patterned features— primarily held together by a tiered structure of labor rather than grades on individual assignments. Through repeated use, various other characteristics have become recognizable, creating definition and expectation. This is why grading contracts are distinguishable from (though sometimes compatible with) other forms of classroom assessment such as portfolios or rubrics-based evaluation. However, contract grading is also not a stable, monolithic practice; rather, the term embodies strands of related practices, some of which operate under the surface in more liminal or occluded spaces. There is just as much variation in grading contracts as any other form of assessment (i.e., points, percentages, letter grades) (Albracht et al. 2019). This is an important point because when contract grading is discussed in scholarship, the authors often focus on one narrowed, localized practice or specific grading contract model. They also tend to ignore the multiple surrounding histories and variables that have called that singular enactment into being, such as the identities, experiences, and strengths of instructors; the types of preparation available to new instructors or graduate teaching assistants; and institutional regulations and policies. Contract grading may be recognizable, but this practice is also infinitely complex.

In a class that uses grading contracts, students meet each writing assignment in a specific way tied to their labor or process rather than through the averages and numbers of traditional grading systems that depend on teacher perceptions of quality (Danielewicz and Elbow 2009; Inoue 2012). This means that there are no partial points; instead, assignments are usually evaluated in terms of pass/fail or acceptable/ unacceptable so that decisions about grades are minimal (Elbow 1998; Potts 2010). Then, to raise their course grade, students opt into a higher number of assignments or variations on those assignments (Danielewicz and Elbow 2009; Potts 2010). For example, students might agree to a specific number of projects, such as X number of essays with Y page count (Danielewicz and Elbow 2009). This usually results in a tiered grading structure, with the requirements for each A–F final course grade made available as a checklist or guide. The document that articulates these conditions—the contract—functions as an agreement between teachers and students at the beginning of the term for the way students will be assessed during the course (Inoue 2015). Usually, teachers include a written statement or rationale for choosing contract grading for the course, perhaps verbalized on the first day of class or brought up throughout the term. The grading contract itself can be embedded within the syllabus or exist as a separate document.

While these recurring features usually define contract grading, several other characteristics may be articulated differently and vary in importance from person to person, class to class, or even over the course of time within a class (Inoue 2019). For example, behavioral expectations like attendance, timeliness, or participation are often tied to the grade tiers within a grading contract. Some teachers might incorporate deadlines into their classroom policies (e.g., Inoue 2019), while others might opt for more flexible approaches like deadline windows (e.g., Womack 2017). Additionally, grading contracts usually account for some aspect of the writing process, but teachers assign and value that labor differently, perhaps through labor logs that track the hours and methods of engagement (e.g., Inoue 2019) or something material, such as required revisions (e.g., Danielewicz and Elbow 2009). These features embody a series of decisions that regulate and structure classroom spaces as well as the people within them; they are choice points every teacher negotiates on some level and are not unique to contract grading. As each teacher engages with assessment choices, sometimes deliberately and sometimes unknowingly, they make a series of decisions for addressing and prioritizing these components.

To see what grading contracts do or accomplish, it is important to realize that teachers employ them for different reasons and, therefore, design them toward different outcomes. There is general agreement among teachers who utilize contract grading: gains in writing come from continuous feedback, self-assessment, and revisions as opposed to grades (Danielewicz and Elbow 2009). This belief, however, stems from different epistemological positions. Grading contracts can operate as an extension of process-based (e.g., Elbow), critical (e.g., Shor), or antiracist (e.g., Inoue) pedagogies. Additionally, grading contracts may emerge within theories of universal design for learning (UDL) that center access for students with invisible and visible disabilities. From a disability studies framework, Anne-Marie Womack (2017) points out the potential flexibility of grading contracts and notes that "critical pedagogy and disability studies share common goals of examining social contexts, empowering disenfranchised groups, and raising political consciousness" (520). Social theories of disability focus on structural processes of othering and, as such, are able to disrupt normalized views of individuals and their environments to (re)imagine ways of creating access (McKinney 2018).

The connection between grading contracts and social justice is not a given, though (Albracht et al. 2019; Villanueva 2014). Contracts may also be part of a process framework, where the course's focus remains on writing in a way where the connection between assessment and social (in)justice is not made explicit to students. In fact, arguably the iteration of grading contracts that circulates most predominantly in scholarship and handbooks is the Danielewicz-Elbow model, which does not allow for student input and focuses "as much time and attention as possible to writing—not politics and culture" (2009, 248). In these cases, teachers tie assessment to learning but do not intentionally engage in classroom discussions about privilege and oppression or education's role in reproducing social inequalities.

Some teachers do include opportunities for students to participate in authoring the central tenants of the grading contract or rubrics for individual assignments, making the assessment structures student-centered and collaborative (Adsanatham 2012; Inoue 2012; Shor 2009). There are several reasons that teachers might elect to co-design grading contracts with their students, including revising classroom structures to be more responsive to student needs, increasing transparency, or cultivating buy-in and engagement. Shor (2009) argues that in order for a document to constitute a "strong contract," it must express mutual obligations between teachers and students; thus, student participation is an essential component of design. Some related variations of co-authorship also encourage students to choose their own projects and/or create their own assignments (Gibbs 2016; Sommers 2011), or even "protest" aspects of the class (Shor 2009) or have a "gimme" for one missed requirement (Inoue 2015). Negotiation remains one of the most contentious aspects of contract grading: To what extent should students be included in the design, revision, or enforcement of the contract? To what extent should students compose assignments, develop rubrics, or direct feedback? What are the processes that would best enable these actions? Importantly, full-class negotiation is not inherently more equitable, and teachers who facilitate this must do so responsibly so that student-student and student-teacher dynamics impacted by race, gender, class, disability, age, and other social identities are always considered.

DOMINANT CONTRACT GRADING MODELS

An analysis of contract grading from the perspective of RGS is predicated on viewing multiple contracts in relation to one another. To understand grading contracts in this way, exploring points of variation gives us just as much information as locating the overlaps and commonalities. As Miller et al. (2018) argue, "Genre awareness can emphasize the local situatedness of rhetoric, with attention to not just the regularity but also the variation within genres" (273). In contract grading design, highlighting these variations and tracing the choice points beneath them is important—not necessarily to reconcile disagreements but to more fully understand the questions and considerations that arise from any one uptake. Therefore, genre awareness gives us a language for comparing many moving parts within and across contexts, tracing the formation of each characteristic and defamiliarizing the contract-grading models those characteristics collectively form. In this sense, studying the genre conventions of grading contracts becomes a "demystifying move" (Freedman and Medway 1994), a way to identify and evaluate specific features within the genre, as well as patterned iterations or model type.

In writing and writing-intensive courses, current views on grading contracts have emerged primarily from a handful of descriptions and models that circulate in published scholarship, namely those given by Danielewicz and Elbow (2009), Shor (2009), and Inoue (2015). The reoccurrence of these three models illustrates that teachers compose grading contracts in response to previous scholarship or, in some cases, conversations with their own teachers and mentors in the field. While these grading contracts are not representative of the full scope of approaches, they can serve as an introduction to the genre *if* coupled with questions and considerations that emerge during/through their composition. Again, in this way, genre analysis moves us beyond prescriptive models that are meant to be copied and instead offers a framework for recognition and evaluation. Below, I offer overviews of three models of grading contracts in order to highlight the typifications and choice-points that constitute key approaches that prioritize process-centered, critical, or labor-based and antiracist pedagogies, respectively. Within these subgenres of grading contracts, there is an infinite number of possible combinations and iterations, and even roughly formed categories are unstable and fluid.

A Process-Centered/Hybrid Grading Contract

Peter Elbow's contract is a well-known version of contract grading and is included in his frequently cited article co-written with Jane Danielewicz (2009), "A Unilateral Grading Contract to Improve Learning and Teaching." This design's purpose is to alleviate the "anxiety and hurt" that grading causes for both students and teachers (Danielewicz and Elbow 2009, 261). In accounting for these emotional components of learning, Danielewicz and Elbow argue that their contract "fosters a deep commitment to process" for students (261), claiming that students will see improvements in their writing. For composition teachers beginning to use grading contracts, this example often serves as the default starting place and, over time, has become synonymous with the concept of contract grading itself. In fact, most empirical research on contracts draws from data on Elbow's contract specifically (e.g., Inman and Powell 2018; Inoue 2012; Spidell and Thelin 2006).

One striking feature in this model—which Asao Inoue (2019) calls the hybrid model due to the fact that its assessment structure incorporates both graded and nongraded elements—is that Elbow and Danielewicz reserve the A course grade for writers who have regularly demonstrated "A-quality" work. This move, they believe, encourages capable students to give extra effort. Thus, the default course grade for all completed work is a B, which each student, regardless of prior knowledge or ability, should be able to receive. In their narrative account of their contract design, Danielewicz and Elbow report that their contract produces more total work from students than traditionally graded courses and observe that "the effect is most striking with skilled writers who must now engage in learning tasks they used to skip" (2009, 256). Thus, even in a contract-graded class, teachers might still privilege traditionally high-achieving students and use some degree of grading as motivation.

A Critical Pedagogy Grading Contract

In "Critical Pedagogy is Too Big to Fail" Ira Shor (2009) directly responds to Danielewicz and Elbow by positioning his contract along-side theirs in terms of grades, negotiation, and an underlying critical pedagogy. His contract, like theirs, focuses on performance minimums and measures levels of student participation through essay length, attendance, and class contributions (the more a student participates in or practices "successful" student behaviors, the higher the grade possibility). However, because of "the impact of place on practice," Shor believes it is necessary to grade his students on individual papers, A–F, rather than for only "above a B," as Danielewicz and Elbow do. He acknowledges that his colleagues' grading system might work when most students arrive to college with B-level skills, but he teaches at City University of New York and works with a range of students, some who come from "non-academic cultures and non-standard literacies" (9, 11). He argues that teachers should grade A–F to note the full range of academic abilities.

While using A–F grading on individual assignments may seem contrary to contract grading, Shor defines contracts through a co-authorship process with students that occurs through negotiation, a practice he has advocated since his 1996 book *When Students Have Power: Negotiating Authority in a Critical Pedagogy*. In sum, whereas Danielewicz and Elbow are most worried about the problematic effects of grades, thus giving up their power over grading (up to a B) but deciding the requirements for a course without direct student input; Shor conversely retains his

authority to grade papers A–F, but instead presents every course requirement and performance minimum initially as a proposal to be discussed
with his students, after which he ultimately drafts the contract with their
consent. "A critical teacher," he argues, "earns the right to propose
only if students exercise the right to dispose" (2009, 21). Shor further
describes this distinction by characterizing a "weak" democratic classroom as one formed by neoliberal, top-down policies and a "strong"
democratic classroom as one that allows collaboration, conflict, and
dissent (2009, 21). Because of Shor's work, negotiations have become a
common feature of grading contracts situated within critical pedagogy.

A Labor-Based, Antiracist Grading Contract

Asao Inoue connects grading contracts to broader movements of social
justice and assessment, specifically antiracism. Over two books, he
details ways that a "labor-based grading contract" affords his classes
opportunities to recognize and intervene in the politics of language
rooted in white supremacy (Inoue 2019, 4). From this perspective, methods of grading should always be called into question for their inherent
biases and disrupting the notion of "A-level writing" should become a
collaborative class endeavor (Inoue 2015, 93). Inoue's labor-based grading contract is an expression of what he calls an "assessment ecology,"
which he describes as

> a complex political system of people, environments, actions, and relations
> of power that produce consciously understand relationships between and
> among people and their environments that help students problematize
> their existential writing assessment situations, which in turn changes or
> (re)creates the ecology so that it is fairer, more livable, and sustainable for
> everyone. (Inoue 2015, 82)

According to Inoue, then, assessment should be responsive to all the
complex parts of a classroom space and the ways those parts interact
with one another. In this ecology, he employs a practice made possible by
contract grading in which feedback becomes a form of problem-posing
rather than directions for revision. Additionally, to further problematize
the idea of quality, Inoue tracks student labor in addition to the writing
projects themselves to assign end-of-course grades. This approach lays
bare connections between assessment, larger educational contexts, and
society. In this way, one could argue that this model foregrounds the
situatedness of assessment.

The significant variation between these three approaches to the
grading contract demonstrates the complex series of rhetorical choices

that can be made when designing particular assessment genres, even within the "narrow" approach of contract grading. Bringing together these models furthers our evaluative capacity in the way that Miller et al. (2018) advocate with RGS, as it highlights "the context of the conventions, ideologies, and histories embedded therein," thus bringing to light their particular (and sometimes interrelated) "power relationships, social agreements, and background presumptions" (272). For example, in some sense, Inoue's approach of *completely* decoupling grades from teacher judgement circles back to earlier articulations of contract grading dating back to the 1960s (e.g., Farber 1990). However, a key practice that usually sets Inoue's labor-based contract grading apart is the incorporation of negotiation for rubrics for each individual assignment and how his feedback is articulated through those rubrics, encouraging students to challenge dominant culture constructions of merit and white language supremacy (Inoue 2019). Though incredibly influential, these three models likely make up a small percentage of grading contract models present in writing classrooms today as teachers continuously adapt and innovate. Nonetheless, examining these contracts as a group hopefully enriches our collective understanding of choice points and their potential impact.

DEVELOPING A CRITICAL AWARENESS OF UPTAKES

By utilizing an RGS perspective, teachers can develop their own expertise to become more familiar with grading contracts and the philosophies and circumstances that shape them. As I have argued elsewhere (Schwarz 2018), in order to better understand various classroom genres, educators must "de-norm" their features and the ways those features both reflect and reproduce multiple (and sometimes conflicting) personal and institutional ideologies.[1] This de-norming process involves several stages—identify, challenge, change, and reflect—and can be defined as a kind of strategic defamiliarization for purposes of invention. Genre theory can support this critique and innovation: theories of uptake can be used to assess prior knowledge, support dialogue across contexts, and ultimately lead to critical self-reflection and more effective

---

1. De-norming is a twist on the common practice of "norming," where teachers meet to assess student writing as a group in order to calibrate teachers' grading through consensus. In contrast, de-norming is a process that highlights and values variance as a way to create dialogue around dissensus, encouraging teachers and other stakeholders to identify, challenge, and change dominant culture assumptions embodied in classroom genres that work against equitable and inclusive ends. For more about de-norming as a method of critique, see Schwarz (2018).

classroom practices. Thus, RGS as a process of studying both reoccurrence and unique instantiation has the very practical application of preparing teachers for the complexities of contract grading as a document (classroom artifact) and its enactment (performance).

Classroom assessment genres are full of arbitrary features that we often take for granted as necessary or "just the way it is." Recognizing that these features are, in fact, choice points rather than a fixed set of rules is challenging, especially when a singular example serves as our only frame of reference. These perceptions about what grading contracts are and the purposes they serve usually come from our own educational histories; we are always fighting our own perceptions of what is possible. Many writing programs have common syllabi or default grading templates that form our earliest understandings of classroom typifications. Some of us walk into our own classrooms repurposing assessment genres, including grading contracts, from our experiences as students. This practice of inheriting can be dangerous because teachers might circulate and enact dominant uptakes without examining the beliefs, values, and assumptions embedded within their construction. Over time, typified moves within our own contracts may also become so habitual that we unconsciously inhabit them, forgetting their original purpose. Maybe we, as teachers, think we're grading to be fair or to encourage process or to be antiracist, but we do not have enough ways of assessing our own assumptions. And just because a grading contract was authored for antiracism does not necessarily mean that its features support additional minoritized identities such as students with disabilities. While there will always be biases inherent in assessment, an awareness of genre and critical approach to uptake provide teachers with more knowledge of design and possible frameworks for accountability.

Often the challenge for teachers and students within contract grading classrooms is learning a basic uptake awareness that allows us to make sense of grading contracts. Thus, genre awareness can be a useful approach to teacher development *and* this genre awareness should also be coupled with RGS as a critical enterprise. An example of a critical approach to professional development might entail faculty and/or graduate students to map out their own perceptions of the above models and their corresponding ideologies. What are their similarities? What are their differences? How might they be grouped, classified, and named differently? What perspectives might be missing? How are equitable outcomes conceptualized and then prioritized? And, importantly, how might our own biases dictate what we see, select, and think to ask while working within assessment genres, including contract grading? Education scholar Kevin Kumashiro (2002) argues that critical teaching—that is, teaching to challenge power and privilege within the classroom—requires an epistemological stance that supposes that people do not move from ignorance to enlightenment. Rather, all teachers and students have different resistances to new knowledge, points of crisis that make learning difficult.

In order for new uptakes in contract grading to emerge, sources of resistance are important to recognize and move through. Genre offers one way to identify these points of resistance; through comparison, we can engage in self-reflection. For example, why have we assigned behaviors like attendance or timeliness such value in our writing classrooms—how is merit being configured in a way that opens access for some and closes access for others? On a disciplinary level, which teachers and students are typically privileged in scholarly discussions of developing pedagogical approaches, such as antiracist assessment? Who is benefitting most from this concept and how do we know? These questions enable teachers to appraise various grading contracts while gaining the knowledge to challenge their design(s) and imagine new alternatives. Thus, RGS addresses our prior conceptual limitations by identifying and affirming possibilities beyond our own experiences.

CONCLUSION

Grading contracts function as contested sites where teachers—and students—negotiate their individual identities, experiences, and values with other contextual pressures. They also originate from distinct concerns that seek to fulfill the pedagogical goals of its author(s) and consequently materialize in the documents' features. Thus, a range of beliefs and values guide and materialize through each uptake. For any assessment genre, educators will need to reach beyond handbooks to build a system that supports rather than undermines their pedagogical or curricular goals. In order to do this, educators need access to a broader range of grading contracts that will allow them to learn the scope of choices possible, question which features might be missing, and imagine new designs for the genre.

Due to the limited empirical research on contract grading as well as its positioning within personal, institutional, and disciplinary ideologies, the contract itself might become fixed over time and end up mirroring other, traditional forms of assessment. Unfortunately, at this stage, versions of Elbow's (2009) model still seem to make up most contract grading research (e.g., Inman and Powell 2018; Inoue 2012; Spidell and

Thelin 2006). This is not a critique of Elbow's grading contract exactly; rather, this is a critique of the field's continued overreliance on any complete model, which leads to an extremely limited view of contracts and the many ways they might be innovated for specific contexts and purposes. Additional scholarship should help us theorize differences in what contracts are and what they do in a way that foregrounds uptakes as ideological and embodied.

RGS offers a framework for teachers, educators, and scholars to identify the common, typified features within grading contracts as documents and also work beyond this step of classification to consider components of enactment—the potential adaptation, use, and impact of various choice points. An RGS perspective allows educators a sociorhetorical method of critical analysis, a way to trace the series of ideological moves within and across features and situations. Centering uptakes and variations, then, democratizes knowledge and builds a capacity among more teachers to effectively engage with various choice points. Teachers can (re)design grading contracts from an always-expanding scope of questions and considerations rather than default definitions and models. With more research into contract grading as a rhetorical genre—not as a singular, static model—we can begin to evaluate and appreciate the multitude of ways grading contracts live in classrooms and transform our teaching.

REFERENCES

Adsanatham, Chanon. 2012. "Integrating Assessment and Instruction: Using Student-Generated Grading Criteria to Evaluate Multimodal Digital Projects." *Computers and Composition* 29 (2): 152–74.

Afros, Elena, and Catherine F. Schryer. 2009. "The Genre of Syllabus in Higher Education." *Journal of English for Academic Purposes* 8 (3): 224–33.

Albracht, Lindsey, Al Harahap, Amanda Pratt, Ranmali Rodrigo, Clare Russel, and Virginia M. Schwarz. 2019. "Response to 'In the Absence of Grades: Dissonance and Desire in Course-Contract Classrooms.'" *College Composition and Communication* 70 (5): 145–51.

Bailey, Lucy E. 2010. "The 'Other' Syllabus: Rendering Teaching Politics Visible in the Graduate Pedagogy Seminar." *Feminist Teacher* 20 (2): 139–56.

Bawarshi, Anis, and Mary Jo Reiff. 2010. *Genre: An Introduction to History, Theory, Research, and Pedagogy.* West Lafayette, IN: Parlor Press.

Danielewicz, Jane, and Peter Elbow. 2009. "A Unilateral Grading Contract to Improve Learning and Teaching." *College Composition and Communication* 61 (2): 244–68.

Elbow, Peter. 1998. "Changing Grading While Working with Grades." In *The Theory and Practice of Grading Writing: Problems and Possibilities,* edited by Frances Zak and Christopher C. Weaver, 171–84. Albany: State University of New York Press.

Farber, Jerry. 1990. "Learning How to Teach: A Progress Report." *College English* 52 (2): 135–41.

Freadman, Anne. 2002. "Uptake." In *The Rhetoric and Ideology of Genre: Strategies for Stability and Change*, edited by Richard M. Coe, Lorelei Lingard, and Tatiana Teslenko, 39–53. Cresskill, NJ: Hampton Press.

Freedman, Aviva, and Peter Medway, eds. 1994. *Genre and the New Rhetoric*. Bristol, PA: Taylor & Francis.

Gibbs, Laura. 2016. "(Un)Grading: It Can Be Done in College." *Education Week-Work in Progress* (blog). March 31, 2016. https://blogs.edweek.org/teachers/work_in_progress /2016/03/ungrading_it_can_be_done_in_co.html.

Inman, Joyce Olewski, and Rebecca A. Powell. 2018. "In the Absence of Grades: Dissonance and Desire in Course-Contract Classrooms." *College Composition and Communication* 70 (1): 30–56.

Inoue, Asao B. 2012. "Grading Contracts: Assessing Their Effectiveness on Different Racial Formations." In *Race and Writing Assessment*, edited by Asao B. Inoue and Mya Poe, 78–94. New York: Peter Lang.

Inoue, Asao B. 2015. *Antiracist Writing Assessment Ecologies: Teaching and Assessing Writing for a Socially Just Future*. Fort Collins, CO: WAC Clearinghouse.

Inoue, Asao B. 2019. *Labor-Based Grading Contracts: Building Equity and Inclusion in the Compassionate Writing Classroom*. Fort Collins, CO: WAC Clearinghouse.

Kumashiro, Kevin. 2002. "Against Repetition: Addressing Resistance to Anti-Oppressive Change in the Practices of Learning, Teaching, Supervising, and Researching." *Harvard Educational Review* 72 (1): 67–93.

McKinney, Charlesia. 2018. "Reassessing Intersectionality: Affirming Difference in Higher Education." *Composition Forum* 39. http://compositionforum.com/issue/39/intersectionality.php.

Miller, Carolyn R. 1984. "Genre as Social Action." *Quarterly Journal of Speech* 70 (2): 151–67.

Miller, Carolyn R. 1994. "Rhetorical Community: The Cultural Basis of Genre." In *Genre and the New Rhetoric*, edited by Aviva Freedman and Peter Medway, 67–78. Bristol, PA: Taylor & Francis.

Miller, Carolyn R., Amy J. Devitt, and Victoria J. Gallagher. 2018. "Genre: Permanence and Change." *Rhetoric Society Quarterly* 48 (3): 269–77.

Neaderhiser, Stephen. 2016. "Hidden in Plain Sight: Occlusion in Pedagogical Genres." *Composition Forum* 33. http://www.compositionforum.com/issue/33/hidden.php.

Potts, Glenda. 2010. "A Simple Alternative to Grading." *Inquiry: The Journal of the Virginia Community Colleges* 15 (1): 29–42.

Schwarz, Virginia M. 2018. "De-Norming the Syllabus: An Analysis Situated in Critical and Caring Pedagogies." In *Critical Theory and Qualitative Data Analysis in Education*, edited by Rachelle Winkle-Wagner, Jamila Lee-Johnson, and Ashley N. Gaskew, 79–92. New York: Routledge.

Shor, Ira. 1996. *When Students Have Power: Negotiating Authority in a Critical Pedagogy*. Chicago: University of Chicago Press.

Shor, Ira. 2009. "Critical Pedagogy Is Too Big to Fail." *Journal of Basic Writing* 28 (2): 6–27.

Sommers, Jeff. 2011. "Self-Designed Points: Turning Responsibility for Learning over to Students." *Teaching English in the Two-Year College* 38 (4): 403–13.

Spidell, Cathy, and William H. Thelin. 2006. "Not Ready to Let Go: A Study of Resistance to Grading Contracts." *Composition Studies* 34 (1): 35–68.

Stommel, Jesse. 2018. "How to Ungrade." March 11, 2018. https://www.jessestommel.com /how-to-ungrade.

Villanueva, Nayelee. 2014. "Impact of a Grade Contract Model in a College Composition Course: A Multiple Case Study." PhD diss., University of Nevada, Las Vegas. https:// digitalscholarship.unlv.edu/thesesdissertations/2308.

Womack, Anne-Marie. 2017. "Teaching Is Accommodation: Universally Designing Composition Classrooms and Syllabi." *College Composition and Communication* 68 (3): 494–525.

4
EVALUATIVE FEEDBACK GENRES
Sites for Exploring Writing Teacher Development

Jessica Rivera-Mueller

Whether working with graduate students in composition practicums or undergraduate students in English education courses, writing teacher educators (WTEs) design course projects and processes to depict the learning activities that they deem important for becoming a teacher of writing. The pedagogical genres that support these learning activities serve a critical function by shaping, in part, the learning conditions for writing teacher development and communicating the pedagogical beliefs and practices that WTEs believe facilitate teacher development. As Dylan Dryer (2012) explains,

> Genres like response papers, seminar papers, rosters, syllabi, notes on office doors, assignments, in-class exercises, and comments on student papers (as well as talk at the seminar table and in offices) help *produce* the identities of novice graduate students/novice composition teachers by operationalizing the routines and subject positions through which these students and teachers become learners and teachers. (442, emphasis added)

Because pedagogical genres are so closely linked with identity production, I have become increasingly invested in learning more about the ways pedagogical genres in my courses help to produce students' understandings of, expectations for, and beliefs about teacher development.

This tension has become most visible in my work with the evaluative feedback I compose to accompany students' grades on course projects. In my process of composing evaluative feedback genres, I aim to construct an approach to teacher development that is rooted in ongoing pedagogical inquiry. This approach, as described by Marilyn Cochran-Smith and Susan L. Lytle (2001), "is associated more with uncertainty, more with posing problems and dilemmas than with solving them, and more with the recognition that inquiry both stems from and generates questions" (56). Inquiry-oriented teaching wades into the complexity

https://doi.org/10.7330/9781646422920.c004

that is inherent in teaching and learning. Rather than simply training teachers to be effective in particular teaching contexts, I also aim to help writing teachers develop practices and habits of mind that foster a career-long process for teacher development (Fecho et al. 2004; Simon 2015; Staunton 2008; Stenberg 2005; Qualley 1997). This aim is especially important in instances when the indicators of teaching effectiveness can be quite narrow. This occurs, for example, when secondary teachers are only evaluated according to how their students perform on standard-ized assessments or when postsecondary teachers are evaluated primar-ily according to the results from their course evaluations. Definitions of teaching effectiveness, such as these, limit who should experience teacher development and what counts as evidence for teacher develop-ment. While I want the curriculum in my courses to prepare students for their future teaching contexts, I don't want my classroom to replicate these narrow definitions. Narrow definitions are in stark contrast to an inquiry-oriented approach, which assumes that all teachers benefit from an ongoing examination of their teaching and works toward aims that may not be immediately or readily visible.

While it is important for evaluative feedback genres to accomplish their job of providing an evaluation and feedback, I am equally con-cerned with the identity work that occurs through its production. The grading criteria in my courses can establish an inquiry-oriented process for teacher development as integral to earning a good grade, but I remain keenly aware of the fact that my courses are just one context through which my students will establish and develop their identities as teachers. Put simply, I don't want students in my courses to *just* read my evaluative feedback as justification for their grades. Instead, I want evaluative feedback to also serve an educational function, helping stu-dents develop beliefs about teacher development that they can continue to examine in their future teaching contexts. As much as students are just that—students in the process of learning—they are also prospective teachers who will take up lessons from my evaluative feedback as part of their development as teachers outside of any WTE course. Equally, the feedback I provide them is grounded in my own ability to both rec-ognize them as current learners and envision them as future teachers beyond my class. Therefore, I care about the overlapping ways both they and I engage with evaluative feedback genres and how that engagement shapes our long-term conceptions of teacher development—how we identify and pursue teaching effectiveness and teacher learning amid the competing definitions that swirl around us. Because evaluative feed-back genres often support both kinds of pedagogical aims, a tension can emerge between the process of learning to become a teacher and the product of earning a grade.

For these reasons, I grapple with how evaluative feedback genres enact particular beliefs about teacher development and how students make sense of those beliefs. To support my own development as a teacher, I conducted a self-study to examine the work of evaluative feedback genres in my teaching. My research questions guiding this project included: How does my evaluative feedback enact particular beliefs about teacher development and how might evaluative feedback genres help students explore their own beliefs about teacher development? In this chapter, I share the results from my self-study to argue that genre analysis can help WTEs examine such questions. To that end, I begin this chapter by explaining how I define and examine evaluative feedback as a genre. I then share how the process of analyzing evaluative feedback genres in my Teaching Writing courses illuminated the beliefs that are enacted in my evaluative feedback and possibilities for engaging in critical conversations with students about their understandings of teacher development.

EXAMINING EVALUATIVE FEEDBACK AS A GENRE

In *Writing Genres*, Amy Devitt argues for a rhetorical theory of genre that "sees genres as types of rhetorical actions that people perform in their everyday interactions with their worlds" (2004, 2). Building from Devitt's conception of genre, *evaluative feedback*—as a term in this chapter—refers to a teacher's action of providing written feedback for students to accompany their grades on course projects. While there are multiple kinds of genres that constitute evaluative feedback, the genres I analyze in this chapter most resemble formal end comments. The evaluative feedback I compose utilizes the formal features of a letter (opening greeting, body, and closing salutation) and employs a personal voice to offer holistic commentary. To accomplish the purpose of offering both an assessment and feedback, my letters contain three specific rhetorical actions: inviting and encouraging dialogue with the student, explaining my understanding of the student's project and my evaluation of the student's attempt to accomplish these goals, and offering possibilities for future thinking and/or development. As outlined in table 4.1, I use specific rhetorical moves to accomplish these actions.

These rhetorical moves help me perform the actions that I aim to accomplish, and studying these rhetorical moves helps me see the beliefs about teacher development that undergird my rhetorical

Table 4.1. Rhetorical actions for evaluative feedback

Rhetorical Actions	Rhetorical Moves	Examples
Invite and encourage dialogue with the student	Open letter with personal salutation; close letter with invitation for further discussion of feedback	"Hi Amanda, [. . .] Please let me know if you'd like to discuss this feedback further. Best, Dr. Rivera-Mueller"
Explain my understanding of the student's project and my evaluation of the student's attempt to accomplish these goals, including praise and/or critique	Report my sense-making	"I think the strongest part of your unit is your focus on listening. The enduring understandings and essential learning questions are beautiful! They are important and wonderful concepts that we really need as people! I absolutely loved how your unit slowly builds to the final challenge in the final lesson to listen as an act of bravery! I initially wondered if this could go earlier, but then I realized how beautiful it is to have this final lesson offer this challenge. Well done! I know it was hard to give up some of the other stuff, but this unit will offer really important groundwork for that larger unit on writing persuasively."
Offer possibilities for further thinking and/or development	Pose questions	"The area I would encourage you to further consider is the notion of bias. In the introduction to bias, you have some really great questions that open the door to an authentic conversation about bias. This is followed up by the next day's lesson about bias and the media. Is this conversation about bias different than the notion of bias you're thinking through in day 3? There seems to be a difference between a deliberate choice to not see (enact a bias) and an inability to see our own bias. Throughout the unit, you're asking students to examine both kinds of bias, and I'm wondering if it might be helpful to make this distinction."

actions. Evaluative feedback as a genre, however, encompasses more than such moves. As a way of understanding the rhetorical nature of evaluative feedback genres, I apply Devitt's conception of genre as "a nexus between an individual's actions and a socially defined context" (2004, 31). In particular, I draw on Devitt's framework for naming the components of the socially defined context, including the immediate learning situation, surrounding cultures, and other genres that inform the rhetorical actions (31). This framework for analyzing the social and rhetorical components of genre proves useful for revealing and exploring beliefs about teacher development that emerge through evaluative feedback genres.

To apply Devitt's framework for rhetorical genre study to my own use of evaluative feedback, I employed the methodology of self-study, a form of practitioner research that enables teacher educators to pursue the questions about teaching and learning that emerge from their own practice (Berry 2007; Borko et al. 2007; Loughran 2002; Schulte 2009; Zeichner 1999). Because the process of self-study draws upon data sources that directly reflect and inform a practitioner's research questions, I studied the evaluative feedback letters that I composed for undergraduate students in my Teaching Writing courses. The letters that I analyzed were composed initially for instructional purposes, and my research questions led me to study these texts in this new way. Analyzing these letters with Devitt's conception of genre allowed me to understand how my evaluative feedback enacts particular beliefs about teacher development and identify possibilities for helping students better explore their own beliefs about teacher development.

My first step in this project involved selecting the specific letters for analysis. I decided to analyze letters from two different iterations of the course to examine how my evaluative feedback might be changing over time. I also decided to analyze all of the letters that I composed for students in response to three different kinds of course projects: a teaching unit, a teaching demonstration, and a group facilitation. (The teaching unit is an individual project, and the teaching demonstration and group facilitation are collaborative projects.) It was important for me to analyze letters for all of these projects because they all contribute to the broader "rhetorical ecosystem" within which my students and I participate (Bawarshi 2001). These projects were important to study because they each represent important aspects of teacher development. As a WTE, in other words, I aim to help students experience particular aspects of teacher development in each project. While students complete the collaborative projects at different times throughout the semester, it is my hope that collectively these projects provide a context for exploring teacher development. For my analysis, I wanted to look for broad patterns and themes across these projects to gain a deeper understanding of the possibilities and constraints that might be integral to evaluative feedback genres. My specific teaching aims are listed in table 4.2.

After selecting these letters, I examined how the rhetorical actions and moves that I outlined earlier seem to function across the letters. I

Table 4.2. Course projects analyzed

Course Project	Role in Teacher Development
Teaching Unit: Individually, create 10–14 lessons focused on some aspect of teaching writing in a secondary setting	This project is the culmination of the work in the course, and I describe it to students as the place to articulate and enact their current beliefs about the teaching of writing.
Teaching Demonstration: In pairs, design and deliver a mini-lesson to the class and lead a reflective talk after the delivery of the lesson	I describe this project to students as an important opportunity to practice learning from the process of designing and delivering a lesson.
Group Facilitation: In a small group, create a question about the teaching of writing, select and study scholarship related to this question, and facilitate a conversation about this question with the class	I describe this project to students as a place to explore the relationship between theory and practice and practice inquiry-based conversations with peers.

paid particular attention to any similarities and differences across the letters for different course projects and across the letters from my first and second iteration of the course. I then applied rhetorical genre analysis to these observations, examining how these letters work as genres, how they inform each other, and how I might be more purposeful as the composer of these letters. Below, I present the pedagogical insights and possibilities that I crafted from this analysis.

REVEALING BELIEFS ABOUT TEACHER DEVELOPMENT

To understand how I might help students experience and explore beliefs about teacher development, I first wanted to better understand the particular beliefs that I enact in my letters. While I had a sense of the rhetorical actions that I wanted to accomplish through this genre, as outlined earlier, I wanted to look more closely at the ways my rhetorical moves perform those actions and how those actions are rooted in particular beliefs about teacher development. Making a distinction, in other words, between my intended rhetorical actions and my rhetorical moves—as genre theory compels me to do—revealed the beliefs that I enact in my letters. I am mindful, however, of the ways my interpretations are partial. Devitt highlights this dynamic in the following way:

> Just as users of the genres are the most reliable definers of a genre, they are also the most reliable interpreters of that genre. On the other hand, people are shaped by their contexts and genres, and no one can be fully aware of the complexities of a group or its genres or fully conscious of their ideological effects. To some extent, interpretations are always informed guesses colored by ideological frames. (2004, 53–54)

As the teacher of this course, I obviously know what I say I value in teacher development, but this analysis helped me see more clearly what I actually do in fostering teacher development. Though my knowledge is incomplete in that I am unable to fully know the context within which my efforts are received, this analysis provides a more thorough understanding of my rhetorical actions, an important understanding for my ultimate goal of exploring these beliefs with students.

First, I noticed the way that my rhetorical moves position students as decision-makers. In my evaluative feedback, I prompt students to make pedagogical decisions and contribute their understandings of these decisions to our class community and their future teaching colleagues. I saw this belief most specifically in my rhetorical move of posing questions. Looking closely, I noticed that my questions prompt students (1) to reflect upon the decision-making they completed in the process of developing their projects and (2) to make further decisions as they continue to refine their projects. For example, in one letter providing evaluative feedback for a group facilitation, I ask the students about their prior experience as theater majors. I write, "Since you all have a background in theatre, did you find the research articles helpful? In what ways were they helpful or not? And what questions and/or concerns do you have about using these strategies?" This small group of students were the only theater majors in the course, and this identity was an important part of their engagement in the course. It was important, then, for me to engage with their shared sense of identity and their contributions to the course. In this evaluative feedback, I ask about their process because I want to acknowledge and interact with them as the agents of their own learning process. I prompt similar thinking when I pose questions that ask students to examine their observations of their teaching demonstrations. For example, in a teaching demonstration focused on the use of passive and active voice, I question how the group's opening video functioned in the lesson. I write,

> I would encourage you to further consider the role of the opening video. How do you feel that it supported the rest of the work in the lesson? Did it achieve its aim? I noticed that we didn't really come back to the ideas in the video during the lesson, so I wonder if you still see it as playing an important instructional role.

I don't provide an answer to this question, compelling students to reflect on their observation of how the lesson unfolded and make decisions for their future classrooms.

Second, I noticed how my rhetorical moves model my belief that teacher-learning is situated. I saw this most clearly in my rhetorical move of reporting my sense-making. As I report how I understand students' projects, I inhabit the role of an expert, rather than the ultimate authority figure. I model, in other words, how my expertise is situated. Throughout the letters, I use several phrases to point out the contextual nature of my evaluation. I use phrases such as: "As a teacher," "For me," "Personally," "Since X is true, I believe Y is true," "I think," "This suggestion might," "In my own courses, I," and "So here's my thinking." Another common way that I situate my perspective is by saying a version of the following: "Your students will teach you the answer to this question." In these moments, I offer options, rather than solutions. In one example, I write,

> I think the biggest thing to consider in the future is whether or not you want students to apply these lessons to a story they've already crafted or use these lessons to develop a story. I think the first option might lead to more depth because they'll be working with the ideas in the context of their own stories/characters. But this unit, as it is currently designed, provides a great introduction to the concepts. I think it's a matter, then, of how this unit will fit into the larger goals of your entire course and where this unit fits within the course as a whole (beginning, middle, or end).

I make these moves because I know that secondary students in different contexts will respond differently. There are no simple answers for what will work in a classroom. Accordingly, I frame my knowledge within the specific contexts that I have taught. Additionally, I ask students to reference contexts that they have inhabited as teachers, such as teaching practicums.

Finally, my analysis revealed my belief in teaching as a shared enterprise. I saw this most clearly in my choice to address the collaborative projects to all group members rather than creating individual letters for each group member. While the group projects do include both individual and group pieces, my evaluative feedback occurs collectively to highlight how teaching is a shared enterprise. As teachers at the secondary level are increasingly asked to collaborate on shared goals, I think it is important to provide opportunities where we focus on the effort of the team rather than just individual performance. I also want students to grapple with the idea that there are many stakeholders involved in education, and different stakeholders bring different expectations to the work of teaching. This is supported by our work throughout the course to critically engage a range of stakeholder perspectives. My move, then, to write one letter affirms these contributions as contributions to our collective learning. Accordingly, I begin these letters by expressing gratitude for their work. For example, I write,

> Thank you for your facilitation on the topic of grading in the English classroom. This is such an important topic, especially as school districts consider moving to "standards-based" grading. I appreciate both the information and questions you shared with the class to support this discussion. Your group's questions helped us successfully grapple with this tough topic.

I hope that speaking to the group collectively helps students consider themselves part of a collective enterprise of teaching rather than individual teachers.

My beliefs that teachers are decision-makers, teacher-learning is situated, and teaching is a shared enterprise are the most prominent beliefs that I could see myself enacting as I actively construct a process for teacher development. While I aim to construct the situation or context for teacher development, the situation is not fully within my control. "People construct situations through genres, but they also construct genres through situations" (Devitt 2004, 22). As a WTE, though, I recognize the ways that evaluative feedback genres traditionally value the individual over the collective. Contemporary assessment scholarship, for example, often privileges individuals over collectives by offering recommendations for improved assessment practices that are rooted in the assumption that student achievement is an individual endeavor (i.e., O'Connor 2007). Applying a framework that considers the rhetorical context of genre helps me name the ways that evaluative feedback genres push back on my intended goals. For example, the tension between individual and group identity becomes more visible through genre analysis. I can see, in other words, how my belief in teaching as a shared enterprise creates actions that are not aligned with common assessment practices.

The choice to write one letter, of course, is not one that I make lightly. My choice violates the logic that assessments are supposed to measure what an individual can do and that evaluative feedback genres are supposed to articulate this measurement. Privileging the collective leads to other consequences as well. For example, I am unable to offer specific details for everyone. Instead, I highlight the moments that seem connected to the contribution of the group. For instance, I use expressions such as "I appreciated the moment when . . ." rather than writing about a specific person's actions. I also address my suggestions to a generic "you." In a teaching demonstration letter, for example, I write,

> In terms of your lesson design, I appreciated the organic nature of your lesson. In each of the activities, your team worked with students' ideas to explore character development. The opening discussion was a huge

success, as learners were passionately engaged in the discussion of some of their favorite characters. This moment allowed learners to share something about their lives as readers, bridging the connection between reading and writing.

While one person clearly led this discussion, as is indicated in my notes that I took while the lesson unfolded, I chose to discuss how I saw the moment functioning pedagogically. In this moment I am evaluating the product, rather than the people. In moments such as these, evaluative feedback genres push back against my aims as a WTE.

I am also able to recognize the push back of evaluative feedback genres (and their traditional conventions) when it comes to the tone that I seek to use in my letters. Because we are working in a moment when evaluations for learning are increasingly standardized, I find myself pressed to create a more formal tone, masking the subjectivity that often occurs during the process of evaluation. This became most clear to me when I observed my tone become more formal in my second year. In my letters for the unit plans in my second year, for example, I use language from my rubric in my closing comments. This same change occurs in my feedback for the second-year group facilitations. While I made the choice to integrate this language more fully because we studied rubric language more specifically in the second year, I also know that this move was motivated in part by my desire to make my role as an evaluator more explicit. As Anis Bawarshi points out,

> when communicants use genres, they are interpreting and enacting the social motives (embedded rhetorically within it) that sustain an environment and make it meaningful, and so are becoming socialized into producing certain kinds of texts, but also certain kinds of context, practices, and identities—ways of being and acting in the world, socially and rhetorically. (2001, 78)

I saw a similar pattern when I examined the letters that I crafted for the teaching demonstrations in the second year. My tone was much more direct, often doing more work to explain why I offer particular suggestions. While I could attribute these changes to a range of factors, I believe it is the genre itself pushing back on my work. As I feel increasingly responsible for the quality of my program's graduates and as I wrestle with my own authority, I want to make sure that the evaluation aspect of my evaluative feedback is not lost. It seems fair to say that the first year's letters operate primarily from my role as a teacher, and the letters in my second year operate increasingly from my role as an institutional member who maintains professional standards in teacher education.

EXPLORING BELIEFS ABOUT TEACHER DEVELOPMENT

The above insights addressed my first research question and are useful for thinking more purposefully about the ways I shape and am shaped by evaluative feedback genres. But I was also interested in seeking ways to more purposely invite students into this exploration. I posed this second research question because I believe student engagement with evaluative feedback can help all classroom members explore, and perhaps alter, their views of teacher development. This can occur, of course, because altering the situation alters the genre, and altering the genre alters the situation (Devitt 2004, 23). As Devitt explains, genre is a reciprocal dynamic within which individuals' actions construct and are constructed by recurring context of situation, context of culture, and context of genres (31). In my analysis, I have come to see how teaching genre more explicitly, discussing the connections between learning to teach and learning to write, and focusing on capacity building are specific pedagogical actions that hold potential for more fully engaging with evaluative feedback genres.

Teach Genre More Explicitly

In conducting this analysis, I was most struck by the limited nature of my knowledge. It should be obvious to me that I am one participant in the genre of evaluative feedback, but this analysis reminded me that the students in my class perceive my rhetorical moves and actions in ways that are not solely up to me to determine. Again, this should be really obvious to me. In the quick pace of teaching, however, I don't often carve out enough mental space to really consider this interaction. I too often hope the letters do their work as I have intended. I know, though, that students are always making sense of writing pedagogy education in their own ways. In other words, students will use their own prior knowledge, experience, values, and goals to come to their own conclusions about our work.

This renewed awareness, provided by genre analysis, has led me to think more deeply about the extent to which I teach genre. Crafting feedback for writers is an important part of the course, as I have designed the course around three central questions: What are meaningful aims for writers? How do writing teachers prompt students to engage in these purposes? What kinds of support do students need to achieve these learning goals? While we currently discuss genre in the Teaching Writing class from the perspective of teachers who help secondary students develop as writers, we haven't yet applied that same thinking to our engagement with evaluative feedback that emerges within the course. I imagine that I haven't engaged in such conversations yet because these iterations of the course occurred during my first two years in a new institution as a tenure-track faculty member. In this new context, I have been in the process of figuring out the course and who I could/should/want to be within that context. Evaluative feedback has been a place where I have most wrestled with my authority and the extent to which I should both guide and judge students' work.

Truthfully, this possibility sounds a bit scary. Prompting this discussion may open myself up to critique in a way that might undermine my role as evaluator. This conversation would become another moment when I pull back the curtain on my practices, and I find that there is a fine balance between establishing the authority that is necessary to lead a group of students and making my decision-making visible to sponsor teacher learning. Considering this pedagogical action reveals why I sometimes prefer evaluative feedback to function as a communication tool rather than a pedagogical tool. However, teaching genre more explicitly would allow me to integrate more perspectives into my own thinking and help learners explore their thinking. It would also better ensure that students critically engage with evaluative feedback genres. As Summer Smith (1997) reminds us, teachers "must heighten our awareness of the constraints of generic conventions and the danger they pose to end comments' effectiveness" (267). In studying end comments composed for her home institution, Smith found that the

> stability of the genre—the very feature that makes end comments recognizable and, perhaps, easier to write—may also reduce the educational effectiveness of the comment. The stronger a generic convention, the more it constrains teachers' choices, encouraging them to write statements that fulfill generic expectations and discouraging them from resisting the genre even when resistance would be rhetorically effective. (266)

For teachers and students, genre expectations can lead to a less critical engagement with evaluative feedback genres. Smith provides the example of a student who discounts a teacher's praise because the student believes that praise is supposed to occur at the beginning of an end comment whether it is warranted or not. To bring this heightened awareness for all classroom members, I could introduce more theoretical work on genre theory to provide language for all of us to critically reflect upon our engagement with evaluative feedback genres. For example, Deborah Dean's (2008) explanations in *Genre Theory: Teaching, Writing, and Being* may provide a useful foundation for such conversations, as she focuses on a range of ways genre can be conceptualized and how those conceptions impact teaching practices.

Discuss Connections between Learning to Teach and Learning to Write

To compose evaluative feedback, I draw from my background as a composition teacher. Because I find many parallels between the activities of learning to write and learning to teach, I have applied my understanding of and practice with composing evaluative feedback for writers to my practice of composing evaluative feedback for writing teachers. In other words, the feedback letters I have composed for writers over the years serve as the basis for my process of composing evaluative feedback in my role as WTE. Conducting this analysis has given me a deeper appreciation for Devitt's idea that genres always exist in the context of other genres. As Devitt explains, "One never writes or speaks in a void. What fills that void is not only cultural context (ideological and material baggage surrounding our every action) and situational context (the people, languages, and purposes involved in every action) but also generic context, the existing genres we have read or written or that others say we should read or write" (2004, 27–28). Prior to this analysis, I knew that I was drawing upon my experience as a composition teacher, but I hadn't fully realized the extent to which my evaluative feedback was shaped by the assumptions that are part of the learning-to-write process.

I saw this theme most clearly when I studied my rhetorical move of posing questions. In these moments, I could see that I raise a lot of questions that we don't necessarily discuss at a later point. Though I could see the value in what I'm aiming to sponsor—teachers as decision-makers—I wondered if I should be coming back to these questions more fully. Or, I wondered, are these questions intended to provoke thought? Ultimately, I came to reflect upon the ways that my questions function differently in these situations. As a teacher of writing, I often dialogued with students about the questions in my letters because they chose to revise their individual projects for a final portfolio. The learning window was open longer than the one for the projects that occur in my Teaching Writing course. While I have increasingly designed more opportunities for revision into my Teaching Writing course, some aspects cannot be revised, as in the case of the teaching demonstrations and group facilitations. Differences such as this matter, and we can better understand the evaluative feedback genres when we consider the assumptions that shape the other pedagogical genres that are a part of the genre system. Discussing the extent to which learning to teach and learning to write are related processes offers another way to both help learners understand their engagement with evaluative feedback genres and reflect upon their beliefs about teacher development.

Focus on Capacity Building

My analysis also indicated that we could further explore our beliefs about teacher development by highlighting and discussing the way the context of culture impacts our engagement with evaluative feedback genres. As Devitt explains, "Ideological and material contexts, contexts beyond the more immediate context of situation of a particular genre, partially construct what genres are and are in turn constructed (reproduced) by people performing genre actions" (2004, 27). This aspect of genre strikes me as particularly important to discuss with students, as it is critical in shaping the kinds of actions I take in my evaluative feedback. I am most aware of this dynamic when my actions contradict common assumptions about learning to teach. For example, I especially feel this way when I knowingly choose to act as a fellow teacher who is coming alongside students in an ongoing process of learning to teach, rather than a professor who has or can provide all of the answers. From this role, there have been instances when I have broken the level of formality that I feel compelled to use in my letters. Often, these instances are to celebrate the work that students have accomplished. One letter, for example, opens with the following statement:

> The short version is: Your team rocked this project! Way to go! I hope you can feel that in your growth as teachers. There are many good things I could say about your overall work in this project, but I'll aim to highlight the ones that I think are currently most helpful.

In this moment, I am drawing from my knowledge of working with this group of students in this course and in a course during the prior semester. I'm accounting for the context of our entire work together, one in which I observed tremendous growth that couldn't be articulated simply by the criteria for the project's evaluation. I wanted to acknowledge and celebrate that growth. This role, however, is in opposition to the kind of context that students experience in other moments, when teaching is made to look discrete and measurable. The subject praxis exam that students are often required to take for teaching certification is one example of a context in which teaching is simplified to right and wrong answers. As a WTE, I've long wrestled with the tension between these two contexts. I want to help students understand the complexity of teaching, and yet I feel responsible for addressing, in some way, this exam that is important for participation in their future careers.

The language of capacity building, though, can help me bridge that gap. I borrow this term from Mark Priestley et al. (2015), who explain that teachers draw from their past experiences (in terms of their skills and knowledge), professional and personal beliefs, and values to act within a given context. Therefore,

> for the teachers of tomorrow, it is important to attend to the nature of what will become those past experiences in the present, which is where the importance of teacher education lies. Such education (both initial education and continuing professional development) should focus on capacity building—and if the focus is to be on developing agents of change and professional developers of the curriculum, then programmes of professional development should focus on developing this capacity, to interrupt habitual ways of thinking about schooling and to encourage an innovative and questioning mindset. (31)

With this language, I am able to reframe my course's situation. Rather than worrying about the extent to which this context is preparatory for contexts rooted in other ideological assumptions, I can affirm my commitment to using the course as a place to facilitate a questioning mindset. In my work with the students in my course, then, I can explain my choice to come alongside them and invite them to wonder about the contexts of culture that shape their experience of this choice, explaining that this thinking has implications for the construction of their beliefs about teacher development.

CONSTRUCTING BELIEFS ABOUT TEACHER DEVELOPMENT

Genre analysis, in this project and others, allows me to examine what is actually occurring in my classroom. It provides the same sense of excitement and anxiety that can arise when I ask my students for their feedback on our work together. I want to know, and I don't want to know. Often these moments involve vulnerability, as I seek to understand how I shape and am shaped by genre. I value the uncertainty, though, as genre analysis can reveal pedagogical possibilities that can enhance our aims. The pedagogical insights and possibilities that I identified through my self-study in this project provide a next step for pursing my goal of sponsoring beliefs that can foster long-term success for teachers. While I'm a bit intimidated by some of my findings, such as teaching genre more explicitly, I believe such conversations will provide opportunities to confront and collectively remake the situation. For me, this process is important because students in writing pedagogy education courses need to wrestle with these questions as students and as teachers. Because genre conventions "are at work in rhetorically shaping and reproducing our social environments, our practices, and our identities as social actors," students need opportunities to critically examine the role of

evaluative feedback genres (Bawarshi 2001, 73). Making these practices
less routine and more explicit can help all classroom members better
understand and negotiate the possibilities and constraints of available
pedagogical genres.

REFERENCES

Bawarshi, Anis. 2001. "The Ecology of Genre." In *Ecocomposition: Theoretical and Pedagogical Approaches*, edited by Christian R. Weisser and Sidney I. Dobrin, 69–80. Albany: State University of New York Press.

Berry, Amanda. 2007. *Tensions in Teaching about Teaching: Understanding Practice as a Teacher Educator*. New York: Springer.

Borko, Hilda, Dan Liston, and Jennifer A. Whitcomb. 2007. "Genres of Empirical Research in Teacher Education." *Journal of Teacher Education* 58 (1): 3–11.

Cochran-Smith, Marilyn, and Susan L. Lytle. 2001. "Beyond Certainty: Taking an Inquiry Stance on Practice." In *Teachers Caught in the Action: Professional Development That Matters*, edited by Ann Lieberman and Lynne Miller, 45–58. New York: Teachers College Press.

Dean, Deborah. 2008. *Genre Theory: Teaching, Writing, and Being*. Urbana, IL: NCTE.

Devitt, Amy J. 2004. *Writing Genres*. Carbondale: Southern Illinois University Press.

Dryer, Dylan B. 2012. "At a Mirror, Darkly: The Imagined Undergraduate Writers of Ten Novice Composition Instructors." *College Composition and Communication* 63 (3): 420–52.

Fecho, Bob, Kim Price, and Chris Read. 2004. "From Tununak to Beaufort: Taking a Critical Inquiry Stance as a First Year Teacher." *English Education* 36 (4): 263–88.

Loughran, John. 2002. "Understanding Self-Study of Teacher Education Practices." In *Improving Teacher Education Practice through Self-Study*, edited by John Loughran and Tom Russell, 239–48. New York: Routledge/Falmer.

O'Connor, Ken. 2007. *A Repair Kit for Grading: 15 Fixes for Broken Grades*. London: Pearson.

Priestley, Mark, Gert Biesta, and Sarah Robinson. 2015. *Teacher Agency: An Ecological Approach*. New York: Bloomsbury.

Qualley, Donna J. 1997. *Turns of Thought: Teaching Composition as Reflexive Inquiry*. Portsmouth, NH: Boynton/Cook.

Schulte, Ann Katherine. 2009. *Seeking Integrity in Teacher Education: Transforming Student Teachers, Transforming My Self*. New York: Springer.

Simon, Rob. 2015. "'I'm Fighting My Fight, and I'm Not Alone Anymore': The Influence of Communities of Inquiry." *English Education* 48 (1): 41–71.

Smith, Summer. 1997. "The Genre of the End Comment: Conventions in Teacher Responses to Student Writing." *College Composition and Communication* 48 (2): 249–68.

Staunton, John A. 2008. *Deranging English/Education: Teacher Inquiry, Literary Studies, and Hybrid Visions of "English" for 21st Century Schools*. Urbana, IL: NCTE.

Stenberg, Shari J. 2005. *Professing and Pedagogy: Learning the Teaching of English*. Urbana, IL: NCTE.

Zeichner, Ken. 1999. "The New Scholarship in Teacher Education." *Educational Researcher* 28 (9): 4–15.

5

OCCLUSION IN A CLASSROOM GENRE SET
Assessing Assignment Sheets and Grading Rubrics

Dustin Morris and Lindsay Clark

The assignment sheet and the grading rubric are two genres, common to the classroom, that work together in important but occluded ways. As Swales (1996) discusses, occlusion in academic genres happens when a genre's knowledge construction is hidden, less visible to a public audience (46). While Swales focuses on research genres such as conference presentations, monographs, and journal articles, his argument can also extend to pedagogical genres (Neaderhiser 2016). In the classroom, instructors develop specific genres, but how and why they are created may be occluded from audiences needing that information the most, specifically students. To that end, it is important to understand the reciprocal relationships conveyed between genres in the same genre set.

We are particularly interested in unpacking the occluded relationship between the assignment sheet and the grading rubric, as these two genres are relatively common within the system of classroom genres. These two genres are utilized by students, maintaining assessment functions in the classroom and serving as guides for completing assignments successfully. However, as Bawarshi and Reiff (2010) note, insight into genres like the grading rubric isn't always as clear to students as it might be to instructors. Therefore, access to pedagogical genres is not equal and can further widen the power relationships between teachers and students (89). By examining how the grading rubric functions in conjunction with the assignment sheet, we can explore how the production of these pragmatic genres (often done in isolation) is often occluded from students, and the implications for both students' uptake and instructors' assessment practices.

To understand the relationship between these two genres, we examined the ways they interact and overlap within the classroom genre system. In this chapter, we discuss our study of assignment sheets in a First-Year

https://doi.org/10.7330/9781646422920.c005

Writing (FYW) program, along with the grading rubrics used to assess the resulting student writing. There is a reciprocal correlation between these two genres, and a thorough understanding of the recurring moves within each can shed light on how instructors compose these documents, offering insight into possible training methods to help accentuate this connection. Additionally, we are interested in the larger context of how instructors and students perceive these genres, and how their composition may be occluded in the larger classroom genre set. By examining these two genres as interrelated classroom genres, rather than just book-ended genres that present a writing task (via the assignment sheet) and then explain how it will be assessed (via the rubric), we aim to uncover the rhetorical nuances that emerge from their otherwise occluded pedagogical roles in the classroom, for teachers and students alike.

ASSIGNMENT SHEETS AND RUBRICS: INSTRUCTION AND ASSESSMENT

There has been significant interest in understanding the type of writing assignments that students do in university settings, including Bridgeman and Carlson's (1984) survey of the writing assigned across first- and second-year writing programs at thirty-four universities, Light's (2001, 2003) study of the writing produced by Harvard undergraduates, and Melzer's (2003, 2009) analysis of assignment types, length, and frequency in Writing Across the Curriculum programs at a national level. However, while the assignment sheet has been analyzed in relation to the syllabus (Graves et al. 2010), what lacks in many of these studies and conversations is an examination of how the assignment sheet operates in conjunction with the grading rubric, within the larger genre system of a classroom that includes a syllabus, tip sheets, handouts, and other texts that guide students through their writing tasks.

The assignment sheet is predominantly understood as an instructional document for students working on the assigned task, whereas the rubric is considered an assessment tool for teachers. However, both provide information to the student on how to complete the assignment and how to earn a grade. The assignment sheet, as Reiff and Middleton (1983) posit, facilitates "communication between teacher and student" (263). According to Connors and Glenn (1995), the goal of the assignment sheet is to help the writer begin the assignment, support invention, and offer a chance for the student to do their best work (58).

Similarly, for Bawarshi (2003), the assignment sheet uses moves that cue students to specific kinds of action (127); however, he also notes that the assignment sheet helps position instructor identity, as both the reader and writer. Bawarshi claims that instructors are situated in this dual role as "a double subject position, a subject subject, one who is doing the action (the subject as writer) and one on whom the action is done (the subject as reader)" (131). Therefore, the instructor relies on a series of rhetorical moves to alert students to the type of writing they should produce. For example, "your task," "you will first need to . . . ," or even "for example" are all moves that are typical in the assignment sheet.

Although writing studies scholars have explored various aspects of the assignment sheet genre, scholarship on grading rubrics has stemmed predominantly from the field of education, where the use of rubrics is largely debated (Turley and Gallagher 2008; Livingston 2012). Rubrics are standard grading criteria used across assignments and "can either be holistic or analytical, or it may be a combination of the two" (Rezaei and Lovorn 2010, 19; O'Neill et al. 2009). Holistic rubrics focus on product rather than process, while an analytical rubric gives multiple scores rather than just one overall score (Finson and Ormsbee 1998). Similar to how Connors and Glenn describe the assignment sheet, an effective rubric offers students an idea of the assignment criteria and should give a clear picture of strengths and weaknesses in their text, supplementing comments on the actual draft. Even though rubrics are considered a common pedagogical genre within education scholarship, there is a correlation between the rise of rubric usage and a general dissatisfaction with traditional essay grading techniques (Rezaei and Lovorn 2010). Still, several studies point toward more reliable grading from the use of rubrics (Jonsson and Svingby 2007; Silvestri and Oescher 2006), while others posit that the use of rubrics may not promise effective assessment (Ross-Fisher 2005; Orsmond and Merry 1996; Tomkins 2003).

For this study, we highlight rubrics that use a mixture of approaches, with the samples based on availability. We do not mean to suggest one is better than the other, but rather that the assignment sheets examined in this study use rubrics that assess both the whole project and individual components. Furthermore, this study does not address the effectiveness of the individual rubrics themselves; rather, we examine the relationship of rubrics in tandem with assignment sheets and the relationship that should develop due to their use functions. While it is important to explore how effective rubrics are for assessment, we are primarily interested in how instructors use rubrics in conjunction with assignment sheets, especially in regard to how clearly expressed that relationship is within those genres. For us, this represents an opportunity to help instructors craft genres that support student learning by uncovering rhetorical connections between these two linked genres that, in their very creation, are often occluded.

STUDY METHODS

The research site for this study is one first-year writing program at a mid-level public university in the southwestern United States. The program's mission states that the two-course sequence, ENGL 1113 and 1213, are intended to develop skills in critical reading and writing at the college level. ENGL 1113 concentrates on developing students' abilities to read analytically and use revision skills to compose essays; ENGL 1213 adds components of college-level research and documentation skills. Both courses teach modes of organization, sentence correction, and revision as integral parts of the writing process rather than as isolated course units. All papers are read at least once by the instructor or by peer reviewers in rough draft form, and students are expected to incorporate that feedback into their final, graded essay. In addition to the required formal essays, students engage in a significant amount of informal exploratory writing. These courses act as an introduction to university writing for students, most of whom take the courses during their first or second year of college.

According to the program's outcomes statements for the FYW sequence, students enrolled in ENGL 1113 should be able to demonstrate an understanding of writing as a process. For ENGL 1213, students should exhibit abilities to locate and use source material and establish supportable theses based on their research findings. While these outcomes are paraphrased from the composition program's website, it is interesting to see another genre influencing the assignment sheets and rubrics genre set.

Sample

We collected a sample set of twenty-two documents—sixteen assignment sheets and six grading rubrics—based on availability via the FYW program's online instructor resources. The program's intraweb site offers two sample assignment sheets for each of the eight required assignments in the FYW sequence: for ENGL 1111, a literacy narrative, a profile essay, a textual analysis, and an evaluation essay; for ENGL 1213, a "making connections" essay, an annotated bibliography, an I-search paper, and a final research paper. The sample documents display the wide variation of approaches within the program, with eight different instructors represented in the sixteen sample assignments. Five of those instructors were also represented in the six grading rubric samples (one instructor wrote two different rubrics); three of the rubrics were linked to specific assignments, and three were general rubrics that covered multiple assignments throughout a semester.

While all of the twenty-two samples were written by instructors, we also took note of any explicit guidelines from the FYW program on how the documents should be composed. As Dana Comi explores in her chapter on departmental teaching handbooks (in this collection), the availability of explicit program guidelines for classroom genres like the syllabus or assignment sheet can be especially helpful for new graduate teaching assistants. As those TAs gain experience, however, it is also important for them to express their evolving pedagogical identities while still adhering to programmatic policies. According to this program's policies, assignment sheets must contain specific criteria (noted in our analysis). However, this set of criteria can either be in the instructors' words or copied verbatim from the policy manual, thereby allowing instructors flexibility depending on their familiarity or comfort composing the genre. In the case of the grading rubrics, there appears to be no programmatic requirements on how they should be constructed.

Artifact Analysis

This study blends a rhetorical genre studies (RGS) approach with English for specific purposes (ESP). While these two schools of genre study tend to be seen as separate approaches aimed at different analytical purposes, Johns (2003) and, more recently, Cheng (2011) have observed that due to ESP scholars' growing attention to context, research blending RGS and ESP analysis has been increasing. Within an RGS framework, genre studies "has been directed toward an understanding of how genres mediate situated practices, interactions, symbolic realities, and 'congruent meanings'" within sites of activity (Bawarshi and Reiff 2010, 59). This was pertinent to our study, as we were interested in examining the mediated relationship between assignment sheets and grading rubrics, as two congruent components within the classroom as a site of activity. We also, however, wanted to draw from ESP methodology, particularly in how the internal rhetorical "moves" a genre makes may be analyzed both textually and linguistically (Swales 1990; Bawarshi 2003). For the purposes of our analysis, we relied on the definition of a rhetorical move as a "bounded communicative act that is designed to achieve one main communicative objective" within the genre (Swales and Feak 2000, 35).

To employ this hybridized analysis, we first isolated moves found in the samples and analyzed them for their communicative purposes, identifying the specific objectives student writers were being asked to achieve with each move. Finally, we used Hyland's (2004) ESP-based approach to genre analysis, which prioritizes a "visible pedagogy" that "seeks to offer writers an explicit understanding of how target texts are structured and why they are written the way they are" so writers know what needs to be learned rather than relying on inductive methods (11). Hyland's theory of visible pedagogy underscores the importance of making occluded genres visible for students and teachers alike. In hybridizing our approach, we were able to understand how the context of the particular communicative act (the move) is the beginning of the analysis, but also how understanding the context of the particular genre is the end goal.

We isolated each move in the assignment sheets and rubrics by tracking patterns in the information given in the documents. If a rubric or assignment sheet displayed the same type of information in three or more examples, we noted that rhetorical feature as a recurring move. For example, the recurring assignment sheet move *Starting* appears as follows in Samples 4 and 5 (the profile essay and rhetorical analysis, respectively):

> "To begin, you should decide who or what you want to profile for this assignment." (Sample 4)

> "Begin by locating a text that makes use of multiple strategies, or that makes use of those strategies in subtle and complex ways." (Sample 5).

Similarly, the recurring rubric move *Rhetorical Awareness* is demonstrated through the following statement about considering audience:

> "The essay demonstrates that the paper is meant to be read by someone and that the writer has thought about the effects of language on the reader." (Sample 21)

In some rubrics, the *Rhetorical Awareness* move was presented as an explicit category, while in others, it was identified by statements about audience and sense of purpose.

Though we are interested in understanding how assignment sheets and grading rubrics coexist and interact with each other, we chose to identify and classify the two genres' rhetorical moves separately. While we do consider assignment sheets and grading rubrics to be interrelated genres—including their use of particular moves—we aimed initially to track the moves that appeared independently in each genre set. Doing this enabled us to consider each genre within its rhetorical context: as independent genres typifying certain acts (giving instruction on a pending assignment, providing insight into the assessment of the completed assignment) as well as connected genres participating in a shared communicative act. We were then able to consider how the two sets of moves fulfilled both of those contexts—or, in some cases, failed to do so. Accordingly, in the next section we have divided our findings into two parts to address assignment sheets and rubrics separately, followed by a discussion of the connections between the two genres.

FINDINGS

Assignment Sheets

Across the sixteen assignment samples, eleven recurring moves were identified. Only one of those eleven moves, the *Description* of the assignment, was found in all of the samples. Three other moves—*Requirements, Length,* and *Criteria*—were present in fifteen of the samples collected. Across the sample set, varied methods of organization were used in arranging the moves. After identifying the recurrent moves, we further noted that the eleven moves could be separated into two categories: content moves, functioning mainly through exposition to stress content-based components important for students to consider while writing, like details on the assignment's topic or organization, and logistical moves, describing more conventional parameters for students to follow, like required lengths or citation style.

Content Moves

In identifying moves regularly used within the assignment sheet samples, we classified five moves primarily focused on the assignment's body or content (table 5.2). These included specifications addressing macro-organization requirements, such as an assignment description and an explanation of the writer's purpose or objective. Typically, the instructors included guidance on how to begin the writing process and how to conclude the assignment, with example excerpts to encourage students' thinking and writing processes. Rather than addressing technical issues (like formatting or grammar), these moves focused more on guiding students through various stages of the writing process, such as building a thesis, finding a topic, or considering modeled examples.

As table 5.3 shows, the *Description* section was the only move that appeared in all sixteen assignments sheets; however, the length of the *Description* was notably different across the samples. Some contained

Table 5.1. Content moves in assignment sheets

Move (# of instances)	Example
Description (16)	"Your task for this essay is to write the story of your own literacy experience."
Objective (12)	"Craft a thesis-driven analytical essay that demonstrates substantial understanding of the rhetorical strategies used in a specific text, and an ability to examine, critique, and interrogate those strategies."
Starting (11)	"In order to write your narrative, you will first need to determine what your relationship to literacy is, determine where that relationship started, and what caused the status of that relationship."
Conclusion (8)	"Be wary of too much summary. Please no more than three sentences of summary."
Examples (4)	"For example, if you are an English major, the question 'Does teaching solely Western literature benefit or harm students?' is too vague. A better question might be 'Is teaching Shakespeare the best way to teach dramatic literature?'"

Table 5.2. Logistical moves in assignment sheets

Move (# of instances)	Example
Requirement (15)	[List of required components] Submission of all drafts Participation in a conference MLA format—include a works cited page 3 source minimum
Length (15)	"Write a 4-6 page profile of an individual, group, place, or event based on your own observation."
Criteria (15)	[List of specific grading expectations] Include a concise description of the subject Include clearly defined criteria Engage in knowledgeable discussion of the subject
Value (12)	[Title of assignment] Essay Two—The Annotated Bibliography (150)
Style (11)	"In addition to your exploratory essay, you will also submit a Works Cited. . . . The items on the list should follow MLA guidelines for proper formatting."
Formal Rubric (4)	[Section heading] Grading Criteria for Final Draft

only one sentence of description, while others offered whole paragraphs explaining the assignment. For example, Sample 2 provides more details about the assignment than other samples by asking students to narrow their approach, use effective organization, and establish a clear perspective.

Table 5.3. Frequency of recurring content moves by assignment type

Assignment (# of samples)	Objective	Description	Starting	Examples	Conclusion
Literacy Narrative (2)	2	2	1	1	2
Profile Essay (2)	2	2	1	1	1
Textual Analysis (2)	2	2	1	0	1
Evaluation Essay (2)	2	2	1	0	1
Making Connections (2)	1	2	1	0	0
Annotated Bibliography (2)	1	2	2	0	1
I-Search Paper (2)	1	2	2	0	2
Research Paper (2)	1	2	2	2	1
Total (n=16)	12	16	11	4	9

While the *Description* move was present in every assignment sheet, it was sometimes preceded by an announcement of the assignment's purpose—the *Objective* move:

> Objective: To craft a thesis-driven essay that explores your experience with reading and/or writing and to connect that experience to a broader cultural issue. (Sample 8)

This method—listing the objective first and not integrating it into a larger paragraph—was only used in six assignment sheets. The more common approach was to incorporate the objective into the actual description of the assignment, illustrated below:

> However you choose to approach this essay, make your point with a strong thesis statement connected by topic sentences supported by organized, appropriate, and specific details. (Sample 8)

Alternatively, other assignments performed several moves at once, combining *Description* with the *Objective, Starting,* and *Requirement* moves:

> The research narrative requires students to employ story-telling techniques with critical component (*Requirement*), thus students must connect their personal research experience to larger cultural contexts. Students will continue investigating their specific research question started in Essay Three A by identifying a personal connection, describing the steps they went through during their investigation, and compiling the information in a way that guides them into Essay Four. (*Starting*)
> This essay should be highly focused, often on a personal experience and/or interest, as well as very descriptive. (*Description*) Students should

include concrete details in their writing that paint a vivid picture for readers (*Requirement*). Students need to synthesize other writers' claims and
how each source shaped or changed their thinking about their research
question (*Objective*). (Sample 13)

As stated before, the *Description* length varied across the assignment sheets
and within the type of assignment. Another variable that influenced the
activity of the move was the assignment's complexity. For example, in the
case of Sample 11 (for the Annotated Bibliography assignment), the *Description* move is employed multiple times at various points in order to
provide specific information, such as describing a source's thesis, providing a summative conclusion, and qualifying how a source should be used.

One of the least utilized content moves was *Examples*: only four assignment sheets offered any illustrative examples for students. In Sample
16, for the Research Paper assignment, the instructor offered thesis
questions for students to consider as they begin writing, demonstrating
the difference between a vague and more developed thesis. However,
the instructor is quick to point out that these are only "jumping off
points," examples to help students in their invention process—not to
be confused with a *Starting* move identifying how to begin the writing
process itself. It is notable that the *Examples* move was so infrequently
used throughout the full assignment sample set; it seems that giving
students jumping-off points would be beneficial for many different types
of assignments. In fact, the Literacy Narrative and Profile Essay assignments are the only ones where it occurs—one time in each—aside from
the final Research Paper at the end of ENGL 1213.

The *Conclusion* move, defined as the summative reminders and directives after the assignment description and other details but before any
final breakdown of requirements or other criteria, was also employed
by only half of the assignment sheets. Typically, *Conclusion* moves offer
students advice about what makes a successful essay:

> A successful essay will answer these questions in a way that is effective, use
> an academic voice, incorporate sources beneficially and ethically, and,
> most importantly, keep your audience engaged in your thoughts and
> research. (Sample 10)

Most instances of the *Conclusion* move appeared as part of an assignment's main body, in paragraph form, although one variation was apparent in an assignment sheet for the Annotated Bibliography, which
contained bullet-pointed "Tips":

- While you may not write these sentences in this exact order, or use
  a whole sentence to address author's credentials, etc. you SHOULD
  NOT mix your summary sections with your evaluation of the article.

- Be wary of too much summary. Please no more than three sentences of summary.

- Do not include direct quotations or paraphrases. (Sample 11)

While these offer more than a way to conclude an essay, we still classify this as a *Conclusion* move based on its position in the assignment sheet. Additionally, the use of imperative statements made these "tips" much more directive than what was common in other rhetorical moves, placing them in alignment with other instances of the *Conclusion* move.

Moves like *Description* were present across all sixteen assignment sheets in the sample, whereas *Examples* and *Conclusions* moves were not consistently found, with four and nine instances, respectively. As stated in the methods, we attribute this to the fact that the FYW program's policies require instructors to explicitly state an essay's outcomes on the assignment sheet, whereas providing illustrative examples or concluding directives (i.e., *Examples* or *Conclusion* moves) is not a programmatic requirement.

As a transitional point, we would also comment on the use of the *Formal Rubric* move. While we discuss it further below as a "logistical" move, it is worth noting that it somewhat blurs the line between content and logistics. A portion of the samples incorporated a formalized rubric-based heuristic directly into the assignment sheet, with moves characterizing the assessment of both content features, such as descriptive requirements valuing "thesis-driven" assignments and logistical expectations, such as length requirements. Ultimately, even though the *Formal Rubric* move may comment on content-based components, it was much more focused on providing answers to students' technical questions about the assignment, as one might expect from logistical moves.

Logistical Moves

Assignment logistics, or conventional expectations, such as required components, criteria, length, assignment value, sources (types and/ or number), and citation style, appeared in various places within the samples. As noted in the analysis of content moves, how explicit these moves were stated seemed to be up to instructors, as departmental policy guidelines provided no specific mandate. Table 5.4 indicates the frequency of each logistical move identified in the assignment sheets, parsed by the assignment type.

The most frequently recurring logistical moves were *Requirement*, *Criteria*, and *Length*, all of which appeared in fifteen of the assignment samples. The FYW program's policy states that all assignment criteria should appear, in some form, on instructors' assignment sheets. This was

Table 5.4. Frequency of recurring logistical moves by assignment type

Assignment (# of samples)	Requirement	Criteria	Length	Value	Sources	Style	Formal Rubric
Literacy Narrative (2)	2	2	2	2	0	0	1
Profile Essay (2)	2	2	2	2	0	0	0
Textual Analysis (2)	2	2	2	2	2	2	1
Evaluation Essay (2)	2	2	2	1	2	2	0
Making Connections (2)	2	2	2	1	2	2	1
Annotated Bibliography (2)	2	2	2	1	2	2	0
I-Search Paper (2)	2	2	2	2	2	2	2
Research Paper (2)	1	1	1	1	2	1	1
Totals (n=16)	15	15	15	12	12	11	6

met without exception, as the *Criteria* move appeared in all fifteen samples. Alternatively, the method of inclusion for the *Requirement, Length,* and *Style* moves was primarily by instructor discretion. The program does dictate several guidelines for each move, but ultimately, instructors are free to maneuver within those guidelines. Subtle variations in *Length* were noted, but all assignment sheets fell within acceptable program expectations. The *Style* move, addressing documentation and citation style, represented another noted variation, since not all assignments in the sample set required sources. In cases where an assignment did ask students to use sources, the instructor usually indicated the required method of documentation—commonly MLA format—but in two samples, instructors allowed their students to select their citation style: "The essay's format and documentation style is in keeping with MLA or APA" (Sample 19).

Each instructor detailed requirements differently in their assignment sheets, but for the most part the only notable differences concerned the *Criteria* and *Formal Rubric* moves. When it came to the *Criteria* move, as a marker of how an assignment would be assessed, the samples revealed one of two things: they either listed the criteria at the very end, thus concluding the entire document, or they integrated the criteria into the overall document. Also of note is that even though *Criteria* and *Formal Rubric* are closely related, we did not consider them to be the same move. We separated them because, while a small number of samples included specific, formal rubric-oriented details to evaluate students, the majority of assignment sheets did not. Much more commonly, instructors relied on the *Criteria* move, thus directly satisfying the FYW program's policy on explicitly stating criteria. For example, as one assignment for the literacy narrative indicates, the criteria (established by the instructor) dictate that students should craft a narrative, create vivid details, convey the significance of the event, and be free from errors (Sample 1). In a similar fashion, the Research Paper (the final assignment for ENGL 1213) uses the *Criteria* move to state that students should demonstrate an evaluation of sources, synthesize and integrate those sources into their prose, enter into a scholarly conversation, articulate a central thesis, and provide correct citations (Sample 16). The *Criteria* move stresses the main outcomes for each assignment, but it does not suggest how the essays would be evaluated, thus marking a difference in how we classified instances of the *Criteria* and *Formal Rubric* moves.

These logistical moves' frequent recurrence suggests the interrelation of instructors' efforts to make students aware of assignment requirements and students' desire to know the technical components that instructors will use to evaluate their writing.

Rubrics

In addition to analyzing the moves in assignment sheets, we sought to analyze the recurring moves within grading rubrics, as separate moves describing how the students' essays would be evaluated. Table 5.5 shows the frequency of six recurring moves across the sample of six rubrics—three general or "holistic" rubrics and three assignment-specific rubrics. Notably, the three general rubrics opted to include ways an essay could receive various scores based on how well it was constructed, employing qualitative descriptions for the score values: "excellent," "good," "fair," and "weak."

The rubrics often included instructors' definitions of the terms used to identify the categorical moves along with a description or examples of what would qualify as successful uptake of each move. For example, one rubric gives this explanation for the *Content* move:

Table 5.5. Frequency of recurring moves in rubric by assignment type

Assignment (sample ID)	Content	Revision	Organization	Style	Documentation	Rhetorical Awareness
Textual Analysis (S 17)	1	1	1	1	1	1
I-Search (S 21)	1	1	1	1	1	1
Research Paper (S 19)	1	1	1	1	1	0
General/ Holistic (S 18)	1	1	1	1	1	1
General/ Holistic (S 20)	1	1	1	1	1	1
General/ Holistic (S 22)	1	1	1	1	1	1
Totals (n=6)	6	6	6	6	6	5

> Measures how well one balances claims and evidence, the complexity of a central controlling idea (or thesis), and the extent to which one has thoroughly dealt with (analyzed) the subject at hand. (Sample 20)

The *Content* move qualified the construction of a student's thesis and how well it was supported by source material, a valued step in this move. One sample, however, included "following directions" in the *Content* section, whereas others identified this move as *Rhetorical Awareness.*

The *Rhetorical Awareness* move mentions the audience reaction to the essay's central claim: three of the six rubrics contained the phrase "so what?," characterizing the importance of why the essay matters and to whom. For instance, an essay with a strong sense of rhetorical awareness "demonstrates an understanding of and accomplishes the assignment" (Sample 20). The *Style* and *Organization* moves stressed the importance of tone, diction, and logical order of information. Of the six rubrics, two used "structure" as a synonym for "organization," but the evaluative criteria paralleled the other four rubrics that exclusively used "organization" to classify the arrangement of ideas and paragraphs within assignments.

One important aspect discovered in the analysis of the rubrics was the arrangement of the individual moves. All six samples used headings to outline their assessment categories. While there were some variations between names, such as "organization" versus "structure," each instance of the move evaluated the same criteria. Therefore, we chose to categorize the larger moves in a standard way. All samples set *Content* as the first criterion graded, followed by *Rhetorical Awareness*. *Style* and *Organization* were the third and fourth moves, but some samples regarded these moves as interchangeable (Samples 19 and 22). Both moves focus on aesthetics of writing, such as sentence types, diction, transitions, introductions, and conclusions. Lastly, *Revision* was organized as the final move in all of the rubrics. Generally, this move examines significant changes to the previous four moves between a rough and final draft but also adds importance to proofreading skills.

General rubrics, as stated before, are used to assess student writing throughout the semester: they do not (or should not) change. Three of the sample rubrics fell into this category, as their moves included generalized commentary applying to multiple assignments. These rubrics were also more complex in their wording than the assignment-specific rubrics. For example, under *Style*, one general rubric is very explicit about what qualifies as an "excellent" essay: writing that engages the reader, practices style that seems effortless, and demonstrates control throughout the whole essay (Sample 20). Its explicitness resides in the language and detail used to describe how "excellent style" can be achieved. "Lively choice," "impressive vocabulary," or "total control of how she says what she says" are all descriptors of what works well in the essay's stylistic choices. Because that rubric is used throughout the semester, the way in which those qualifications will be assessed may be different. Clearly, an instructor cannot grade the first essay and the last essay with the same expectations, but the purpose of a single, general rubric seems to showcase what essays should achieve or be like by the end of the semester. For example, under *Style*, Sample 18 states that students should use "appropriate academic tone." However, in the Literacy Narrative assignment sheet, the style recommendation is to be personal and creative, which may be at odds with an "appropriate academic tone." This is further complicated with such assignments as the Annotated Bibliography, which recommends students not even use whole sentences to describe the individual source. Therefore, the specific criteria on the assignment sheet would suggest a superseding of the general rubric. This is another example of occlusion between the assignment sheet and rubric genre: while the distinctions of style or tone may be clear to instructors, students may be left trying to ascertain which document—the assignment sheet or rubric—they should follow.

DISCUSSION AND IMPLICATIONS

Bazerman (1994) states that genres, "in-so-far as they identify a reper-
toire of possible actions that may be taken in a set of circumstances,
identify the possible intentions one may have" (82). The relationship
between the assignment sheet and grading rubric is complicated, but
teachers and students should be aware that these genres can and will
orient people toward specific actions, as Bazerman suggests. For us,
focusing on the assignment sequence in FYW courses is just one way
of understanding the relationship between the assignment sheet and
grading rubric, when both genres coexist within a classroom genre set.
In the writing classroom, the assignment sheet often signals the start of
students' uptake of the writing process, which in turn concludes when
instructors apply the rubric as part of their grading process. Both genres
facilitate their own ways in which students react to the process of writing essays. However, they also share a reciprocal relationship in shaping
how students and instructors behave. To this end, this study uncovers
two problems: a misunderstanding of how general rubrics are used
through a semester, and an unawareness of how individual genres function within a genre set.

While each assignment sheet contained specific criteria, the corresponding rubrics did not consistently carry the same emphasis. By highlighting specific objectives for a given assignment, a rubric provides the
opportunity to communicate to students how the act of assessment is
accomplished: students are able to see the impact their writing will have
based on how well they can meet those objectives. The general rubrics
we analyzed did not reflect that opportunity. Since these documents
were used throughout the semester, they contained assessment criteria
students may not yet recognize at a given point in the class schedule
before certain course topics had been addressed. For instance, the
Textual Analysis assignment requires an analytical thesis. However, that
assignment is the third essay in the FYW program's scaffolded sequence
for ENGL 1111. Therefore, by using one rubric throughout the semester,
instructors might confuse students about the assessment goals for the
individual assignments in that sequence—the two essays preceding the
Textual Analysis, for which the requirement of an analytical thesis does
not apply, and the essays following the Textual Analysis, which may or
may not continue to be evaluated based on whether elements from the
preceding assignments are still incorporated.

It also became increasingly clear across the assignment sheets that
Objective and *Requirement* moves comprised an implicit rubric, independent of whether a more formal corresponding rubric existed. In such

cases, the inclusion of a much more developed, general rubric, again, may have implications on student uptake. This is especially so if an instructor places higher priority on requirements like word count or page count, sources used, or formatting issues than on content. From our own experiences, first as new instructors and later as mentors, new instructors like graduate teaching assistants may rely more heavily on logistical moves rather than content moves as a way to maintain an authoritative teacherly identity when the seemingly limitless possibilities of instruction become overwhelming. However, as Sands (2017) and Leahy (2017) point out, rubrics may capture important moves about writing, but they cannot contain them all. Therefore, we are not advocating for the exclusive use of rubrics in the writing classroom, but perhaps instead that instructors should ensure those implicit rubric features—reflected in both content moves and logistical moves—are further explicated in assignment sheets themselves rather than in a separate, formal grading rubric. Discussion of how a rubric will be used to assess the final essays should work in tandem with the assignment sheets and explore the many ways in which writing and composing in academic settings can change.

Another concern with these paired or "bookended" genres is the inattention to how an instructor's pedagogical goals function between the two genres. As previously stated, general rubrics may prioritize moves not yet covered and thus penalize students for not meeting those requirements on an assignment. While instructors may use rubrics in an attempt to be less subjective in their assessment or to be more transparent in their grading process, the moves identified within the rubric genre indicate that instructors still end up weighing some criteria over others. This is an important qualification to consider in order to ensure an instructor's pedagogical intent is prioritized across the genres they present to their students. Instructors should understand how assignment sheets and rubrics are part of goal and outcome teaching (Kendall 2008); if those genres are composed without proper attention, it can complicate how students respond in their writing. By examining the specific rhetorical moves of these two genres, we noticed that specific assignment outcomes and goals did not always translate to the formal rubrics. This occurred in specific rubrics less frequently, since the formal rubrics were written with singular assignments in mind. An awareness of how these genres work in tandem to express the values and outcomes of classroom assignments cannot be understated.

Finally, the third issue uncovered by this study presents the greatest implications for how rubrics and assignment sheets function in an FYW class, as well as how these findings might relate to other departments and disciplines incorporating assignment sheets and rubrics into their curriculum. Implicitly, instructors understand that assignment sheets and rubrics should work in tandem, but that connection is not always explicit within the documents that students ultimately receive. For these two genres to successfully work together, instructors need to create assignment sheets that visibly interact with the rubrics that ultimately guide their assessment. For example, if an assignment sheet contains specific objectives to be met, those objectives should appear on the grading rubric. As Woodard et al. (2013) stress, the construction of rubrics has largely been ignored in teacher education and development. They note, "composing an effective rubric—particularly for instructional or formative contexts—is a complex task that requires teachers to think meta-cognitively about their goals for a writing assignment" (442). Instructors need to be mindful when using rubrics to communicate assignment goals to students. When we compose these genres, we must be aware of our expectations and be able to articulate those expectations clearly in these documents and to our students.

The implications of this study extend beyond first-year writing classes, including upper-level courses and graduate writing courses inside and outside of the humanities. In general training books for teaching assistants, the literature often stresses the importance of developing thoughtful assignment sheets and rubrics, but they do not state if these should be developed at the same time (White 2007). It takes time and energy to craft effective assignment sheets and rubrics, and even more time to shape those genres to speak in tandem and avoid occlusion for their intended audiences. As many RGS scholars recognize, genres identify particular social actions users can take up. If we want our students to be able to understand how these two genres work together—both for their purposes and ours—then we need to recognize that how we create assignment sheets and rubrics matters, that they represent an opportunity to make our pedagogy apparent. The more explicit we can be in our assignment direction and assessment, the more accessible those expectations will be to students. By addressing occlusion in these two classroom genres, we can make the rhetorical nuances that shape student and teacher writing more visible.

REFERENCES

Bawarshi, Anis. 2003. *Genre and the Invention of the Writer: Reconsidering the Place of Invention in Composition.* Logan: Utah State University Press.

Bawarshi, Anis, and Mary Jo Reiff. 2010. *Genre: An Introduction to History, Theory, Research, and Pedagogy*. West Lafayette, IN: Parlor Press.

Bazerman, Charles. 1994. "Systems of Genres and the Enactment of Social Intentions." In *Genre and the New Rhetoric*, edited by Aviva Freedman and Peter Medway, 67–85. Bristol, PA: Taylor & Francis.

Bridgeman, Brent, and Sybil B. Carlson. 1984. "Survey of Academic Writing Tasks." *Written Communication* 1 (2): 247–80.

Cheng, An. 2011. "Language Features as the Pathways to Genre: Students' Attention to Non-Prototypical Features and Its Implications." *Journal of Second Language Writing* 20 (1): 69–82.

Connors, Robert J., and Cheryl Glenn. 1995. *The St. Martin's Guide to Teaching Writing*. 3rd ed. New York: St. Martin's Press.

Finson, Kevin D., and Christine K. Ormsbee. 1998. "Rubrics and Their Use in Inclusive Science." *Intervention in School and Clinic* 34 (2): 79–88.

Graves, Roger, Theresa Hyland, and Boba M. Samuels. 2010. "Undergraduate Writing Assignments: An Analysis of Syllabi at One Canadian College." *Written Communication* 27 (3): 293–317.

Hyland, Ken. 2004. *Genre and Second Language Writing*. Ann Arbor: University of Michigan Press.

Johns, Ann M. 2003. "Genre and ESL/EFL Composition Instruction." In *Exploring the Dynamics of Second Language Writing*, edited by Barbara Kroll, 195–217. New York: Cambridge University Press.

Jonsson, Anders, and Gunilla Svingby. 2007. "The Use of Scoring Rubrics: Reliability, Validity and Educational Consequences." *Educational Research Review* 2 (2): 130–44.

Kendall, Anna. 2008. "The Assignment Sheet Mystery." *The Writing Lab Newsletter* 33 (1): 1–5.

Leahy, Anne. 2017. "Rubrics Save Time and Make Grading Visible." In *Bad Ideas about Writing*, edited by Cheryl E. Ball and Drew M. Loewe, 259–63. Morgantown: West Virginia University Libraries Digital Publishing Institute.

Light, Richard J. 2001. *Making the Most of College: Students Speak Their Minds*. Cambridge, MA: Harvard University Press.

Light, Richard J. 2003. "Writing and Students' Engagement." *Peer Review* 6 (1): 28–31.

Livingston, Michael. 2012. "The Infamy of Grading Rubrics." *The English Journal* 102 (2): 108–13.

Melzer, Dan. 2003. "Assignments across the Curriculum: A Survey of College Writing." *Language and Learning Across the Disciplines* 6 (1): 86–110.

Melzer, Dan. 2009. "Writing Assignments across the Curriculum: A National Study of College Writing." *College Composition and Communication* 61 (2): 240–61.

Neaderhiser, Stephen. 2016. "Hidden in Plain Sight: Occlusion in Pedagogical Genres." *Composition Forum* 33. http://www.compositionforum.com/issue/33/hidden.php.

O'Neill, Peggy, Cindy Moore, and Brian Huot. 2009. *A Guide to College Writing Assessment*. Logan: Utah State University Press.

Orsmond, Paul, and Stephen Merry. 1996. "The Importance of Marking Criteria in the Use of Peer Assessment." *Assessment & Evaluation in Higher Education* 21 (3): 239–50.

Reiff, John D., and James E. Middleton. 1983. "A Model for Designing and Revising Assignments." In *Forum: Essays on Theory and Practice in the Teaching of Writing*, edited by Patricia L. Stock, 263–69. Montclair, NJ: Boynton/Cook.

Rezaei, Ali Reza, and Michael Lovorn. 2010. "Reliability and Validity of Rubrics for Assessment through Writing." *Assessing Writing* 15 (1): 18–39.

Ross-Fisher, Roberta L. 2005. "Developing Effective Success Rubrics." *Kappa Delta Pi Record* 41 (3): 131–35.

Sands, Crystal. 2017. "Rubrics Oversimplify the Writing Process." In *Bad Ideas about Writing*, edited by Cheryl E. Ball and Drew M. Loewe, 264–67. Morgantown: West Virginia University Libraries Digital Publishing Institute.

Silvestri, Lynette, and Jeffrey Oescher. 2006. "Using Rubrics to Increase the Reliability of Assessment in Health Classes." *International Electronic Journal of Health Education* 9: 25–30.

Swales, John M. 1990. *Genre Analysis: English in Academic and Research Settings.* Cambridge: Cambridge University Press.

Swales, John M. 1996. "Occluded Genres in the Academy: The Case of the Submission Letter." In *Academic Writing: Intercultural and Textual Issues*, edited by Eija Ventola and Anna Mauranen, 45–58. Philadelphia, PA: John Benjamins.

Swales, John M., and Christine B. Feak. 2000. *English in Today's Research World: A Writing Guide.* Ann Arbor: University of Michigan Press.

Tomkins, Margaret. 2003. "Trouble Comes in Threes." *Times Educational Supplement* no. 4547 (August): 23.

Turley, Eric D., and Chris W. Gallagher. 2008. "On the 'Uses' of Rubrics: Reframing the Great Rubric Debate." *The English Journal* 97 (4): 87–92.

White, Edward M. 2007. *Assigning, Responding, Evaluating: A Writing Teacher's Guide.* 4th ed. New York: Bedford/St. Martin's.

Woodard, Rebecca, Alecia Marie Magnifico, and Sarah McCarthey. 2013. "Supporting Teacher Metacognition about Formative Assessment in Online Writing Environments." *E-Learning and Digital Media* 10 (4): 442–69.

PART 2

Genres Surrounding the Classroom

6

"BUT NOBODY LOOKS AT THESE!"
Making the Rhetorical Case for Syllabi of Record

Amy Ferdinandt Stolley and Christopher Toth

In the thirty years since Ernest L. Boyer (1990) articulated a more expansive definition of academic scholarship, faculty across disciplines have paid closer attention to the scholarship of teaching and learning, identifying how our work in the classroom can both improve student learning and connect our teaching with our own scholarly interests and identities. Boyer's work pushed against the notion that scholarship was only published or publishable research; instead, he explored the complexity of academic scholarship, claiming that teaching is both an important byproduct of and an important influence on the more traditional research academics' conduct. As a result, faculty have used classroom documents such as assignment descriptions, lesson plans, and course syllabi to illustrate how their scholarship informs their teaching and vice versa. The syllabus has become a central document in this context; it is a text all instructors use, yet one that many instructors seem to use differently. As Albers (2003) notes, syllabi have become a standard element in faculty's professional portfolios, job applications, and evaluation processes as a means of demonstrating teaching effectiveness. At the same time, faculty have become interested in thinking more critically about the role the syllabus plays in student learning, classroom climate, and the teacher–student relationship (Doolittle and Siudzinski 2010; Fink 2012; Parkes and Harris 2002).

In the fall of 2017, the course syllabus—and specifically the syllabus of record (SOR) for each course we offer—became a major point of discussion within the Department of Writing at Grand Valley State University. The SOR is a document that includes a course title, course catalog description, student learning objectives, topics, methods of evaluation, and sample textbooks or readings for the course. Names for this genre may vary depending on the institution; the document may be called a common syllabus, master syllabus, or basic data sheet. (Throughout

https://doi.org/10.7330/9781646422920.c006

this chapter, we will refer to this document as the syllabus of record or SOR.) At many institutions, the SOR is a utilitarian genre shared among instructors and administrators but rarely shared with students. The SOR functions as a syllabus template that faculty can (and usually do) add content and details to before they share it with students, but the SOR also creates a consistent set of information that, at least at Grand Valley State University, must appear on every instructor's version of a course's syllabus.

Our attention was turned to syllabi of record as a result of a directive from the Provost's Office. Faculty were informed that to prepare for our 2018 Higher Learning Commission accreditation visit, every department needed to have an updated syllabus of record on file for every course offered. This external impetus forced us, as a department, to take stock of our SORs to identify which courses had no SOR and which SORs were so outdated they no longer resembled the courses we were actually teaching. Through this process, we came to understand the SOR as a central document within what we're calling a "curriculum genre set," which includes the SOR, the individual course syllabi we give to students, and the one-page curriculum guide document we share with students during advising meetings.[1] More importantly, we discovered how the SOR could be a much more generative genre that created an occasion for a productive conversation among colleagues.

SITUATING SORS WITHIN EXISTING SYLLABI RESEARCH

Studies on the classroom syllabus have focused primarily on the purpose of the syllabus. In their study of classroom syllabi, Matejka and Kurke (1994) found that "great" syllabi serve "four distinct purposes: as a contract, a communication device, a plan, and a cognitive map" (115). Parkes and Harris (2002) argued that the functions of a syllabus "include (a) serving as a contract, (b) serving as a permanent record, and (c) serving as an aid to student learning" (55). Finally, Fink's study (2012) found more specific functions of the classroom syllabus, including serving as communication mechanism for course content, an instructor planning tool, a course plan for students, a teaching tool/resource for student learning, an artifact for teacher evaluation, a record keeping tool, a

---

1. The curriculum genre set is not limited to these genres and could likely include other genres such as course catalog descriptions, evaluation rubrics, and even sample assignments. However, we expect that the contents of these genre sets might vary across institutions and even differ across academic units or departments at the same institution because genre sets are necessarily context-specific (Devitt 2004).

contract, a tool for socialization to the academy, and as a scholarship opportunity for instructors. Although these studies of classroom syllabi vary in the degree to which they provide specific purposes for the genre, there seems to be general agreement that an effective course syllabus is both a communication tool for teachers and a learning tool for students.

For many faculty, the audience of the course syllabus is solely the students enrolled in a class. Fink's analysis of course syllabi found that instructors did not typically see larger institutional needs or curricular planning/assessment as a central purpose of the course syllabus; instead, they understood it more as a document shared between instructor and students rather than audiences outside the classroom. However, there are certainly audiences outside the teacher–student relationship who have an interest in the course syllabus, including administrators and accreditation officials who "all use the document for different purposes," such as conducting assessment, evaluating transfer credit, adjudicating grade appeals, and meeting accreditation requirements (Fink 2012, 1).

Beyond the limited scholarship on the course syllabus, there are even fewer studies of shared, common, or departmental syllabi. For many departments and programs, the common syllabus, which *all* instructors teaching a given course use, creates curricular consistency across instructors and sections, serving a primary audience of instructors and students. Brosman (1998) describes the common departmental syllabus as "particularly appropriate in a humanities core curriculum, as an assurance that all students have covered, for instance, Plato's Symposium before they advance to the next level" (60). Moreover, Brosman argues that the common syllabus "can be viewed as supporting standards in more than one way, protecting students, facilitating multi-section arrangements, and contributing to a shared educational experience among enrollees. It is a tool of consistency, rationality, and rigor," a point that is particularly relevant in today's climate that focuses on accountability, assessment, cost reduction, and student retention (62).

Brosman's description of the common syllabus invokes Janet Giltrow's (2002) concept of the meta-genre. As Bawarshi and Reiff (2010) describe it, a meta-genre operates by providing guidance on how to produce other genres that helps to "teach and stabilize uptakes" by creating models for other genres (94). In our case, the SOR served as a meta-genre, or a model, that informed other documents such as the individual course syllabus. Bawarshi and Reiff also claim that "knowledge of meta-genres can signal insider and outside status" (94), further illustrating the norming function that common departmental syllabi like the SOR provide. For that reason, Brosman explains that common syllabi can create problems: they are too authoritarian, centralizing curricular power in one or two individuals rather than in the entire teaching faculty; they create too much uniformity; and they impose on a faculty member's academic freedom. Further, as Albright argues in his chapter in this collection, common syllabi can contribute to eliminating instructors' autonomy and professional identity, especially for contingent faculty.

The SOR shares some generic qualities with both the single course syllabus, which is unique to each instructor and class, and the common departmental syllabus, which is shared across all sections and instructors. However, the SOR, too, has a distinct audience and purpose of its own. Like Brosman, who examined common syllabi and found "no history" of it (1998, footnote 1), we found no existing scholarship on the genre of the SOR; however, we expect that many universities, like ours, have such templates and require faculty to generate and share this genre with colleagues, administrators, and accreditors.

At Grand Valley State University, the SOR is described in our faculty handbook as "the official record of minimum course content—that is, content that must be present in every section of a course. In essence, it describes a department's vision of what should be taught, and (to a lesser extent) how it should be taught." (Grand Valley State University [GVSU] 2018). Our university identifies four primary audiences for the SOR who use the document for different purposes: faculty who use the document as a "blueprint for designing course syllabi"; students who can use the SOR to understand what learning outcomes they can hope to achieve; faculty at other universities who can refer to the SOR to evaluate transfer credit; and faculty curriculum review and assessment committees who use the SOR to evaluate and assess courses (GVSU 2018). These audiences and purposes make sense in theory; however, in practice we do not believe the SOR is often used by students. Students currently have no means of accessing SORs because they are stored online behind a login page only available to faculty and administrators. Students would have to ask for an SOR from faculty, advisors, or administrators, but we would expect that students do not even know to ask for the document and instead rely on their social networks of peers for information about a course. Therefore, it is reasonable to assume that students are a secondary audience for the SOR, while faculty, administrators, and outside accreditors are the primary audiences and users of the documents.

If we view academic communities of students, faculty, administrators, and accreditors as an activity system—a group with some shared goals and actions—we are able, as Amy Devitt notes, to see "a clearer depiction of diverse participants and roles, of an overarching purpose for multiple genres, and of multiple genres as the means of achieving that purpose" (2004, 55). In our department, our curricular activity is guided by "the curriculum genre set," which includes the individual course syllabi, the SOR, and the one-page curriculum guide that illustrates our modular curriculum for students. The goals and audiences for these documents vary, and our group members—faculty colleagues in the department and administrators—value these documents differently. Faculty's greatest interest centers on student learning, curriculum coherence, and the quality/usability of the documents, whereas administrators seem primarily concerned with whether or not the document met the minimum guidelines necessary for accreditation purposes. Moreover, while students are the primary audiences of our individual course syllabi and the curriculum guide, they have little exposure—if any—to the SOR. In theory, the SOR should function as an important element of this genre set, as it functions as a meta-genre upon which the individual course syllabi and curriculum guide are based. In practice, however, it has been more likely that the SOR is orphaned in a file cabinet, rarely used or referenced by faculty, administrators, or students until it's time for accreditation. Yet through our department's work with the SOR, instigated by the accreditation process, we discovered a much more complex network of genre and activity, and because we engaged fully in the process of reviewing and revising our SORs, we learned a great deal about our colleagues, classes, students, and curriculum as a result.

RECONSIDERING AND REVISING SORS

Before discussing our specific case study, we want to provide readers with a general description of our independent writing major to help illustrate the larger curricular system in which the SOR operates.

At GVSU, writing majors complete four core writing courses in professional writing, style, creative writing, and document design. Next, writing majors complete four modules of two courses each. Each module course has some combination of the core courses as prerequisites. This modular part of the curriculum allows students maximum flexibility by permitting them to select the courses where their interests lie and/or where they foresee gaining the theoretical grounding and skills necessary for their future careers. Since writing majors can chart their own path through the curriculum, almost every graduate will have taken a different set of writing major courses by the time they get to our two culminating courses, which include an internship and capstone courses that every student is required to take.

To communicate our program requirements with writing majors and prospective majors, faculty rely on a one-page curriculum guide (see Appendix for a textual rendition) that presents a visual representation of the course offerings and requirements. Before we developed and adopted this modular approach in 2012, our curriculum offered linear tracks that funneled students through either a creative writing or professional writing track, resulting in a program that offered little flexibility for students and limited their ability to conceive of writing studies—and their own professional goals—more broadly.

State of SORs

As mentioned earlier, all departments across our university were required to have SORs on file for each course in preparation for an upcoming accreditation by the Higher Learning Commission. Many faculty were not aware of which courses did or did not have SORs on file, and a few faculty were not even aware that these documents existed. When new faculty joined the department or when existing faculty were asked to teach a course for the first time, they rarely looked at SORs. Instead of referencing this master document, faculty more often looked at individual course syllabi from other faculty members. So, while many of the SOR documents were on file, they were relegated to a role that existed primarily for administrative purposes.

Our department was asked by the Provost's and Registrar's Offices to create six new syllabi of record for writing courses in our curriculum where none existed. Given that our department had undergone a major curriculum revision a few years earlier, a majority of the twenty-eight courses offered in the Department of Writing already had SORs on file. We were willing to do the work that was asked of us by administration, but in the back of our minds, we grumbled, "But nobody looks at these!"

DESCRIPTION OF SOR REVIEW PROCESS

There were two types of processes the fifteen tenured or tenure-track faculty in our department used to create the six new SORs: "divide and conquer" or "fully immersive collaboration." The description of these two processes below illustrates how our group of faculty engaged with the genre of the SOR and put it in conversation with other genres in the curriculum genre set.

Process I: Divide and Conquer

For upper-level writing module courses, faculty split in teams of two or three to draft an SOR. These teams consisted of tenured or tenure-track faculty volunteers who routinely taught a particular course and/or had disciplinary expertise. While faculty don't "own" courses in our department, this divide-and-conquer approach seemed logical given that the faculty with the biggest stake in a course (i.e., those who teach it most frequently) should get to draft the SOR. For example, faculty who specialize in creative nonfiction met and developed learning outcomes and revised the course description based on their experiences teaching creative nonfiction courses and writing and publishing in the genre.

After drafting the SOR, these faculty presented a draft of their SOR to the rest of the writing faculty or, at a minimum, gave them to the department chair for review and to ensure consistency. The department faculty or chair ensured that the objectives and material presented in these upper-level SORs were connected to and expanded upon the competencies required in the core courses of the major. Next, the SORs were submitted into the university's curriculum review system for approval by the college and university curriculum committees respectively. A majority of the SORs we revised followed this "divide and conquer" process.

Process II: Fully Immersive Collaboration

The other type of SOR review process our department engaged in was much more collaborative. The courses that received this type of treatment were the core courses, such as WRT 210: Introduction to Style, and the internship and capstone courses. For this process, the faculty devoted time during our weekly meetings to generate the SOR together as a group. The faculty began by collectively looking at some individual instructors' syllabi. Our conversations about an SOR generally revolved around questions of content and alignment with the rest of the curriculum, such as:

- What should students be learning in this course?
- Why do we value that students learn these particular writing concepts, skills, or strategies?
- How does the content of this course help to fill a gap that students will not get in other writing courses?
- What content is important enough to be stated as a learning objective and what content can be agreed upon as a common feature or activity of the course?
- How accurate is the course title? (Is it both descriptive and interesting to students?)

- How clearly does the description align with what should be (or has been) routinely taught in the course?
- How can we make the course catalog description clearer so that it reflects our values for the course while not misleading students about the content?
- To what extent will the knowledge gained in this course be re-examined in the capstone courses?
- How will students learning about X or Z be prepared for success in future writing courses that require this course as a prerequisite?

Faculty who routinely teach the particular course under discussion offered answers to these types of questions while the rest of the faculty asked follow-up questions. Individual faculty also had the chance to voice concerns about a course or express ideas on how information about the course might be clearer for students.

After the meeting in which we discussed a course, one or two faculty would volunteer to create an SOR draft that incorporated everyone's viewpoints and bring this draft back for final approval at a future faculty meeting. Once the revisions were accepted by faculty, the SOR was submitted into our curriculum review system for approval by the college and university curriculum committees.

RE-CENTERING SORS WITHIN THE DEPARTMENT

Ultimately, these processes for creating and reviewing SORs encouraged dialogue and a space for faculty to reflect on what we were teaching in specific writing courses and why we were teaching those specific lessons, skills, and strategies. It also allowed time and space for faculty, even if they were not teaching a particular writing course, to verbalize the purpose of a specific course and how it fits into the larger curriculum. At the same time, the two processes we engaged in were messily discursive.

In the "divide and conquer" process, conversations about one course created a domino effect and invoked other courses. For example, when we discussed the creative nonfiction workshops' student learning objectives, it quickly became apparent that other workshop genre courses should probably be aligned too, especially between the intermediate and advanced courses and across genres. If we were creating a coherent set of learning objectives for the nonfiction workshop, shouldn't we also revise the poetry and fiction workshops as well? While this process was messy, it also helped our courses, and specific elements of the courses (especially the student learning objectives), to have more uniformity across the major.

The "fully immersive collaboration" process created an opportunity for us to talk about courses that faculty were meaning to examine and discuss but just never got around to until the SOR process required us to do so. This was especially important for WRT 210: Introduction to Style, a course that we often said we should really figure out but never turned our attention to. Over half of the writing faculty taught this course at some point in time in its nearly twenty-year history, and while almost every instructor included some form of student learning objectives on their individualized syllabus, these were never codified into a coherent set of outcomes that appeared in each instructor's syllabus. Our lack of consistent learning objectives illustrates Christy Desmet's (2005) claim that part of what influences a writing program's coherence (or lack thereof) results from "the frequent paucity of local history for most programs" (47). There may have been conversations about learning objectives for WRT 210 in the past, but those discussions were not accessible to the instructors as they wrote their own syllabus for the course either because they weren't present for the conversation, or they didn't remember them. As a result, we used the extant learning objectives as a starting point for our group discussions to come to a common understanding of the course's goals.

Throughout the collaboration process for WRT 210, the writing faculty made significant revisions. We changed the name of the course from Writing with Style to Introduction to Style to better align with the names of the other introductory courses and to clarify to students that this was a theoretical, analytical course rather than a production-oriented course that the former name had previously communicated. We rewrote the course catalog description with two purposes in mind: to capture students' interest in the course and to align it to the newly written student learning objectives. We created new, shared student learning objectives that previously did not exist. We revised the course topics and methods of evaluation as well as updated the list of sample sources of information, which had not been revised in almost twenty years since the course was first created.

The collaborative process allowed faculty to verbalize their hidden assumptions about a particular course, realize how those assumptions compared with other faculty, and then negotiate those assumptions into an SOR on which everyone could reach consensus. Our experience with this process and our understanding of hidden assumptions and professional identities is similar to those experienced by Micciche and Arduser as well as Pengilly (see their chapters in this collection) when they proposed new curricula within their departments. All writing faculty in the department were engaged in the process, so even when philosophical differences arose about course content or pedagogical approaches in a particular course, we used open dialogue that allowed us to reach an agreement. Overall, the process also helped faculty to be more in tune to the larger curriculum, even for modules or courses they would never teach.

Our two approaches to drafting and revising SORs reflect an overall culture in the department that respects individual faculty members' expertise and disciplinary knowledge while prioritizing the collective goals and vision of the group. For example, we recognized that practicing poets who frequently teach the poetry workshop would have much more to say about the poetry workshop model than those who teach professional writing (and vice versa). However, our department's commitment to viewing the different curriculum modules as interconnected and interdependent drove our desire to collaborate on courses in which we all have a stake, as it were, including the core introductory courses and the capstone courses. As such, we were able to equally engage and represent each of our own individual academic identities within the context of our shared identity as a department.

It's worth noting that the creation and revision of the SORs took place at the same time the department faculty were brainstorming ways to retain writing majors and recruit more. We had been concerned with how to make the major more enticing to current students and how to attract new potential majors. As a result of this larger context, many of our SOR discussions also filtered through this lens of seeking clarity and coherence for students. For example, the changing of course names during the SOR revisions arose out of a sense of obligation to students. We wanted to make the major as transparent and clear for students as possible, especially those prospective students who were first learning about it. As a result of our efforts to develop and revise our department's SORs, we believe an unintended but positive result is an overall improvement in our advising practices, as the SOR, functioning as a meta-genre, has influenced other genres within the curriculum genre set. We each now have a clearer understanding of each course in the curriculum—especially those we don't teach ourselves—and how they fit together to prepare students for the myriad of professional and/or graduate education paths they might pursue.

Whether we used the "divide and conquer" or the "fully immersive collaboration" approach, both processes concluded with sending the newly created SORs to the college and university curriculum committees. Once approved by those committees, the SORs were then filed with the Registrar's Office and the Department of Writing.

Although students will likely not see the revised SORs, the information generated through and by the SOR revision process is communicated to students through the individual course syllabi they receive from their instructors on the first day of class. In preparation for the accreditation visit, departments were required to verify that the updated learning objectives were included on all syllabi distributed to students at the beginning of the semester. Instructors who did not include the updated SOR learning objectives had to update their syllabi and redistribute them to students to ensure that the students had copies of the correct objectives. To some, this felt like a bit of administrative hoop-jumping; however, it was one direct way in which traces of the SOR, which typically was seen as a genre with little connection to other, more meaningful curriculum documents, became visible for students.

The university administration was most interested in whether or not the SORs were written and submitted by the deadline; we didn't receive feedback on the documents aside from confirming that they had been submitted, and we don't know how or if the administration or accreditors evaluated the SORs, though we do know that our accreditation visit was successful. However, by engaging in the collaboration of creating the SORs, writing faculty realized the value of the process. They noticed how their own individual writing courses could be better described for students or use learning objectives that more accurately and concretely reflected the content of their courses. The process itself became a mechanism for clarifying relationships between courses in the writing curriculum. Because faculty found this process so valuable and generative, the Department of Writing faculty decided to update the SORs for ten additional courses, revising outdated learning objectives, course descriptions, course titles, and sample sources of information. By the end of the process, we had either written or revised SORs for over 50 percent of our writing curriculum.

THEORIZING THE SOR THROUGH GENRE SETS

Writing scholars (Bawarshi 2003; Bawarshi and Reiff 2010; Bazerman 1994) have acknowledged that an individual course syllabus is an enacted genre that helps to construct the classroom within university contexts. As our discussion above demonstrates, the course syllabus and SOR are complex activities that do not occur in isolation, and in fact they work together in a larger genre set that also includes, in our case, the curriculum guide and other classroom genres. The curriculum genre set communicates information about courses and curriculum to a wide range of audiences, illustrating the "inherent relatedness of genres within the same social group and its actions" (Devitt 2004, 55). Bawarshi (2003) claims that the syllabus is a "site of action that produces subjects who desire to act in certain ideological and discursive ways. It establishes the habitat within which students and teachers rhetorically enact their situated relations, subjectivities, and activities" (125). We would extend Bawarshi's claim to genres beyond the classroom syllabus; based on our experiences revising SORs for our curriculum, it is clear that the larger curriculum genre set creates a habitat in which faculty and students write, learn, and interact with each other.

It was important that we work on revising our SORs together so that our department's habitat, guided by the curriculum genre set, was collectively understood, described, and enacted. Our collaborative revision of our department's SORs created an environment wherein we could be more sensitive and responsive to disciplinary differences, student needs, and our shared goals as a community of scholars and writers. By focusing our attention on the SOR, one genre within the curriculum genre set, we were able to see how the SOR functions as a meta-genre that "helps coordinate how its participants manage their way through and perform the various genres that operationalize this system" (Bawarshi 2003, 126). Because we did this work together rather than in isolation or simply delegating the responsibility to the department chair, we developed SORs that were responsive to other genres in the genre set (such as our individual course syllabi or our advising documents and practices), allowing them each to remain flexible "site[s] of invention within which teachers and students assume and enact a complex set of textured actions, relations, and subjectivities" (Bawarshi 2003, 126).

Viewing our department's SOR revision process through the lens of genre theory helps to illustrate how curriculum genres such as the SOR, curriculum guide, and individual course syllabus can and should work in concert with one another. As Amy Devitt's (2004) work illustrates, "A group usually operates through a set of genres to achieve the group's purposes" (64), though genres are added to or dropped from the genre set as the needs and activities of the group change, "thereby . . . changing the larger contexts of genres" (64). By focusing on one neglected genre, the SOR, we were able to understand its relationship to others within the genre set, illustrating how these documents "sequence how we relate to and assign roles to one another, how we define the limits of our agency, how we come to know and learn, and how we construct, value, and experience ourselves in social time and space" (Bawarshi and Reiff 2010, 90).

CONCLUSION

Before beginning the process of reviewing and revising our department's SORs, we viewed it as a disposable genre with little impact or meaning, a genre "nobody looks at." More cynically, some may have viewed it as a purely administrative genre, a text we wrote and generated because it was required by the Provost's Office or by college curriculum review committees, but not one that we integrated into our thinking and conversations about our curriculum with much serious consideration. However, what the process of re-examining and revising our department's SORs taught us was that the SOR instead had been a dormant genre, one that was underutilized by our faculty. By taking a closer look at these documents as an interrelated genre set, we now understand that the SOR can—and should—be an active part of the genre set that includes the SOR, our curriculum guide, and our individual class syllabi. Rather than staying locked in a file cabinet in the main department office or saved digitally behind a password, our SORs now influence and will be influenced by all future curricular and departmental discussions about individual classes, modules within the curriculum, and our curriculum as a whole.

Through the revision process, the SOR has become an important, better integrated component of the curricular system, the genre set of curriculum materials, and, most importantly, the activity of the department, ensuring that it will be a central part of our conversations in the future. The SOR has become an *active* genre that, as Carolyn Miller (1984) describes, "acquires meaning from situation and from the social context in which the situation arose" (163). Miller explains that exigency is an "objectified social need" that drives the creation and interpretation of genre (157). Because our work as faculty is driven primarily by the exigency of the classroom and the needs of our students, we work to communicate our curriculum—and the place of each course within that curriculum—clearly with students to meet those needs. What we didn't know before was that the SOR, a genre previously seen as having little connection to the work we do with students, was a critical piece in the genre set, even if it remains mostly invisible to students. The SOR is translated and interpreted for students through more reader-friendly, student-centered documents—namely, the course syllabus and our curriculum guide—that provide students the information that they need to know in the contexts—the classroom and in our advising meetings—that matter most to them.

External administrative and accreditation forces initiated our department's work on our curriculum's SORs, but the process demonstrated both the value of the SOR as an individual genre and the role it can play in the broader genre set of curricular documents used to communicate the standards, outcomes, and practices of both individual courses and the program as a whole. We recognize that our department may be unique in many ways. We are an independent writing department that does not have to negotiate significant disciplinary differences as faculty in more traditional English departments do, like those described by Micciche and Arduser in their chapter on proposing a new certificate program. Because of this, we may be able to conceive of our program with more flexibility through our module courses, when other writing faculty may be limited to tracks or concentrations within a broader English major. Likewise, our institution requires SORs for curricular approval, assessment, and revision, and it has centralized the document as a part of the accreditation process in ways other institutions may not.

Despite the ways that our university, department, and curriculum may differ from other universities, we believe that the SOR—or some other standardized syllabus template on which faculty can base their individual course syllabi—is an important genre for departments and programs to incorporate into their work. The SOR provides consistency in both content and learning objectives while still affording academic freedom to the faculty who adapt the syllabus to their interests and strengths. More importantly, however, we believe that the syllabus of record can be a genre that invites conversation and plays an important rhetorical role in the work of any department, regardless of the unique rhetorical contexts of different programs, groups of faculty, student populations, or university systems.

APPENDIX 6.A

CURRICULUM GUIDE FOR THE WRITING MAJOR

GRAND VALLEY STATE UNIVERSITY

The Writing Major
An individualized 42-credit program of study

Core Requirements (12 credits)
- WRT 200 Introduction to Professional Writing
- WRT 210 Introduction to Style
- WRT 219 Introduction to Creative Writing
- WRT 253 Document Production and Design

Modules (complete three; 18 credits)

- **Working with Writers & Manuscripts**
  - WRT 307 Consulting with Writers
  - WRT 308 Editing and Publishing
- **Reading as Writers**
  - WRT 316 Style & Technique
  - WRT 411 Style & the Book
- **Poetry Workshops**
  - WRT 320 Int. Poetry Workshop
  - WRT 420 Adv. Poetry Workshop
- **Fiction Workshops**
  - WRT 330 Int. Fiction Workshop
  - WRT 430 Adv. Fiction Workshop
- **Writing for the Web**
  - WRT 351 Writing for the Web
  - 451 Adv. Writing for the Web
- **Writing with Technologies**
  - WRT 353 Visual Rhetoric & Doc Design
  - WRT 455 Multimodal Composing
- **Nonfiction Workshops**
  - WRT 360 Int. Creative Nonfiction Workshop
  - WRT 460 Adv. Creative Nonfiction Workshop
- **Magazine Writing**
  - WRT 365 Int. Magazine Writing
  - WRT 465 Adv. Magazine Writing

Electives (6 credits)

- **Interdisciplinary Electives**
  - Advisor Approved Courses
  - Study Abroad Courses
- **Writing Electives**
  - Any WRT Module Courses
  - WRT 350 Business Communication
  - WRT 354 Writing in the Global Context
  - WRT 381 Sports and Writing

Capstones (6 credits)

- WRT 490 Writing Internship
- WRT 495 Genre and Writing

REFERENCES

Albers, Cheryl. 2003. "Using the Syllabus to Document the Scholarship of Teaching." *Teaching Sociology* 31 (1): 60–72.

Bawarshi, Anis. 2003. *Genre and the Invention of the Writer: Reconsidering the Place of Invention in Composition.* Logan: Utah State University Press.

Bawarshi, Anis, and Mary Jo Reiff. 2010. *Genre: An Introduction to History, Theory, Research, and Pedagogy.* West Lafayette, IN: Parlor Press.

Bazerman, Charles. 1994. *Constructing Experience.* Carbondale: Southern Illinois University Press.

Boyer, Ernest L. 1990. *Scholarship Reconsidered: Priorities of the Professoriate.* Princeton, NJ: The Carnegie Foundation for the Advancement of Teaching.

Brosman, Catharine Savage. 1998. "The Case for (and against) Departmental Syllabi." *Academic Questions* 11 (4): 58–65.

Desmet, Christy. 2005. "Beyond Accommodation: Individual and Collective in a Large Writing Program." In *Discord and Direction: The Postmodern Writing Program Administrator,* edited by Sharon James McGee and Carolyn Handa, 40–58. Logan: Utah State University Press.

Devitt, Amy J. 2004. *Writing Genres.* Carbondale: Southern Illinois University Press.

Doolittle, Peter E., and Robert A. Siudzinski. 2010. "Recommended Syllabus Components: What Do Higher Education Faculty Include in Their Syllabi?" *Journal on Excellence in College Teaching* 20 (3): 29–61.

Fink, Susan B. 2012. "The Many Purposes of Course Syllabi: Which Are Essential and Useful?" *Syllabus* 1 (1): 1–12.

Giltrow, Janet. 2002. "Meta-Genre." In *The Rhetoric and Ideology of Genre: Strategies for Stability and Change,* edited by Richard M. Coe, Lorelei Lingard, and Tatiana Teslenko, 187–205. Cresskill, NJ: Hampton Press.

Grand Valley State University. 2018. "Faculty Academic Policies-Curriculum." Grand Valley State University. https://www.gvsu.edu/policies/policy.htm?policyId=A3DFC850-DA53-502E-888E40A7B3024EB6.

Matejka, Ken, and Lance B. Kurke. 1994. "Designing a Great Syllabus." *College Teaching* 42 (3): 115–17.

Miller, Carolyn R. 1984. "Genre as Social Action." *Quarterly Journal of Speech* 70 (2): 151–67.

Parkes, Jay, and Mary B. Harris. 2002. "The Purposes of a Syllabus." *College Teaching* 50 (2): 55–61.

7

"IS IT IN THE HANDBOOK?"
The Role of Departmental Teaching Handbooks in Developing Pedagogical Identity

Dana Comi

A teacher's pedagogical identity formation occurs, in part, through their course materials. When interacting with course materials, either by developing, adjusting, or composing them for the first time, teachers not only enact pedagogical genres, but "do business within a specific community [and] occupy the subject positions offered by the genres or genres at hand" (Helscher 1997, 29). For graduate students entering the role of a teacher, many for the first time, pedagogical meta-genres like the departmental teaching handbook are often one of their first resources, directing the evolution of their pedagogical identity through future classroom genres, such as syllabi, assignment prompts, and rubrics. As Melanie Kill (2006) describes, new teachers must ascertain "the generic actions and interactions that are valued in particular communities" and "develop identities appropriate to the places and spaces [they] want to occupy" (217). Departmental teaching handbooks are, as Dylan Dryer (2012) suggests with rosters, syllabi, notes on office doors, and assignments, critical locations where graduate teaching assistants (GTAs) "[operationalize] the routines and subject positions through which . . . students and teachers *become* learners and teachers" (442). These genres construct and maintain subjectivities for both teacher and student, and therefore stand as critically important not only for the academic development of students but also the pedagogical development of new teachers.

However, although writing researchers have discussed the connection between identity formation and pedagogical genres, less attention has been given to the evolving pedagogical identities of GTAs as they interact with meta-genres that guide their teaching, like teaching handbooks. Jennifer Grouling (2015) highlights the need for attention to "assignment sheets, syllabi, comments on student writing . . . [and] how these

https://doi.org/10.7330/9781646422920.c007

genres and [graduate student/teaching] identities interact to form a more complete picture of GTA identity." Grouling argues that a GTA's course materials are "[where] programmatic identity and individual teaching identity intersect," foregrounding the ongoing development of graduate students' pedagogical identities as influenced and mediated by disciplinary expectations. Restaino (2012) similarly calls for researchers to examine "the preparation and support of graduate students as they *become* teachers of first-year writing" (106, emphasis added). As GTAs become familiarized and eventually participate in pedagogical genres, they don't only learn to write in these kinds of ways, they also learn to step into genred subjectivities of "teacher" in and beyond their classroom.

I aim to take up these calls to examine GTAs' pedagogical identity development and performance of pedagogical genres by analyzing the meta-genre of the departmental teaching handbook. By focusing on the role of the departmental teaching handbook as a meta-genre in shaping and directing GTAs' identities, I emphasize that, as with any genre, the creation of course materials (including syllabi, assignment prompts, and class plans) is directed in part by other genres that explain, warn, and otherwise influence teachers as they interact with new genres. My research questions are:

1. How do graduate teaching assistants rely on departmental teaching handbooks when creating their course materials?

2. In what ways do graduate teaching assistants' characterizations of departmental teaching handbooks influence how they understand their roles as teachers and describe their pedagogies?

3. How does graduate teaching assistants' utilization of departmental teaching handbooks shape the ongoing development of their pedagogical identities?

Exploring how GTAs perceive and utilize departmental teaching handbooks can reveal key insights about the genre, especially regarding its meta-generic role in the ongoing formation of pedagogical identity. In the section below, I articulate the connections between meta-genres and pedagogical identity, then provide an overview of the study of eight GTAs' perceptions of and interactions with one school's departmental teaching handbook, followed by brief case studies detailing the experiences of three of those GTAs. While my findings suggest the GTAs had similar understandings of the role the teaching handbook played in directing and shaping their course materials, there were a range of ways they used that handbook. As a result, I conclude that even within shared perceptions of a meta-genre like the departmental teaching handbook, different engagements with that genre means its influence varies, thus affecting GTAs' pedagogical identities in both constructive and limiting ways.

META-GENRE AND PEDAGOGICAL IDENTITY

Extending from Carolyn Miller's (1984) foundational definition of rhetorical genre, genres can be understood as habitats for social action, wherein writers can dynamically enact identity formation. As Janet Giltrow (2002) explains, meta-genres exist at the borders of these habitats,

> flourish[ing] at the boundaries, at the thresholds of communities of discourse, patrolling or controlling individuals' participations in the collective, foreseeing or suspecting their involvements elsewhere, differentiating, initiating, restricting, inducing forms of activity, rationalizing and representing the relations of the genre to the community that uses it. (203)

Like genres, meta-genres promote and constrain particular actions, are socially situated, and are used by members of discourse communities to understand how to act in particular genres, who to be. Meta-genres help familiarize writers with unfamiliar genres via explicit or implicit commentary, helping "teach and stabilize uptake" while also signifying "insider and outside status" in a community (Bawarshi and Reiff 2010, 94).

For teachers, meta-genres are important resources that signal external expectations, requirements, and regulations for their pedagogical activity. Pedagogical meta-genres are what Bazerman (1994) describes as the "genres that flow from the surrounding institutions into the classroom to regulate it" (60), thereby affecting the genres circulating within and out of the classroom. For graduate teaching assistants, pedagogical meta-genres can give insight into not only how to create course materials, but also how to begin enacting the genred subjectivities associated with being a teacher. Paying attention to how GTAs interact with pedagogical meta-genres like the departmental teaching handbook can provide a snapshot of new instructors' "pedagogical identities in action," as they work to understand, produce, and participate in classroom genres like the syllabus and writing prompts (Neaderhiser 2016). Additionally, increased attention to the influence of meta-genres on the production of course materials foregrounds a key site of graduate student identity formation, adding to existing work on graduate students' acculturation in academic contexts (Berkenkotter et al. 1988; Prior 2013).

DEPARTMENTAL TEACHING HANDBOOKS AS META-GENRES

While a myriad of meta-genres may influence the production of class-room genres, this study focuses on departmental teaching handbooks, as given to graduate students before or during their first semester of teaching. Departmental teaching handbooks have not been examined specifically as a pedagogical genre, perhaps because they exist on the margins, as opposed to texts that directly operate and circulate as classroom genres, like the syllabus, assignment prompt, or student essay (Bawarshi 2003, 119; see also Christie 1993; Russell 1997). However, these handbooks often include formal policies and statements, orientation materials, and pedagogical resources vital to new graduate student teachers. A departmental teaching handbook[1] serves as a kind of touchstone, a text layered with statewide, institutional, and departmental guidelines and expectations, many of which both implicitly and explicitly relate to the pedagogical choices of graduate teaching assistants. The departmental teaching handbook I highlight in this study also served as a primary text constellated across other spaces, including a Blackboard page, a Facebook group, and a departmental web page for first and second-year graduate teaching assistants, thereby acting as a diffused influence across multiple pedagogical resources for new GTAs. This study foregrounds how GTAs both perceived and utilized the handbook, thus highlighting the mediating role of the meta-genre in the production of not only GTAs' course materials but also their identities as teachers.

RESEARCH DESIGN AND METHOD

Located in the midwestern United States, Public U is a large, public research institution with a two-part writing sequence, ENGL 101: Composition and ENGL 102: Critical Reading and Writing, required for incoming undergraduates. In the English graduate program at Public U, new students are admitted as either graduate teaching assistants, who teach two sections of ENGL 101 starting in their first semester, or graduate research assistants, who begin teaching during their second year. A week prior to their first semester of teaching, new GTAs attend a week-long orientation designed and conducted by the writing program, where they receive an overview of the writing program's goals and expectations, practice teaching and grading, and receive their teaching handbooks as a resource to begin creating their course materials.

---

1. I use "departmental teaching handbook" in order to differentiate from departmental handbooks that only include information pertinent to *being* a graduate student (graduate program procedures, academic requirements, progress to degree completion).

The departmental teaching handbook they receive, the Manual for Teachers (nicknamed "the MAT"), is an eighty-eight-page document, organized into two main sections (as its table of contents shows, see Appendix). On the handbook's first page, there is a short explanation of its central purpose:

> The MAT articulates the common goals that bind the [writing program] together and offers support for individual teachers. To meet these goals, it has three more specific functions: to clarify policies and expectations:
>
> 1. to clarify policies and expectations of the [writing program]
> 2. to provide resources to assist teachers in daily classroom activities
> 3. to provoke reflection and assessment of teachers' own developing teaching philosophies and practices

The first section, "Course Goals, Requirements, and Policies," includes a wide range of policies, guidelines, and resources for teaching writing at Public U, including statewide learning outcomes, university core goals, and departmental goals for both ENGL 101 and 102. Additionally, this section outlines class policies applied to all writing program courses, including early semester procedures (enrollment, rosters), late semester procedures (course withdrawal, grade inquiries), plagiarism and attendance, and grading requirements and options. Also included are policies specifically for graduate teaching assistants: guidelines for office hours, teaching absences, and professional development protocols (required development sessions, priorities for assigning courses). The second section, "A Pedagogical Guide to Creating Your Own Course," contains guidelines for creating course materials and activities, including syllabi, writing assignments, class discussion and writing prompts, and peer-response workshops. This section also provides advice for dealing with classroom disruptions, accommodating students with disabilities, and a series of "attitudes" to take on as a writing instructor in order to teach writing successfully.

In order to explore how departmental teaching handbooks influence GTA pedagogical identity and activity, I interviewed a group of GTAs at the end of their first year of teaching at Public U about their own experiences and negotiations with the MAT. The participant group comprised eight MA and PhD students, with concentrations ranging from literature to rhetoric and composition. Although all participants were in their first year as GTAs at Public U, two participants had prior teaching experience from previous graduate programs. I conducted two interviews with each teaching assistant: the first set of interviews provided an overview of how they perceived the MAT in terms of its design and purpose, how it influenced the production of their course materials, and how they took

Table 7.1. Study participant profiles

GTA	Program (Degree)	Prior Teaching Experience (Secondary/College Level)	Year in Program
Jones	Literature (MA)	None	1
Andrew	Literature (MA)	None	1
Cash	Literature (MA)	None	1
Marley	Fiction (MFA)	1 year (Secondary)	1
Stephen	Fiction (MFA)	None	1
Leslie	Rhetoric & Composition (PhD)	2 years (College)	2
Daniel	Literature (PhD)	2 years (College)	2
Kira	Literature (PhD)	None	1

up the handbook during their first year. The second set of interviews involved discourse-based interviews (DBI), where I gathered course materials from each teaching assistant prior to the interview and identified a series of rhetorical and linguistic patterns across the materials they used for both ENGL 101 and 102, changes they made to the departmentally provided syllabus template and sequence of unit projects, and key differences between their materials for the two-course sequence.

During the DBI stage, each graduate teaching assistant provided explanations for the patterns apparent in their course materials. Given that many of them adjusted the assignment sheets and syllabus template provided by the writing program, these second interviews were an opportunity for me to investigate when and why the GTAs made changes to departmental materials rather than creating their own, which areas they felt comfortable innovating or departing from preapproved materials, and which policies and structures they felt they should not—or could not—change.

I analyzed the interview transcripts with in vivo coding, drawing on words and phrases from the language of the raw data (Saldaña 2009, 74). I wanted to prioritize and preserve the voices of the graduate teaching assistants I interviewed, so in vivo coding enabled me to carefully attune to not only what the teaching assistants had to say, but also *how* they chose to describe their writing and teaching. I developed themes inductively out of the first set of coded interviews, and then developed three profiles that complicate those themes, highlighting how three of the GTAs' responses during their DBI interviews represent a range of uses for the MAT, even within shared perceptions and descriptions of the handbook.

FINDINGS

The graduate teaching assistants' perceptions and descriptions of the departmental teaching handbook (the MAT) affected the ways that they used the handbook and, to different extents, shaped the course materials for their ENGL 101 and 102 courses. During orientation, the new GTAs received a physical copy of the MAT to prepare for the upcoming semester.[2] While several GTAs only made minor (if any) changes to the assignment prompts provided for the ENGL 101 preset assignment sequence, they were all encouraged to generate their own syllabi, using the template drawn from the MAT. The MAT presents itself as a tripartite document, one that articulates common goals, provides support, and prompts teachers to reflect and assess their pedagogical identities as they develop. However, not all of the GTAs perceived of the handbook as carrying out these purposes, which had a significant effect on the ways they referenced it while developing their course materials. Three prominent themes emerged from the first set of interviews, in regard to the GTAs' shared understandings, varying interpretations, and self-reported uses of the MAT.

Getting Everyone on the Same Page

During the first round of interviews, several GTAs discussed the MAT's primary purpose as being to centralize the varied backgrounds and experiences of the new cohort into a cohesive and standardized pedagogy, a kind of protocol. Table 7.2 outlines GTAs' initial explanations of the primary purpose of MAT's design.

For GTAs with no prior teaching experience before entering into the program at Public U, such as Jones and Cash, their explanation of the handbook's ability to "get everyone on the same page" was primarily informative: the handbook outlined and explained all they needed to know before stepping into the classroom. Daniel, however, who had two years of teaching college-level writing during his master's program, emphasized the need for the "language, the policies, and the goals to be consistent" between his course materials and the handbook. For Daniel, then, the handbook served as a way to make sure some of his pre-existing course materials were in alignment with the language of the handbook, adjusting as necessary.

---

2. A copy was also available online via a Blackboard resource page, along with several other separate teaching materials (e.g., a syllabus template, sample assignment sheets) that mirrored content from the MAT.

Table 7.2. The handbook as protocol

GTA	The handbook . . .
Jones	"is designed to give all GTAs a framework from which to work . . . a way to sort of centralize all their knowledge and give a starting point."
Andrew	"is an attempt to just have everything is one place that might come to mind, frequently asked questions, general standards and regulations . . . if there happens to be someone who doesn't think about [a policy] in the same way the department does."
Cash	"helped me navigate my first year . . . made me feel like I was part of a team."
Marley	"informs GTAs on how to conduct themselves and how students should conduct themselves."
Stephen	"has the standard practices and requirements for GTAs, and the procedures."
Leslie	"provides answers to scenarios . . . what to do when a student wants to withdraw or wants an incomplete . . . along with syllabus language and course goals"
Daniel	"[tells GTAs] what to do if they don't know where to find an answer"
Kira	"shows how to best navigate teaching composition classes here at [Public U]."

Like Jones and Cash, Marley had no prior teaching experience before Public U and saw the handbook as a way to provide an informative background and "keep things consistent" across the introductory writing courses. However, the handbook served Marley not only as an instructional resource and a way to check his materials against institutional and departmental guidelines, but also as a way to orient his pedagogy and set clear goals for his teaching. He described how the handbook allowed him to continue aligning and shaping his pedagogy:

> The handbook helped me orient myself and re-orient myself when I was, at certain times, hazy about what I was doing . . . at some point, the goals [listed in the handbook] became my goals, so this was something I internalized and thought: "this is what my students need to know."

Marley returned to the MAT again and again during his first year of teaching, especially when he started to forget broader departmental outcomes. The MAT, then, assisted in Marley's pedagogical identity development by generating meaningful (and ongoing) goals for his teaching.

Policy, Not Pedagogy

In addition to identifying one role of the handbook as "getting everyone on the same page," the GTAs also emphasized the extent to which the handbook was policy-driven. As table 7.3 demonstrates, each GTA explained how the handbook was to an extent useful as an informative

Table 7.3. The handbook as rulebook

GTA	The handbook is . . .	. . . but not . . .
Jones	"a way for us to know policies we might not know about"	"for in-class . . . pedagogical stuff"
Andrew	"an outline of the regulations and the things that an instructor should keep in mind throughout the semester and at any point they're teaching"	"for the actual content of the course"
Cash	"designed as a general reference for heading off big problems like plagiarism"	"for writing your course description"
Marley	"a lot of policies . . . includes everything a GTA needs to know before they walk into the classroom"	"for your teaching . . . or helping students"
Stephen	"a wealth of information . . . what we can and can't do"	"on the spot pedagogy moments"
Leslie	"the rulebook"	"[a guide] for how to build your course"
Daniel	"a list of guidelines for what a GTA can and can't do"	"helpful for building a course"
Kira	"a collection of policies"	"for student behavior"

text, an outline of regulations and policies, or a guide for addressing problems. However, they commonly positioned the MAT as not relevant or useful for pedagogy—or, as Andrew described it, "for the actual content of the course."

The general perception of the handbook as a rulebook is somewhat surprising given that only part 1 of the MAT contains policies. Part 2, which comprises about half of the handbook, offers pedagogical resources, rather than direct language from state, institutional, or departmental policies. However, that perception remained and was reinforced by many GTAs' tendency to use the handbook in what Cash described as a "purely referential" manner. All of the GTAs who used the handbook mentioned the table of contents and index as key tools for navigating the large document. Marley observed that the MAT, when brought up during discussions with his cohort, "comes up in terms of policies and not as a text on its own," highlighting the extent to which the MAT was referenced to figure out which policies needed to be included in their syllabi or to understand options for implementing policies like attendance, technology use, and classroom civility.

Two patterns emerged within this shared view of the handbook as a rulebook: more experienced GTAs referenced the MAT to see which policies they could transfer from their prior teaching experiences into their new courses, while new GTAs chose from policy options listed in the MAT, waiting until their second semester to make changes (if any)—even if they questioned or didn't understand the policies they were implementing. Leslie emphasized her initial worry that she wouldn't be able to teach first-year writing the way she had at her previous university:

> There were a lot of things that I did there that I wanted to make sure that I did here. I use a lot of laptops in my room, so I wanted to know if I could require or recommend laptop use. . . . I wanted to know if there were absence or late policies set by the department or if I got to set them. . . . I usually allow past final grade revision, because that's the way writing works. But I had heard that maybe that wasn't allowed.

Notably, Leslie's desire to use similar policies from her previous institution wasn't out of convenience or consistency, but because they aligned with her pedagogical philosophy: that writing takes practice, so past final grade revision should be allowed. Likewise, Daniel used the MAT to "make sure the language and policies were consistent" in his syllabus, that nothing was contradictory policy-wise. Even though Leslie and Daniel considered the handbook to be driven by policy, not pedagogy, they made sure their policies aligned because their pedagogies and policies *were* meaningfully connected.

Leslie's navigation of departmental policies listed in the MAT differed significantly from Andrew's approach, who made clear distinctions between policy and pedagogy:

> I relied both semesters on the MAT more for all the institutional and departmental policies than I did for subject matter, content, the actual content of the courses. I thought of [the MAT] mainly as having to do with structure and regulation, as opposed to course content.

Andrew relied on the MAT's explanation of policies, choosing from the set of sample policies included in part 2's syllabus template. He didn't see a meaningful connection between the policies he included on his syllabus and the "actual content" of the course; instead, the act of including the required and recommended policies from the syllabus template reflected his adherence to "general standards and regulations." Andrew understood his syllabus-building as a way to make sure his policies aligned with departmental (and institutional, and state) expectations, an altogether separate endeavor from his teaching.

The Final Word

Each GTA had a sense of the MAT as having the final say in conversations or questions about how much freedom GTAs had to make and enforce pedagogical decisions.

Table 7.4. The handbook as final word

GTA	The handbook is . . .
Jones	"a contingency plan, a failsafe, if someone fucks up we have this here to say, that they fucked up and we didn't"
Andrew	"the first word with regard to policies [and] the final word"
Cash	"a resource to check first before you go asking about [a policy] to [the writing program director]"
Marley	"not so much a recommendation as a requirement"
Stephen	"[a way] to address if something happens . . . the university can be like, hey, we gave them the MAT, so accountability is probably part of it"
Leslie	"the last word . . . the final authority or the final word on what you can and cannot do . . . I'm always afraid I'm going to be breaking the rules"
Kira	"[why] my hands were tied during the first year"
Daniel	"a support . . . I was supported by the handbook, the handbook says 'this,' no conversation needed"

GTAs characterized the MAT as the final word in two ways: first, as a text protecting the department and university from liability if a GTA failed to follow proper policies or procedures, and second, as a text serving as the ultimate authority over GTAs' decision-making. In her first interview, Leslie spoke about going into the writing program director's office to ask a question about offering revision opportunities for students. In response, the director pulled a copy of the MAT out of her desk to show Leslie the specific requirements for revision for ENGL 101, which conflicted with Leslie's plans. Leslie saw the MAT, then, as "the final authority or final word on what you can and cannot do." If a student came to her during her first semester and asked whether they could still pass the class, Leslie "would pull out the MAT with them, and say, okay, here are your options . . . it kind of took some of the pressure off, it made it less like I was telling them they couldn't pass or telling them to withdraw, so I found that really helpful." Cash similarly treated the MAT as a resource to which he could defer on departmental policies related to his students:

> I wanted to be fair to students but then also adhere to whatever departmental policy was. I found myself first semester spelling out for a student . . . what they needed to do in order to do all right in the course. I spelled out some information using the manual saying, you know, I'm not allowed to give you anything other than a failing grade.

For Leslie and Cash, the handbook functioned as a way to support their own authorities as teachers through the formal institutional and departmental policies that were non-negotiable, invoking the authority of both the institutional policies of the university and of the department. However, they did not use the MAT to avoid the responsibility of having to justify their pedagogical decisions; rather, they referred to it in order to understand what their pedagogical decision "must be." In this sense, the MAT actually established Leslie and Cash's pedagogical identities, as it established the final word in terms of policy, both for Leslie and Cash, as well as for their students.

This understanding of the MAT also helped Daniel, who described a situation in which he utilized the handbook to defend his point system for major assignments when questioned by another GTA: "I was told [my point system] was inconsistent with the handbook . . . so I went to the handbook and I was supported by the handbook. No conversation needed." Kira described a similar sense of finality, although perhaps from a less satisfactory perspective: even as she wished to have more freedom with grading and setting her own grading scale, she felt that her "hands were tied" because of the specific guidelines for grading options outlined in the MAT and the lack of alternatives for letter grading. As with Leslie, Cash, and Daniel, the MAT served Kira as the final word on policy-related questions. However, this sense of the MAT clearly restricted her choices for the pedagogical structures she wanted to implement.

The common understanding of the MAT as the final word led some of the GTAs to perceive the handbook as a rulebook even when deciding whether to adhere to recommendations or advice provided as a resource, rather than the set of policy requirements outlined in part 1. Although Cash had ideas for changing up the course as he entered into his second year of teaching, he decided not to alter his course materials because he wanted to adhere to the policies *and* recommendations outlined in the MAT. The MAT functioned as a "coercive genre" (Bawarshi 2003, 120), where Cash felt tied to the handbook, even when his gained experience enabled him to consider alternative policies or structures in his courses. When asked whether he disagreed with or challenged any of the formal policies or recommendations included in the MAT during his first year of teaching, Cash replied, "No. I had no desire to resist it."

THREE CASES OF GTA UPTAKE

The GTAs at Public U perceived the MAT as being a calibrating protocol, rulebook, and final word: as a way to rein GTAs in, a way to get GTAs to follow the rules, a way to discourage departure from institutional and departmental goals, thereby creating a more cohesive, united writing program. However, these perceptions of the MAT did not result in identical uptakes, what Freadman (1994, 2002) outlines as the range of responses and actions cued by a genre. The genre uptake knowledge of the GTAs was "tacitly acquired, ideologically consequential, deeply remembered and affective . . . connected not only to memories of prior, habitual responses to a genre, but also memories of prior engagements with other, related genres" (Bawarshi and Reiff 2010, 86), and therefore, varied despite the GTAs' shared perceptions of the MAT.

In this section, I detail three GTAs' uptakes from the MAT, outlining three profiles (which I term the anarchist, the innovator, and the risk-taker) in order to complicate the themes developed in the previous section. Stephen, the anarchist, is the only GTA to not use the MAT at all during his first semester, which had significant implications for not only the production of his course materials, but also his understanding of his identity as an instructor. Leslie, the innovator, wove her prior pedagogical experience and sense of identity into her new university context, engaging with the MAT to find spaces for creativity and flexibility—even within what she considered the authoritative "rulebook." Jones, the risk-taker, began their[3] first semester as a new GTA strongly adhering to the course materials provided to them, but then branched out in their second semester to take more risks with their materials and gain a stronger sense of their own pedagogical identity. Stephen, Leslie, and Jones's uptake profiles demonstrate that even within shared perceptions of departmental teaching handbook as a meta-genre, their interactions with the MAT did not result in similar pedagogical decisions. Each of their pedagogical identities were affected differently depending on their uptakes of the MAT, showing the complex ways in which meta-genres can influence the pedagogical identities of new teachers.

Stephen, the Anarchist

While Stephen, like the other GTAs, described the MAT as "a list of guidelines" that "tells incoming GTAs what they can and can't do," his uptake was markedly different. Namely, he did not use the MAT, at least not directly. Stephen initially stated that he "kind of forgot" he had the MAT; however, he also described himself confidently as "pretty much a rebel" who decided not to use the MAT, stating, "If I needed to know anything, [the department] would tell me." Stephen received the MAT

---

3. Jones's pronouns are "they/them/theirs."

at orientation, put it under a stack of books on his new desk, and never referred to it.

When talking about his syllabus, he explained that he didn't write any of his own policies; instead, he relied on the policies included on the syllabus template provided on the Blackboard resource page because "they must be approved and good." This syllabus template was also available in part 2 of the MAT, which indicates that because he had neglected to consult the MAT, he didn't recognize that the templates were identical. As a result, he did use the MAT somewhat indirectly; due to a general lack of familiarity with the larger system of pedagogical genres updated and maintained by the department, he didn't realize how the MAT connected to the resources constellated across the department's teaching website and Blackboard page.

In short, even though Stephen didn't directly utilize the MAT, it still shaped and influenced his pedagogical identity, namely in the way that it distanced him from meaningfully connecting with his own teaching materials. In our first interview, I asked Stephen to point to a section of the syllabus that most represented his teaching style and who he was as a teacher. He paused, then said, "I mean, I just copied and pasted it. Let me see." After several minutes of silence and looking through his syllabus, he said, "No. I don't see anything." Although he had referenced these teaching materials, only slightly adjusting the language of major assignment prompts from ENGL 101 to 102, he didn't see meaningful connections between his course materials and his pedagogical identity.

Here, we get a sense of Stephen's teaching style, along with the role he took up in the classroom: someone responsible for being authoritative and discipline-driven, deciding whether students merited particular grades or merited allowances for being absent or distracted while in class. Unlike the GTAs who used the MAT as a final word in making and justifying pedagogical decisions, Stephen made a concerted effort to circumvent the MAT's authority by avoiding it altogether. Instead, he worked to develop his pedagogy outside of what he perceived to be the limiting constraints of having to refer to and interact with the MAT, which he described as "all rules [with] not really any space for options."

Somewhat ironically, Stephen's anarchist tendency to forgo using the MAT may have limited the possibilities he was able to imagine for his role in the classroom, other than that of disciplinarian. Even as he drew from sample policies he viewed as pre-approved and therefore effective, after his second semester he described his efforts to enforce those policies as "an exercise in futility" because of their rigidity. Whether increased interaction with the MAT would have resulted in him taking up the handbook's call, as stated on its first page, to assess one's own "developing teaching philosophies and practices" through "[reflecting] on course materials and teaching practices," it is impossible to say. However, Stephen's modeling of his course materials off of his experience with strict teachers and inflexible policies came into conflict with his own experience teaching, where a hawk-eyed monitoring for students on their phones began to overwhelm any larger pedagogical goals he had. Stephen's developing identity as an instructor seems to have been hindered by course materials from which he felt disconnected, specifically those policies that seemed to lock him into a role of disciplinarian even as he felt the pull to move into less authoritative roles. Stephen's interactions with the MAT signal its influence as a meta-genre that indirectly, yet meaningfully, shaped the composing of his syllabus.

Leslie, the Innovator

Leslie, like Stephen, perceived the MAT as a rulebook and as having the final say, but she was able to find spaces for innovation and creativity within the requirements and limitations she saw in the handbook. Leslie entered Public U with two years of prior experience teaching college-level writing as a GTA at another university, where she had taken a teaching practicum that gave her experience creating course materials. Leslie described one activity from that practicum in which each GTA began with a syllabus template that they then individually revised over the course of the semester "until [the syllabus] was mostly us." Because of her experience developing a syllabus and other course materials from a template into more representative and personalized texts, she was more concerned about the transfer of her teaching materials to Public U than she was about understanding *how* to create course materials.

Unlike Stephen, who struggled to identify moments in his course materials that represented his pedagogy, Leslie had thought critically about the language and organization of her materials and how it set the tone of her class. For instance, she explained her desire to resist the "knowledge-flowing-from-me-to-the-students model" and therefore used the "we" pronoun throughout many sections of her syllabus in order to establish the class "as a co-learning experience." Leslie also included the verb "explore" consistently throughout her ENGL 101 and 102 materials, emphasizing that her classes "are not [spaces] where we 'master' a certain genre or become experts at writing" but instead places to explore and practice different kinds of writing.

Although Leslie carried this pedagogical identity of a co-learner and facilitator of exploration with her from her previous institution, some aspects of her pedagogical identity didn't transfer over so easily, like her preference for portfolio grading. Leslie initially met resistance—not by an official policy stated in the MAT but by an unspoken policy of first-years not being allowed to implement a portfolio grading system. Given that this policy wasn't explicitly stated in the MAT, she used that gap to her advantage, developing an innovative "mini-portfolio" grading system that adhered to the requirements for this alternative assessment system. Leslie met with the director of the writing program and was able to gain approval for her modified portfolio grading. In this way, her utilization of the MAT supported her pedagogical identity in a constructive way.

Leslie was careful, however, to recognize spaces where innovation could be unproductive or damaging to herself as an instructor. As she explained, statewide and institutional policies seemed like mandates she couldn't reword or adjust, even while recognizing there was some space for potential innovation:

> These policies felt like things that were rules, I didn't feel like I could change them. I could probably write my own diversity and civility statement, but even that felt like . . . I need to defer to the big dogs. What happens when you plagiarize? I needed to make sure I didn't get that wrong. Classroom safety? Those are actual rules from the university, I need them to be word for word. These were things that could get me in trouble as an instructor. I needed those on my syllabus to be exact. There are legal consequences to all of these.

Leslie drew on the established language of these policies from the MAT, choosing not to innovate in those instances. Overall, her utilization of the MAT indicates that she knew when to protect herself as a new GTA, but also when to challenge boundaries in order to enable new avenues that would allow her to represent her pedagogical identity and teach the way she wanted to, based on her pedagogical philosophy and values.

Jones, the Risk-Taker

Like Stephen, Jones had no prior teaching experience before entering Public U, and they did not innovate or move significantly away from the provided materials in their first semester. Jones explained that they mostly "copy-pasted" course materials from the MAT for their first semester, choosing from the available sample statements for standard policies like attendance and late work. However, in their second semester, Jones began to take risks, developing new project assignments and making changes to key policies.

Jones made significant changes to their course materials over the winter break before returning to teach ENGL 102 in the second semester, due to their newly gained teaching experience and developing pedagogical identity. One such change was to their attendance policy, which they shifted from a penalty-based model to a points-based model. The sample attendance policies listed in the MAT each had a variation of the same penalty: if students missed a certain number of classes, their grade would be deducted a certain percentage. For the spring semester, Jones reframed their policy so students would receive points for *attending* class, rather than losing a grade percentage for *missing* class. These points functioned as participation points and were recorded "as a kind of extra credit." While Jones hadn't experienced any student resistance to the penalty-based model in the fall, they realized that this policy did not actually reflect who they were as an instructor: "I noticed . . . that students that were already getting a penalty because they were missing out on important information and brainstorming and invention activities . . . I didn't want to make it even worse." This new model allowed Jones to better represent their desired identity as an instructor—someone who was "accessible, straightforward, and open, and equitable." By reinforcing students' choice to come to class and recognizing that students would face negative consequences in general for missing class, Jones established a clearer connection between their pedagogical identity and their course materials.

Jones's risk-taking also extended beyond the syllabus, as they became more comfortable experimenting with new kinds of project assignments. For their ENGL 102 course, Jones chose to create an assignment from scratch for the final unit, which allowed them to insert "a lot more of 'me' [into the prompt]." Jones acknowledged that their cohort "had more freedom for creating the assignment sequence [for ENGL 102 compared to ENGL 101], but we still had to stay with certain bounds." Given those limitations, Jones drew on the MAT and met with the writing program director to ensure their new assignments still fulfilled course goals. Like Leslie, Jones used the MAT to support their pedagogical risk-taking, venturing beyond the provided syllabus template and assignment sheets into creating materials that better represented them. Unlike Leslie, however, Jones still seemed to largely defer to the perceived "rulebook" status of MAT and did not seek out spaces to create significantly different course structures. Instead, Jones checked their new materials against the MAT, treating it as the final word against proposed revisions.

CONCLUSION

Stephen, Leslie, and Jones's varied responses to and utilizations of the MAT, even within their shared understanding of the handbook as protocol, rulebook, and final word, highlight the influence departmental teaching handbooks have as a meta-genre influencing pedagogical identity. In recognizing the role of this meta-genre in how GTAs develop ownership of their course materials, and more importantly, their identities as instructors, it is crucial that graduate programs critically consider the resources they provide to graduate students, as well as the productive and limiting influences these materials may carry. Part of this examination must include a review of pedagogical meta-genres like departmental handbooks and other guides for creating course materials. The Public U English Department's MAT, even as a text equally split into an overview of policies and guidelines and a pedagogical guide, was largely perceived to be a set of required procedures and practices, perhaps because it was named and structured as a manual, not a teacher's guide or resource collection.

Further studies might also consider the role of other meta-genres and genre systems like departmental websites, faculty development materials, and practicum texts (i.e., handouts and exercises) in shaping and directing GTAs' pedagogical decisions. While this study drew on self-reports from graduate students reflecting on their first year of teaching, studies able to observe and understand the ongoing (and perhaps changing) perceptions and uptakes of meta-genres by new teachers moving through their first years of teaching would help illuminate the complex and varied role of meta-genres in developing pedagogical identity.

This study's focus on the role of the departmental teaching handbook reveals how a resource like the MAT has significant meta-generic influence on new GTAs' pedagogical identities. While not all teachers fit neatly into identities like "anarchist," "innovator," or "risk-taker," these uptake profiles do show that pedagogical resources play an important role in establishing teachers' pedagogical identity, particularly during their first year in a new program. Better understanding how teachers draw on and engage with pedagogical meta-genres like teaching handbooks can help departments anticipate and prepare resources for new teachers, as well as critically interrogate the resources already in place. For new teachers like GTAs, meta-genres like the departmental teaching handbook not only support the ongoing development of their pedagogical identity but are also integral to the shaping of their pedagogical experience even before entering the classroom.

APPENDIX 7.A

MANUAL FOR TEACHERS (MAT)

REFERENCES

Bawarshi, Anis. 2003. *Genre and the Invention of the Writer: Reconsidering the Place of Invention in Composition.* Logan: Utah State University Press.

Bawarshi, Anis, and Mary Jo Reiff. 2010. *Genre: An Introduction to History, Theory, Research, and Pedagogy.* West Lafayette, IN: Parlor Press.

Bazerman, Charles. 1994. *Constructing Experience*. Carbondale: Southern Illinois University Press.

Berkenkotter, Carol, Thomas N. Huckin, and John Ackerman. 1988. "Conventions, Conversations, and the Writer: Case Study of a Student in a Rhetoric Ph.D. Program." *Research in the Teaching of English* 22 (1): 9–44.

Christie, Frances. 1993. "Curriculum Genres: Planning for Effective Teaching." In *The Powers of Literacy: A Genre Approach to Teaching Writing*, edited by Bill Cope and Mary Kalantzis, 154–78. New York: Routledge.

Dryer, Dylan B. 2012. "At a Mirror, Darkly: The Imagined Undergraduate Writers of Ten Novice Composition Instructors." *College Composition and Communication* 63 (3): 420–52.

Freedman, Anne. 1994. "Anyone for Tennis?" In *Genre and the New Rhetoric, edited by Aviva Freedman and Peter Medway*, 37–56. Bristol, PA: Taylor & Francis.

Freedman, Anne. 2002. "Uptake." In *The Rhetoric and Ideology of Genre: Strategies for Stability and Change*, edited by Richard M. Coe, Lorelei Lingard, and Tatiana Teslenko, 39–53. Cresskill, NJ: Hampton Press.

Giltrow, Janet. 2002. "Meta-Genre." In *The Rhetoric and Ideology of Genre: Strategies for Stability and Change*, edited by Richard M. Coe, Lorelei Lingard, and Tatiana Teslenko, 187–205. Cresskill, NJ: Hampton Press.

Grouling, Jennifer. 2015. "Resistance and Identity Formation: The Journey of the Graduate Student-Teacher." *Composition Forum* 32. http://compositionforum.com/issue/32/resistance.php.

Helscher, Thomas P. 1997. "The Subject of Genre." In *Genre and Writing: Issues, Arguments, Alternatives*, edited by Wendy Bishop and Hans A. Ostrom, 27–36. Portsmouth, NH: Boynton/Cook.

Kill, Melanie. 2006. "Acknowledging the Rough Edges of Resistance: Negotiation of Identities for First-Year Composition." *College Composition and Communication* 58 (2): 213–35.

Miller, Carolyn R. 1984. "Genre as Social Action." *Quarterly Journal of Speech* 70 (2): 151–67.

Neaderhiser, Stephen. 2016. "Hidden in Plain Sight: Occlusion in Pedagogical Genres." *Composition Forum* 33. http://www.compositionforum.com/issue/33/hidden.php.

Prior, Paul. 2013. *Writing/Disciplinarity: A Sociohistoric Account of Literate Activity in the Academy*. New York: Routledge.

Restaino, Jessica. 2012. *First Semester: Graduate Students, Teaching Writing, and the Challenge of Middle Ground*. Carbondale: Southern Illinois University Press.

Russell, David R. 1997. "Rethinking Genre in School and Society: An Activity Theory Analysis." *Written Communication* 14 (4): 504–54.

Saldaña, Johnny. 2009. *The Coding Manual for Qualitative Researchers*. New York: SAGE.

8

"AM I COVERED FOR THAT?"
Examining the "Work" of Policy Documents in the First-Year Course

Mark A. Hannah and Christina Saidy

Administratively, writing programs employ a range of documents to facilitate the implementation of their programmatic visions. Examples of these documents include policy statements, goals and objectives, assessment plans, instructor manuals, values statements, and mission statements. Our specific writing program has a policy document—listing specific writing program policies—that all instructors must place in their syllabi verbatim.

Anecdotally, and in our experience, we have come to see that this policy document, which is designed to guide instructor decision-making and practices as well as communicate expectations and acceptable behavior for students, is used in a variety of ways. We have both taught the practicum for new instructors at our institutions and at past institutions. In this capacity, we mentor new-to-us teaching assistants and instructors to teach first-year writing and technical and professional writing at our institutions. While neither of us currently serve as the writing program administrator (WPA), our positions as facilitators of the writing practica put us in the position to transmit or pass on the program's values, practices, and administrative vision. After we have passed on the policy document to instructors, we see three general responses. The first is that instructors put the policies in their syllabi and completely adhere to the policies without questions. Second, and most infrequently, instructors vocally resist the policies. Typically, in these cases, the instructors put the policies in their syllabi verbatim, but we spend much time and energy in discussion. Third, and most commonly, instructors ask questions, clarify, and express some reservations. In these situations, and often in the second response above, instructors place the policies in their syllabi but develop workarounds or ad-hoc hacks of the policies. That is, the policies are placed in the syllabi, but the instructors spend

https://doi.org/10.7330/9781646422920.c008

time and energy with students both addressing the spirit of the policy and discussing how the policy aligns with the instructors' teacherly identity and practice.

Over the years, as we have observed the many varieties of instructor workarounds and addressed the many questions and concerns instructors have about our specific program policy document, we have observed tensions. There is often a tension between what a program values and what its instructors need or value. There are also tensions at times between programmatic or teacher values, expressed in program policies, and students' needs, wants, and values in their writing courses (Hannah and Saidy 2014). However, as we have noticed these tensions anecdotally in the programs in which we work, we have also come to realize that while most programs have stated program policies, not much research exists in the literature of writing program administration about what these policies do, how they function, and who they serve. In response, we set out to descriptively study program policy documents. We wanted to know what these policy documents contain, how they express a program's concerns and values, and who the documents serve. In this chapter, we offer a brief review of scholarship about pedagogical genres and directly address work regarding policy documents. We then describe our method, coding procedure, and findings; discuss key findings; and conclude with our reflections on possible ways for programs to innovate on their current use of policy documents in the first-year course.

THE ROLE OF POLICY DOCUMENTS

Much important work has been directed at understanding the genre of pedagogical documents at macro and micro levels. For example, Bazerman (1994), Bawarshi (2003), and Devitt (2004) discuss how certain pedagogical genres, such as the syllabus, act as a meta-genre and facilitate various forms of genred activity in the classroom as well as in other nonclassroom, extracurricular contexts. Taking a less meta perspective, various scholars have examined micro examples of genres of pedagogy. Examples of this work include examinations of syllabi (Baecker 1998; Eberly, Newton, and Wiggins 2001; Fink 2012), assignment prompts (Clark 2005), end comment responses to student writing (Smith 1997), instructor manuals (Reynolds 1995), and teaching statements (Chism 1998). Across this work are acknowledgments of the complex and various kinds of work these genres simultaneously perform for different audiences and for different rhetorical contexts. Ultimately, the simultaneity of work, audience, and context lead to the emergence of "tensions" (Neaderhiser 2016) that stem from competing expectations of how the genre documents are to operate inside and outside of the classroom.

With our interest in policy documents as a pedagogical genre, we turned to writing program administration scholarship. In their survey of writing program administrators (WPAs) and department chairs, Rose et al. (2013) discovered that a key component of WPAs' jobs is creating, implementing, and maintaining program policy (57). But despite the reported importance of program policy work, policy documents as a genre have received little critical attention in our discipline's scholarship (Nicolas 2017). This dearth of literature is somewhat surprising given that successful teaching depends on providing students with clear expectations and guidelines for how the work and environment of the writing classroom will be managed. Furthermore, successful classroom experiences require the coordination of a mix of competing values, expectations, goals, and requirements, and the program policy document appears ready as the prime programmatic tool for facilitating the "coordinating game" that teachers manage in the first-year classroom. To facilitate this coordination, writing program policies "[ensure] all students receive equitable treatment" and "function to standardize experience across multiple sections of what is supposed to be the same course" (Nicolas 2017, 16). Through creating static criteria, program policies aim to facilitate students' decision-making by simplifying the complexity and variety of their day-to-day lives.

In focusing on standardization, simplification, and the like, writing program policies appear to generate a tension between writing studies' "democratic aspirations" (Gallagher 2019, 476) and its treatment of students and instructors. As a discipline, writing studies aims to build meaningful learning experiences that promote access and are suited to students' unique goals and needs. However, policy documents' impulse toward standardization potentially undermines these aspirations by cultivating an "ideology of normalcy" (Oswal and Meloncon 2017) in which student and instructor differences are ignored. More specifically, policy documents have the potential to suppress a writing program's ability to imagine fully the differences between its stakeholders, which thus makes it very difficult for a writing program to "find approaches that speak to the salient features of its unique culture and community" (Endres 2006, 86). Recent work that draws on disabilities studies scholarship has further encouraged program administrators to think beyond the culture of normalcy (Fedukovich and Morse 2017; Nicolas 2017; Shea 2017; Vidali

2015; Yergeau 2016). Specifically, this scholarship asks administrators to adopt policies that are attuned to the unique positionality of their students and teachers, as well as to teachers' responsibility for evaluating student behavior and work product in a way that is responsive to student needs rather than simply to administrative ones.

In light of both the general lack of research about the role of writing program policies in the first-year course and the recent calls to think more broadly about policy beyond the ideology of normalcy, we designed a study of writing program policy documents to examine and document the features of this genre in order to assess the kinds of work these documents do. In particular, we want to look at the content of policy documents and begin to evaluate how they create conditions for supporting writing development and training.

METHODS

To identify writing programs whose policies may be representative of national trends, we turned to the Conference on College Composition and Communication (CCCC) Writing Program Certificate of Excellence Award winners. Part of the criteria for the CCCC Certificate of Excellence is that award-winning programs must "exhibit coherence in terms of disciplinary expectations" (CCCC 2018). Beyond this expectation for disciplinary coherence, CCCC Certificate of Excellence winners are viewed as imaginative and exemplary models of writing programs on a national scale. The list contains sixty-eight award winners for the years 2004–2018 and includes writing centers and writing-in-the disciplines programs in addition to first-year writing programs. Since we were seeking specific policy documents for first-year composition (FYC) programs, we reviewed the list and excluded writing centers and programs that are outside of FYC, such as engineering writing.

After eliminating programs not related to FYC, we were left with thirty-one programs. We reviewed each of these programs looking for public-facing policy documents available via web search. The public-facing nature of these policy documents was of particular importance to us because we were interested in the ways that writing program policy documents publicly construct what it means to be a student and instructor in the program. The nature of these public-facing documents varied. For example, some of the program websites had a link called some variation of "Writing Program Policies." More common, however, was the policy document genre, which was often directed toward writing program faculty and included specific policies that must be included in syllabi. One program had a syllabus checklist that also included program policies. Therefore, we found it important to define what we are referring to as a policy document. For our purposes, a policy document is any public-facing document that details a writing program's policies that must be included on syllabi used by instructors in the program. Once we identified a public-facing policy document for a program, we searched for a recent and publicly available syllabus for the introductory composition course within that program. This syllabus was used to verify that the public-facing document we located truly represented the program policies as communicated by faculty to students in syllabi.

Coding Policy Documents

The search yielded nine programs with publicly available policy documents.[1] Of these programs, seven are R1 (doctoral university—highest research activity), one is an R2 (doctoral university—higher research activity), and one is an R3 (doctoral university—moderate research activity). We suspect that the large number of R1 institutions reflects the size of the faculty and staff available to complete the application process for the CCCC award designation. However, these larger institutions also may require more public policies, as they have a larger teaching faculty and serve more students. These institutions represented a range of geographical locations in the United States: two in the West, three in the East/Northeast, two in the South, and two in the Midwest.

Once we obtained the sample policy documents, we conducted a summative content analysis (Hsieh and Shannon 2005; Huckin 2003) of each of the policy documents individually. We applied the same coding method to each of the nine documents. In our coding, we made three passes through each document. In the first pass, we looked for major topics or ideas. These broad ideas were typically section headers. In the second pass, we looked for language that further defined the big ideas. In the third pass, we looked deeper for implied topics or moves the policy documents made to further define the topics. At the end of our coding, we pulled out major topics that were easily identifiable (Level 1 codes) and their subtopics (Level 2 codes). We then looked at the remaining, or miscellaneous, topics in order to find any unifying themes among them, which lead us to identify three additional themes. In all, we had ten Level 1 codes (see table 8.1) and three miscellaneous themes.

---

1. In our analysis and report of findings, we chose not to identify individual programs by name. We did this to keep the focus on the policies themselves rather than on specific programs.

Table 8.1. Level 1 codes

Policy Topic	Frequency (n=9)
Academic Integrity	9
Attendance	9
Disability Accommodations/Accessibility	7
Late Work/Work Completion	4
Classroom Behavior (Civility, Tolerance, etc.)	5
Writing Lab/Writing Center/Writing Support	4
Technology	3
University Honor Pledge	2
Participation/Student Engagement	2
Counseling Services	2

FINDINGS

In this section, we detail key findings of our content analysis and provide examples for each of the codes.

Academic Integrity and Attendance

Every program articulated policies related to academic integrity and attendance, but the categories were described in a variety of ways. For academic integrity, we saw headers such as *Academic Integrity* (3), *Academic Honesty* (2), *Plagiarism* (3), and *Academic Integrity and Civility* (1). Despite the differing headings, the majority of these policies are plagiarism focused. They typically offer a definition of plagiarism and emphasize the impact to the student, such as a description of what will happen to the student if they commit plagiarism. Furthermore, many of these documents link, intertextually, to a university office—such as an office of student conduct or dean of students—that deals with plagiarism cases. In one exception, the university with the Academic Integrity and Civility policy focuses heavily on the communal aspects of writing and encourages students to use faculty as a resource if the student is struggling with course materials. The policy notes that "acts of academic dishonesty may solve problems temporarily . . . [but] they are always detrimental in the long run." This is the only policy that encourages students to get help rather than plagiarize and acknowledges the reason that many students plagiarize—a misunderstanding of course content and/or time constraints in getting the assignment done. The instructor is positioned as a *helper* in avoiding plagiarism rather than as a *reporter* of plagiarism, as is the case in many of the other documents where the professor identifies and reports plagiarism to a writing program director or a university level administrator who evaluates the case.

The Attendance category is also present in all of the policy documents, and a number of terms are used for this particular code: *Attendance* (4), *Absences* (2), *Attendance Policy* (1), *Attendance and Assignments* (1), and *Participation and Attendance* (1). Six of the policy documents discuss consequences or punishments for violating the attendance policy. These consequences include grade reductions, recommendations to drop the course, or even course failure. Six policies justify why attendance is important and is often tied to student performance in the course or the highly collaborative nature of writing. For example, one policy reads, "In a class as small as this one, your absence will be noticed. Other students depend on your feedback in class discussions and workshops. In short, your presence counts in this course." Furthermore, five of the policies discuss the number of allowable absences in the course. Of these five, three policies go a step further and distinguish between excused and unexcused absences. Four of the nine policies describe the student's responsibility in the case of absence, such as, "If you must miss a class, you are responsible for finding out what you missed and for keeping up with assignments. If you know in advance that you will have to miss a class, it's a good idea to let your instructor know ahead of time by e-mail or, better yet, by making an appointment." One policy takes this a step further and discusses the role of the teacher in absences informing the student that in the case of excessive absences, "please let me know as soon as possible. Based on this discussion, I may be able to refer you to the appropriate campus resource for help and possible accommodations." Only one of the policies comments on what it means to be present beyond just showing up for class. This is described in terms of a participation requirement that states, "You are expected to be prepared for class and to participate in class discussions, to be able to respond to questions posed to you, to have drafts when they are due, and to complete in-class writing activities. Your participation will contribute to your final grade." In doing so, this document explicitly links a particular type of participation with attendance.

Disability Accommodations and Accessibility

Disability accommodations and accessibility codes are present in seven of the policy documents. We saw three major moves in these documents.

First, two of the policies express a value statement that acknowledges that students may need accommodations and that these accommodations will be made available to them. Second, five of the policies instruct students how to initiate the accommodation process. This ranges from contacting the instructor to contacting the appropriate disability resource office on campus. Finally, all of the policies include a link or phone number for the appropriate disability resource office.

Acceptable Classroom Behavior or Civility

Five of the policy documents address classroom behavior and/or civility. Three of these documents begin by defining appropriate classroom behavior in a positive way. For example, one document reads, "Civility is genuine respect and regard for others: politeness, consideration, tact, good manners, graciousness, cordiality, affability, amiability, and courteousness," while another reads, "We will build a classroom environment built on mutual respect, which includes behaviors such as listening to others before responding, critiquing our peers' ideas rather than our peers themselves, and framing disagreement as an opportunity to develop and nuance our own views." While the content of these two documents is different, they both explore the positive aspects of civil behavior. In contrast, another document defined classroom behaviors that will not be tolerated. It reads, "Inappropriate language or tone of voice, interruptions, dominating class discussions, and other behaviors that might impede the creation of a safe and comfortable learning environment will not be tolerated." In this definitional move, the program takes a hard line in response to inappropriate student behaviors.

Beyond defining behaviors, many of the documents connect appropriate behaviors to the importance of communal goals and values to further learning. For example, one policy reads, "Community members affect each other's well-being and have a shared interest in creating and sustaining an environment where all community members and their points of view and values are respected." Two of the policy documents encourage communication between faculty and students to further civility and appropriate behavior. One encourages students, "Please come and talk to me if you feel like I can better facilitate a respectful and productive learning space." The other example develops this further noting, "It is always a good idea to talk to your professor or take advantage of other provided resources if you are having trouble with a classroom discussion, a topic in class, or an assignment. Remember, we are here to support you, but we can only do so when the lines of communication are kept open." These civility/behavior statements focus largely on ways that civil behavior is a collaborative endeavor.

In two of the behavior policies, there are mentions of the role of technology in the classroom. One notes, "Instructors will use their discretion on permitting the use of laptops and other electronics, but these devices should always be used in support of classroom activities and never for personal reasons during class." The other specifies that cell phones should be turned off, and that other use of technology is at the professor's discretion. As an aside, we did identify two of the policy documents that also included a university honor code, which is another way that universities define acceptable behavior and civility for all students.

Late or Incomplete Work

Four of the documents contained policies on late or incomplete work. Three of the policies define what is considered late work. For example, one reads: "Papers are due on the date and time designated on the course syllabus." One policy discusses incomplete work and defines what it means: "Incomplete work, meaning writing that does not meet the minimum count." Three policies have a consequence for late work, such as: "Late papers will be marked down one letter grade per day late, including weekends." Three of the policies describe the student's responsibility or what the student needs to do in relation to this policy. For example, one policy reads: "Instructors are not required to accept late work; at the very least, most require that you make arrangements with them in advance." Another policy builds on this student responsibility: "If you must submit a late paper, you should contact me the day the paper is due, so that I know when to expect your paper and how you will submit it." Overall, these policies all discourage late work and, for the most part, place the onus of responsibility upon the student if or when work is late or incomplete.

Writing Support and Writing Centers

Four of the documents contained writing support or writing center policies that generally position writing support as beneficial. For example, one policy reads: "All writers benefit from feedback and support." Another policy focuses on the benefits to students' grades when attending the writing center: "Did you know working with a tutor, whether for English or any other discipline, leads to better course grades, high GPAs, greater academic success?" All four of the documents provide contact information for the writing center and links to the writing center website.

Miscellaneous Policies

The remaining codes were grouped into three common themes: (1) Grading, (2) Programmatic Values About Writing, and (3) Understanding the University Context.

In Grading, four schools were represented, and the grading section included information such as *criteria for evaluation, grade requirements for the course,* and *grade appeals.* One institution has a policy that the course evaluation must be completed as part of the citizenship grade. These grading policies were direct and program specific.

The Programmatic Values About Writing codes focused on programmatic practices that reflected the values of a program. Three schools were included in this theme, and the topics included: *draft workshops, paper formatting, making the library useful,* and *revision policy.* For example, the policy on draft workshops states:

> Draft workshops enable you to develop two major writing skills that are integral to this course: (1) learning to be a critic of your own writing and the writing of others, and (2) learning how to revise your work given comments and questions from your peers. Your writing will improve by having others read it and respond to it.

This policy clearly communicates a value about the importance of audience in the development of the writer and their writing. While the policy goes on to state the specifics about the workings of draft workshops and their due dates, this information is clearly foregrounded by the program's values about drafting, workshops, and writing development. The policies in this category tended to work this way—they defined a programmatic value and the policy that derives from that value.

The final theme is Understanding the University Context, and three programs had policies that fit under this theme. One of these schools had four such policies, another school had two, and one school had one. The topics of these policies included: *transfer credit, placement, honors policy,* and *enrollment/maintaining class enrollment caps.* Each defined the policy and also directed students how to act in response to the policy. For example, one of the policies on enrollment caps states:

> Capped at just 19 students, First-Year Writing and Rhetoric is likely to be one of the smallest classes you take at [university]. The [program] believes strongly that writing courses should be kept small so that students can work closely with their instructor and also with one another on their

writing. Instructors are therefore asked not to over-enroll their courses. If you find yourself on a waitlist you have several options.

This policy situates the place of first-year writing in the larger university context, details the policy, and offers students appropriate ways of dealing with the policy. Like the other policies under this theme, this policy helps the student to understand and navigate the university context, while clearly communicating the program's policy.

Noted Absences

Outside of these main codes, we want to note things that we did not find but expected to find in our sample. First, we anticipated a higher frequency of explicitly legal language—i.e., statements that are clearly legal in nature like disability accommodations—in the policy documents. When such legal matters were addressed in the documents, we noted how the description was passed off intertextually with a link to the appropriate university resource, such as the disability services center or the Dean's Office or Provost's Office for disciplinary matters. Second, in light of the ubiquity of technology in everyday life, we assumed that many policy documents would have explicit technology policies that covered a range of technology types and practices. However, few programs addressed technology, and when it occurred it was limited primarily to cell phone usage in the classroom. Third, we anticipated more statements about inclusiveness broadly conceived, but only one program had such a statement, which was a personal pronoun policy that included a link to services for LGBTQ students.

DISCUSSION

Through our analysis, we noted a number of tensions in policy documents. These tensions developed as policies address varying audiences and program values. In doing so, policies employ a range of voice that attempts to account for these audiences and values. In what follows, we discuss the tensions that became apparent to us in our analysis.

Program Values

Policy documents largely worked to communicate larger program values about what it means to be a writer, an instructor, or a learner in the program and in the larger university setting. Some of the documents cast what it means to be an ideal learner at the university and in the writing program. For example, one document notes, "The Writing Program expects students to be active and engaged learners, including through collaboration, and practicing a commitment to the materials, their own writing processes, and to their peers." This description is then followed by an example of how instructors may evaluate "average," "superior," and "weak" engagement. The juxtaposition of a value statement with a criteria or evaluative statement illustrates the potential tension between programmatic values and the need to manage or provide guidelines for student behavior. In this example, we notice two levels of potential tension for teachers that develop from how a program articulates part of its values. First, the program's definition of an ideal student may or may not align with the teacher's idea of an ideal student. Second, once criteria for assessment are introduced, a potential tension between teachers and students arises. This policy asks teachers to assess students according to predetermined criteria, which places limitations on the teacher and student in conceptualizing classroom performance and behavior. In both examples, teachers are asked to accommodate program values to their own notions of student behavior and engagement.

This pairing of values followed by ideal behaviors or consequences is particularly evident in categories such as plagiarism/academic dishonesty statements. Most programs stated values regarding authorship or appropriate sharing of ideas. For example, one policy reads, "Trusting one another to create original work, this community respects one of the central challenges of college education: working through unfamiliar and potentially uncomfortable ideas together." This description captures the ideal, or even idyllic, college setting as an opportunity space for learning together through writing and cultivating an understanding that writing is a property of both individuals and communities, i.e., the very way the program values authorship. However, the next sentence begins, "To violate these principles in the classroom and the course injures the larger university community," and it goes on to discuss how academic dishonesty will be treated. This particular pairing of an ideal notion of collaboration and authorship with information about consequences for misbehavior produces a unique tension for students regarding how they understand plagiarism. Specifically, this pairing of an ideal with a consequence casts plagiarism as something that is cut-and-dry and straightforward rather than a complex phenomenon. While the policy describes writing as a communal endeavor, it also casts the individual's potential plagiarism as the thing that injures this community. In doing so, the policy potentially short circuits or cuts off discussion or reflection opportunities for students to think through and reflect on their own notions of authorship in the classroom. This particular tension is important to consider since all of the policy documents contained some type of plagiarism policy.

Audience: Who Do Policy Documents Serve?

A potential tension arises from the way that policy documents attempt to address multiple audiences and serve many purposes. Primary among these audiences are instructors and students. Universities and their administrations are a third but much less visible audience. Yet, often the audience cannot be pinned down to a singular individual, as the documents work to meet the needs of all of these audiences simultaneously.

Policy documents are typically filtered through instructors to students. Sometimes, the policy document is directed at instructors clearly with the understanding that the policies will be communicated to students. For example, a school that provides a checklist for instructors directs them to use the checklist for their syllabi to ensure that they cover all the required points. In each of these bullet points, there is a section directing the instructors how to use the text and a section on the policy itself. A section on grading methods reads:

> Your students have a right to know how many papers they will write, how much each will count towards their final grade, and what other factors enter into their grade (exercises and other assignments, attendance, class participation, etc.). If you provide students with this information in writing at the beginning of the semester, you protect yourself from later complaint about your grading system.

In this case, it is clear that the audience for this document is the instructor, as it directs the instructor of the policy requirement and the ways policy documents are used by students. We see the complexity in simultaneously writing a policy for one audience—instructors—that anticipates the response of another audience—students, parents, or even university administrators charged with handling escalated grade appeals.

In the second way, policies are written explicitly for students. For example, one program contained a policy on class enrollment caps directed toward students. The policy reads, "The First-Year Writing Program is invested in a high-quality experience for all of its students. Because this experience is heavily dependent on class size, it is the policy of the First-Year Writing Program not to override the number of available seats offered." The statement then goes on to encourage students to address questions to the director of First-Year Writing rather than individual instructors. This statement clearly communicates the policy and course of action to the student and removes the instructor. However, many of these policies directed toward students also implicitly communicate program expectations and practices to instructors, as well as the reasons underlying those practices.

In the third way programs structure policy documents, institutional audiences are explicitly addressed along with instructors and students. In using this kind of structure, programs accomplish two distinct ends: program visibility and legal compliance. This structuring technique positions programs to communicate their values to the administration or the larger university community as well as illustrate how the writing program either is in conversation with or collaborating with other campus groups. For example, one policy document reads, "The Office of the Provost asks that we include the [University] honor pledge," followed by the pledge. This language suggests a relationship of courtesy with upper administration since the writing program chooses to include this policy in program syllabi, even though the honor pledge would be in place whether or not instructors include it on the syllabus. As such, this policy example demonstrates the complexity writing programs face in "playing ball" with upper administration demands, while at the same time clearly apprising students of the criteria that will be used to evaluate their behaviors not only in the first-year course but also in other institutional contexts.

Together, each of the examples discussed in this section illustrate how addressing multiple audiences through policy documents reflects the complexity of writing programs' efforts to serve many people. There are efforts to make information clear for instructors, such as information about what must be included and what can be changed, moves to communicate policies to students, including reasons for those policies or resources available for support, and efforts to clearly communicate values to stakeholders across the university. Giving clarity to a large group of people is challenging, as is reflected in the ways these documents address multiple audiences.

Range of Voice

The complexity of values and audience carried over into something we call the range of voice. In our analysis, we noticed three different general levels of voice: authoritarian; authoritative; and permissive.

Authoritarian policies contain top-down, direct, and unchangeable language. In these cases, instructors are directed to copy and paste the policy into the syllabus verbatim. While many of the policy documents had some authoritarian sections specifically related to issues such as attendance or university-wide policies, purely authoritarian policies were less frequent than authoritative policies. Of the three types of voice we observed, the authoritarian comes closest to preserving or operating through an ideology of normalcy. That is, through their top-down nature, these statements view all students through a universal standard that transcends and does not admit difference, and in doing so simplifies students in the hopes of rendering them easily manageable. This lack of flexibility or malleability potentially impacts instructors' ability to shape their teacherly or pedagogical identities in ways that either promote effective teaching or, as Michael Albright argues (in this collection) in regard to the "common" or shared syllabus, limits them from representing and promoting their own professional identities.

Authoritative policy documents also contained direct and clear policies, but they also may offer some flexibility. The majority of the policy documents we analyzed contained some, if not many, authoritative policies. At times, directions to instructors at the beginning of a policy document provided the degree to which the instructor should adhere to the policies. For example, one document specified, "Individual faculty members may revise these policies for tone, style, and degree of explanation, and some policies provide a range of supported options." These instructions communicate clearly that some elements of the policies are malleable while others are not. Some documents address this more on a policy-by-policy basis. For example, one document provides a specific plagiarism policy, directs instructors to include that policy on the syllabus, and then adds, "You may also add your own comments." In that case, the policy itself is unchangeable, but the instructor may add additional information to this section. This provides opportunities for instructors to include language that represents their own values and supports their teacherly identity, which positions policies as the first move in establishing teacher–student relationships.

Lastly, permissive policy statements detail the policies that must be included but offer quite a bit of flexibility to instructors to shape their own policies. For example, the policy document at one of the universities that provided the greatest degree of permissiveness describes the attendance policy, saying, "Your attendance policy should be clearly stated on your syllabus, must align with [the university's] overall policy, and must be enforceable. [The student health center] does not provide absence notes, but if a student must be hospitalized or must return home for medical reasons you will be notified by the Office of the Dean of Students." This policy document offers instructors a great deal of freedom in determining attendance policies as long as they do not violate larger university policies. In this way, the instructor is positioned professionally as a person with agency and choice. Yet, even in these more permissive policy statements, we saw the imposition of university policies and a need for a writing program to adhere to these policies. That is, policy documents can never be fully permissive, since writing programs function as a small part of a larger university and thus operate under and are constrained by the university's own policies.

REFLECTIONS

We undertook this content analysis to more clearly understand the ways that policy documents work within writing programs. In part, this was personal, as we wanted to more deeply understand the ways that policy documents work so that we could understand how the instructors in our own program negotiate the program policies they are required to include in their syllabi. We knew this negotiation was happening, but we did not have the analytical framework to account for and make transparent the tensions that exist in policy documents and necessitate negotiation. Despite our study's limitations—our sample was relatively small, the schools were mainly R1 institutions, and we pulled from public materials rather than solicited documents—our analysis provides potential insight into how this negotiating work occurs.

What struck us most in our analysis was the complexity of the balancing act that policy documents perform. That is, the work of balancing competing programmatic, instructor, student, and institutional interests and values was present in all of the documents in our sample. As we note in our discussion, there are varying values, audiences, and degrees of permissiveness that come into play as programs work to balance the needs and expectations of stakeholders. Yet, when language was unable to account for the full range of behaviors that may emerge in the classroom environment, documents tended to simplify in an authoritarian way.

The idea of simplification, though, contrasted with our observation of how different policies rhetorically bleed (Edbauer 2005). For example, a program might offer a simple and authoritative description of academic integrity, using plagiarism as its focus, and then in another section describe appropriate behaviors in the classroom that either explicitly discuss academic integrity or imply such behaviors' relation to academic integrity. While this bleeding is likely more representative of the complexity of program policies, it brings about tensions that can be confusing for users, especially new instructors and students trying to find their way in the first-year course. We see such bleeding as a more accurate view of the nature of program administration work, and we see an opportunity to make the prevalence of rhetorical bleeding transparent to instructors and students as an inherent part of the work of writing.

To promote transparency, we encourage program administrators to view policy documents as an opportunity space for modeling how pedagogical genres generate tensions for varied audiences—instructors, students, administrators, etc. As Porter et al. (2000) and, more recently, Nicolas (2017) note, writing programs have the power to harness the rhetorical power of what they create. In his chapter on the genre of outcomes statements (in this collection), Logan Bearden demonstrates how revising outcomes statements can positively transform a program's culture. This too is true for policy documents, as they generate rhetorical power that often is occluded by their administrative function. Program administrators have the opportunity to rewrite their programmatic policies in ways that enable instructors and students to see and understand the constitutive, rhetorical work these documents do. Recent writing program administration scholarship drawing from disability theory offers program administrators a useful starting point for broadening the rhetorical capacity of policy documents and thinking beyond the constraints of administrative documentation. As we note above, rhetorical genres in policy documents bleed. If programs work to make this bleeding transparent, policy documents can be more than administrative rules that require compliance.

We see a pedagogical opportunity here as well. Since many first-year writing syllabi require rhetorical analysis, we see an opportunity to use the findings of this study in a pedagogical exercise in which students rhetorically analyze the required policies in their syllabi to identify ways that student and instructor identity are constructed via required policies. This exercise offers instructors and students an opportunity to analyze and discuss the ways that rhetorical genres bleed. Further, this student-centered exercise would help students to understand that policy documents are more than simply "the rules," they are documents that reflect a program's values, practices, and position within the larger university.

Creating space for programmatic discussions about policy documents that more clearly address the ways to account for instructor and student identity and its potential construction in program policies is a sometimes missed yet readily available opportunity for program administrators. We see opportunities for programmatic discussion on policy documents to promote awareness of how competing voices (e.g., the range of voice we discussed), create some dissonance for readers in their decision-making about how to adapt their behavior and ultimate production of writing for the class. We noted that policies with more authoritative and permissive voices offered space for instructors to construct and reflect their identities in their policies. This is an important affordance, yet it is one that is not readily available or seen as accessible, especially to new instructors.

Together, these suggestions offer preliminary ways for programs to more clearly address the tensions that arise in policy documents as they seek to articulate a program's values, goals, and practices while simultaneously accounting for instructor and student needs, practices, and identities. Furthermore, if instructors and students can see policy documents as rhetorical documents rather than simply a set of rules, they can ask more than "Am I covered?" Instead, they can ask, how do these policies participate in the construction of their identity and what does that mean in the first-year course?

REFERENCES

Baecker, Diann L. 1998. "Uncovering the Rhetoric of the Syllabus: The Case of the Missing *I.*" *College Teaching* 46 (2): 58–62.

Bawarshi, Anis. 2003. *Genre and the Invention of the Writer: Reconsidering the Place of Invention in Composition.* Logan: Utah State University Press.

Bazerman, Charles. 1994. "Systems of Genres and the Enactment of Social Intentions." In *Genre and the New Rhetoric,* edited by Aviva Freedman and Peter Medway, 67–85. Bristol, PA: Taylor & Francis.

Conference on College Composition & Communication (CCCC). 2018. "Writing Program Certificate of Excellence." National Council of Teachers of English. https://cccc.ncte .org/cccc/awards/writingprogramcert.

Chism, Nancy Van Note. 1998. "Developing a Philosophy of Teaching Statement." *Essays on Teaching Excellence: Toward the Best in the Academy* 9 (3): 1–2.

Clark, Irene. 2005. "A Genre Approach to Writing Assignments." *Composition Forum* 14 (2). http://compositionforum.com/issue/14.2/clark-genre-writing.php.

Devitt, Amy J. 2004. *Writing Genres.* Carbondale: Southern Illinois University Press.

Eberly, Mary B., Sarah E. Newton, and Robert A. Wiggins. 2001. "The Syllabus as a Tool for Student-Centered Learning." *The Journal of General Education* 50 (1): 56–74.

Edbauer, Jenny. 2005. "Unframing Models of Public Distribution: From Rhetorical Situation to Rhetorical Ecologies." *Rhetoric Society Quarterly* 35 (4): 5–24.

Endres, William. 2006. "Communicative Strategies for Administrative Practices: Evaluating Weblogs, Their Benefits, and Uses." *WPA: Writing Program Administration* 29 (3): 85–106.

Fedukovich, Casie J., and Tracy Ann Morse. 2017. "Failures to Accommodate: GTA Preparation as a Site for a Transformative Culture of Access." *WPA: Writing Program Administration* 40 (3): 39–60.

Fink, Susan B. 2012. "The Many Purposes of Course Syllabi: Which Are Essential and Useful?" *Syllabus* 1 (1): 1–12.

Gallagher, Chris W. 2019. "Standardization, Democratization, and Writing Programs." *College Composition and Communication* 70 (3): 476–507.

Hannah, Mark A., and Christina Saidy. 2014. "Locating the Terms of Engagement: Shared Language Development in Secondary to Postsecondary Writing Transitions." *College Composition and Communication* 66 (1): 120–44.

Hsieh, Hsiu-Fang, and Sarah E. Shannon. 2005. "Three Approaches to Qualitative Content Analysis." *Qualitative Health Research* 15 (9): 1277–88.

Huckin, Thomas. 2003. "Content Analysis: What Texts Talk About." In *What Writing Does and How It Does It: An Introduction to Analyzing Texts and Textual Practices*, edited by Charles Bazerman and Paul Prior, 19–38. New York: Routledge.

Neaderhiser, Stephen. 2016. "Conceiving of a Teacherly Identity: Metaphors of Composition in Teaching Statements." *Pedagogy* 16 (3): 413–43.

Nicolas, Melissa. 2017. "Ma(r)king a Difference: Challenging Ableist Assumptions in Writing Program Policies." *WPA: Writing Program Administration* 40 (3): 10–22.

Oswal, Sushil K., and Lisa Meloncon. 2017. "Saying No to the Checklist: Shifting from an Ideology of Normalcy to an Ideology of Inclusion in Online Writing Instruction." *WPA: Writing Program Administration* 40 (3): 61–77.

Porter, James E., Patricia Sullivan, Stuart Blythe, Jeffrey T. Grabill, and Libby Miles. 2000. "Institutional Critique: A Rhetorical Methodology for Change." *College Composition and Communication* 51 (4): 610–42.

Reynolds, Nedra. 1995. "Dusting off Instructor's Manuals: The Teachers and Practices They Assume." *WPA: Writing Program Administration* 19 (1/2): 7–23.

Rose, Shirley K., Lisa S. Mastrangelo, and Barbara L'Eplattenier. 2013. "Directing First-Year Writing: The New Limits of Authority." *College Composition and Communication* 65 (1): 43–66.

Shea, Kelly A. 2017. "Kindness in the Writing Classroom: Accommodations for All Students." *WPA: Writing Program Administration* 40 (3): 78–93.

Smith, Summer. 1997. "The Genre of the End Comment: Conventions in Teacher Responses to Student Writing." *College Composition and Communication* 48 (2): 249–68.

Vidali, Amy. 2015. "Disabling Writing Program Administration." *WPA: Writing Program Administration* 38 (2): 32–55.

Yergeau, M. Remi. 2016. "Creating a Culture of Access in Writing Program Administration." *WPA: Writing Program Administration* 40 (1): 155–65.

9

RECOMMENDATION, REQUIREMENT, AND REPRODUCTION
Sanctioned Uptake in Classroom Accessibility Statements

Matt Dowell

I write this chapter as a writing program administrator (WPA) who writes or (more often) interprets policy statements to be used and followed by the many instructors within my university's first-year writing program. Simultaneously, I write as an instructor who is sometimes (likely often) suspicious of the work policy statements can (or are meant to) do, particularly those originating from contexts outside of my pedagogical planning. I also write as a disabled instructor and administrator informed by Nicolas's (2017) call to create classroom policies and practices that resist impulses to "fix difference" by privileging the "normate" student body (16), as well as Vidali's (2015) call to "disable" the administrative work of writing programs by "knowingly and innovatively thinking through and with disability, particularly in terms of the stories we tell about ourselves" (33). Due to these overlapping, conflicting subject positions, I've become very conscious of what is made explicit and what remains occluded in institutional policy statements, especially when it comes to statements addressing classroom accessibility and the actions they invite. This chapter represents an opportunity for me to interrogate the sanction of such statements. Additionally, I want to consider how the endorsement of required or recommended policy statements by program administrators might reify the very sanction imposed upon—or granted to—instructors as they take up those policies within their own pedagogical documents.

When starting a new class, a teacher might learn that a student "needs" classroom accommodations when the student presents paperwork from the campus disability/accessibility office, accompanied by the words, "I have a disability form for you," or even just, "I was told to give you this." This moment is often anticipated by a statement in the instructor's syllabus announcing the university's policy-driven process

https://doi.org/10.7330/9781646422920.c009

for procuring classroom accommodations. Much like how the syllabus acts as a meta-genre "carry[ing] out the mandate" of regulating the flow of information into and out of the classroom (Bazerman 1994, 60), a policy statement like the accessibility statement exists in superposition: it reflects the university's legal obligation to provide accommodations, while also articulating the social actions to be taken up by students and instructors in order to establish a need for accommodations (from students) and a commitment to fulfill those accommodations (from instructors).

Within a syllabus, the classroom accessibility statement[1] acts as a variable prompting tool. Some students reading the statement will be informed to initiate a relationship with the campus office that approves accommodations; others will be reminded to provide their teacher with previously acquired paperwork; and still others may be prompted to check on the status of a pending request. In any case, the classroom accessibility statement is typically considered to exist primarily for the benefit of students—not only as the audience but also as actors performing an expected uptake action outside of the classroom to secure approval for accommodations, thereby enabling them to fully engage the class. However, the statement's ability to prompt that uptake is dependent on the instructor's inclusion of the statement within their syllabus, an action often mandated by universities, departments, or programs.

The inclusion of the accessibility statement within a syllabus highlights an uptake not typically acknowledged within the genre of policy statements, one which instructors are expected to perform as they integrate institutional policies into their own classroom genres. Given how educational accessibility is normatively situated around students acquiring approval for accommodations they need (and are legally entitled to), the instructor seems to occupy a minor role in the university-established process for *securing* accommodations—that their primary role is instead after the fact, in *providing* accommodations once the process has concluded. But, when viewed as an example of how policy statements operate as part of an instructor's extended pedagogical genre system, the accessibility statement represents a rhetorical moment that enables, endorses, or restricts specific social actions, thus leading to questions about the expected role instructors are to take in generating, distributing, and acting upon (and within)

1. These policies frequently have titles highlighting accommodation or disability. I use the term *classroom accessibility statement* to instead privilege the circulation of language that more broadly acknowledges *access*.

such statements. I qualify this rhetorical uptake as being sanctioned due to the inherent tensions within the word's dual meaning, indicating not only what is required or mandated, but also what is allowed or permitted.

Uncovering the embedded uptakes within classroom accessibility statements can help identify the social actions that institutional policies—even beyond disability/accessibility—privilege, limit, or allow. Additionally, such an analysis reveals how classroom instructors are included in—or excluded from—the sanctioned uptakes in recommended or required statements. The occluded authorship of many policies, along with explicit or implied requirements to use particular statements or language, often invites a faculty uptake that adheres to institutional expectations that may differ from their own pedagogical values. As I demonstrate in this chapter, instructors may be incorporating accessibility statements into their syllabi that both name and erase the social actions they have agency to commit, without authorial control over the policy's content or language. Exposing how instructors are ventriloquized in or, worse, erased from institutional policy statements offers one avenue through which instructors and program administrators can ask questions about these statements and advocate for faculty in designing and facilitating classroom accessibility, including through the authorship of syllabus statements.

To investigate the classroom accessibility statement as a genred example of institutional policy statements, and to examine the uptakes sanctioned by the genre, I coded and analyzed the speech acts within a modest corpus of public-facing accessibility statements. Additionally, I analyzed the framing language of the headings and discursive text surrounding the statements within faculty support resources. I wanted to understand the social actions invited and obscured by those statements, as well as how instructors were made present within the statements. I offer in my findings what I see as the sanctioned faculty uptake of the classroom accessibility statement, as well as the implications not only for classroom teachers but also for department or program administrators compelled by a managerial imperative that informs and influences the uptake they might sanction for instructors under their purview.

ACCOMMODATION, COERCION, AND MANAGEMENT VIA POLICY STATEMENTS

In recent years, scholars have brought disability to the forefront of writing studies, critiquing classroom inaccessibility (Dolmage 2017; Price

2011) but also offering strategies for dis-abling policy creation and curricular design (Garrett 2018; Womack 2017). Oswal and Meloncon (2017), for example, show how uncritical reliance on rubrics for online teaching accessibility ultimately results in an "ideology of normalcy" (64). Wood et al. (2014) similarly argue that classroom accessibility is often viewed reductively through a checklist approach that characterizes disability as "something that must be fixed or accommodated minimally" (147). The critique of the continued centering of able-bodiedness in writing classrooms has also been extended to question the exclusion of disability from writing program administration (Vidali 2015; Yergeau 2016). What scholarship has shown is that shortcuts toward accessible classroom design, as is often prioritized in university disability/accessibility policies, still position disability as a deficit and accommodations as deviations from ideal classroom conditions and practices.

Policy statements function by carrying the weight of a formal, *organizational* endorsement: "An official statement, adopted by organizational leadership, that guides organizational practice" (Gallagher 2019, 398). As a genre, policies can appear as self-contained documents (as Hannah and Saidy explore in this collection), but they also proliferate through other formal genres in different academic contexts, including teaching handbooks, syllabi of record, and course proposal protocols (exemplified in this collection by Comi, Stolley and Toth, and Pengilly), as well as informal genres like syllabus checklists or departmental email reminders. Such proliferation shows policy statements as performing within a fairly "meta-generically rich atmosphere" (Giltrow 2002, 197).

Of those policies, Vidali (2011) cites statements on plagiarism and disability as the most common syllabus policies to carry the weight of organizational endorsement, both of which she characterizes as "anxious attempts to contain and control their ambiguity and indeterminacy" (254). In the case of disability accommodations, statements typically declare a university's legally mandated adherence to a process for ensuring equal access to educational opportunities "without compromising quality or content" (Rocco and Collins 2017, 328). The "legal or legal-like language" (Vidali 2011, 261) in policy phrases like "accommodations are not retroactive" and "students must first disclose their need for accommodations" emphasizes how these policies respond to requirements in Section 504 of the Rehabilitation Act, the Americans with Disabilities Act, and the ADA Amendments Act (Rocco and Collins 2017). Given how policies emphasize legal compliance, it comes as little surprise when I, as a WPA, am asked by instructors if a particular accommodation is reasonable or even allowed, what they *must* do if a student notifies them of accommodation needs later in the semester, or whether they can provide accommodations even if a student hasn't supplied documentation. Reminiscent of the anxiety Vidali identifies in policy efforts to control the ambiguity of disability, instructors experience their own anxiety related to the actions they are sanctioned, empowered, or even coerced to perform, based on the dicta outlining what they are expected to include in their syllabi.

Bawarshi (2003) characterizes the syllabus genre as coercive, at least in the way that all genres are coercive:

> It establishes the situated rules for conduct students and teacher will be expected to meet, including penalties for disobeying them. But even more than that, the syllabus also establishes a set of social roles and subjectivities that student and teacher have available to them in the course. (120)

These "social roles and subjectivities" result, in part, from the uptake of the syllabus, as performed by students and teachers. As Freadman (2002) explains, social action isn't exclusively found in the intended result or response to a genre, but instead begins with the "taking of an object": "[a] step in which our uptake selects, defines, or represents its object" (48). For accessibility statements, the "taking of an object" in question exposes a tension between competing uptakes: the statement's content articulates the process students must "take up" in order to receive accommodations, but also concretizes the role instructors have as part of that process. However, even before the statement can establish the subjectivities available to students or teachers *within* the classroom, the interinstitutional circulation of accessibility policies informs instructors of what sanctions are in place, dictating how they are expected to take up (i.e., *include*) the policy within their *syllabi*.

Sanctioned uptake addresses the relationship between a policy's institutional purpose of initiating a process compliant with legal requirements, and the framing language used in the circulation and advisement on how a syllabus statement should be published by instructors—language that informs the taking up of not just the presented policy but also the larger enforced institutional contexts within which an instructor operates. According to Dryer's (2016) work to disambiguate uptake, the accessibility statement as I have positioned it operates as an "intermediary genre that facilitates the uptake of one genre by another" (65): it instigates the social action of connecting students who need accommodations with the office that authorizes such accommodations, thereby staging an uptake that produces documentation *for* accommodations. However, that is only part of the uptake activity within accessibility statements. Dryer separates the notions of *uptake affordances*, which focus on the "conventions that precede and shape the encounter," and *uptake enactments*, which involve an act of "deliberate repurposing of" a text "in response to uptake affordances" (65). These separated notions apply to the accessibility statement, which not only establishes uptake for students—generating the required accommodations paperwork—but also presents uptake expectations for instructors, especially when connected to the framing language qualifying how instructors should deploy the statement. Capturing that language, found in the meta-generic atmosphere of faculty resources like teaching handbooks and best-practices guides, offers opportunities to analyze how instructors are required, recommended, or encouraged to employ institutionally created accessibility statements within their own syllabi. Meloncon (2018), for example, warns that incorporating "strongly encourage[d]" and "highly recommend[ed]" policies into one's syllabus reifies institutional norms of inclusion that move accessibility *away* from the forefront of the classroom (42). Framing language highlights the uptake enactments available to instructors: what possibilities for deliberate repurposing exist when instructors take up both the generic conventions common to accessibility statements and the directives given for how those statements should be used.

As a final point, faculty uptake can be complicated by administrative intercessions made within institutional employment hierarchies. Faculty administrators like WPAs often face a managerial imperative that undergirds much of the work they are expected to do (Strickland 2011, 3), including engaging with policies that impact the classrooms and instructors they manage. This managerial imperative can produce tension for WPAs, however, since many are also classroom teachers themselves. As Leverenz (2002) argues, a WPA's personal policy decisions "might not be appropriate as requirements for all teachers in the program [they] supervise" (105). Similarly, Nicolas (2017) acknowledges this tension, admitting that although "cripping" (discarding) ableist policies might help individual teachers "avoid fixating on difference in their own syllabi," there could be "scaling up" challenges if that were mandated program-wide (18). Calling to mind Bazerman's reminder of how institutional genres regulate classrooms, Bawarshi's assertion that all genres are coercive, and Vidali's argument about how policies attempt to control the ambiguity of disability, the tension between managerial control and pedagogical autonomy weighs on the decision-making processes of program administrators and the actions they might sanction for the instructors they oversee.

METHODOLOGY

In order to analyze sanctioned faculty uptake within accessibility statements, I employed a purposeful sampling methodology (Patton 2015) that prioritizes a small homogeneous sample—in this case, a set of accessibility policy statements from twelve universities, including my own, considered to be institutional performance peers: public, comprehensive universities with comparable diversity in student populations, course offerings, and academic activity.[2] Using the public data method demonstrated by Emily Isaacs and Melinda Knight (Isaacs and Knight 2014; Isaacs 2018), I collected the statements from online sources hosted by the universities, such as faculty resource pages, university policy registers, teaching and learning centers, offices of academic affairs, offices of disability services, and, in one case, an office of legal affairs.

My data collection focused on four aspects of the larger activity systems within which these statements existed: the text of the statement itself, the title of the statement and/or webpage hosting it, any explanatory or framing language immediately surrounding the statement, and the institutional office or resource hosting the statement. I located the policies through keyword searches for language commonly linked to accessibility statements (such as "accommodations," "disability," or "American Disabilities Act"), and I recorded every instance where a university's accessibility statement was published through formal channels (such as those described above).[3] Even though identifying *every* instance may seem unnecessary, I did so not only to account for the locations housing the statement but also to establish the statement's (re)production across multiple locations—or the production of *different* language across those locations.

Rather than locating twelve accessibility statements (one for each university), my collection resulted in twenty uniquely distinct policy statements across the twelve institutions. For six of the universities, including my own, I found multiple notably different statements demonstrating no awareness or acknowledgment that other versions of the statement existed at other locations. In most of those cases, one statement was hosted through an office of academic affairs (such as a provost's office), and the other by the campus office in charge of accommodations. For the purpose of creating a coded corpus, I privileged the statement most explicitly connected to each university's office for disability or

2. As reported by my university's Office of Institutional Research.

3. I did not include individual class syllabi in my collection, as I was primarily interested in how these statements were initially presented for *faculty* uptake, with directives or expectations targeted at instructors themselves.

accommodations support—either by way of being hosted by that office or by the presence of referential links showing the statement as being endorsed by the office. I did, however, take those multiple locations into account when coding the framing language that accompanied the policy statements.

Coding and Content Analysis

I conducted a qualitative, inductive conceptual content analysis (Huckin 2003) by coding the individual statements for speech acts related to disability, accommodation, accessibility, and the actors involved therein (students, faculty, offices, or institutions). I first coded for locutionary acts—explicit declarative statements announcing the university's commitment to provide accommodations, prescriptive statements specifying a student's necessary actions, or informative statements identifying the location or contact details for the accommodations office. Then, through the discovery of related acts, I created additional categories of illocutionary acts—those intended to be interpreted more subjectively, such as conditional statements qualifying student eligibility, or descriptive statements projecting a student's rationale for taking action or seeking to understand the accommodation process. I ultimately established fourteen speech acts occurring at varying levels of frequency across the twelve accessibility statements.

Considering Meloncon's (2018) warning to faculty regarding university policies qualified by descriptors like "strongly encouraged" or "highly recommended," I was also interested in any phrasing expressing—explicitly or implicitly—how faculty are expected to share the statements with students. Accordingly, I analyzed the language that accompanied the statements, in thirty-one official locations across the twelve universities. These locations represent a variety of genres within the broader academic genre ecosystem, including departmental handbooks, best-practice guides, reference pages, and disability support resources. Nearly all of these locations provided framing language contextualizing, explaining, or mandating how faculty should take up the policy statements within their own classroom syllabi.

I qualified framing language as a variety of textual forms, including webpage/section headings (like Recommended Accessibility Statement), as well as discursive text (like introductory explanations, callout text, or bullet points) describing how (or why) faculty should employ the statements. I coded the framing language using a grounded theory approach (Charmaz 2006), beginning with common phrases and terms, like *required* or *sample*, as well as verb forms emphasizing

varying degrees of what *must*, *should*, or even *can* be done. I then refined
the categories through a second round of coding to account for more
implicit interpretation, such as differentiations between an imperative
given with direct references ("include *this statement* on your syllabus,"
mandating the specific use of "*this statement*") and an expectation given
with implied compliance ("use *a statement* on your syllabus," assuming
"*a statement*" to be similar to a provided sample). Ultimately, I established four different coded categories: Explicit Directive (emphasizing
required use), Implied Expectation (inferring assumed compliance),
Presumptive Recommendation (offering approved suggestions or examples), and Permissive Option (allowing individual faculty choices).[4]

While the coded speech acts from the accessibility statements narrowly define instructors' roles in—or exclusion from—the accommodation process, the framing language presents a more conflicted
portrayal of the agency afforded to instructors seeking to integrate the
policy statement into their own pedagogical materials. In the following
sections, I explore how my findings demonstrate options for faculty
uptake as articulated (or proscribed) within the statements themselves,
as well as the sanctioning of faculty uptake as expressed within the
framing language accompanying those statements through faculty-
facing resources.

FACULTY UPTAKE WITHIN ACCESSIBILITY STATEMENTS

The statements largely erase instructors from the matter of accommodation, instead inviting an uptake requiring students to move outside
the classroom to gain accommodations *for* the classroom, through a
process that only includes instructors as part of the foregone conclusion
that accommodations will be provided as long as students follow the
proper channels. As table 9.1 indicates, the most common speech acts
focus on key information a student needs to know in order to pursue
accommodations: articulations of student eligibility and need as well as
specific identification and contact information for the office authorized
to confer accommodation approval.

Even the most minimal of the collected statements included this
information, as seen in the following full statement:

> [University 1] is committed to providing an inclusive experience, acces-
> sible learning environments and equal opportunity to individuals with
> disabilities in accordance with the Americans with Disabilities Act of

---

4. Given the subjective nature of this type of coding, a second coder analyzed the corpus for intercoder reliability, with 85 percent agreement.

Table 9.1. Speech acts appearing within university accommodations statements

Speech Act	Statement Type	Count (n=12)
University commitment to or provision of accessibility	Declarative	9
Establishment of student eligibility	Conditional	12
Establishment of student need	Conditional	11
Reference to applicable laws or policy	Declarative	4
Necessary student action (at accommodations office)	Prescriptive	8
Identification of accommodations office	Informative	11
Rationale for contacting accommodations office	Descriptive	6
Necessary student action (with instructor)	Prescriptive	6
Rationale for engaging with instructor	Descriptive	4
Details about accommodation process	Descriptive	3
Details about how accommodations operate	Descriptive	3
Directive for acquiring more information	Conditional	6
Location of accommodations office	Informative	6
Contact information for accommodations office	Informative	11

1990, and Section 504 of the Rehabilitation Act of 1973. Individuals needing reasonable accommodations should contact the Office of Disability Resources ([phone number] or [URL]).[5]

The expected purpose of facilitating student uptake is thus established: a student self-identifying as an individual with disabilities eligible for reasonable accommodation is invited to contact the specific office and initiate the accommodation process.

This statement, however, does more than just invite student uptake: it also references the laws governing the university's compliance, explicitly citing the ADA and Rehabilitation Act. This inclusion reflects what Wood and Madden (2013) characterize as "meeting legal obligations," confirming that the accommodation process satisfies "minimum legal or institutional requirements to provide [students] with access to learning." It also reinforces the statement's conditional qualification of "reasonable accommodations" as contingent upon that legal compliance, echoing Nicolas's (2017) description of accommodation processes as being "steeped in biomedical authorization," placing student need secondary to "meeting legal standards and medical definitions of disability" as established by "some sort of institutional authority" (14). Only five

---

5. Although these statements are public documents, administrative details are not permanent. Therefore, I have redacted contact information subject to change.

statements included direct citation of legal compliance, but the broader corpus's use of conditional and prescriptive phrases to qualify student uptake demonstrated that emphasis on institutional authority. These acts ranged from saying very little about accommodations beyond the directive to "contact the Office of Disability Services," to using legal-like language to describe student requirements, such as "must self-disclose and initiate the request" or "must be registered and provide official documentation." When these directives were given, they almost exclusively focused on student interaction with the accommodations office, external of the classroom—and the instructor.

Given that accessibility policies are largely established at institutional levels (as reflected in the legal or formalistic language), the policy statements not only invite students to a certain uptake but also inform instructors of how they are expected to take up the action of fulfilling university policy—even if their uptake is not explicitly articulated within the statements. Classroom instructors were directly referenced in nine statements, but those references fall into three distinct categories, with faculty interpolated as (1) part of an institutional collective, (2) the final stage of the accommodation process, or (3) in cooperative interaction with students.

In the first category, two statements invoked faculty as members of a larger university collective committed to accessibility, stating how "faculty and staff partner with [the office] in the implementation of accommodations," or how "responsibility for disability-related accommodations and access is shared by [the office] and faculty." In both instances, faculty's uptake actions are folded into those of the overall university: the "taking of an object" is simply the endorsement of the university's broadly expressed commitment to accessibility, an ambiguous action faculty share with the accommodations office. Notably, how instructors might perform that commitment is left unstated, whereas the accommodations office's uptake actions are explicitly outlined—not only in specific declarations but also in the prescriptive speech acts telling students they must "first contact" or "be registered with" the office. What is communicated to faculty is that they have a responsibility to follow the mandate of accommodation, but that their actions are subsumed by to the office's act of authorization.

Four statements did connect faculty more directly to a specific type of interaction with students, albeit a passive one wherein instructors are simply expected to *receive* information. In two statements, students are instructed to "send" or "present" their instructor with an accommodation letter, thus activating the instructor within the process—once the student has obtained the required documentation. The other two statements direct students to "inform the instructor during the first week of classes" of accommodation needs *before* contacting the accommodations office. In one case, the statement tells students to "notify me [the instructor] with a memo from [the accommodations office]," with the condition that "accommodations are not retroactive" and a recommendation that "you provide me with notification as early as possible in the term," before concluding by directing students to the office both "to register" and "if you have any questions about disability accommodations." This demonstrates how an instructor may exist within the policy statement only to the extent of being acknowledged as someone to be notified and *not* someone authorized to direct the accommodation process, provide accommodations as they see fit, or to answer questions about accommodations. Even when a statement directs students to notify their instructor of accommodation needs at the start of the term, it presents a logic wherein notification simply precedes the process of documenting disability, with the presumed conclusion of accommodations being provided, but still only after the instructor receives official documentation—an uptake in which they have no active role.

Finally, three statements positioned faculty in a cooperative relationship with students. In one statement, students—if they have a disability—are "encouraged to meet with me [the instructor] to discuss the accommodations outlined in the letter," which students should "send . . . as early as possible." Another statement similarly pairs the accommodations letter with a request to "meet with me as soon as possible" so the instructor can "support your successes in an informed way." A more curious (but telling) example is the third statement, which explicitly articulates that students must first "document their disabilities" through the accommodations office, and concludes by telling the student to "contact me if needed." There is no hint of what the instructor's uptake *will* be, should an "if needed" situation arise—simply that they should be contacted (much like the initial notification of an accommodations need). Perhaps it is assumed that the instructor already knows what to do in such situations, but even so, the statement offers no indication of that action. The reoccurring speech acts—not only in this example but broadly through the corpus—invite a student uptake positioning students in direct relationship with institutional processes of authorization, and a faculty uptake positioning instructors in a passive or perfunctory role merely due to their presence in the classroom.

FACULTY UPTAKE WITHIN FRAMING LANGUAGE

The typified genre of classroom accessibility statements places near-exclusive priority on student uptake; the uptake afforded to instructors is largely diminished or occluded. However, as Neaderhiser (2016) notes, the classroom isn't the only context within which a genre like the accessibility statement may appear. Students may view the statement as just part of the class syllabus, but that policy often predates any particular syllabus, published or circulated to faculty via other genres—along with language giving instructors a framework for understanding how the policy applies to them. It is within that framing language that I found the most active articulations of the sanctioned uptake available to faculty—not so much regarding their role *within* the accommodation process, but rather how they must, should, or might take up the statement during their own process of composing syllabi.

I found a broad variance in the framing language used on the thirty-one administrative webpages and faculty resources where the twelve universities' accessibility statements were introduced or described. As tables 9.2 and 9.3 show, this language included instances explicitly emphasizing a directive, through words like *required* or direct imperatives, as well as instances asserting more implicitly how instructors were "expected" to take up the statement, including cases where a "template" or "sample" was provided (thus implying that sample should still be *followed*). The language also included more subjectively qualified recommendations, where suggestions or "examples" were presented as "strongly encouraged" (but typically *only*) instructor choices. The final category (also the least common) marked "permissive" options that offered faculty some freedom to dictate their uptake enactments, through phrases indicating how instructors could "modify" or even "craft your own" statements.

Interestingly, one of my initial assumptions was that the four categories would represent a sort of sliding scale, with some schools showing heavy use of explicit directives and others having gradually less authoritarian implied, presumptive, or permissive approaches. However, my findings showed a more mixed use of categorical types within *each* university's framing language, with "required" or "expected" language co-occurring with more passive or permissive instances—sometimes even within a single sentence, such as one case stating that faculty should "copy and paste the following statements or craft your own." That sentence gives both an explicit directive ("copy and paste the following") and a permissive option ("craft your own"). Mixed messages like this appeared in nearly every location I analyzed, suggesting internal contradictions

Table 9.2. Framing language articulating faculty uptake: Section headings and titles

Type (# of instances)	Select Examples (n=23)
Explicit Directive (9)	"Sample Paragraph **to Include** on Class Syllabus" "[University]'s **Required** Elements" "**Use** a Syllabus Statement"
Implied Expectation (15)	"Statements **Common to All** Syllabi" "Course Syllabus **Template**" "**Sample** Disability Statements"
Presumptive Recommendation (10)	"General **Suggestions** for Teaching Students with Disabilities" "**Recommended** Course Syllabi/Website Statements" "**Tips** for Successful Syllabus Construction"

Table 9.3. Framing language articulating faculty uptake: Discursive text

Type (# of instances)	Select Examples (n=22)
Explicit Directive (10)	"At a minimum, your syllabus **must include** [the] Disability Accommodation statement" "The information on this page **is required**." "**Copy and paste the following statements**."
Implied Expectation (11)	"Please review these policies and **refer to them when needed**." "See the [learning center] **template**" "The **following syllabus statement may be used**"
Presumptive Recommendation (21)	"The [office] **recommends using the following text** on syllabi" "[University] **strongly encourages the inclusion** of a syllabus statement" "**An example of such a statement would be** . . ."
Permissive Option (8)	"Copy and paste the following statements **or craft your own**." "These guidelines **allow individual discretion** with regard to additional information which may be included." "Following are samples that **could be used [or] adapted** for your syllabus."

within the framing language regarding the level of uptake for (or by) which instructors are sanctioned.

In one of the more consistent genre ecologies I encountered, one university's accessibility policy was hosted in two locations: an Accessibility Resources page hosted by University Life, and the Center for Excellence in Teaching and Learning (CETL) site. On the Accessibility Resources page, the statement is preceded by the subtitle Sample Paragraph to Include on Class Syllabi, which is mirrored discursively in a description further down the page: "This page provides **a sample paragraph for professors to use** on their syllabus when communicating to students their willingness to provide equal access" (emphasis added). On the CETL site, the accessibility statement—as articulated—is likewise marked as compulsory. Under the heading What Information is Required? (duplicated in a subheading, What Information is Required to Be in a Course Syllabus?), a bullet point list is introduced by the phrase, "At a minimum, your syllabus must include the following elements," one of which is listed simply as "the institution's Disability Accommodation statement." The page links to a syllabus template providing "an example of required, recommended, and optional content for your syllabus." That document is where the actual Disability Accommodation statement is found, under a heading in red type reading, "**The information on this page is required.**" While the framing language from the Accessibility Resources and CETL pages is phrased differently, both sets make clear the instructor's sanctioned uptake, through language depicting the action of including the statement in their syllabi as being explicitly mandatory and emphatically required.

Given the obligatory nature of language such as "for professors to use," "to include," and "is required," the word *sample* appears rather out of place. If we imagine a sample to be representative of a larger collection (such as a corpus of classroom accommodations statements) then offering a single policy statement as a sample instructors *must* use seems to deviate from the point of calling it a sample in the first place. This is further established in cases where framing language presented faculty with permissive options in their uptake choices. In only eight instances, instructors were given sanction to choose their own path for their syllabus's accessibility statement (still, as long as they *did* include one), with phrases such as the following:

- "Copy and paste the following statements **or craft your own.**"
- "The following is a sample . . . which may be used **or modified to suit your course.**"
- "The following syllabus statement may be used as is by faculty **or varied to suit individual style.**"

In each instance, instructors are informed of two different sanctioned uptakes: either use the provided statement or make changes according to your own judgment (ranging from modifications to a completely different statement). What I find most interesting about this type of framing language is how it suggestively reframes the possibility of the policy statement, centered on the sanctioned faculty uptake. With the option to reject the singular sample in preference for one's own policy statement, the sanction shifts to a range of possibilities that may or may not invite the authorized or approved uptakes as written into the typified genre of the accessibility statement as traced in the previous section. The invitation to "craft your own" statement allows instructors to deviate from genre expectations, which could result in a separation from the generic boundaries of the policy statement. Such a deviation raises questions about what roles antecedent genres might play in constructing such a statement, assuming that instructors would draw on prior knowledge to compose—or, calling back to Dryer (2016), to *repurpose*—their statement.

The permissive option to craft, modify, or refashion the accessibility statement also sanctions a change in the statement's otherwise occluded authorship: the teacher-author would not be ventriloquized by the compulsory duplication of required or strongly encouraged language, but would instead be authoring the genre in their own voice. However, that is just one potential implication of having a more developed awareness of the sanctioned uptake invited by the accessibility statement genre.

THE IMPLICATIONS OF SANCTIONING FACULTY UPTAKE

The uptake affordances articulated within the statements I analyzed largely cast faculty as external to the process of accessibility—their narrowly defined role is simply *to accommodate* once a student's need *has been approved*. In examining motive and intention within genres, Bawarshi (2003) notes how the exigence of a genre's invited social action can become "so sedimented . . . , so ideologically naturalized" that we no longer realize the controlling ideologies that influence the genre and compel us to act. We don't pause, he argues, "to consider how or why we come to recognize a situation as requiring a certain action. We just act" (89). For institutional policy statements like the classroom accessibility statement, it is easy to dismiss them simply as boilerplate language we just have to include on syllabi, a formality with little influence on the faculty actions that actually support student accessibility. However, that statement comes encoded with institutional endorsements of ableist ideology that compel not only students but also instructors to act in ways that treat disability as something to be codified and institutionalized, authorized and managed outside of the classroom. Additionally, the framing language describing how faculty should address disability in their syllabi—and by extension the classroom itself—reinforces that sanction, explicitly and implicitly emphasizing the specific social actions instructors are expected to take up.

Before this project, I had only spent meaningful time with three accessibility statements: the one recommended in my graduate program's departmental teaching handbook, the one required at my first faculty job, and the one I use at my current institution, which is a combination of the university's "recommended" model and my own textual additions—something I felt comfortable doing as a WPA empowered to interpret and add to institutional policy. Yet, even given those modifications, I still feel conflicted, as both a disabled faculty member and administrator. As a teacher, I question including a policy that implicates me as endorsing an institutional model, knowing the hurdles and hardships students face when contemplating disability disclosure (Carroll-Miranda 2017), as well as the biomedical bias privileged by universities when defining and approving accommodations (Nicolas 2017). As a WPA, I advocate for accessible, inclusive course design and pedagogical practices, and yet I find myself uncertain of how to inform and shape programmatic policy, torn between knowing how the smooth operations promised by the "managerial imperative" (Strickland 2011) align with dominant ableist ideology in higher education (Dolmage 2017) and resisting authoring policy that ascribes responsibilities and actions to instructors within my program.

Given how the language framing accessibility statements often highlights "what is allowed and what is not," the sanction for faculty uptake can be seen as having a policing function, amplified by articulations that require, or recommend faculty choices. Hannah and Saidy (in this collection) come to similar conclusions in their identification of authoritarian and authoritative voices in broader policy documents. Much like the authority to approve accommodations for students, the university is positioned as having authority to approve and sanction uptake of the accessibility statement as part of individual instructors' syllabi—not only the authoritarian *power* to impose sanctions, but also the authoritative *genre knowledge* to ensure that required or recommended sample statements embody the rhetorical exigencies of institutional compliance *and* pedagogical accessibility. Even despite incongruities in how coercive the framing language might be—at times in direct conflict with language located at other institutional locations—the sanctioned actions available to faculty assume an uptake that reproduces the policy as authorized by the university.

For instructors, the most consequential implications of this analysis center on their ability to situate themselves within the sanctioned uptake of the statement. Wood and Madden (2013) offer suggested practices for composing accessibility statements, which include encouragements to "create your own disability statement (even if it's in addition to an official required statement)." Authoring an individual statement (or addendum to an institutional one), they argue, "allows you to position yourself rhetorically as an instructor" invested in creating inclusive spaces and providing individualized responses to students. They also cite multiple statements composed by various scholars in disability studies, such as Margaret Price, whose statement combines her university's official policy with her own additions. This example highlights a second important point related to my study: in order to understand both the sanctioned uptake instructors are expected to perform with policy statements and how those uptake enactments might be repurposed, it is vital to have access to a body of genre samples that count more than the single sample a university might offer—especially in more permissive instances where faculty are given sanction to craft or modify a statement to suit their individual pedagogy. Recommended and required statements preemptively prevent or deter faculty acquisition of such meta-knowledge by limiting the genre artifacts an instructor encounters. In fact, only one university in my study provided multiple examples in a single location for faculty to examine or choose from. My hope is that the data presented in this chapter can contribute to a broader genre awareness allowing instructors and WPAs to consider the uptakes sanctioned by both recommended (or required) and self-authored statements.

This study also underscores the fraught position of WPAs and other faculty administrators when authoring policies or circulating university-sanctioned ones. By endorsing recommended or required policies within departmental genres such as handbooks and syllabus checklists, WPAs can become aligned with the sanctioned processes articulated within those statements and, possibly worse, might enable further sanctioning of how instructors are inscribed *into* those statements. But, as Nicolas (2017) noted, composing a different programmatic policy presents scaling issues, further complicated by the inevitability that newly written policies will also ascribe values and responsibilities to instructors, many of whom are contingent and beholden to a WPA, within the employment hierarchy through which the managerial imperative functions.

For both WPAs and teachers, meta-generic knowledge of accessibility statements and the institutional framing language contextualizing them invites new uptakes of the genre, including the creation of new models. But my study also presses for a critical genre awareness of policy statements, for the same reason Devitt (2009) values teaching genre within the classroom: in order to invite "a conscious attention to genres and their potential influences on people and the ability to consider acting differently within genres" (347). Attention to the social actions faculty are expected to take up from university-sanctioned policy statements can facilitate conversations on the reasons, uses, and limitations of such statements. That attention to generic features and uptakes better situates instructors and WPAs—individually and collaboratively—to advocate for their own policy statements, especially when paired with knowledge about statements endorsed by experts in disabilities studies. Even when instructors and programs must use a required accessibility statement, critical awareness of the genre can only help instructors understand what affordances those statements privilege and how they may want to speak and act in response to such sanctions.

REFERENCES

Bawarshi, Anis. 2003. *Genre and the Invention of the Writer: Reconsidering the Place of Invention in Composition*. Logan: Utah State University Press.

Bazerman, Charles. 1994. *Constructing Experience*. Carbondale: Southern Illinois University Press.

Carroll-Miranda, Moira A. 2017. "Access to Higher Education Mediated by Acts of Self Disclosure." In *Negotiating Disability: Disclosure and Higher Education*, edited by Stephanie L. Kerschbaum, Laura T. Eisenman, and James M. Jones, 275–90. Ann Arbor: University of Michigan Press.

Charmaz, Kathy. 2006. *Constructing Grounded Theory: A Practical Guide through Qualitative Analysis*. Thousand Oaks, CA: SAGE.

Devitt, Amy J. 2009. "Teaching Critical Genre Awareness." In *Genre in a Changing World*, edited by Charles Bazerman, Adair Bonini, and Débora Figueiredo, 337–51. Fort Collins, CO: WAC Clearinghouse.

Dolmage, Jay Timothy. 2017. *Academic Ableism: Disability and Higher Education*. Ann Arbor: University of Michigan Press.

Dryer, Dylan B. 2016. "Disambiguating Uptake: Toward a Tactical Research Agenda on Citizens' Writing." In *Genre and the Performance of Publics*, edited by Mary Jo Reiff and Anis Bawarshi, 60–79. Logan: Utah State University Press.

Freadman, Anne. 2002. "Uptake." In *The Rhetoric and Ideology of Genre: Strategies for Stability and Change*, edited by Richard M. Coe, Lorelei Lingard, and Tatiana Teslenko, 39–53. Cresskill, NJ: Hampton Press.

Gallagher, Chris W. 2019. "Standardization, Democratization, and Writing Programs." *College Composition and Communication* 70 (3): 476–507.

Garrett, Bre. 2018. "Hacking the Curriculum, Disabling Composition Pedagogy: The Affordances of Writing Studio Design." *Composition Forum* 39. http://compositionforum.com/issue/39/hacking.php.

Giltrow, Janet. 2002. "Meta-Genre." In *The Rhetoric and Ideology of Genre: Strategies for Stability and Change*, edited by Richard M. Coe, Lorelei Lingard, and Tatiana Teslenko, 187–205. Cresskill, NJ: Hampton Press.

Huckin, Thomas. 2003. "Content Analysis: What Texts Talk About." In *What Writing Does and How It Does It: An Introduction to Analyzing Texts and Textual Practices*, edited by Charles Bazerman and Paul Prior, 19–38. New York: Routledge.

Isaacs, Emily. 2018. *Writing at the State U: Instruction and Administration at 106 Comprehensive Universities*. Logan: Utah State University Press.

Isaacs, Emily, and Melinda Knight. 2014. "A Bird's Eye View of Writing Centers: Institutional Infrastructure, Scope and Programmatic Issues, Reported Practices." *WPA: Writing Program Administration* 37 (2): 36–67.

Leverenz, Carrie Shively. 2002. "Theorizing Ethical Issues in Writing Program Administration." In *The Writing Program Administrator as Theorist: Making Knowledge Work*, edited by Shirley K. Rose and Irwin Weiser, 103–15. Portsmouth, NH: Boynton/Cook.

Meloncon, Lisa. 2018. "Orienting Access in Our Business and Professional Communication Classrooms." *Business and Professional Communication Quarterly* 81 (1): 34–51.

Neaderhiser, Stephen. 2016. "Hidden in Plain Sight: Occlusion in Pedagogical Genres." *Composition Forum* 33. http://www.compositionforum.com/issue/33/hidden.php.

Nicolas, Melissa. 2017. "Ma(r)king a Difference: Challenging Ableist Assumptions in Writing Program Policies." *WPA: Writing Program Administration* 40 (3): 10–22.

Oswal, Sushil K., and Lisa Meloncon. 2017. "Saying No to the Checklist: Shifting from an Ideology of Normalcy to an Ideology of Inclusion in Online Writing Instruction." *WPA: Writing Program Administration* 40 (3): 61–77.

Patton, Michael Quinn. 2015. *Qualitative Research and Evaluation Methods: Integrating Theory and Practice.* 4th ed. Thousand Oaks, CA: SAGE Publications.

Price, Margaret. 2011. *Mad at School: Rhetorics of Mental Disability and Academic Life.* Ann Arbor: University of Michigan Press.

Rocco, Tonette S., and Joshua C. Collins. 2017. "An Initial Model for Accommodation Communication between Students with Disabilities and Faculty." *In Negotiating Disability: Disclosure and Higher Education,* edited by Stephanie L. Kerschbaum, Laura T. Eisenman, and James M. Jones, 327–44. Ann Arbor: University of Michigan Press.

Strickland, Donna. 2011. *The Managerial Unconscious in the History of Composition Studies.* Carbondale: Southern Illinois University Press.

Vidali, Amy. 2011. "Embodying/Disabling Plagiarism." *JAC* 31 (1/2): 248–66.

Vidali, Amy. 2015. "Disabling Writing Program Administration." *WPA: Writing Program Administration* 38 (2): 32–55.

Womack, Anne-Marie. 2017. "Teaching Is Accommodation: Universally Designing Composition Classrooms and Syllabi." *College Composition and Communication* 68 (3): 494–525.

Wood, Tara, Jay Dolmage, Margaret Price, and Cynthia Lewiecki-Wilson. 2014. "Moving beyond Disability 2.0 in Composition Studies." *Composition Studies* 42 (2): 147–50.

Wood, Tara, and Shannon Madden. 2013. "Suggested Practices for Syllabus Accessibility Statements." *Kairos: Rhetoric, Technology, and Pedagogy* 18 (1). http://praxis.technorhetoric.net/tiki-index.php?page=Suggested_Practices_for_Syllabus_Accessibility_Statements.

Yergeau, M. Remi. 2016. "Creating a Culture of Access in Writing Program Administration." *WPA: Writing Program Administration* 40 (1): 155–65.

10

WRITTEN IN HOMELY DISCOURSE
A Case Study of Intellectual and Institutional Identity in Teaching Genres

Megan Schoen, Jim Nugent, Cindy Mooty, and Lori Ostergaard

In "Genre as Social Action," Carolyn Miller (1984) advocated for a more expansive rhetorical study of genre, including "such homely discourse as the letter of recommendation, the user manual, the progress report, the ransom note, the lecture, and the white paper" (155). This broad view of genre, Miller claimed, would not diminish genre study, but would instead affirm the serious critical attention given to "the rhetoric in which we are immersed and the situations in which we find ourselves." (155). That serious attention has been exemplified in analyses of academic genres, such as John Swales's (1996) exploration of the discourse of research-based academic genres. There, he argued that documents such as manuscript submission letters, while typically occluded by the larger, more public genres they functionally support, such as books and articles, are worthy of study in their own right.

While Swales focused on occluded academic genres that support faculty scholarship, Stephen Neaderhiser (2016a; 2016b) noted that Swales's concept of occlusion could also be applied to pedagogical genres such as teaching statements, syllabi, and assignment descriptions. Neaderhiser contended that these documents are also worthy of study as occluded genres, even as they are in some ways more conspicuous than the research-based genres Swales described. He argued that academics might resist understanding teaching genres like syllabi as occluded because these documents are visible both in the classroom and in scholarship about how to write them effectively; however, he argued, the purposes for which syllabi are used by and for other audiences outside the classroom remain fairly obscure and undertheorized (2016b). In calling for a different kind of attention to such genres, Neaderhiser joined a small number of other scholars who have treated pedagogical genres as subjects for serious inquiry, including scholars examining the genres of

https://doi.org/10.7330/9781646422920.c010

teacher end comments (Smith 1997), teacher reflections (Dryer 2012), and writing assignment descriptions (Melzer 2009).

In this chapter, we turn our critical attention to the "homely discourse" and occluded genres of syllabi and assignment descriptions within Oakland University's first-year writing program during the 2010 and 2017 academic years. These years encompass an important era of evolution for OU's department of writing and rhetoric, an independent department that was created in 2008 and needed to move quickly to forge its institutional and intellectual identity. In this study, we seek to describe our collective identity formation by performing computer-aided textual analysis of the "homely" pedagogical genres of FYW syllabi and assignment descriptions from the 2010 and 2017 academic years and by performing interviews with 13 program instructors. We identify how certain processes in the evolution of our program—processes that we describe as waves—were enacted as classroom genres. In doing so, we hope to avoid chronicling our department's emergence in the familiar form of an administration-centric historiographic narrative, but rather to provide an account of its dynamic and recursive evolution as an "ecology of genres" (Spinnuzi 2003).

INSTITUTIONAL CONTEXT

Founded in 1957, Oakland University (OU) is an R2 state university located twenty-five miles north of Detroit and home to almost sixteen thousand undergraduate students. In OU's relatively short history, first-year writing (FYW) has never been affiliated with the discipline of English; the program was housed at various times in the departments of learning skills; rhetoric; and then rhetoric, communication, and journalism, before moving into a newly created department of writing and rhetoric in 2008 (Chong and Nugent 2015; Ostergaard and Giberson 2010). Concurrently, a new major in writing and rhetoric was created, which included tracks in professional writing, writing for digital media, and writing studies. Many new faculty members were hired and contributed to a newfound sense of excitement and possibility in the young department.

OU's FYW program comprises five courses: WRT 1040: Critical Thinking and Reading, WRT 1000: Supervised Study, WRT 1020: Basic Writing, WRT 1050: Composition I, and WRT 1060: Composition II. During the first two years of the department's existence, the program was without a writing program administrator (WPA) and oversight of the program was assumed by the department chair and junior faculty. In the 2010 academic year, the department assessed WRT 1060: Composition II for the first time, appointed Lori Ostergaard to serve as inaugural WPA, and developed a syllabus template for Composition II that conformed with both the general education syllabus requirements and our own newly created course outcomes. Because Composition II is the required first-year writing course in OU's general education program, the results of our assessments of the course informed our revisions to the entire first-year writing program, including Composition II's prerequisite courses (Basic Writing and Composition I). Between 2010 and 2014, Lori used the assessment of Composition II to make incremental improvements to the writing program, leading the department through a complete revision of our student evaluations of teaching, engaging full- and part-time faculty in revisions of Basic Writing and Composition I and creating a new first-year writing guide for the program, *Grizz Writes*. Megan Schoen was hired in 2016 to serve as WPA, and she has significantly improved the first-year writing guide, developed new committees to administer individual courses, and organized professional development events to further address issues with course instruction.

THEORETICAL FRAMEWORK AND METHODOLOGY

Our study draws on five salient understandings of genre, as reflected in the literature of genre theory, namely: (1) genres are an inherently social phenomenon (Berkenkotter and Huckin 1993; Miller 1984); (2) genres are reflective of the values, norms, and ideologies of discourse communities (Bawarshi and Reiff 2010; Berkenkotter and Huckin 1993; Devitt 2009); (3) genres are dynamic, both reflecting and bringing about change within discourse communities (Bazerman and Russell 2003; Devitt 2009; Russell 1997; Smart 2003); (4) genres are sites of negotiation between individual and community/professional values (Bazerman and Russell 2003; Miller 1984; Neaderhiser 2016a); and (5) genres are a facet of rhetorical ecologies (Afros and Schryer 2009; Bawarshi 2001; Prior and Shipka 2003; Spinnuzi 2003).

In this study, we describe how our individual and collective identities have formed within the genre ecology of our FYW program and how the evolution of those identities exemplifies the social action of pedagogical genres as expressed through various processes of endorsement, acceptance, and resistance. In order to characterize this genre ecology, we undertook an IRB-approved study that compared syllabi and assignment descriptions from our required first-year writing course, WRT 1060: Composition II, during the 2010 and 2017 academic years. In order to compare potential differences between these two distinct periods in our department's history, we identified instructors who taught in the department during both academic years and restricted participation in the study to those twenty individuals. After collecting syllabi and assignment descriptions from these instructors, we performed computer-aided textual analysis on them to determine the frequency of words and phrases used during each of the two periods. By examining both the particular and the macro-level revisions these twenty instructors made to their teaching genres over time, our intent was to chronicle how syllabi and assignment descriptions have served as "crucial constructors" (Neaderhiser 2016b) of our new department's identity. These homely discourses are not just evidence of or artifacts from particular moments of institutional evolution. Rather, course syllabi and assignment descriptions represent social action in the recursive and ecological forms described by Miller, Bawarshi, and other genre scholars.

In addition to our keyword analysis, we also interviewed faculty to determine their approach to syllabus and assignment development in their WRT 1060: Composition II classes between the 2010 and 2017 academic years. Of the twenty faculty who taught during both periods, thirteen agreed to participate in an interview about the changes they made to their syllabi and assignment descriptions. These interviews allowed us to determine how these colleagues used pedagogical genres to construct themselves as members of our nascent department; how they established their own ethos as knowledgeable teachers, writers, and researchers within this new discourse community; and how they conveyed the social/political/educational mission of our department to their students (see Appendix for interview questions). These interviews served to illuminate the ideologies embedded within their course documents (Bawarshi and Reiff 2010). At a time when an increasing number of writing programs stand independent from English departments (see Everett and Hanganu-Bresch 2017), a study of teaching genres can help to provide an understanding of these emerging discourse communities. The homely discourses of teaching genres "reflect and shape" (Neaderhiser 2016b) our institutional identities and reveal how we view the social, political, and educational work of new departments. This study also shows what can be gained when departments move beyond assessing only student genres to adopt mixed-method, longitudinal approaches to analyzing the often-occluded aspects of teaching genres.

OCCLUDED GENRES AND WAVES OF CHANGE

OU's Department of Writing and Rhetoric and its programs are, like most institutions, caught in dynamic tension between the forces of stasis and renewal, preservation and transformation, autonomy and interdependence. Citing Mikhail Bakhtin, Berkenkotter and Huckin (1993) noted that genres represent the very "sites of tension between unifying ('centripetal') forces and stratifying ('centrifugal') forces" (476). In our decade of existence as an independent department, we identify a number of different periods, or "waves," when such inward and outward forces acted on the intellectual ecology of our FYW program. As they moved, these waves were variously reflected, rejected, amplified, ridden, and resisted by members of the department. In the sections that follow, we put our keyword frequency analysis and interview research into conversation with some of the narratives of change that have been told and retold by members of our department community over the past decade. In doing so, we seek to map some of the traces that these waves left within the homely genres of our teaching. Our research enables us to see often occluded features and functions of these document genres: rather than focusing on their more visible and obvious roles as instruments for teaching, we seek to understand how they might reveal important information about our evolving department identity.

Wave 1: Multimodality and New Media

In 2008, multimodality and new media pedagogy were very much in the air of OU's Department of Writing and Rhetoric. The department's new major featured a track in new media writing, and hiring soon began for tenure-track faculty lines in new media. That year, the department chair Marshall Kitchens created two positions for special instructors to serve as technology liaisons to the department and to help faculty with scanning and uploading PDF documents, using the university's course management system, developing new video and audio assignments for the first-year classroom, and performing other technological tasks. As might be expected, some faculty were unnerved by the unprecedented emphasis on digital technologies and multimodality. In the earliest years of the department, the push for multimodality was recognized as a top-down initiative; reflecting on these years in an interview, instructor Armando[1] noted, "I'm not sure if it was a mandate or not but there was some conversations about incorporating multimedia genres at the time. Having a digital project was considered a good thing during that era."

---

1. All instructor names in this article are pseudonymous.

Table 10.1. Keyword frequencies in syllabi, 2010 and 2017 academic years

Keyword	2010	2017	% Change
Annotated Bibliography	17	23	+35
Audience(s)	9	11	+22
Conference/Conferencing	9	23	+156
Draft/Drafting	41	62	+51
Essay/Essays	62	44	−29
Exam	21	15	−29
Exercises	6	2	−67
Grammar/Grammatical	5	3	−40
Multimodal/Multimedia	8	3	−63
Paper/Papers	161	151	−6
Peer Review	18	26	+44
Primary Research/Sources	8	16	+100
Project(s)	82	106	+29
Quiz/Quizzes	26	13	−50
Reflection	21	40	+90
Revise/Rewrite	46	95	+107
Rhetorical/Rhetoric	11	17	+55
Scholar/Scholarly	14	24	+71
Secondary Research/Sources	5	6	+20

Taken together, the phrases "multimedia," "new media," "unimodal," and "multimodal" appeared seventeen times in 2010 assignment descriptions and they appeared ten times in 2010 syllabi (see tables 10.1 and 10.2). In 2017 these had fallen by 59 percent (to seven) and 60 percent (to three), respectively. Meanwhile, mentions of "visual" in assignment descriptions fell by 69 percent (from sixteen to five), although "video" increased by 50 percent (from eighteen to twenty-seven). In these data we see an interesting ebb, flow, and counterflow of multimodal pedagogy within the ecology of the department. As the initial shock of the push for multimodal and new media projects took hold, faculty may have felt immediate pressure to explicitly label their assignments as multimodal or the like. One faculty member, Catrice, recalled that the technology liaisons were instrumental in explaining multimodal pedagogy to her and "really helped solidify that there had to be different ways to have students remediate information." Despite this, however,

Table 10.2. Keyword frequencies in assignment descriptions, 2010 and 2017 academic years

Keyword	2010	2017	% Change
Academic	34	57	+68
Analysis/Analyses/Analyze	32	94	+194
Audience(s)	25	67	+168
Bibliography	6	25	+317
Context	1	14	+1300
Credible	8	12	+50
Culture	20	3	–85
Discussion	10	35	+250
Essay	60	170	+183
Grammar/Grammatically	3	13	+333
IMRAD/IMRD	0	9	N/A
Interview(s)	25	66	+164
Literature Review	0	5	N/A
Method(s)/Methodology	14	38	+171
Paper	151	293	+94
Primary Research/Sources	19	46	+142
Project	80	175	+94
Research	148	172	+16
Results	8	24	+200
Rhetoric/Rhetorical	10	13	+30
Secondary Sources	10	20	+100
Spelling	1	9	+800
Study/Studies	28	50	+79
Synthesis/Synthesizing	1	12	+1100

she admitted that multimedia approaches were not overtly present in her earliest major assignment descriptions, even if they were present in smaller, online activities. Multimodality appears to have transitioned from an overt to tacit part of our classroom genres during these years, a phenomenon explained by a number of factors. When Lori began her term as WPA in 2010, in addition to reassuring faculty about their abilities to teach digital composition, she also began offering professional development seminars and a free graduate course in multimodal composition pedagogy. As an understanding of the intellectual justifications for multimodal pedagogy suffused within the department culture—and as the apparent mandate to "train up or else" dissipated—it's likely that instructors no longer felt the need to outwardly present themselves as a certain kind of pedagogue. As a result, these outward markers fell out of the assignment and syllabus genres and became less prominent within the genre ecology of our department.

Wave 2: Grammar

In a *Composition Forum* profile of our first-year writing program, Allan et al. (2015) detailed the ways our department has engaged part-time faculty in professional development, assessment, and research studies to improve pedagogy. The authors described our efforts to "create a program-wide research culture" that can "empower faculty to better understand their own classroom practices through research." While this profile summarized our department's commitment to, and success with, engaging colleagues in researching best practices, it also documented a conversation that Lori had with an instructor when she was the WPA in 2010. That colleague was resistant to the department's "prohibition against direct instruction in standardized English grammar," and insisted that the way she taught grammar was both an ethical and deliberate choice: she felt she had an obligation to teach grammar so that her students would be successful in their majors and careers. Lori struggled to convince this colleague of what foundational research in the discipline of writing studies has long demonstrated: direct, prescriptive instruction in grammar through worksheets, quizzes, and other means divorced from real writing in context does little to improve writing and can even be detrimental to a writer's development (Hartwell 1985; Hillocks 1987). However, with time this colleague significantly revised her position, leading us to wonder what role the genre ecology of the department may have played in the evolution of her pedagogical values.

When viewed in isolation, our keyword analysis of the genres of course syllabi and assignment descriptions suggests that, in regard to grammar instruction, the impact of our professional development, mentoring, and shared research might not have been as great as we had hoped. Our keyword analysis of course syllabi suggests only a slight decline in grammar instruction over seven years—in 2010, "grammar/grammatical" appeared five times in syllabi, but only three times in 2017. However, there was also an increase over that same period in the use of "grammar/grammatical" in assignment descriptions, from three to thirteen instances. In our initial analysis of these data, we suspected that this increase could be attributed to the different roles these genres play in the classroom and department ecology. For example, all faculty in the department are required to upload syllabi to a shared online space every semester, but they are not required to share individual assignment descriptions. Syllabi, which are regularly reviewed by department administrators, are uploaded for the purpose of assessment and university accreditation, shared with new colleagues as models, and forwarded to students and advisors for transfer course reviews; as such, they are likely perceived as more public-facing (i.e., less occluded) documents than assignment descriptions. Our interviews support this interpretation: even as our colleagues described the syllabus as a kind of contract between themselves and their students, they were also conscious of external audiences for these documents. In speaking of their syllabi, six of the thirteen colleagues we interviewed mentioned the pedagogical recommendations they received from the WPA, suggesting that they are aware of the syllabus's "rhetorical functions both in and outside of the classroom" (Neaderhiser 2016b).

By contrast with the more overtly public-facing syllabus, our colleagues may assume that because assignment descriptions' "primary (or singular) purpose binds them to the classroom" (Neaderhiser 2016b), these genres open up spaces where faculty may be free to enact their own values. Our keyword analysis of assignment descriptions could, therefore, indicate that, in the seeming privacy of their own classrooms and assignment descriptions, instruction in grammar remains a pedagogical priority for some. However, a closer examination of those descriptions revealed that the increase in the use of "grammar/grammatical" resulted from our colleagues' adaptation of the assignment description genre to include their grading rubrics. Instead of flouting department guidance against direct instruction in standardized English grammar, then, our study suggests that instructors have transformed the assignment description to better reflect and support our department ecology.

Despite the increased presence of "grammar/grammatical" in Composition II assignment descriptions between 2010 and 2017, our review suggests that grammar instruction may be valued less by our colleagues than it was seven years ago. For example, Belen assigned 20 percent of her research paper grade to grammar and another 20 percent to citations in 2010, but her grading criteria in 2017 combined grammar and citations into 26 percent of the total assignment grade. In her interview, Belen noted that she eliminated grammar quizzes from her syllabi because "Lori pointed out it is not effective to look at spelling, punctuation, and grammar." The department ecology impacted more than just Belen's grammar quizzes: in syllabus comparisons, the use of the keyword "quiz/quizzes" was halved (from twenty-six to thirteen), the keyword "exam" decreased 28 percent (from twenty-one instances to fifteen), and "exercises" decreased by two-thirds (from six instances to two). By contrast, keywords associated with higher-order skills increased dramatically. The use of "analysis" in assignment descriptions jumped almost 194 percent (from thirty-two to ninety-four), and "synthesis," which appeared only once in any assignment description in 2010, was used twelve times in the 2017 descriptions. We also find evidence of the department's shift towards rhetorical instruction in assignment descriptions requiring an "audience" for student work, with use of that keyword in assignment descriptions rising 168 percent, from 25 instances in 2010 to 67 in 2017.

Wave 3: Teaching Writing as a Process

Another tale of resistance shaped a third wave within our department ecology. Based in part on the findings of our 2010 assessment of Composition II, we wanted to create a discourse community where writing instruction would be viewed as a metacognitive process focused on drafting, revising, peer review, conferencing, and reflection. Adapting to this new pedagogy was difficult for instructors like Robert, who had been teaching social construction theories since 1994. His 2010 syllabus required students to write four papers on the theme of social construction, and it included only two process-related keywords: "revision" of at least one paper during the semester and a suggested "conference" with him if students received a failing paper grade. There was no mention of drafts, peer review, or reflection within his 2010 syllabus or assignment description.

Robert admitted that after his "pedagogy was taken away" (an allusion to an intervention made by the WPA during a review of his teaching), he went through multiple steps to reinvent himself to be consistent with the new department direction. He examined sample syllabi, attended professional development sessions, collaborated with colleagues, and was mentored by the associate WPA. While he mentioned that his "pedagogy was taken away" twice during the interview, he also noted, "I would say I kind of upped my game a little bit especially in this way on my syllabus . . . I like the changes that I have made." His 2017 documents suggested that his work was more in line with departmental norms; his 2017 syllabus used the same language for revision and conferences mentioned above (allowing students to revise papers preferably after attending a conference with him), but he added "reflection" and "revision" as weighted grade categories. Robert's increased reliance on these processes mirrors what we saw in other syllabi. Collectively, the terms "revise" and "rewrite" jumped 107 percent (from forty-six to ninety-five instances) between 2010 and 2017, while "reflection" increased 90 percent (from twenty-one to forty) and instances of "conference" and "conferencing" increased 156 percent (from nine to twenty-three).

Two other process-related keywords increased between 2010 and 2017: "draft/drafting" increased 52 percent (from forty-one to sixty-two instances), and "peer review" rose 44 percent (from eighteen to twenty-six). There is no mention of these terms within Robert's syllabus, which might indicate that he does not incorporate these practices within his class. However, in his 2017 assignment description, he informs students that their "rough draft is due on April 10 in class for peer review." This simple phrase indicates that Robert is teaching his students important steps within the writing process; however, his syllabus may still be a site of negotiation between his personal disposition to teach critical theory and his attempts to incorporate the values of the department discourse community.

Wave 4: Teaching Research Writing

In the early days of the department, research was not an explicitly integral aspect of WRT 1060: Composition II. A key recommendation of the 2010 assessment was to increase attention to research writing in the course through instructor professional development, including demonstration of the IMRAD organization typical of research writing in the sciences. The program also began placing a greater emphasis on primary research and APA format, and it promoted feedback groups and teaching circles as a way to encourage instructors to share ideas and resources for teaching research. Our analysis of syllabi and assignment descriptions suggests that our department's teaching of research and research-based writing has evolved significantly between 2010 and 2017.

Our keyword analysis revealed an increase between the two assessment periods in terminology associated with academic research. For example, in WRT 1060 assignment descriptions, the frequency of the word "academic" rose by 68 percent (from thirty-four to fifty-seven), and "research" itself rose 16 percent (from 148 to 172). "Primary research" or "primary sources" rose 142 percent (from nineteen to forty-six), while other keywords associated with primary research such as "interview" increased 164 percent (from twenty-five to sixty-six). Additionally, "secondary sources" doubled (from ten to twenty). Keywords associated with the organizational structure of research articles increased: "IMRAD" and "IMRD" went from zero to nine instances, "literature review" went from zero to five instances, "methods/methodology" increased 171 percent (from fourteen to thirty-eight), "results" increased 200 percent (from eight to twenty-four), "discussion" increased 250 percent (from ten to thirty-five), and "bibliography" increased 317 percent (from six to twenty-five).

Our interviews also suggested that the collective understanding of teaching research writing is maturing in our FYW program. As faculty discussed the changes they made to their syllabi and assignment descriptions, we began to understand not only how department-initiated activities and policies helped to facilitate these changes, but also how individual faculty initiatives and informal faculty collaborations served to foster faculty identity as teachers of research writing. During the 2010 academic year, only five of the thirteen colleagues we interviewed (38%) were teaching research-based themes such as ethnography or open inquiry research. Of the other eight colleagues, four were teaching thematic courses including pop culture, oral history, critical theory, and working-class studies; the other four were teaching what they describe as "traditional English courses," focusing on introducing students to various essay genres (summary, book reviews, argument, etc.). By 2017, however, twelve of the thirteen colleagues we interviewed (92%) described their course as "research based" or "open inquiry." Some instructors noted during the interviews how departmental policies and professional development helped them to move toward new teaching methods, while others noted how their own self-sponsored professional development assisted them. For instance, Gloria admitted, "I didn't do any primary research at all in 2011. It's funny because it's in the course objectives, but I seemed to have ignored that." She said she became comfortable teaching primary research through various department resources, having conversations with her colleagues, and working on her own dissertation. She explained,

> I think I had a very general knowledge of what IMRAD style was, and then when we were doing the feedback group [a department committee that used interviews and surveys to assess effective paper response practices], someone said "you should write it up," and I thought, "I wouldn't even know how to do that." I think concurrent with changing my class, and starting school myself, it was kind of the "eureka!" Oh my gosh, I'm asking them to do what I'm trying to do. So then I felt like I got even better at explaining the stages because I was doing it myself.

Here, we see how a colleague's own graduate research, along with informal research collaboration with colleagues, helped her to professionalize as a teacher of research writing beyond what the department's regular professional development could offer.

Our shifting understanding of the role of research in WRT 1060 was reflected in these teaching documents and faculty interviews. The changes that appear in these teaching genres over time reflect the evolving norms and values of the department. The ways in which our faculty became more comfortable with and knowledgeable about the teaching of research writing appear to have been the result of both top-down initiatives such as department policies and professional development workshops as well as the individual efforts of faculty to professionalize themselves, including through the pursuit of graduate coursework and degrees. These teaching genres can be seen as sites of negotiation among departmental and institutional values and the values of individual instructors developing their professional identities as teachers of writing.

COERCION AND MATERIALITY IN THE ECOLOGY

While our study focused on two ostensibly student-addressed genres, the more public-facing syllabus and the less public assignment description, the evolution of this discourse community is also evident in the transformation of the course description for WRT 1060: Composition II. Because course descriptions address audiences of instructors, students, parents, advisors, administrators, articulation coordinators, state legislatures, and other stakeholders, the course description genre may serve as an important site of identity formation and negotiation for a department. When our department was created in 2008, the course catalog description for WRT 1060 assured readers that the course

> emphasizes the process of writing in increasingly complex rhetorical situations with focus on developing analytic thinking and problem-solving strategies in writing. Students learn methods of academic research including evaluation and documentation of sources and are expected to create at least one research paper.

In the years after our 2010 assessment, we revised the description to focus on the "methods of research and writing, including the use of rhetorical strategies and synthesis of scholarly sources to create academic arguments." The new course description further notes that WRT 1060 "emphasizes processes of writing and revision with a focus on information literacy, critical thinking, and effective communication in diverse rhetorical contexts."

In 2010, the course catalog description served as a site for "disciplining" our faculty—it was, in essence, a mini-syllabus instructing our colleagues on best practices for writing instruction. We still expect our instructors to scaffold assignments, introduce students to source evaluation and documentation, and require a research paper or project, but it is no longer necessary for the course description itself to dictate these practices. Instead, the top-down language of our original course description has been replaced with both our agreed-upon departmental outcomes—research, rhetoric, and revision—and the university learning outcomes that the course addresses: information literacy, critical thinking, and effective communication. Our revised course description is a testament to the disciplinary expertise of our faculty and the pedagogical consensus we have built within the department.

To be sure, genre ecologies—like real ecologies—can be coercive. As Bawarshi (2003) described,

> The syllabus is a coercive genre, in the same way that all genres are coercive to some degree or another. It establishes the situated rules of conduct students and teacher will be expected to meet, including penalties for disobeying them. But even more than that, the syllabus also establishes a set of social relations and subjectivities that students and teacher have available to them in the course. (120)

Essential to our understanding of genres as social action (Miller 1984) and as "sites of tension between unifying ('centripetal') forces and stratifying ('centrifugal') forces" (Berkenkotter and Huckin 1993) is the understanding that genres necessarily make some forceful impact on individuals and society. As such, we accept that genres must always be in some way coercive. However, we believe that this study reinforces the emerging scholarly understanding that genres work as the agents of social change in recursive and dynamic ways that go beyond mere coercion. Genres—even the most homely, templatized, and over-prescribed teaching genres—always leave gaps in their responses to recurrent rhetorical situations to enable their own iterative and organic evolution. Indeed, the potential for individual innovation within the construct of a fairly prescriptive genre is documented elsewhere in this collection, for example, in Michael Albright's chapter on the contradictory functions of the syllabus as gateway and gatekeeper, as well as in Mark Hannah and Christina Saidy's study of course policy documents. Like these authors, we found that rhetors will inevitably find ways to push at the edges of genres and, in doing so, shape the larger genre ecology itself in some way.

In their interviews, our colleagues consistently identified a threat to our department's genre ecology. In eleven out of thirteen interviews, faculty acknowledged the important role informal conversations with colleagues had on shaping their syllabi, assignment descriptions, and pedagogy. Many, like Catrice, described their reliance on colleagues for insights and ideas: "I would go back to my office and ask for opinions about an assignment and purpose, attendance language when it comes to designing my syllabus." Catrice echoed the opinion of most of her colleagues when she described these interactions with colleagues to be "very fulfilling." Unfortunately, because the college appropriated 65 percent of our office space two years ago and required half of our colleagues to move to a building across campus, several of our interview subjects lamented the loss of community: Deena talked about "how hard that was for some of us," Belen described the move as a "trial," and Catrice suggested that the conversations she had with colleagues were "very much missed at this point." The interview responses demonstrated that our separate office spaces undermined the department's cohesive identity and removed opportunities for department members to share ideas about teaching materials such as syllabi and assignment guidelines. These data point to the important impact that material conditions such as offices can have on a discourse community's ability to communicate and collaboratively innovate pedagogical genres.

CONCLUSION

As both the transformation of our course description and our research into course syllabi and assignment descriptions demonstrate, the homely discourse of these pedagogical genres can be incredibly rich sources of information about the academic departments that produce and use them, and they can be particularly helpful for understanding how departments emerge and evolve over time. As genres within complex and dynamic rhetorical ecologies, these texts help us map the development of discourse communities, isolate positive changes within those communities, and identify threats to our department ecologies. These occluded genres illuminate the diverse array of individual, departmental, and institutional actants that together negotiate the identity of an academic unit. In the case of our department at OU, for example, the initial syllabi template that department administrators created in 2010 facilitated top-down changes to our departmental culture, including an articulation of shared outcomes that promoted multimodal composing, process approaches, and rigorous research while de-emphasizing explicit instruction in grammar. In this way, the department used the syllabi template for Composition II to "establish . . . the situated rules of conduct students and teacher will be expected to meet" (Bawarshi 2003, 120). At the same time, individual instructors used these documents to develop and enact their own pedagogical identities, filling their personal guidelines into the gaps and fissures of templates, and in some cases adapting or eschewing top-down administrative policies to assert their own practices. Moreover, small groups of instructors often worked together informally in offices and hallways to share ideas for developing policies and assignments that were less formally codified by the genres. This complex interaction of agents is both reflected in and constituted by the homely syllabi and assignment descriptions we examined in this study.

Syllabi and assignment descriptions are important sites of analysis for understanding what and how we attempt to teach students. But, as this research shows, they are also powerful lenses through which to view our own pedagogical identities, whether as individuals or as institutions. The relationship between evolving genres and changing programmatic identity is similarly explored in Logan Bearden's study of programmatic outcomes statements, in this collection. Bearden examines how outcomes statements perform "at the intersection of institutional requirements and disciplinary knowledge," suggesting that these documents can act as "vehicle[s] through which meaningful and transformative curricular revisions can be made." Bearden identified program outcomes as meta-genres that impact the construction of "programmatic genres like assignment sheets, assessment materials, and teachers' guides," and he suggested that revisions to these meta-genres can "fundamentally transform the values and therefore the culture in and around the program." Our research similarly demonstrates that changes to programmatic documents like syllabi and assignment descriptions can both reflect and produce significant cultural shifts within a department.

The methods employed in this study could be adapted by other departments to understand more fully their own ecologies and the evolution of those ecologies over time. This self-analysis through pedagogical genres offers the opportunity for departments to develop a clearer sense of what they have been in the past, what they are currently, and perhaps how they can become what they aspire to be. Such reflection might be particularly important for newer departments trying to find their way (such as the many independent departments of writing, like our own, that have emerged on college campuses across the nation), but also well-established departments of English looking to reinvent themselves and chart a new course. While departments might be accustomed to examining such homely pedagogical documents for program assessment and accreditation reviews, we suggest that these texts can also be analyzed as genres within a complex ecological system in order to provide important insights about the workings of that very system itself.

APPENDIX 10.A

INTERVIEW QUESTIONS

1. What big changes did you make to your assignment descriptions? Why?

2. What were some things you kept the same in your assignment descriptions? Why?

3. Did any new departmental policies, documents, or guidelines lead to changes in your course syllabi or assignment descriptions? If so, what were they?

4. Did any department professional development workshops influence changes you made to either your syllabi or assignment descriptions? If so, what were they?

5. Did any professional development activities outside the department (e.g., CETL [Center for Excellence in Teaching and Learning] workshops, local conferences, national conferences, graduate classes, etc.) influence changes you made to your syllabi or assignment descriptions?

6. Did any individual mentoring in the department (official/unofficial) influence changes you made to your syllabi or assignment descriptions? If so, what were they?

7. Did any reviews of your courses (formative and summative) influence changes you made to your syllabi or assignment descriptions? (For example, when you were reviewed during your first year, or when you were reviewed for your first two-year contract or contract renewal.)

8. Did informal conversations with colleagues (e.g., in your office, hallways, at lunch, etc.) influence changes you made to your syllabus or assignment descriptions?

9. What other factors influenced or brought about changes you made to your syllabi and/or assignment descriptions between the 2010 assessment and this most recent assessment? (For example, student course evaluations or other forms of input?)

10. What do you think these changes in your syllabi and/or assignment descriptions signal about your own development as a teacher between 2010 and 2017?

11. Do you think you've made any significant changes to your pedagogy overall since the first assessment? If so, what are the greatest ways you have changed as a teacher between 2010 and 2017?

12. What do you think these changes in your syllabi and/or assignment descriptions signal about our development as a department between 2010 and 2017?

13. What are the greatest ways in which the department has changed/developed between 2010 and 2017, from your perspective?

REFERENCES

Afros, Elena, and Catherine F. Schryer. 2009. "The Genre of Syllabus in Higher Education." *Journal of English for Academic Purposes* 8 (3): 224–33.

Allan, Elizabeth G., Dana Lynn Driscoll, D. R. Hammontree, Marshall Kitchens, and Lori Ostergaard. 2015. "The Source of Our Ethos: Using Evidence-Based Practices to Affect a Program-Wide Shift from 'I Think' to 'We Know.'" *Composition Forum* 32. https://compositionforum.com/issue/32/oakland.php.

Bawarshi, Anis. 2001. "The Ecology of Genre." In *Ecocomposition: Theoretical and Pedagogical Approaches*, edited by Christian R. Weisser and Sidney I. Dobrin, 69–80. Albany: State University of New York Press.

Bawarshi, Anis. 2003. *Genre and the Invention of the Writer: Reconsidering the Place of Invention in Composition*. Logan: Utah State University Press.

Bawarshi, Anis, and Mary Jo Reiff. 2010. *Genre: An Introduction to History, Theory, Research, and Pedagogy*. West Lafayette, IN: Parlor Press.

Bazerman, Charles, and David R. Russell. 2003. "Introduction." In *Writing Selves/Writing Societies: Research from Activity Perspectives*, edited by Charles Bazerman and David R. Russell, 1–6. Fort Collins, CO: WAC Clearinghouse.

Berkenkotter, Carol, and Thomas N. Huckin. 1993. "Rethinking Genre from a Sociocognitive Perspective." *Written Communication* 10 (4): 475–509.

Chong, Felicia, and Jim Nugent. 2015. "A New Major in the Shadow of the Past: The Professional Writing Track at Oakland University." *Programmatic Perspectives* 7 (2): 173–88.

Devitt, Amy J. 2009. "Teaching Critical Genre Awareness." In *Genre in a Changing World*, edited by Charles Bazerman, Adair Bonini, and Débora Figueiredo, 337–51. Fort Collins, CO: WAC Clearinghouse.

Dryer, Dylan B. 2012. "At a Mirror, Darkly: The Imagined Undergraduate Writers of Ten Novice Composition Instructors." *College Composition and Communication* 63 (3): 420–52.

Everett, Justin, and Cristina Hanganu-Bresch, eds. 2017. *A Minefield of Dreams: Triumphs and Travails of Independent Writing Programs*. Fort Collins, CO: WAC Clearinghouse.

Hartwell, Patrick. 1985. "Grammar, Grammars, and the Teaching of Grammar." *College English* 47 (2): 105–27.

Hillocks, George. 1987. "Synthesis of Research on Teaching Writing." *Educational Leadership* 44 (8): 71–82.

Melzer, Dan. 2009. "Writing Assignments across the Curriculum: A National Study of College Writing." *College Composition and Communication* 61 (2): 240–61.

Miller, Carolyn R. 1984. "Genre as Social Action." *Quarterly Journal of Speech* 70 (2): 151–67.

Neaderhiser, Stephen. 2016a. "Conceiving of a Teacherly Identity: Metaphors of Composition in Teaching Statements." *Pedagogy* 16 (3): 413–43.

Neaderhiser, Stephen. 2016b. "Hidden in Plain Sight: Occlusion in Pedagogical Genres." *Composition Forum* 33. http://www.compositionforum.com/issue/33/hidden.php.

Ostergaard, Lori, and Greg A. Giberson. 2010. "Unifying Program Goals: Developing and Implementing a Writing and Rhetoric Major at Oakland University." *Composition Forum* 22. http://compositionforum.com/issue/22/oakland.php.

Prior, Paul, and Jody Shipka. 2003. "Chronotopic Lamination: Tracing the Contours of Literate Activity." In *Writing Selves/Writing Societies: Research from Activity Perspectives*, edited by Charles Bazerman and David R. Russell, 180–238. Fort Collins, CO: WAC Clearinghouse.

Russell, David R. 1997. "Rethinking Genre in School and Society: An Activity Theory Analysis." *Written Communication* 14 (4): 504–54.

Smart, Graham. 2003. "A Central Bank's 'Communications Strategy': The Interplay of Activity, Discourse Genres, and Technology in a Time of Organizational Change." In *Writing Selves/Writing Societies: Research from Activity Perspectives*, edited by Charles Bazerman and David R. Russell, 9–61. Fort Collins, CO: WAC Clearinghouse.

Smith, Summer. 1997. "The Genre of the End Comment: Conventions in Teacher Responses to Student Writing." *College Composition and Communication* 48 (2): 249–68.

Spinnuzi, Clay. 2003. "Compound Mediation in Software Development: Using Genre Ecologies to Study Textual Artifacts." In *Writing Selves/Writing Societies: Research from Activity Perspectives*, edited by Charles Bazerman and David R. Russell, 97–124. Fort Collins, CO: WAC Clearinghouse.

Swales, John M. 1996. "Occluded Genres in the Academy: The Case of the Submission Letter." In *Academic Writing: Intercultural and Textual Issues*, edited by Eija Ventola and Anna Mauranen, 45–58. Philadelphia, PA: John Benjamins.

11

PERFORMING REFLECTION IN INSTITUTIONAL CONTEXTS
A Genre Approach to Compelled Reflective Writing

Lesley Erin Bartlett

Reflective writing endures as a curricular mainstay in many if not most university writing programs and it is increasingly present in curricula across disciplines, perhaps particularly in institutions with campus-wide ePortfolio initiatives. Often invoking Dewey (1910), teacher-scholars cite myriad positive learning effects of reflection, including increased capacities for metacognition, transfer, and lifelong learning (Yancey 1998; Schön 1983; Cambridge 2010). Although scholarship that offers sharp critiques of the efficacy of reflective writing in institutional contexts exists alongside the wealth of scholarship that outlines (or assumes) the efficacy of reflective writing for students (Jung 2011; Scott 2005), most writing programs and teachers seem settled on the idea that reflection, in general, is a good thing. I am one of those writing teachers, but caveats abound—mostly concerning how institutional purposes for reflective writing influence and sometimes shape the work of writing teachers and students. In short, reflective writing occupies a complicated space between student learning and institutional assessment imperatives.

In this chapter, I focus on what I call *compelled reflective writing* to illuminate the tensions that can exist between pedagogical values and institutional assessment needs. To illustrate these tensions, I explore the institutional position of compelled reflective writing in particular contexts; more specifically, I show how compelled reflective writing in institutional contexts is often an uptake (Freadman 2002) of more powerful, often occluded genres (Swales 1996; Neaderhiser 2016b). In doing so, I invite writing teachers and writing program administrators to consider how the institutional position of compelled reflective writing could influence everyday teaching and learning. Studying pedagogical and institutional genres related to reflective writing allows for a better understanding of how writing programs and teachers

https://doi.org/10.7330/9781646422920.c011

straddle the often-competing values of student learning and assessment imperatives—and the potential consequences of such straddling for students and writing programs alike.

I am writing from at least three mutually informing perspectives. Primarily, I am writing from the perspective of a writing teacher who values reflective practice and reflective writing and wants to teach both the processes and products of reflection in ways that benefit students. I have been teaching writing (and studying the teaching of writing) for upwards of fifteen years, and I have been consistently concerned that reflective writing assignments in my classes are not living up to the promise of what reflective practice is supposed to make possible for students.

Another perspective I am bringing to this work is that of a former campus-wide ePortfolio project runner and faculty developer. Reflective writing is a hallmark of most ePortfolios, and I spent three years helping faculty across disciplines think about how to implement ePortfolios in their programs and departments at a large land grant institution. Even though our ePortfolio project was tied to regional accreditation and thus had high-stakes expectations and defined student learning outcomes, it was designed for flexible implementation across departments and programs. That is, individual departments and programs in large part determined their own purposes for ePortfolios, and participation in the ePortfolio project was not required of departments and programs. Unsurprisingly, students' reflective writing in their ePortfolios varied widely depending on the ePortfolio's primary purpose—e.g., to help students gain employment, to help programs assess themselves internally, or to help programs prove to their external accreditors that their students were meeting expected outcomes. The differences in the reflective writing were telling.

Finally, I come to this work from the perspective of a person who keeps journals. I have used personal reflective writing to make meaning for myself since I was a teenager. I suspect this self-motivated reflective writing contributed in some ways to my *hating* reflective writing assignments when I was a student. I resented the requirement to perform what felt like a contrived version of myself—on demand—in order to be successful in a course. I am aware that reflective writing in school is not the same as the writing I do in my journals. The rub is that it is perhaps not enough *unlike* the writing I do in my journals. Compelled reflective writing, unlike most other school writing assignments but very much like personal journal writing, requires an overt performance of self. Because compelled reflective writing in school is imbricated in an institutional context that involves uneven power relationships and stakeholders with various priorities, responsibilities, and values, the expectations for the resulting performance can be coercive.

My aim in this chapter is to invite writing teachers from across disciplines and writing program administrators to consider how the institutional position of compelled reflective writing in their own institutional contexts influences how it is taught and taken up—and to craft our pedagogies and programs with these realities in mind. While compelled reflective writing assignments are, importantly, taken up by students, this chapter focuses on the institutional uptakes that compelled reflective writing often anticipates. Because there are so many different characteristics of reflective writing, so many reflective writing genres, and so many different ways of teaching reflective writing across various contexts, I invite writing teachers and WPAs to pay careful attention to (1) the *purpose(s)* of reflective writing in our institutional contexts and (2) the potential misalignment of our pedagogical aims with our pedagogical practice.

FROM REFLECTION TO REFLECTIVE WRITING
TO EVIDENCE OF STUDENT LEARNING

In Michael Neal's contribution to Kathleen Blake Yancey's 2016 collection, *A Rhetoric of Reflection*, he outlines some of the reasons reflection took such hold in composition pedagogies, particularly as it related to portfolio assessment—which, he writes, "became so ubiquitous it was being presented as the solution for seemingly every writing situation and problem" (68). He cites a long list of reasons for the field's interest in reflection, including but not limited to "encourage[s] metacognition"; "make[s] pedagogy more dialogic"; "help[s] students assume control of their own development as writers"; and "integrate[s] literacy learning and authentic writing with assessment" (69), and goes on to acknowledge that "anything in the field with this level of optimism is bound to be tempered to some degree in time, but I include this list to show how enthusiastic we were and how well reflective writing matched our goals with the goals of the community. It seemed a perfect fit for both our values and the problems we faced with student learning and assessment" (69). Though unmitigated enthusiasm may have waned in some corners of composition studies, reflection and reflective writing still feature prominently in the curricula of many writing programs. The enduring presence of reflective writing is undoubtedly tied to pedagogical goals; however, institutional assessment imperatives that use reflective writing as evidence of student learning also help explain the continued presence and proliferation of reflective writing assignments.

What I am calling *compelled reflective writing* is externally required writing that involves an overt performance of self—examples include writing that is assigned by an instructor or required as part of a job application. Several scholars have written about different genres of what I would identify as compelled reflective writing; for example, Julie Jung (2011) takes up process descriptions, Kimberly Emmons (2003) explores portfolio cover letters, and Stephen Neaderhiser (2016a) addresses statements of teaching philosophy. What is unique about compelled reflective writing compared to other required assignments is the assumption that writers will turn themselves inside out: writers are expected to make their internal thoughts, their *reflection*, visible to external audiences. Sometimes those thoughts are quite personal and vulnerable. Writers do this in personal journals and diaries, for instance, which could also be considered a type of compelled reflective writing—but internally compelled. When reflective writing is externally compelled, there is an anticipated audience beyond oneself—with expectations, preferences, biases, and power—who will presumably read the reflective writing and thus judge the writer's performance of self. This chapter focuses on compelled reflective writing in classroom settings, but it is important to note that compelled reflective writing genres exist outside classrooms as well—and both have complicated relationships with identity performance and power.

Because of these complicated relationships, separating the *practice* of reflection from the *performance* of reflective writing is illuminating and instructive. In this calculus, *reflection* turns inward and *reflective writing* turns outward. Though these practices and performances can be mutually informative and may overlap at times, it is useful to consider that reflection and reflective writing are not one and the same. Reflection is a practice that is often invisible to external audiences and reflective writing is a performance that is, to some degree, *for* external audiences. This is not to say that compelled reflective writing cannot also be for the student's benefit. Some students may be able to approach compelled reflective writing assignments in a relatively unencumbered way that allows them to translate their reflective practice into reflective writing that genuinely satisfies their learning goals without fretting too much about the expectations and needs of external audiences. However, many students likely cannot—and there are consequences to teaching and assessing writing (and writing programs) as though they can.

In scholarship, assignment sheets, class discussions, and elsewhere, the terms *reflection* and *reflective writing* are often used interchangeably.

The assumption seems to be that the *performance* of reflective writing is always evidence of the *practice* of reflection. In fact, in the conclusion of Kathleen Blake Yancey's most recent book about reflection, she writes that reflection "is both a practice and a text; the practice is always implicitly in the text; and it is sometimes explicitly so" (2016, 318). While the practice may well be implicit in the text at times, I'm skeptical about whether or not reflective writing *always* represents the kind of reflective practice in which most teachers hope our students will engage.[1] Writers cannot help but make choices about what to make visible (and what to conceal) in writing; in other words, writers are compelled to make performative choices. This is perhaps particularly relevant when writers are compelled to perform their identity in a text that serves multiple purposes—some pedagogical (e.g., to gauge students' understanding of a course concept), some personal (e.g., to consider individual growth in a particular area, like writing introductions), and some institutional (e.g., to provide evidence that a course is meeting general education outcomes).

Compelled reflective writing in school serves to provide evidence of student learning—that is often the rhetorical purpose in institutional contexts, even though reflection and reflective writing can serve many other purposes. Consider a common transactional trajectory: first, reflective writing is a transaction between teacher and student (pedagogical purpose), then between teacher and program (presumably higher stakes assessment purpose), and often then between program and institution (presumably even higher stakes assessment purpose). Sometimes the transaction continues between educational institutions and accreditors and/or state legislatures (presumably even *higher* stakes assessment purpose). For many teachers, the ideal first transaction would be between a student and themself (personal purpose related to learning); however, students' reflective practice can get short-circuited by the rhetorical purpose of much reflective writing in institutional contexts. Yancey (2016) writes, "To think of reflection only or exclusively as a mechanism for evaluation is to waste its potential: reflection can assist with assessment, certainly, but its larger value is linked to supporting writers in a myriad of ways as they develop both writing knowledge and practice" (11). With Yancey, I want to stress that reflective writing can "assist with assessment," but I also want to emphasize that assessment purposes can subsume other, more student-focused purposes for reflective writing. As Yancey and others argue, reflection is rhetorical.

---

1. Earlier in her conclusion, Yancey acknowledges that "even where reflection is valued, it can become a practice too routinized, too familiar and thus not useful" (308).

When the practice of reflection is externally compelled and must be performed in reflective writing, the rhetorical purpose of the reflective writing in the institutional context can understandably take precedence.

UPTAKE AND THE INSTITUTIONAL POSITION
OF COMPELLED REFLECTIVE WRITING

Increasingly, compelled reflective writing is becoming a mechanism by which students prove that they have learned what institutions want them to learn. Put another way, compelled reflective writing is often used for the institutional purpose of validating existing curriculum—and this purpose has consequences for writing teachers and students. In "Rethinking Regulation in the Age of the Literacy Machine," Mary Soliday and Jennifer Seibel Trainor (2016) take up "the bureaucratization of literacy" and report on a study they conducted at their comprehensive state university, which they claim, like other state institutions, is "vulnerable . . . to acts of regulation at all levels" (126). Soliday and Trainor found that, in our current assessment-focused educational climate, students were "unable to see the rhetorical purposes [of] assignments . . . or the opportunities for authorship they provided" (126). My experience teaching writing has occurred in the context of five different state universities—all with elaborate bureaucracies of assessment (to riff on Soliday and Trainor's term), which I was more or less aware of (more as a full-time administrator and tenure-track faculty member and much less as a graduate student and lecturer, differences I will explore in the pages ahead). The reality of Soliday and Trainor's finding is tricky when it comes to compelled reflective writing because students often understand the rhetorical purpose of such writing to be convincing their teacher that they have learned what they were supposed to learn.

Some writing studies research shows the consequences of regulating and bureaucratizing reflective writing. Tony Scott's (2005) article, "Creating the Subject of Portfolios: Reflective Writing and the Conveyance of Institutional Prerogatives," offers an in-depth illustration of how "large-scale assessments influence everyday pedagogy" (5). His article "presents research from a qualitative study of the way that reflective writing is solicited, taught, composed, and assessed within a state-mandated portfolio curriculum" (3). Scott focuses on the effects on students' reflective writing, but I am most interested in the institutional genres surrounding students' reflective writing. Because of the focus of his study, his level of access, and the opportune nature of his research site (within a statewide mandated portfolio assessment system), Scott was able to do something I want to invite readers to do as well: consider the institutional position of reflective writing in particular contexts and question the extent to which reflective writing assignments anticipate institutional uptakes.

Scott's research emphasizes how reflective writing in institutional contexts can coerce students' identity performances. That is, an important rhetorical purpose of students' performances of self is to validate the curriculum. He writes, "The system encourages the construction of a generic reflective subject that reproduces the system's ideal of a portfolio student. In the classes I observed, the composition of the reflective letter is best described as bureaucratic practice—a socializing process that reproduces the values of the sponsoring institution" (2005, 5). According to Scott, the "ideal portfolio student" in the Kentucky system (from which he drew the data for his study) is "[a] student who makes her own choices concerning what to include in her portfolio, is able to assess her own writing and growth, works in partnership with her teacher, and writes the pieces that she wants to write—those that 'grow naturally out of instruction'—seemingly without regard to the requirements of the portfolio" (12). Scott's example seems particularly insidious because students are coerced to perform an agentive identity on the page.

Scott's research also highlights the tension between the multiple purposes compelled reflective writing serves. He writes, "Another potential problem with reflective writing is that it is a somewhat unwieldy hybrid of personal and public writing. Students are often asked to reflect both for their own enrichment *and* to aid in their own evaluation. The practice is intended to lend students independence *while* providing a wealth of information for assessment" (2005, 7). Educators surely hope this both/and approach to reflective writing will be possible to accomplish, but skepticism is reasonable. Students are understandably accustomed to prioritizing what "counts" for their grade. Those criteria are also often more concrete and straightforward than the more amorphous direction to write for your own enrichment. Scott sums up the double-bind of both teaching and writing compelled reflective writing genres when he writes, "From a wide-angle, systemic view, the portfolio is characterized by requirements, annual measurements, curricular consistency, and accountability. As a pedagogical tool in particular classrooms, however, the same portfolio is intended to serve as a means through which students can gain agency and a sense of ownership of their work" (11). When institutional, systemic purposes are high-stakes, concrete, measured, and accounted for, and pedagogical purposes are, from an institutional perspective, lower-stakes, amorphous, and difficult to measure and account for, then the potential for misalignment of pedagogical aims and pedagogical practices is very high.

A SUCCESSION OF UPTAKES: AN ILLUSTRATIVE EXAMPLE

The first-year composition program at my home institution, ISUComm Foundations Courses, offers an illustrative example of the ways that reflective writing can be enmeshed in institutional assessment imperatives. The role of reflective writing within this particular institutional assessment structure at Iowa State University illuminates how the relationships between genres in a bureaucratic succession—some visible to teachers and students, some not so visible—influence and potentially shape what is possible for writing teachers and students. In offering this example, I aim to invite writing teachers from across disciplines and writing program administrators to consider the institutional positioning of reflective writing in their own contexts.

In the state of Iowa, "state legislation requires that all undergraduate courses typically enrolling 100 students or more must have a continuous improvement plan in place" (ISU Office of the Senior Vice President and Provost 2018). According to the webpage about continuous improvement plans (CIP) on the Senior Vice President and Provost's Office website,

> there are many effective ways to facilitate and assess student learning, which will vary based on such factors as academic discipline, specific course content, academic level of course, class size, and instructor/student learning preferences. Therefore, faculty members will have great flexibility in the implementation of course-level improvement plans for each course. However, there is an expectation that the plans will:
> - be based on course-level outcomes,
> - make use of formative and/or summative assessments,
> - make decisions related to course changes based on assessments, and
> - include a feedback loop to reflect upon the impact/success of changes.

Complying with the CIP mandate is not optional, but *how* a course fulfills the mandate is somewhat flexible. The web page goes on to say, "The legislation requires that the Board of Regents submit an annual report to the legislature on the continuous improvement plans. To meet this requirement, Iowa State compiles an annual summary report based on the Qualtrics survey responses." To my knowledge, the CIP is the most powerful institutional genre that would influence genres in ISUComm. Because ISUComm chose to use ePortfolios to fulfill the mandate, students' compelled reflective writing was enmeshed in this institutional assessment process.

The Board of Regents sends the culminating assessment report to the legislature, but, of course, several other transactions must be made to make the report possible (see table 10.1 for a breakdown of the succession of transactional genres). Some of the transactions involve choices, and some do not. In the case of ISUComm Foundations Courses (the first-year composition sequence, English 150 and 250), every student creates an ePortfolio, and these are assessed for CIP data. A defining feature of ePortfolios is the reflective writing they entail. In the 2015–2016 Annual Report that ISU sent to the Board of Regents, one of the ISUComm courses was highlighted in a section entitled "Examples of Impact":

> ENGL 250 (Written, Oral, Visual, and Electronic Composition)-We have identified that our students, while performing relatively well on other aspects of their ePortfolios, are less successful with reflecting deeply and authentically on their strategies and learning. Inasmuch as this metacognition is tied to transfer potential, we want to re-emphasize reflection in ENGL 250. We have additional activities and new reflection prompts to use beginning in Fall 2016. (ISU Office of the Senior Vice President and Provost 2017)

According to the report, ISUComm was dissatisfied with students' reflective writing in their ePortfolios and planned to take steps to try to improve it. Readers can look to another important institutional genre, the *ISUComm Foundation Courses Student Guide for English 150 and 250 (2017–2019)*, for evidence of the renewed emphasis on reflection and reflective writing that the report discusses.

The *Student Guide* is one of the most visible institutional genres to ISUComm writing teachers and students, and the 2017–2019 edition goes to great lengths to explain the importance of reflection in writing development, offering reasons for why reflection is so central to the curriculum (some of which are detailed in the quotation below) and backing up its claims about reflection with scholarship. As the 2015–2016 Annual Report foreshadowed, much is made of reflection for the student (and teacher) audience in the *Student Guide*, which straddles the personal and institutional purposes of reflective writing. For example,

> Reflection is how you make your learning meaningful to yourself and available to you for future access. . . . [W]hen you reflect you are articulating—representing—your learning and the process by which you

gained that learning for yourself and your instructor. By reflecting, you are engaging with the course content of English 150 and 250 in a way that renders it personally meaningful to you and your educational trajectory. Don't be surprised if your reflections reveal ways in which you have modified or diversified learning processes from the past. In fact, that's evidence that you are adding necessary sophistication to your communication toolbox. (ISUComm 2017)

This description conflates the practice of reflection and the performance of reflective writing. It goes back and forth between emphasizing personal and institutional meaning-making, and it privileges evidence. The *Student Guide* represents a writing program doing its very best to build reflective writing into the curriculum in a pedagogically meaningful way that also fulfills institutional assessment imperatives.

Another institutional genre that surrounds compelled reflective writing in the particular context of ISUComm is the *Instructor Guide for Foundational Communication Courses*, a teaching guide that provides policies, rationale, and guidance for teachers within the program. Like the *Student Guide* (and most scholarship about reflection), the *Instructor Guide* conflates the practice of reflection and the performance of reflective writing. One section, entitled "Reflection—Both Process and Product," starts by quoting John Dewey's *Democracy and Education* and emphasizes the learning potential of reflection, but soon acknowledges the difficulties associated with teaching reflective writing:

> Our educational ideal is that students will engage in the authentic but vulnerable self-assessment process that promotes growth. The reality, however, is that students who know that teachers will assess a reflection product assigned at the end of a project are often more concerned with what they think the teacher wants to hear than with how the process of reflecting can help them grow. They can reflect dutifully in response to a reflection prompt but not experience the kind of deep learning the assignment was created to inspire. (ISUComm 2018)

The use of the word *ideal* here is telling; the writers of the *Instructor Guide* are upfront in their acknowledgment that reflective writing in institutional contexts often fails to fulfill writing teachers' pedagogical goals—juxtaposing the "ideal" with what they call "reality." The honesty is refreshing, if a bit disheartening. Their advice to combat merely "dutiful" approaches to reflection is to focus on low-stakes practice and, interestingly, assessment:

> So it is important to offer discussions and activities throughout the semester where students can engage in self-assessment without fear of being judged for their weaknesses. A major boon to helping your students reflect

> productively is to remind them frequently of the Reflection Continuum on page 92 of the Student Guide. This shows them the characteristics of a good reflection (e.g., using course terminology, showing how they have taken accountability for their work, making rhetorical decisions, using feedback). (ISUComm 2018)

Note that "discussion and activities"—not reflective writing—are the classroom genres associated with "self-assessment without fear of being judged for their weaknesses." In the *Student Guide*, the reflection continuum referenced above is entitled General Reflection Rubric and is almost certainly meant to assess the performance of reflective writing (but not other genres that invite reflection). Furthermore, the criterion to "us[e] course terminology" signals the institutional assessment purpose for the reflective writing and suggests the circular nature of the use of reflective writing for assessment purposes. That is, often programs determine learning outcomes and then create reflective writing assignments and rubrics that prompt students to repeat the language from those outcomes in their reflective writing, which in turn can be used to provide evidence that the programs are meeting the learning outcomes they had established.

A characteristic of compelled reflective writing in institutional contexts is that it is often a product in a series of bureaucratic transactions. While the practice of reflection can turn inward and be put to student-driven uses, the performance of reflective writing in institutional contexts most often turns outward and serves multiple bureaucratic purposes. As Tony Scott (2005) writes, "The practice [of using reflective writing for institutional assessment purposes] highlights the tensions between the unique development of individual students and the broad aims and bureaucratic practices of an educational system. The goals that teachers, students, state assessors, and curriculum developers have for reflective texts are not easily congruent" (8). The practice of reflection is meant to contribute to and enrich student development. No doubt the same pedagogical aim exists for the performance of reflective writing; however, the multiple purposes reflective writing serves increase the potential for misalignment of pedagogical aims with pedagogical practice.

Both the *Student Guide* and *Instructor Guide* are institutional genres that surround the reflective writing that occurs in ISUComm foundations courses. They describe programmatic values and practices and offer the scholarly basis for those values and practices. However, the *guides* do not call the reflective writing into being. A highly detailed four-and-a-half-page programmatic ePortfolio assignment sheet does.

Table 11.1. Transactions in CIP process

General Process	ISUComm Example
Program or course administrators give teachers (more or less) direction regarding the parts of the curriculum that will eventually be used for CIP data for courses enrolling more than 100 students	Writing program gives writing teachers ePortfolio assignment sheet (and requires all sections to assign ePortfolios)
Teachers in courses enrolling more than 100 students assign work to students	Writing teachers give students programmatic ePortfolio assignment sheet
Students in courses enrolling more than 100 students complete work	Students complete ePortfolios
Program or course administrators ("reporters") for courses enrolling more than 100 students conduct assessment of their chosen evidence of student learning	Writing program assesses ePortfolios to measure student learning
Provost's Office solicits CIP data from courses enrolling more than 100 students	Provost's Office solicits CIP data from writing program
Program or course administrators ("reporters") for courses enrolling more than 100 students report CIP data to Provost's Office	Writing program reports CIP data to Provost's Office
Provost's Office reports CIP data to Board of Regents	Provost's Office reports CIP data to Board of Regents
Board of Regents reports CIP data to state legislature	Board of Regents reports CIP data to state legislature

In table 11.1, I describe the succession of genres in the CIP assessment process that culminates in an annual report to the state legislature. Each row describes an action that prompts and anticipates another action. The concept of uptake, as conceived by Anne Freadman (2002), helps explain that succession of genres. Drawing on Freadman's work, Irene Clark (2005) writes, "Noting that certain texts are contrived to generate certain kinds of 'uptakes,' Freadman maintains that 'the interpretant, or the uptake text, confirms its generic status by conforming itself to this contrivance' and that it does so by '"taking it as an" invitation or a request.'" Each transaction calls into being a deliverable—sometimes in the form of reflective writing, other times in the form of an assessment report.

There are also other, less visible genres that surround the transactional genres highlighted in table 11.1.[2] For instance, prior to the first

2. I learned about the less visible genres from a colleague who is a designated reporter for a course enrolling over one hundred students. Because I am not a designated reporter, I would not have otherwise known about all of the steps in the CIP reporting process.

transaction—that is, prior to when a program decides what to standardize for assessment—colleges solicit plans for CIP data collection and measurement through email to designated "reporters" for courses that enroll over one hundred students. Presumably, reporters submit their assessment plans to the college before they communicate with instructors and students about the curriculum. Reporters also receive emails from departmental administrators to remind them of their CIP responsibilities and drive them to fulfill them. Unlike the *Guides* and the provost's website, these genres are invisible to teachers and students but nevertheless affect what is asked of them in classrooms.

An important difference between the institutional context in Tony Scott's (2005) study and my home institution context is that the teachers and students in Scott's study seemed fully aware of the assessment purposes for which their reflective writing was being used. For better or worse, this awareness among teachers and students of the assessment apparatus surrounding reflective writing assignments is not always the case. As a teacher who often teaches foundational courses (and has done so at several different institutions), I wondered about the assessment apparatus surrounding our curriculum and so went looking for information. My experience administering an ePortfolio project also prompted curiosity about the purposes for which the required ePortfolio was being used. As I mentioned early in the chapter, my awareness of institutional assessment at the several state institutions where I have been employed has varied based on my position within those institutions. As a graduate student and lecturer, I was much less aware than I have been as an administrator and tenure-track faculty member. My lack of awareness as a graduate student was surely due in part to my relative inexperience with institutional assessment structures and my lack of responsibility for reporting. My subsequent work as an administrator with faculty from across disciplines helped me learn about the various nonnegotiable, high-stakes assessment demands that many programs and departments have to meet as a matter of course. Writing programs are rarely exempt from such demands, though most teachers and students are likely unaware of these pressures. Writing program administrators are often intimately familiar with and acutely aware of such demands. This awareness no doubt affects curricular choices.

Although there is nothing inherently negative about teachers' and students' lack of knowledge about how reflective writing is being used in the larger institutional assessment apparatus, it is still important for teachers and writing program administrators to consider the pedagogical consequences of the institutional position of compelled reflective writing. As Scott writes, "Adopting a genre for reflection is not necessarily bad. As much prior research has shown, sophisticated writers learn to recognize and adapt genres to achieve their goals in particular situations" (2005, 26). However, there are potential consequences not only for the student writing itself but also for students' views of literacy:

> There is an unmistakable systemic logic at work here that exerts considerable influence on students' thinking and writing. The curriculum seeks to foster a sense of ownership among students. Therefore, the reflecting student, encouraged by the genre, presents her work as though she wrote it for herself and then included it in the portfolio because it happens to be her best work. . . . It may be, however, that ownership and empowerment are more contextually prescribed rhetorical stances than actual dispositions. Most student participants saw the composition of the reflective letter primarily as a bureaucratic exercise rather than as an empowering or even worthwhile learning event. (26)

Within the context of Scott's study, the institutional position of the portfolio created conditions that caused students' reflective writing to validate the curriculum. Scott's example may seem extreme and unique because of the statewide, high-stakes mandate in Kentucky, but his example is instructive for any writing teacher or writing program administrator who values reflective practice and reflective writing. Though he was writing in 2005, the regulatory nature of large-scale assessments has arguably become even more pervasive in higher education—and has become more "common sense." While we may not all teach in contexts that have such defined institutional purposes for reflective writing, we are all teaching in more or less regulated contexts, and understanding how that regulation potentially affects our pedagogical practices makes constraints visible in ways that help us see possibilities for intervention and positive change.

CONCLUSIONS AND IMPLICATIONS

Even though many, if not most, writing teachers understand the constraints of compelled reflective writing and acknowledge that students are often (and understandably) writing what they think we want to read, programs and institutions still imbue reflective writing with a great deal of weight and meaning; it is used to understand and assess students, courses, curricula, and programs. It is used as though it is true, as though the performance of reflective writing is a translation of an authentic, unencumbered practice of reflection. Understanding reflective writing in this way can have negative consequences for everyday teaching and learning. Reflective practice and reflective writing have potential to aid in students' learning and development. Their potential is too often diminished and undercut in institutional contexts. Because reflective writing *can be* good for student learning, we may embed it in our programs and classes without paying enough attention to *how* it is being taught and *what* students are actually gaining. More research is needed to understand whether, how, and under what circumstances—and through which genres—students experience the purported benefits of reflective practice and reflective writing.

I have focused on reflective writing genres and illustrated the complexities of compelled reflective writing in a particular institutional context; however, it is important to note that the pedagogical effects of institutional genres and bureaucratic systems discussed here are not exclusive to reflective writing—or, of course, to any individual institutional context. Any time a pedagogical genre is enmeshed in a larger system of institutional genres (which is often), it is subject to the power relationships that influence the system. The consequences of this entanglement on everyday teaching and learning are not inherently negative, but they can be negative—and they deserve critical attention.

One place to look for examples of the relationship between institutional genres and pedagogical practice is the genres that surround curricular certifications, such as guidelines for courses to count for a general education requirement or to receive a writing intensive designation. Going through these certification processes and encountering their attendant regulatory genres may reveal tensions between institutional mandates and pedagogical goals. Taking a deep analytical dive into the genres that surround every curricular requirement an instructor encounters is not feasible, but asking a brief series of questions is: Do I know the origin of the mandate? Do I understand the reasoning behind the mandate? Does the reasoning behind the mandate align with my pedagogical values and goals for my students?

While writing teachers from across disciplines and writing program administrators work within institutional contexts that are more or less regulated, and while institutional genres often seem nonnegotiable and immutable, it is important to look for opportunities for choice, negotiation, and change. As Charles Bazerman (1994) points out, if we recognize how various genres "flow" into and out of the classroom, carrying with them the "mandate of regulation," then we must consider the implications of whether we endorse those mandates: "It is our choice whether these definitions of the classroom and the genres that act out these definitions are wholeheartedly accepted, wholeheartedly resisted, compromised with, or sublated into some fuller understanding of our tasks. Whichever choice we make, we must consider the prices and responsibilities of our institutional places" (60). Remembering our institutional places is undoubtedly important as we make choices about how to respond to the genres flowing in and out of our classrooms. We may also consider personal roles. As a personal journal writer, I have experienced the benefits of self-directed reflective writing—so much so that I have sometimes resented reflective writing assignments that felt coercive to me. At the same time, I remind myself that not every student experiences reflective writing assignments the way I did. As a former ePortfolio project administrator, I am keenly aware of the pressures that programs face as they try simultaneously to meet institutional assessment demands and prioritize student learning. As a teacher, I hope to teach the practice of reflection and the performance of reflective writing in ways that students can use to their benefit. In all of these roles, with Anis Bawarshi (2003), I acknowledge that "all genres are coercive to some degree or another" (120). Perhaps the key is to find—and help our students find—possibilities within the constraints.

REFERENCES

Bawarshi, Anis. 2003. *Genre and the Invention of the Writer: Reconsidering the Place of Invention in Composition.* Logan: Utah State University Press.

Bazerman, Charles. 1994. *Constructing Experience.* Carbondale: Southern Illinois University Press.

Cambridge, Darren. 2010. *Eportfolios for Lifelong Learning and Assessment.* San Francisco: Jossey-Bass.

Clark, Irene. 2005. "A Genre Approach to Writing Assignments." *Composition Forum* 14 (2). http://compositionforum.com/issue/14.2/clark-genre-writing.php.

Dewey, John. 1910. *How We Think.* Boston: D. C. Heath & Company.

Emmons, Kimberly. 2003. "Rethinking Genres of Reflection: Student Portfolio Cover Letters and the Narrative of Progress." *Composition Studies* 31 (1): 43–62.

Freadman, Anne. 2002. "Uptake." In *The Rhetoric and Ideology of Genre: Strategies for Stability and Change,* edited by Richard M. Coe, Lorelei Lingard, and Tatiana Teslenko, 39–53. Cresskill, NJ: Hampton Press.

ISU Office of the Senior Vice President and Provost. 2017. "2015–2016 Annual Report on Course-Level Compliance with Quality Improvement Legislation." Board of Regents, State of Iowa. Archived at https://www.legis.iowa.gov/docs/publications/DF/851433 .pdf.

ISU Office of the Senior Vice President and Provost. 2018. "Course-Level Continuous Improvement Plans." Iowa State University. Accessed April 8, 2020. https://www.provost.iastate .edu/academic-programs/student-outcomes/course-level-continuous-improvement -plans. Archived at https://web.archive.org/web/20200408003646/https://www .provost.iastate.edu/academic-programs/student-outcomes/course-level-continuous -improvement-plans.

ISUComm. 2017. *ISUComm Foundation Courses Student Guide for English 150 and 250 (2017–2019).* Ames: Iowa State University.

ISUComm. 2018. "Reflections—Both Process and Product." Instructor Guide for Foundation Communication Courses. https://support.isucomm.iastate.edu/foundation-instructor-guide/teaching/reflections-both-process-and-product.

Jung, Julie. 2011. "Reflective Writing's Synecdochic Imperative: Process Descriptions Redescribed." *College English* 73 (6): 628–47.

Neaderhiser, Stephen. 2016a. "Conceiving of a Teacherly Identity: Metaphors of Composition in Teaching Statements." *Pedagogy* 16 (3): 413–43.

Neaderhiser, Stephen. 2016b. "Hidden in Plain Sight: Occlusion in Pedagogical Genres." *Composition Forum* 33. http://www.compositionforum.com/issue/33/hidden.php.

Neal, Michael. 2016. "The Perils of Standing Alone: Reflective Writing in Relationship to Other Texts." In *A Rhetoric of Reflection*, edited by Kathleen Yancey, 64–83. Logan: Utah State University Press.

Schön, Donald A. 1983. *The Reflective Practitioner: How Professionals Think in Action.* New York: Basic Books.

Scott, Tony. 2005. "Creating the Subject of Portfolios: Reflective Writing and the Conveyance of Institutional Prerogatives." *Written Communication* 22 (1): 3–35.

Soliday, Mary, and Jennifer Seibel Trainor. 2016. "Rethinking Regulation in the Age of the Literacy Machine." *College Composition and Communication* 68 (1): 125–51.

Swales, John M. 1996. "Occluded Genres in the Academy: The Case of the Submission Letter." In *Academic Writing: Intercultural and Textual Issues*, edited by Eija Ventola and Anna Mauranen, 45–58. Philadelphia, PA: John Benjamins.

Yancey, Kathleen. 1998. *Reflection in the Writing Classroom.* Logan: Utah State University Press.

Yancey, Kathleen, ed. 2016. *A Rhetoric of Reflection.* Logan: Utah State University Press.

PART 3

Genres beyond the Classroom

12

GENRE ANXIETY
The Pedagogical, Political, and Emotional Work of Making a Certificate

Laura R. Micciche and Lora Arduser

In this chapter we recount our experiences developing an undergraduate certificate for copyediting and publishing (CP), within an English department. The two of us work in the complementary but, in our department, distinct subfields of rhetoric and professional writing, and rhetoric and composition. Our collaboration on this certificate, within a department that also includes tracks in literary and cultural studies (LCS) and creative writing, brings together courses across English as well as beyond it. In so doing, the certificate structures knowledge as technical, practical, and conceptual. The first two forms of knowledge—technical and practical—generated concerns among our faculty in literature. Namely, they worried that the certificate would decrease the number of students enrolled in their classes and that course offerings like Editing Professional Documents and Desktop Publishing were overly instrumental. Reflecting on these concerns (and others), we read the certificate proposal as an anxious genre as well as an institutional and curricular one.

While the certificate drafting process evoked pedagogical concerns— How will the proposed courses fit into the existing curriculum? Who will teach them?—it also exposed emotioned concerns about the identity of "English" at a moment when, like English departments across the United States, ours has seen student enrollment decrease and faculty lines go unfilled. As such, the certificate proposal is a complex rhetorical genre that is more than goal-directed and communicative—familiar descriptions of genre work. It also operates as an expressive genre that elicits anxiety about community and identity and serves a pedagogical function by teaching our colleagues how to understand the work we do. In addition to the pragmatic work mundane genres such as proposals do, these genres are *reacted to* as well as created and interpreted (Miller 1984). As

https://doi.org/10.7330/9781646422920.c012

such, we found that the certificate proposal shaped the performance of teaching identities outside of the classroom in unexpected ways.

Our analysis of the institutional proposal genre illuminates the extent to which genre expresses and challenges power relations while also transmitting and manufacturing emotions through the process of circulation. Moreover, we reveal how the certificate proposal mediates between discourse communities—including departmental faculty, university department heads, faculty senate, the Dean's Office and the Provost's Office. We contend that the curriculum proposal genre is a seemingly stable, even innocuous form in institutional life that nonetheless has the potential to destabilize disciplinary relations and identity concepts. This destabilization is both riddled with conflict and rife with productive potential for pedagogical innovation. We reflect on pedagogical functions of the certificate proposal genre: on the one hand, it instructed colleagues how to understand the work of writing studies within the English Department and the College of Arts and Sciences; on the other, the proposal genre taught our colleagues how to feel about a coalition of writing teachers building a non-compulsory program.

MAKING AN ACADEMIC CERTIFICATE

Academic certificate programs at four-year institutions are designed to provide students with specialized skills and knowledge that complement or add a practical dimension to an undergraduate or graduate degree curriculum (Meloncon 2012). Data on freestanding certification programs and certificates completed at two-year colleges is easily accessible (see Georgetown University 2018; NSC Research Center 2016). With the exception of research on technical/professional writing certificates (Harner and Rich 2005; Meloncon 2012; Norman and Wells 1997), however, data on certificate programs that supplement a student's major at four-year institutions is much harder to come by.

Even at our own institution, we have been hard-pressed to locate an outward-facing, robust definition of the certificate beyond its general description and set of required courses. The certificate proposal form, an inward-facing document that we discuss more fully below, likewise reveals little about the function of a certificate program, expected integration into existing programming, and distinctions between a certificate, a minor, and a major.

With those vagaries in mind, we begin with what we know. Undergraduate certificate programs at University of Cincinnati require students to complete eighteen credit hours on average. Existing certificates across the university range from interdisciplinary (African studies, biblical studies, international human rights), disciplinary (ancient Greek, bioethics, chemistry), to paraprofessional (animation, accounting technology, and broadcast media). A combination of the three, the CP program requires students to take courses in rhetoric and professional writing, creative writing, style and grammar, and book arts (the latter is a collaboration between faculty in literature and staff in The Preservation Lab, whose primary mission is to conserve and preserve university and public library collections). The certificate also requires an internship through which students have the opportunity to apply what they have learned in a variety of professional, academic, and publishing settings. The CP certificate's aim is to prepare students to work in print and digital editing, literary and trade publishing, and corporate communications as editors, copywriters, content strategists, and web content editors (see Appendix for the proposal). When we designed the certificate program, we sought a balance between practical and conceptual coursework, resulting in a blended curriculum and culminating in a paraprofessional credential as well as an immersion in critical thinking, rhetorical flexibility, stylistic awareness, and visual literacy.

In the spring of 2017, we began drafting a proposal for the CP. The production and circulation of a variety of proposal formats were delivered to different audiences and presented in meetings, collaborative discussions, email threads, and an online database designed to maintain the university's program and course offerings. The proposal's activity system was both dispersed across discourse communities and contained within the larger academic approval process (Rude 2009). The specific approval process for certificate programs at our university requires submission to the following bodies:

- Departmental undergraduate studies committee
- Departmental steering committee
- Department faculty
- University undergraduate studies committee
- College of Arts & Sciences (A&S) faculty senate
- Department heads committee
- University academic curriculum committee

Each of these approvals necessitated that one or both of us attend a meeting with the particular committee to explain our rationale for creating the certificate and to answer any questions committee members had. At each step in the process, we learned something about how our immediate colleagues in English and those across A&S understand the work of our fields and of this conjoined certificate. For example, at the macro level, A&S faculty senate members interpreted our proposal as traversing disciplines and adding value to coursework in communications and journalism. At the micro level, the undergraduate studies committee in our department viewed the certificate as a step toward bridge-building across areas within English, an effort in the making for several years now as faculty members cope with a shrinking population of student majors and a desire to amplify the value of what we do in practical terms. One form this valuation has taken is an emphasis on transferable skills, both at department and college levels. In the department, this emphasis has been integrated into activities at departmental retreats. At the college level, all faculty in A&S were recently asked by the dean to include language on our syllabi highlighting transferable skills in the form of outcomes. The goal is to help students appreciate the value of the liberal arts beyond classroom walls, as communicated in an email distributed to faculty in September 2018: "Our students need to understand how our liberal arts courses prepare them for a diversity of satisfying career paths, and they need to develop the ability to present their transferable skill strengths to future employers."

GENRE AND THE TRANSMISSION OF AFFECT

On first glance, a workhorse genre like the institutional certificate proposal hardly seems likely to generate emotion beyond the expected worries about disciplinary turf common in academic culture. However, because the proposal form outlines a proposed future that, wittingly or not, includes and excludes participants and stages new or reconfigured coalitions within an organization, we suggest that this seemingly antiseptic genre can function as a generator of affective contagion, a source for the spread of emotions across bodies. Teresa Brennan offers a detailed explanation of this concept in *The Transmission of Affect* (2004). Affective transmission, explains Brennan, refers to the idea "that the emotions or affects of one person, and the enhancing or depressing energies these affects entail, can enter into another" (3). Transmission is a social process, enabled by proximity and permeable boundaries between individuals who "are not self-contained in terms of our energies" (6). Further, transmission can result in people becoming "alike" as well as taking up "opposing positions in relation to a common affective thread" (9). This process of becoming is similar to Sara Ahmed's (2004) description of sticky emotions. In her model, emotions circulate, creating relationships between like and unlike things—relationships that then become sticky. Sticky emotions bind people together and bind individual to collective.

Genres, too, can become sticky when they circulate within organizations and accrue meanings that exceed their original intention or that make visible feeling norms within an organization otherwise obscured. This conception of genre draws both from affect studies and rhetorical genre studies, the latter of which defines genre as "typified rhetorical actions based in recurrent situations" (Miller 1984, 159). Miller describes genre as a fusion of form and substance, noting that form "shapes the response of the reader or listener to substance by providing instruction, so to speak, about how to perceive and interpret; this guidance disposes the audience to anticipate, to be gratified, to respond in a certain way" (1984, 159). Genre's pedagogical function is entangled with "the structures of power that institutions wield" (Miller 1994, 71). We can't fully understand genres without "understanding the system of commonality of which they are a constituent, without exploring further the nature of the collectivity" (Miller 1994, 72). And collectivity contains a dialectic of "sameness and difference . . . agreement and dissent . . . identification and division" (Miller 1994, 74).

Power, identification, and division—these elements of genre and its usage are amplified through circulation. The circulation of genre influences its meaning and uptake; that is, genre "acquires meaning from situation and from the social context in which that situation arose" (Miller 1984, 163). And, in turn, genres "endow situations with a 'logic' or 'common sense,'" (Bawarshi 2003)—an articulation that echoes Miller's view that "genre embodies an aspect of cultural rationality" (1984, 165). Miller's conclusion emphasizes understanding social knowledge so that we are successful in creating, communicating, and interpreting appropriate discourse for particular audiences. This conclusion seems to assume that shared community values and knowledge make for smooth communication processes. What we are interested in here, however, is the less understood ways in which genres function as sticky, emotioned conduits for identity as they circulate across speech acts and communities.

Understanding the ideology driving affective speech acts adds to our understanding of genres as sites of ideological action in organizational contexts (Berkenkotter 2001; Berkenkotter and Ravotas 1997; Paré 2002; Popham 2005; Schryer 1993). More specifically, it can illuminate how instrumental documents influence identity, reproducing and challenging relationships between individuals and groups in academic settings. This work of identity- and relationship-making and unmaking forms a pedagogical text instructing close and distant colleagues how to make sense of work and how to envision students. In our proposal, for example, we describe a concept of work that is practical and technical, and students as applied learners—constructions that unearthed anxieties around what English is and should be.

STICKY EMOTIONS AND DEPARTMENTAL IDENTITY

Studying what genres *do* rather than what they *are* affiliates genre with action and movement, both of which are linked to social views of emotion. Shaped by cultural and social systems like genres, emotions are expressed through physical sensations and responses. Much as genres become sites upon which "battles over values are played out" (Freedman and Medway 1994, ix), emotions, too, embody value systems through their alignment or misalignment with cultural expectations and feeling rules.

Not that any of this was apparent to us when we began this process. In the first stages of our certificate proposal process, the genre did indeed seem innocuous. When we presented our initial draft of the certificate proposal to the undergraduate studies committee composed of faculty from all four areas of our department, committee members were enthusiastic. In fact, in one of our early email exchanges, the undergraduate director described it as a "phenomenal idea." In a meeting in November 2017 the committee unanimously approved the proposal with minor changes.

We began to see the dissonance generated by the proposal in our next step of the approval process, a full department faculty meeting. A senior literary and cultural studies (LCS) faculty member raised concerns that the certificate would exclusively benefit students in the rhetoric and professional writing track and lure students away from the LCS major, already struggling to attract students and fill classes. Though we included classes from all tracks in the proposed certificate, only one of the required six classes was an LCS course, and that one, Book Arts, was newly developed just for the certificate. It is true that LCS courses were not central to the proposed program, but since we did not set out to reproduce the work of the major, this choice seemed appropriate. During our initial conversations about the certificate, we viewed it as additive to the English major, while some (not all) of our LCS colleagues came to view it as subtractive, as taking away something essential from English.

As conversation continued in the faculty meeting, and the undergraduate director and department head presented evidence to assuage concerns about, in essence, poaching students from what had long been the center of the department, another anxiety became apparent: the feeling of exclusion on the part of LCS faculty was tied to an apparent discomfort with this proposal's assertion of an alternative identity for English. That identity was perceived as rooted in the application of skills rather than the broadening of perspective, empathic capabilities, and literary knowledge. In other words, skills and literary cultural knowledge were viewed as mutually exclusive, one trumping the other. Perhaps, too, beneath the objections to a proposed future that did not center LCS courses was a sense that this certificate was a capitulation to the talk of transferable skills and to worries, both within and beyond university culture, about the marketability of humanities degrees generally.

Nationally, the traditional English literature degree—anchored by survey, period, and single-author courses—has been undergoing changes for several years. In our department, literature faculty, especially those trained during earlier eras who have formed their identities around an instantiation of literary study frequently viewed as outdated by non-literature colleagues, are anxious about changes that seem to further marginalize literary content and ethics and, in effect, reshape the idea of "English." In our department these national anxieties are coupled with concerns about changes to our English core curriculum. As our CP certificate was moving through the department approval process, the undergraduate studies committee was also working on a revision of our core, which a majority of faculty, including LCS members, perceived as heavily weighted with English literature courses:

- Intro to English Studies
- Intro to Shakespeare
- Survey: American Literature
- Survey: British Literature
- One Global, Ethnic, and Minority Literature course

In our environment, the proposal became a risky pedagogical document in ways we hadn't anticipated. We discovered that a proposal is more than a generic form. It runs the risk of representing a proposed future, a direction, in which some feel included and others do not. In that sense, we learned to see the proposal as a tool for building collectives as well as a mechanism for exposing fissures within collectives.

The adhesive properties of these various anxieties were strengthened by the value of "effective, transparent, democratic decision-making within the department" (University of Cincinnati 2018, 8) described in our departmental bylaws. Our department bylaws require decisions to be passed by a majority, but we and several departmental committees acted as if all faculty needed to approve the certificate. This inward-facing desire for harmony is likely a product of intermittent efforts over the past twenty years to achieve cohesiveness across the diverse tracks of our department. We have come to see the CP proposal as staking a claim of autonomy that threatened the promise of cohesiveness, a point that was underscored by comments from LCS faculty that the certificate needed to be more engaged with "English," by which we understood colleagues to mean traditional literature courses.

While, like us, a cohort of faculty were excited by the prospect of link-ing professional writing and composition in a shared mission to serve students, others responded to this linkage as a problematic destabilizing of our identity as a department. And while this tension between liter-ary studies and writing programs is in many ways a familiar, tired story within English departments, what strikes us as usable for the future is that an institutional document like a proposal should be treated as a roadmap for the future, a tool for envisioning a "we," and for teaching one another the value and risks of newly configured conceptions of "us." Alongside discussions about classes, personnel, and resources, then, institutional proposals can—perhaps *should*—generate hard talks about program identities and be treated as maps for a collective future rather than as compulsory documents that fulfill requirements and little else. This is to say that we underestimated the cultural work we were doing when building a certificate and then a proposal.

EXTRA-DEPARTMENTAL RESPONSES

That cultural work was not limited to our department. It applied also to the broad ecosystem beyond the department, to governing bodies that determine the pedagogical direction of the college and university, both what will be taught and how it will be taught. As we moved our proposal to the next approval stage—when we would meet with the university undergraduate studies committee, the A&S faculty senate, department heads committee, and the university academic curriculum committee—we prepared by considering how to frame our certificate for different discourse communities (Berkenkotter and Ravotas 1997), expecting to teach a range of audiences how to understand key terms like rhetoric, publishing, and editing and to assure those with whom we compete for dollars that our certificate would require minimal extra resources from the college.

Coming off the heels of our departmental meeting, we began the extra-departmental meeting circuit harboring our own anxieties about persuading committee members of the value and need for the certificate. Surprised by the unanticipated arguments against the CP in our department, we found that the anxieties pronounced in our departmental meetings took on an element of contagion that bonded to us. Therefore, we began to anticipate resistance based on the non-literary aspect of the proposal.

As it turns out, however, we were less bound by internal identity matters than to outside pressures related to the viability of English and the humanities in the wider marketplace. Our proposal became a teaching tool for explaining how the department proposed to integrate English skills—reading, writing, editing, digital composing and delivery—into an outward-facing credential (that is, one that could conceivably help students get jobs).

We talked about transferable skills students would gain from our coursework, with particular emphasis on the internship as an opportunity for students to apply their knowledge in contexts beyond the classroom. During this meeting one of the committee members noted that the certificate would be attractive for students in other majors as well, at which point we began to realize that the departmental impressions and concerns did not transfer to our new audiences.

At each stop, from the A&S faculty senate to the meeting of the department heads and the university academic curriculum committee, the responses were overwhelmingly positive. The heads committee instantly saw the value for our students, with heads of classics and sociology requesting that students consider internships on projects in their departments. Similarly, the academic curriculum committee head did not even include some of the changes other committee members suggested for revision because she did not see them as necessary and, we assume, wanted the certificate to move through the final stages of approval unencumbered.

Our proposal was read positively because of the potential for pedagogical innovation and collaboration that was ascribed to it by an interdisciplinary audience. Emotions attached to the proposal and to the vision we were describing for future students were unconflicted, not burdened by the weight of competing for students or altering the construct of "English." It is difficult to aim for innovation and new curricular opportunities when economic and identity issues are on the line. In this sense, pedagogical innovation is linked to overlapping contexts that come to the surface as institutional documents travel through various discourse communities. A proposal, in other words, is not read and interpreted based solely on whether it makes sense, can be implemented, and is well-written and researched. The life of a proposal and the uptake of its vision are also woven with feeling and concepts of community, the focus of our final section.

CONCLUSION

Much like other institutional genres that tend to pass into the commonsense of a place without much notice (mission statements, annual reports, official course descriptions), the proposal genre is not a neutral document that merely fulfills a requirement. Rather, the curriculum proposal genre works within the complex and contradictory relationships between individuals and social groups. Through its circulation, our proposal had the potential to destabilize in a manner that revealed aspects of group identity and challenged the idea of a collective, cohesive departmental identity. At the same time, circulation revealed alliances where they weren't expected or sought, as was the case in our meetings with extra-departmental committees, resulting in new potential relationships with the departments of sociology and classics.

In either instance, the proposal served multiple pedagogical functions laced with affective significance. On the one hand, our proposal taught departmental and university colleagues to see the work of our proposed certificate as, at least in part, applied and thereby responsive to cultural misgivings about the impracticality of humanities degrees. On the other hand, responses to the proposal from our departmental colleagues taught us something about the fragile ecosystem of a department when instrumental approaches to education loom, threatening identities that have provided coherence and meaning for generations. The economics of education, however, was not the only factor generating anxiety from our colleagues. Longstanding tensions around "English" and who gets to claim belonging contributed as well. For example, when we took the proposal outside of our department, we shed associated feelings of our particular subfields as being "largely invisible to those who explain what English is, does, or should do" (Rentz et al. 2010, 281) and of being "undervalued, overworked, and underpaid" (Crowley 1998, 5). In other words, outside of the department we had to position ourselves as central members of a discourse community (the English Department) rather than as marginalized members of the department. In doing so, we inadvertently positioned our literature colleagues as decentralized members of the English Department.

As a living document that partially functions to destabilize departmental identities, the certificate proposal genre, and perhaps other institutional genres that internally shape curriculum, can unstick long-standing identities that have outlived their usefulness for the sake of pedagogical innovation. However, in our case, the institutional history of rifts within the department suggests that genre's reputation as a tool for communicating shared goals and visions may be overstated when it circulates in a less than harmonic discourse community. If we do in fact work in liminal environments, both risky and harmonious, we can draw insights from Gloria Anzaldúa (2012), who writes about identity and community from her perspective as a feminist of color who grew up in the border town of Rio Grande Valley of South Texas. In her discussion of the limits of identity politics, Anzaldúa finds that feminists "need new categories, new conceptions of community" (263) that can help navigate risky "alliances with others who do not fit into the categories of our self-identity" (264). Applying lessons from Anzaldúa to a very different context, we see that relinquishing old divisions that no longer serve a larger concept of community is important for innovation and for student-centered programming. That is, while some of our LCS colleagues held on to a notion of English centered on literary studies, we too held on to a notion of English that figured us as playing defense against (some of) our LCS colleagues. We learned from our extra-departmental audiences that both stances are limiting wastes of energy; those audiences taught us to look more closely at the work we are doing as a unit. In sum, the work that mundane genres, such as the certificate proposal discussed in this chapter, do in pedagogical-intellectual communities shape both teaching identities and teaching behind the scenes.

APPENDIX 12.A

Proposed Certificate Name and College Offering It:
Copyediting & Publishing Certificate College: McMicken A&S

Proposing unit(s), department(s) or school(s):
Department of English and Comparative Literature Rhetoric and Professional Writing Track

Describe the initiative and rationale for which approval is being sought:
The goal of this certificate is to provide students with skills essential for being successful in careers that involve the production and delivery of

both print and digital texts. The program will prepare students to work in a range of professional environments where close reading and editing skills are imperative to generating clear and effective communication.

Summary of proposed program:

The copyediting and publishing certificate draws on the strengths of all three undergraduate English tracks (Rhetoric and Professional Writing, Creative Writing, and Literary and Cultural Studies). The goal of the certificate is to create skilled copyeditors, editorial assistants and publishing professionals who can compete in a diverse local and national marketplace that includes editing opportunities in book publishing, literary and trade publications, online content editing, and corporate communications. These opportunities include positions as digital editors, associate editors, copywriters, content strategists, and web content editors.

Section I: Need and Demand

The American Academy of Arts & Sciences recently reported a nearly 9 percent decrease in humanities degrees conferred across US institutions between 2014 and 2015. Academy researchers noted that, since 2014, the number of students earning bachelor's degrees in English fell 17 percent, mirroring a similar decline overall in humanities degrees. We read this decline as an expression of the disconnect between the humanities and job prospects.

In an effort to address this disconnect, our certificate program will build on the success of our rhetoric and professional writing track by offering a practical, applied program of study to undergraduates who are passionate about verbal and visual communication and who seek opportunities to apply their skill set directly to existing editorial job openings. Students who complete the certificate will earn a credential with easily recognizable value in the publishing world. More specialized and specific than a bachelor's degree in English, the certificate will communicate to potential employers students' readiness to meet the growing demand for editors in a variety of fields, genres, and professional contexts. In a 2016 Forbes article, George Anders describes 14 high-paying jobs for which English majors are typically hired. Near the top of the list are editor positions. The need for effective communication is not limited by genre, medium, or purpose; we aim to prepare students to meet this need.

Section II: Educational Requirements

The certificate requires students to complete 6 required courses, or 18 credit hours, including an internship.

- Required Courses (4 courses; 12 credit hours total)
    - ENGL 2004: Introduction to Copyediting and Publishing (new course)
    - ENGL 3046: Modern English Grammar (average enrollment: 35)
    - ENGL 4107: Copyediting and Publishing Internship (new course)
    - ENGUPWRT 5124: Editing Professional Documents (average enrollment: 15)
- Choose 1 of the following courses (3 credit hours)
    - ENGL 3070: Desktop Publishing (average enrollment: 20)
    - ENGL 4097: Digital and Visual Editing (new course)
    - ENGL 5128: Publishing and New Media (average enrollment: 15)
- Choose 1 of the following courses (3 credit hours)
    - ENGL 3076: Writing with Style (average enrollment: 25)
    - ENGL 3096: Creative Writing and Publishing (new course)
    - ENGL 3097: Book Arts (new course)

Student Learning Outcomes
- Students earning a copyediting and publishing certificate should be able to
    - Consult, interpret and apply appropriate stylistic, grammatical, and formatting guidelines during the editing process
    - Communicate with web and print designers during production stages of manuscript and/or text development
    - Use digital tools fluently for copyediting purposes (e.g., Microsoft Word's Track Changes, Google docs, Adobe Acrobat Pro commenting tools)
    - Apply copyediting knowledge according to audience, purpose, and situational needs
    - Collaborate on and contribute to team-based projects and develop individual ones
    - Recount/summarize the history of print publishing to digital publishing processes by accruing knowledge of the materials, processes, and tools necessary for the creation of each form
    - Work in a professional setting during the completion of the internship and act responsibly (be on time, communicate effectively, meet deadlines, etc.)

REFERENCES

Ahmed, Sara. 2004. *The Cultural Politics of Emotion.* New York: Routledge.

Anzaldúa, Gloria. 2012. *Borderlands / La Frontera: The New Mestiza.* 4th ed. San Francisco: Aunt Lute Books.

Bawarshi, Anis. 2003. *Genre and the Invention of the Writer: Reconsidering the Place of Invention in Composition.* Logan: Utah State University Press.

Berkenkotter, Carol. 2001. "Genre Systems at Work: DSM-IV and Rhetorical Recontextualization in Psychotherapy Paperwork." *Written Communication* 18 (3): 326–49.

Berkenkotter, Carol, and Doris Ravotas. 1997. "Genre as Tool in the Transmission of Practice over Time and across Professional Boundaries." *Mind, Culture, and Activity* 4 (4): 256–74.

Brennan, Teresa. 2004. *The Transmission of Affect.* Ithaca, NY: Cornell University Press.

Crowley, Sharon. 1998. *Composition in the University: Historical and Polemical Essays.* Pittsburgh, PA: University of Pittsburgh Press.

Freedman, Aviva, and Peter Medway, eds. 1994. *Genre and the New Rhetoric.* Bristol, PA: Taylor & Francis.

Georgetown University. 2018. "Oregon Certificate Holders Can Double Earnings, Research Shows." Center on Education and the Workforce. https://cew.georgetown.edu/?s =certificate.

Harner, Sandi, and Anne Rich. 2005. "Trends in Undergraduate Curriculum in Scientific and Technical Communication Programs." *Technical Communication* 52 (2): 209–20.

Meloncon, Lisa. 2012. "Current Overview of Academic Certificates in Technical and Professional Communication in the United States." *Technical Communication* 59 (3): 207–22.

Miller, Carolyn R. 1984. "Genre as Social Action." *Quarterly Journal of Speech* 70 (2): 151–67.

Miller, Carolyn R. 1994. "Rhetorical Community: The Cultural Basis of Genre." In *Genre and the New Rhetoric*, edited by Aviva Freedman and Peter Medway, 67–78. Bristol, PA: Taylor & Francis.

National Student Clearinghouse (NSC) Research Center. 2016. "Undergraduate Degree Earners—2016." NSC Research Center. https://nscresearchcenter.org/undergraduate degreeearners-2014-15.

Norman, Rose, and Kim Pruett Wells. 1997. "Certificate Programs." In *Education in Scientific and Technical Communication: Academic Programs That Work*, edited by Michael L. Keene, 125–49. Arlington, VA: Society for Technical Communication Press.

Paré, Anthony. 2002. "Genre and Identity: Individuals, Institutions, and Ideology." In *The Rhetoric and Ideology of Genre: Strategies for Stability and Change*, edited by Richard M. Coe, Lorelei Lingard, and Tatiana Teslenko, 57–71. Cresskill, NJ: Hampton Press.

Popham, Susan L. 2005. "Forms as Boundary Genres in Medicine, Science, and Business." *Journal of Business and Technical Communication* 19 (3): 279–303.

Rentz, Kathryn, Mary Beth Debs, and Lisa Meloncon. 2010. "Getting an Invitation to the English Table—and Whether or Not to Accept It." *Technical Communication Quarterly* 19 (3): 281–99.

Rude, Carolyn D. 2009. "Mapping the Research Questions in Technical Communication." *Journal of Business and Technical Communication* 23 (2): 174–215.

Schryer, Catherine F. 1993. "Records as Genre." *Written Communication* 10 (2): 200–34.

University of Cincinnati. 2018. "English Department Policy Documents." Department of English and Comparative Literature. https://www.artsci.uc.edu/departments/english .html.

13

PEDAGOGICAL IDENTITY IN A DIGITAL WORLD
Challenge and Collaboration in the Course Proposal Genre

Cynthia Pengilly

In today's digital world, it has become increasingly normal, perhaps even expected, for various genres related to academic activity to be stored and shared online. On one hand, the digitalization of academic genres can lead to greater transparency and visibility, especially when it comes to genres related to pedagogy that have been previously obscured or unavailable for critical analysis. On the other hand, however, that shift brings with it a number of other potential professional challenges, of which we know little about.

In her 2005 piece, "Beyond Accommodation: Individual and Collective in a Large Writing Program," Christy Desmet describes the pedagogical identities of writing instructors in a writing program as existing along a continuum of ideological positions, located somewhere between accommodation and resistance. She also identifies how pedagogical genres, such as the syllabus and other internal curriculum documents, often obscure the related conversations, negotiations, and collaboration that took place during the production of those genres. In other words, the process behind that of pedagogical genre creation is often lost to institutional and/or program memory. Desmet's description of those "hidden decisions" (117) is reminiscent of the phenomenon documented by Swales (1996), when he identifies how genres related to academic research and scholarship, such as the manuscript submission letter, are often occluded from public view. Bawarshi (2003) has built on Swales's notion of occlusion, in his persuasive account of classroom genres, such as the syllabus, assignment prompt, and student essay, many of which he identifies as being occluded—not publicly visible but critical in constructing the interrelated genre network of the classroom. Neaderhiser (2016) has expanded this conversation by tracing the complexity of pedagogical

https://doi.org/10.7330/9781646422920.c013

genres across multiple contexts, both within and beyond the walls of the classroom. According to Neaderhiser, teachers' professional identities have always been shaped by pedagogical genres and actions extending beyond the classroom, but such genres are often "restricted to how [they] speak directly to or about the classroom rather than how [they] might also represent a teacher's *pedagogical identity in those other contexts*" (emphasis added).

I was afforded an opportunity to reflect upon this body of scholarship, albeit in hindsight, after recently submitting a course proposal at my home institution, Central Washington University. Until that point, I had considered such pedagogical work to be a uniquely personal endeavor, even if I did occasionally solicit feedback from others, but this notion, and my own pedagogical identity by extension, was called into question by CWU's highly transparent and visible curriculum review process (which I was not grateful for at the time). So, naturally, when the course description and associated learning outcomes in my course proposal were challenged by another department within my own college, I found myself in a unique and uncomfortable position; I was thrust into a series of interdisciplinary collaborations to reach an amicable agreement for all parties. The redesign process brought to light the tensions between individual and collective ownership of curriculum, which, in this case, included two different departments as well as the larger institution. While I may have resisted the notion of the redesign process early on, by the end of the process, I welcomed the opinions and advice of others, as I gained greater appreciation for the intersecting disciplinary and pedagogical identities available from both departments. This chapter, then, attempts to record this institutional memory—of pedagogical genre creation—to reveal the hidden collaboration process behind the creation of the course proposal genre while also exploring the ideological positions taken up by faculty along the way.

This chapter explores these ideological positions by highlighting the significance of *collaboration* in one writing professor's creation of the course proposal genre and the sense of professional and pedagogical identity around/within the resultant interdisciplinary *collaborations* to revise the course. With regard to Neaderhiser's (2016) conception of pedagogical identity, this chapter describes a particular process of collaboration in one traditionally occluded, isolated, and personal pedagogical genre of the course proposal. For example, in this case, the collaborative space was used for negotiation and expression of diverse ideas and disciplinary perspectives resulting in a decidedly improved course proposal. Furthermore, this case highlights how the act of making peda-gogical genres public can influence both individual and disciplinary pedagogical identities.

INSTITUTIONAL CONTEXT: COURSE REVIEW PROCESS

At CWU, several layers of curriculum review exist when proposing a new course. I had successfully proposed two previous courses, so I was familiar with my institution's informal and formal review process, which involved the sharing and publication of the course proposal at the department, college, and institutional levels. The review process varies slightly at the department and college levels, but all courses are formally (and publicly) reviewed at the institutional level through the online curriculum management system, Curriculog. The proposed course was titled ENG 315: Visual Rhetoric and Document Design. As someone with industry experience as a technical writer and a master's degree in technical communication, I felt relatively secure in my disciplinary knowledge and pedagogical identity. Hence, of all the courses I'd sub-mitted for review as new tenure-track faculty, this was the course I was least prepared to defend when the time came.

English Department Review Process

The CWU English Department comprises thirteen tenured or tenure-track faculty (including myself) and twenty-eight non-tenure-track fac-ulty (nine of whom are senior lecturers with voting rights), with a range of specialties covering literature, professional and technical writing, lin-guistics and TESOL, language arts and teacher education, and creative writing. The idea for a new course is first pitched at a program commit-tee meeting comprising tenured and tenure-track faculty, such as the Professional and Creative Writing committee. The program committee is responsible for program development, curriculum matters (i.e., cur-riculum review, development, and assessment), and advising students in the major. After a course has been approved at the program committee level, the faculty is given permission to design the course and formally propose it at the next department meeting.

When the course is formally proposed at that subsequent meeting, department faculty are provided with the genre ecology, or collection, of artifacts associated with the course proposal, and the faculty member proposing the course is allotted time on the agenda to present and dis-cuss the course. The course proposal process and genred expectations include a number of other "helper" genres such as the course rationale, course description, outcomes and assessments, and a list of activities and/or description of one or two major assignments. The course proposal process involves several intersecting pedagogical genres, each requiring a certain degree of genre mastery and pedagogical acuity in their own right. In the case of ENG 315: Visual Rhetoric and Document Design, I provided written documentation outlining the basic elements of the course and how it would be used as an elective in our BA in professional and creative writing (PCW) program and as a required option in the new technical writing minor (to fulfill the information design criteria). The course also filled two specific needs for the program and students. First, the course aligned the professional writing course offerings with other professional and technical writing programs in the discipline by offering a dedicated course about information design. Second, the course addressed a direct request from PCW alumni who cited basic design skills and knowledge of industry software as areas where they initially struggled in their careers as journalists, book editors, and technical writers, among other professions.

During open discussion time, which sometimes continues via follow-up emails, department members provide feedback and recommendations such as supplemental texts or readings, improved phrasing for course outcomes, or other pedagogical suggestions. The entire process, from course presentation to open discussion, typically takes approximately ten to fifteen minutes, depending on (1) the type and level of course, (2) the clarity of the course materials, and (3) discussion of any anticipated problems. What I describe here is more of an informal review process in terms of atmosphere and overall acceptance of ideas. There are rarely objections to a course proposal since the first level of review already occurred at the program committee level. However, the course outcomes are sometimes subjected to wordsmithing, which is to be expected in an English department. After discussion has resolved, the department takes a formal vote on the course and successful courses move to the next stage of review, which requires the course to be submitted to Curriculog for institutional review.

For the ENG 315 course proposal, the open discussion time was extended to twenty-five minutes, and a majority of that time was spent troubleshooting the university's software license for Adobe Suite, which did not extend to online students. In the end, the course was approved without a resolution to the software access issue (which is still an ongoing matter) and without recommendations to the course outcomes, though some of the major assignments were discussed, including a useful recommendation from our online pedagogy expert about converting one of the projects to a group assignment. ENG 315 passed through the discussion stage, and I submitted the course to Curriculog the following week.

Institutional Review Process

After a course is approved at the department level, it must be formally proposed through the online curriculum management system, Curriculog, which is then reviewed by the university's Faculty Senate Curriculum Committee (FSCC). The FSCC has primary jurisdiction for all curriculum matters to include newly proposed courses, programs, minors, and certificates, as well as any revisions. The Curriculog system was clearly adopted to align with the institution's initiative for greater transparency as anyone with the website address can view curriculum proposals during any stage in the process (in-progress/active, rejected, or approved/completed). However, only authorized users with password protected accounts can initiate new proposals or make curriculum revisions. In short, CWU has shifted the entire pedagogical process of curriculum design to the online platform, thus revealing the multiple layers and levels of this pedagogical process for all to see, which can sometimes involve several departments (as is the case with cross-listed courses) and/or multiple levels of approval depending on the type of course (i.e., reviews by FSCC, General Education Committee, and/or Graduate Committee).

For undergrad courses that are not within the General Education program, the course must pass through three levels of Curriculog approval before reaching FSCC (department chair, college dean, and registrar services). During the FSCC review phase, the course is shared with the entire academic community outside of the Curriculog system, via an Excel spreadsheet known as the Curriculum Summary Log, which is emailed to all faculty and departments for review. This duplication exists because the Curriculum Summary Log predates the Curriculog system (i.e., faculty are familiar with the process), and a large number of faculty are not responsible for developing new curriculum or have not had the need/opportunity to do so, which made the required use of Curriculog seem punitive toward this group of faculty, who still require a means of equal access to proposed and finalized curriculum changes. Per the FSCC email template detailing the review period, "If there are no concerns [with proposed courses], the curriculum will be approved" (FSCC, email to author, 2018), thus prompting academic departments to act quickly if they would like to place a hold on a course.

The Department of Art + Design first became aware of the ENG 315 course at an FSCC meeting, where the Curriculum Summary Log was openly discussed on the senate floor. According to CWU policy, "Any member of the academic community can request a hold on FSCC action by submitting a completed hold petition form" (CWUR Policy 2-50-040), which provides departments with two weeks to reach an amicable solution or else FSCC will make the final decision. In the case of the ENG 315 course proposal, a formal hold was never submitted to FSCC, but an email inquiry about the course from the Department of Art + Design was interpreted as a "soft" challenge requiring our immediate attention.

CHALLENGE, COLLABORATION, AND CONTROL

After the soft challenge was received, a joint meeting was scheduled between English and Art + Design, with three faculty from each department. There were two department chairs and four faculty members, including myself, and I was the only faculty without tenure. The process of collaboration that took place following the soft course challenge involved three stages of understanding and awareness, each of which challenged our individual pedagogical identities. Our first obstacle to overcome was our differing understandings of the FSCC course hold or petition process, specifically which aspects of a new course could be challenged. Next, we were forced to cross disciplinary boundaries and gain awareness of other disciplinary practices; in short, we had to retrain our brains to think of disciplinary identity not as demarcations but as intersections—spaces that enable us to grow and learn from one another. Finally, we revised the ENG 315 course description and outcomes while considering the recently acquired cross-disciplinary knowledge. This last stage involved the difficult task of balancing collaboration and control in the course proposal redesign, especially considering the traditionally occluded and isolated practices associated with this pedagogical genre.

Stage 1: Understanding the institutional policy for course challenges.
Since both departments are a part of the same college, College of Arts and Humanities (CAH), we were expected to resolve the issue without a formal hold through FSCC, so the email inquiry between departments was enough exigence to initiate the review process. The initial email caused quite a stir of emotion, personally speaking, as it seemed to assert

that the problem was with my course thus calling into question my own disciplinary understanding. The email read as follows:

> Hi Cynthia. You[r] new course proposal, ENG 315, Visual Rhetoric and Document Design caught the attention of several art + design faculty. I spoke with [name removed] today about this. We think it might be best for us to meet and discuss the course content and how you might be able to rewrite some of the course description and learner outcomes that might better describe the course. The way it reads, it seems very similar to what we teach over here.

Initially, I was quite upset about the email because I knew that many technical communication programs offered such courses, which clearly identified it as part of my discipline's practice. As a result, my first response was to outline a few talking points to use in our first meeting, with the sole purpose of defending the course on its disciplinary merits (see Appendix, "Talking Points").

The talking points served as a sort of mini-genre, one which contributed to my ideological positioning in regard to the course proposal. In this document, I began by addressing three important points about the intentionality behind the course design: it was (a) intended for non-art majors, (b) developed in response to our English alumni who lacked essential design knowledge and industry software experience, and (c) aligned with technical and professional writing/communication programs around the nation. I also highlighted how the course would be taught exclusively online to serve our growing online student population, especially noting the lack of online courses offered by the Art + Design Department. Finally, I concluded the talking points with what I thought was an amicable solution—to simply rename the course.

As is the standard practice in a genre aptly named "talking points," I decided to email the document ahead of the meeting with the hopes of getting everyone on the same page; however, the email only made matters worse since tensions were high. The follow-up questions grew in number and were often buried in long email chains due to the number of stakeholders involved. This response to the talking points email was significant for a number of reasons but especially with regard to how institutional expectations of the course proposal genre would impose itself on our cross-departmental collaboration, thus rendering the talking points less useful than even I had intended.

To be specific, sometime during the barrage of emails, I reached out to FSCC for guidance on how to proceed, especially in light of the obvious tensions in the email chain. I was informed in no uncertain terms that (1) *an academic department cannot own a concept* and thereby restrict others from its use and (2) new courses are automatically approved *permitted that there is not a duplication in course outcomes.* In other words, as it was explained to me, "English does not own the concept of writing any more than Art owns the concept of design" (personal email, 2017). For example, the Art + Design Department can offer writing courses for their students and English can offer design courses, provided that there is not a duplication in course outcomes. So, following the guidance of FSCC, I shifted our collaborative focus to duplicate course outcomes, as opposed to pedagogical approaches, which were not valid grounds for a course petition hold. Coincidentally, that is precisely what the talking points document set out to defend—my pedagogical and disciplinary positioning—which were less fruitful in achieving the overall goals of the course proposal redesign, at least according to my institution's policy for course challenges.

When I shared this vital information from FSCC with both departments, it resulted in another round of follow-up questions. However, having the knowledge of these two FSCC policies regarding our institution's curriculum review process ultimately helped us to better understand the daunting task ahead. Below is a short excerpt of an email exchange that took place the day before the multi-department meeting:

> **My comments to the entire group**: Thank you [names removed]. According to the information received from FSCC, we are to focus our attention on "duplicate outcomes" not individual teaching style, practices, or project deliverables (for example, every discipline includes writing as a final project or deliverable, but ENG does not have jurisdiction to oppose such courses on those grounds alone).
>
> **Response from one Art + Design colleague**: I am confused, but again it is because I am unfamiliar with this process. But, if for example, I wanted to include creative writing in our curriculum (which I have thought about at times), are you saying I could teach creative writing, or technical writing, or maybe editing in the graphic design curriculum so long as the outcomes were not duplicated? I had no idea we could do things like this if it is the case.

What these excerpts demonstrate is how a clear understanding of FSCC's less-publicized policies—such as how a department cannot own a concept or course topic as long as the course outcomes are unique—helped us to better navigate our institutional context, thus providing opportunity for each collaborator to further define, and even sharpen, our individual pedagogical identities. In short, once both departments realized the function of the hold process and what aspects of a course could be challenged, we were able to move forward to the next stage of collaborative process: crossing disciplinary boundaries.

Stage 2: Crossing disciplinary boundaries to gain true awareness of others.
As English faculty, one of our primary goals at the meeting was to help our Art + Design Department colleagues understand the value of design principles in the field of professional and technical writing and why our student population needed the course to be offered online and with fewer prerequisite courses (art and design students completed at least four courses before being introduced to InDesign software). We also stressed how the course content would be limited to coverage of basic design principles and beginner-level use of industry software, such as Adobe InDesign, as opposed to the more advanced study of design offered in their own department. Furthermore, we used our own industry experience as examples of the need for the course, as both I and another English colleague at the meeting had previously held positions in information technology firms as technical writers. It was important to us to prepare our students for the type of work and skills—both theoretical and practical/technical—that they would be expected to know in industry, and we used this opportunity to share our experiences. We hoped that such examples would help our art and design colleagues to better understand our disciplinary training and practices and how the teaching of basic design principles could exist simultaneously in the English Department and the Art + Design Department so that we, collectively speaking, could get back to the task of preparing CWU students for long-term success.

It took some time to reach cross-disciplinary understanding as a group, but we discovered some important things about our intersecting disciplinary interests along the way. For example, while discussing basic design principles, the group shifted to a discussion of possible texts that might be considered in such a course. The Art + Design Department faculty were pleased to discover that I was familiar with key introductory texts in the field and had already selected William's *Non-Designer's Design Book* along with selected readings from Tufte's *Visual Explanations*. At another point, the English Department faculty were asked to define or explain what we meant by "visual rhetoric" since it held a prominent position in our original course outcomes (see table 13.1). This discussion allowed us to piece together our fractured understanding of design studies, caused by disciplinary boundaries, via a groupwide exploration of the various distinctions between document design, information design, design literacy, and visual rhetoric from the perspective of designers, design educators, and rhetoricians. Within the group, it would seem that we actually shared a great deal of design terminology as well as a few major theorists, which helped to bridge the gap between our respective disciplines.

Furthermore, upon the realization that the course would be offered primarily (if not exclusively) online, we brainstormed strategies to address the theoretical and practical aspects of the course in the span of a ten-week quarter. This led us to a discussion about how an institutional license to Lynda.com would be essential in an online course such as ours because it could help students learn the practical aspects of Adobe's InDesign to mitigate the burden on the instructor. In fact, we discovered that each of our departments had previously reached out to the university about purchasing Adobe software licenses for online students but without much success. Both departments were in such agreement about this matter that the Art + Design Department chair offered to advocate for the software on our behalf, reaching out via email after the meeting: "I am happy to go with you . . . to talk about the need for Lynda.com. I think that would be a big help with a class such as this" (personal email, 2018). In this moment of solidarity, both departments bonded over the pedagogical problem of providing equitable access to online students, and we agreed about the solution to this problem, which made this moment particularly memorable for me as a scholar of digital pedagogy and online writing instruction.

What began as a turf war about whether the English Department should teach design classes shifted to an understanding of why design principles were necessary to both disciplines and how such skills are essential for landing (and keeping) a job in the private sector. However, even with our newfound understanding of cross-disciplinary practices, there were several moments of tension in the room, especially during the act of revising course outcomes, which required an active negotiation on my part between collaboration and control.

Stage 3: Balancing collaboration and control in the course proposal redesign.
The entire meeting was a practice in collaborative learning and collaborative writing. Because I am a former writing center director, this experience brought to mind Bruffee (1996) and Lunsford's (1995) work on the challenges of collaboration. Lunsford asserts that collaboration is most successful when the environment and tasks "demand collaboration" (39), which is not easy to achieve in contexts where there is an unequal balance of power and participant knowledge. In other words, there must be an opportunity for everyone to learn from the process in order for true collaboration to occur. This is not unlike Dively's (2015) experience with genre uptake and program reform in the training and preparation of graduate teaching assistants (GTAs),

where a standardized curriculum was adopted and implemented for teaching first-year writing. In this account, the GTAs were instrumental to the curriculum redesign process by providing ongoing feedback to program administrators, which increased their sense of agency and further highlighted the tension between pedagogical freedom and control. This account demonstrates Bruffee and Lunsford's work by highlighting the role of conversation in successful collaborations, and their research is especially useful when writing remains the primary outcome of the collaboration, much like it was during the course proposal collaboration.

As the course proposal author, I found it especially difficult at times to balance the task of collaboration with that of control. One such example was a discussion with my own English department colleagues about who might teach the course. I did not dispute my secondary knowledge of the design field behind that of my art and design colleagues, but I was wary about the prospect of handing my course over to someone else. Would they address industry expectations for non-design professions, such as technical writing and usability studies? Could they teach my students how to apply design principles to workplace documents intended for everyday users? Would they offer the course online at least once a year? This was one of my initial run-ins with the delicate balance of collaboration and control, and I struggled to reach a decision that addressed my personal, pedagogical, and disciplinary concerns.

For my English Department colleagues, however, they were working from a different source of knowledge, as they possessed a deeper understanding of CWU's institutional culture. Our academic departments had an established history of working across disciplinary boundaries, and this course challenge experience was a coaching opportunity for my colleagues to acclimate me to this new world of collaboration. First, I was reminded by my English colleagues that we had a similar arrangement with the Business Department for ENG 311: Business Writing, though in reverse order, where business faculty worked closely with the English Department to develop outcomes, assignments, and assessment criteria, and then they turned the course over to English faculty to teach it. I also recalled that I was scheduled to teach CS 325: Technical Writing in Computer Science the following academic year in a similar arrangement, thereby loaning my expertise to the Computer Science Department. These examples revealed a pattern of institutional practice that I had been unaccustomed to at previous institutions while also leading to my persuasion. The power of conversation within my own department helped me realize that I did not need to be the teacher of the ENG 315 class in order to affirm my pedagogical identity. I only needed to defend the merits of the course and advocate on behalf of our students to ensure the course was eventually offered. In other words, I had transitioned to a place where I was willing to relinquish control, or ownership, of the course in the name of collaboration. The shift in my ideological positioning demonstrates the effect of conversation and collaboration in challenging and reshaping my pedagogical identity, especially with regard to the different pedagogical roles I might inhabit during the course of my tenure at CWU, besides that of teaching.

The next pedagogical role expected of me was that of facilitator, as I was responsible for guiding the redesign process to an agreeable conclusion. As the group shifted its attention to the course proposal itself, I was charged again with the difficult task of balancing collaboration and pedagogical control. My pedagogical identity was unveiled for all to see during this process. We gathered around the table with ink pens and copies of the course proposal in hand, talking about each outcome as we revised, rearranged, and deleted entire passages. Indeed, the clarity with which I had originally imagined the course was beginning to fade. There were moments, for instance, when I was forced to explain my pedagogical reasoning, which was akin to being under a microscope—I had to convince not only myself (due to the increasing doubt I was feeling) but also the five other pedagogical experts in the room. Sometimes I succeeded in explaining my pedagogical intent for a particular outcome, as was the case with the first outcome, which asked students to "demonstrate an understanding of theories of visual rhetoric." On other occasions, however, I was not as successful, which provided further practice, and opportunity, in balancing the tasks of collaboration, collaborative writing, and pedagogical control.

As table 13.1 demonstrates, we made several significant revisions to the course outcomes. The first and second outcomes were lightly wordsmithed for improvement in phrasing and style, but the overall intent remained the same. The most significant changes took place in outcomes 3–6, as the fifth outcome was moved up higher in the list (to position 3), and outcomes 3 and 4 were simplified and combined into a single outcome. The outcomes would go through a third round of revision with FSCC to further refine the verb choice and alignment with Bloom's taxonomy (last column in table 13.1). By the end of the process, our collective pedagogical team of two departments and the FSCC had completely overhauled the course outcomes to something that was, admittedly, quite improved from the original.

Table 13.1. Copy of the original, revised, and final course outcomes for ENG 315

Original Outcomes	Revised Outcomes	Final Outcomes
1. Demonstrate understanding of theories of visual rhetoric.	1. Demonstrate an understanding of theories of visual rhetoric.	1. Describe theories of visual rhetoric.
2. Develop the vocabulary and rhetorical awareness to critique a design based on rhetorical purpose and goals.	2. Develop the vocabulary and rhetorical awareness to critique design elements based on audience, purpose, and goals.	2. Develop the vocabulary and rhetorical awareness to critique design elements based on audience, purpose, and goals.
3. Design rhetorically effective documents by manipulating color, type, image, and page layout.	3. Evaluate how basic design principles affect readability, functionality, interpretation, and communication of information.	3. Analyze how design principles affect readability, functionality, interpretation, and communication of information.
4. Implement principles of effective design for both print and web-based documents according to theoretical foundations.	4. Design rhetorically effective documents, for both print and web, by applying basic design principles.	4. Design rhetorically effective documents, for both print and web, by applying basic design principles.
5. Understand how design principles affect readability, functionality, interpretation, and communication of information.	5. Develop a basic understanding of appropriate, industry-specific software used in the design process.	5. Demonstrate basic technical skills required for industry-specific design software.
6. Develop technical skills with design software to create rhetorically effective designs.		

Note: The original outcomes were written by Cynthia Pengilly, Feb. 2018. The revised outcomes were collaboratively written by English and Art + Design faculty, Apr. 2018. The final course outcomes represent the version that was published in the course catalog, after consultation with CWU's Faculty Senate Curriculum Committee.

We also made significant changes to the course description to allow for greater flexibility, pedagogically speaking, regardless of which department offers the course. These changes included removing the list of specific design principles to be covered in the class and identification of specific design software (table 13.2). Furthermore, the revision allowed the industry software to be selected by the instructor teaching the course, thus accounting for industry variations (e.g., the movement toward more open-source software, buyouts/mergers in the software industry, and the introduction of entirely new software competitors).

The redesign process revealed a number of possible scenarios that I had not considered, or envisioned, when working on the course proposal design on my own, in isolation from the surveying eye of other pedagogical experts. For instance, the fact that I designed the course with the sole intent of teaching it myself revealed my pedagogical shortcomings and my rather narrow, or limited, view of the audience in the

Table 13.2. Copy of the original and revised course description for ENG 315

Original Course Description	Revised Course Description
This course surveys the basic theories and elements of visual rhetoric, as well as principles of document design, information graphics, typography, and color. Students will gain practical experience using design software, including Adobe InDesign and Illustrator.	This course surveys the basic theories and elements of visual rhetoric, as well as principles of document design. Students will also gain practical experience using industry-specific design software.

Note: The original course description was written by Cynthia Pengilly, Feb. 2018. The revised course description was collaboratively written by English and Art + Design faculty, Apr. 2018.

course proposal process. First and foremost, it may not always be practical or feasible to teach every course that I design, especially as my duties shift, and most likely expand, in the future. And, in terms of audience, I was so focused on the administrative audience—the individuals and entities that needed to approve my proposal for it to move forward—that I failed to consider the teacher audience, or those instructors that would be teaching the course long after I am gone. These realizations have both broadened and sharpened my pedagogical acumen, which further speaks to the transformative aspects of collaboration with regard to pedagogical identity.

CONCLUSION AND IMPLICATIONS

CWU's curriculum review process has an unusually high level of transparency and visibility, which shifted traditionally occluded pedagogical genres, such as the course proposal, into the forefront for analysis. The experience of drafting and revising the course proposal genre led me to identify three intersecting levels of collaboration, each with implications on my own pedagogical identity: the institutional policy for course challenges; cross-disciplinary boundaries and pedagogical differences; and understanding when to relinquish pedagogical control.

One of the goals of this chapter, then, is to contribute to the demystification of the course proposal genre. It is not an occluded genre *strictly* because of its lack of visibility, though that is certainly a contributing factor, but also because of its operation as a de facto or routinized genre (borrowed from Miller 1984). This sentiment is echoed by Dryer's (2008) study of institutional genre networks that collectively "have a way of surreptitiously reconstituting social relations" (32), and he also addresses the importance of "de-routinizing" such pedagogical genres.

The fact that the course proposal genre often resides locally at the department and/or college level only increases its routinized nature. However, analyzing how the genre operates at the department and institutional levels exposes a much more complex connection to disciplinary (and cross-disciplinary) practices, its multiple audiences, and the roles of the varied authors/writers of the proposal. In response to the call by Bawarshi and Reiff (2010) and Neaderhiser (2016), this case reveals the tensions and complexities of the course proposal genre, to better understand how this unique institutional genre influences the pedagogical identity of several instructors, including myself.

The most surprising aspect of this experience was the role of collaboration, which eventually became the means by which we understood our own professional and pedagogical identity in relation to others. As Lunsford (1995) pointed out, true collaboration is the standard in many professions, including engineering, technical communication, and even education. I instinctively knew this from my industry experience as a programmer, technical writer, and business analyst but had yet to experience that level of collaboration as an academic, with specific implications to my pedagogical identity. I am not suggesting that collaboration is a new concept for academia, only that we know surprisingly little about it outside of research-based academic genres (Swales 1996; Clark 1995). This experience provides insight into an entirely different academic collaborative process, through the lens of pedagogical rather than scholarly (or researcher) identity, which can be extended in future studies to improve our understanding of the complex relationship between the individual and collective pedagogical identities associated with a particular genre.

Furthermore, this case contributes to the ongoing scholarly conversation about occluded pedagogical genres, especially genres with professional and pedagogical implications outside the classroom. While the use of online pedagogical systems, such as Curriculog, may not represent all institutional contexts, they are still meaningful sites of investigation because of their ability to reveal previously occluded pedagogical genres, the occlusion of the situational contexts related to those genres (Neaderhiser 2016), and the occluded conversations and collaborations that take place during the production of such genres (Desmet 2005). Finally, this case suggests that a more engaged and collaborative curriculum development process has the potential to lead to greater cross-disciplinary understanding, with the potential for positive shifts in pedagogical identity.

APPENDIX 13.A

Talking Points for Meeting with Art + Design Department

- The disciplinary perspective of this course is quite different from an art course, taking more of a new-media and professional/technical communication approach, though some of the course outcomes may overlap. Ultimately, this course is *designed* and *intended* for non-art majors.

- PCW alumni survey responses indicate a demand for this specific course and the software skills it provides, as reported by students currently employed in various industries as usability experts, book publishers, book editors, and technical writers.

- This class is an essential, core required class in technical and professional writing/communication programs around the nation; CWU's PCW program is merely aligning itself to disciplinary standards so our students remain competitive in the field (see point #2 above). The following list represents a sampling of such courses from various institutional make-ups, including regional institutions. [I think it is important to note that each institution on this list has maintained a thriving Art/Design Department alongside its Professional and Technical Writing offerings, which speaks to the disciplinary focus of such courses.]

  - ENG 3385, Information Design & Visual Rhetoric, University of Texas Arlington
  - WRIT 4260, Visual Rhetoric & Culture, University of Minnesota Duluth
  - ENG 3380, Visual Rhetoric-Document Design, Our Lady of the Lake University
  - WRIT 3671, Visual Rhetoric and Document Design, University of Minnesota
  - ENG 4030, Document Design in Professional & Technical Comm, Auburn University
  - WRA 360, Visual Rhetoric/Document Design for Prof Writers, Michigan State University
  - ENG 466, Writing, Layout, & Publication of Technical Documents (document design), University of Tennessee at Knoxville
  - ENG 2123, Rhetoric of Visuals and Infographics, Midwestern State University
  - ENG 4218, Visual Rhetoric, University of South Florida
  - ENG 3130, Document Design (emphasis on visual rhetoric and usability), University of Colorado, Colorado Springs

- The course benefits current PCW students—both sides of the program—as students are introduced to leading industry software used in professions on both sides of the major (also serves an immediate need in *Manastash*, a student run publication).

- The course benefits future initiatives in the department, such as the series or sequence of graphic narrative courses being requested by PCW students, which would blend the creative writing and professional writing sides of the program. Again, this points to the disciplinary and program-specific nature of the proposed course, which relies on basic principles of design but is fundamentally centered on rhetoric, writing, and developing transferable workplace skills in PCW.

- Finally, due to the nature of our student population, this course will be offered primarily, if not exclusively, online. To the best of my knowledge, I do not believe that any similar design-oriented courses are available to CWU's online student population.

Possible Solutions

- Add language to the course description that re-directs Art majors away from the class; this is used in CWU's History program, as I recently learned (roughly stated: "This course is not intended for history majors and will not count towards degree requirements.").

- Consider a slight modification to the course title that still captures the true essence and goals of the course (i.e., training PCW majors in basic design principles and industry-related software from a disciplinary perspective), for example, *Visual Design for Professional Writers*.

    - We already have a course titled *Rhetoric for Professional Writers*, so I'd want to avoid *Visual Rhetoric for Professional Writers*, due to the nearly identical titles, and I really want to emphasize the applied/hands-on aspect of the course which isn't captured in a rhetoric-only titled course.

    - Also, the course provides disciplinary-based training in the design of posters, infographics, visual confections, and data visualizations, so a pure document-design titled course also misses the mark. [In fact, I might actually prefer the revised course title to the original, if everyone else agrees.]

REFERENCES

Bawarshi, Anis. 2003. *Genre and the Invention of the Writer: Reconsidering the Place of Invention in Composition.* Logan: Utah State University Press.

Bawarshi, Anis, and Mary Jo Reiff. 2010. *Genre: An Introduction to History, Theory, Research, and Pedagogy.* West Lafayette, IN: Parlor Press.

Bruffee, Kenneth A. 1996. "Collaborative Learning and the 'Conversation of Mankind.'" In *Composition in Four Keys: Inquiring into the Field,* edited by Mark Wiley, Barbara Gleason, and Louise Wetherbee Phelps, 84–97. Mountain View, CA: Mayfield.

Clark, Irene L. 1995. "Collaboration and Ethics in Writing Center Pedagogy." In *The St. Martin's Sourcebook for Writing Tutors,* edited by Christina Murphy and Steve Sherwood, 88–96. New York: St. Martin's Press.

Desmet, Christy. 2005. "Beyond Accommodation: Individual and Collective in a Large Writing Program." In *Discord and Direction: The Postmodern Writing Program Administrator*, edited by Sharon James McGee and Carolyn Handa, 40–58. Logan: Utah State University Press.

Dively, Ronda Leathers. 2015. "Standardizing English 101 at Southern Illinois University Carbondale: Reflections on the Promise of Improved GTA Preparation and More Effective Writing Instruction." In *Ecologies of Writing Programs: Program Profiles in Context*, edited by Mary Jo Reiff, Anis Bawarshi, and Michelle Ballif, 41–67. Anderson, SC: Parlor Press.

Dryer, Dylan B. 2008. "The Persistence of Institutional Memory: Genre Uptake and Program Reform." *WPA: Writing Program Administration* 31 (3): 32–51.

Lunsford, Andrea A. 1995. "Collaboration, Control, and the Idea of a Writing Center." In *The St. Martin's Sourcebook for Writing Tutors*, edited by Christina Murphy and Steve Sherwood, 36–42. New York: St. Martin's Press.

Miller, Carolyn R. 1984. "Genre as Social Action." *Quarterly Journal of Speech* 70 (2): 151–67.

Neaderhiser, Stephen. 2016. "Hidden in Plain Sight: Occlusion in Pedagogical Genres." *Composition Forum* 33. http://www.compositionforum.com/issue/33/hidden.php.

Swales, John M. 1996. "Occluded Genres in the Academy: The Case of the Submission Letter." In *Academic Writing: Intercultural and Textual Issues*, edited by Eija Ventola and Anna Mauranen, 45–58. Philadelphia, PA: John Benjamins.

14

TOWARD THE LEARNING TO TEACH STATEMENT

Megan Knight and Kate Nesbit

KATE'S CONFESSION

I was first tasked with writing a statement of teaching philosophy in my second semester as a graduate instructor. I had some previous teaching experience. I had served as a college preparation mentor and ACT/SAT instructor for a college access nonprofit in St. Paul, Minnesota, and I had taught discussion sections as a teaching assistant for two years, one at my undergraduate institution and the other in the English Department at the University of Iowa. But honestly, when I set out to craft my first teaching philosophy, I had only been designing courses and running a college classroom for a matter of months. I had a lot of ideas and loads of enthusiasm. What I lacked was precisely what most guides and instructions described as central to the teaching statement: principles. How could I articulate the philosophy or principles of my teaching when I had only taught for four months? After all, I was only just learning to teach.

Still, I had significantly more teaching experience than most graduate students do when they sit down to compose a teaching statement for their job dossier. Many of my colleagues in PhD programs within the biomedical sciences, for example, write their teaching statements after having only taught one class—or after having never taught at all. Many disciplinary programs limit their graduate students' teaching opportunities for the sake of protecting research time, even though teaching will almost certainly be a part (and, for many, a significant part) of their future careers. Yet, write a teaching statement we must, regardless of how much or how little experience we have in the classroom. So, how do we reflect on our personal values and beliefs about teaching—and provide a number of fascinating and innovative examples—when we are just getting our feet wet?

After many hours spent drafting (and developing a love affair with my delete key), I wrote my first statement of teaching philosophy. Now

https://doi.org/10.7330/9781646422920.c014

that I look back on it, the statement wasn't that bad. I would describe it as a statement of how-I-want-to-be-teaching philosophy. The draft was more aspirational than descriptive, but it was full of examples and, perhaps more importantly, full of me, full of my personality. The thing I liked about this first statement of teaching philosophy was that it helped me become a better teacher: I could, with direction and intentionality, better understand and try to resemble the teacher I truly wanted to be.

But I was very unhappy with that first statement because I felt it would not help me get what it needed to help me get: a job. The statement was full of me—and that was precisely the problem. I came across as too youthful, too goofy, too emotional, too much like a friendly, smiling, maternal woman teacher. Which I am. I knew I had to incorporate pedagogical theory, relate my teaching to my own research interests, showcase my innovative use of technology and digital media, foreground rigor, and—somehow—also avoid using the saccharine or stale turns of phrase that many commentators complain about and caution against. The next semester I rewrote my teaching philosophy. And the next, I rewrote it again. And again. Each time, the teacher I described became less and less like me.

MEGAN'S CONFESSION

If anybody should have a rock-solid statement of teaching philosophy, surely it's me, who guides new teachers in writing theirs every semester in my graduate pedagogy courses. But much of my most intensive writing anxiety has focused around producing this document. I follow none of my own best advice. I flounder. I write fragments and rants and vignettes, then struggle to structure them into a coherent narrative. I have probably written a dozen versions of a statement over the course of my two decades in higher education, and I am happy with exactly none of them. Some are precious, some are abstract or dry; some just do not make very much sense. And I strongly suspect that none of them go very far in capturing what my students and I actually do in the classroom. In this way, I am someone who does not practice what she preaches—nor preach what she practices.

Over a decade ago, when I was first nominated for a teaching award, I found myself panicking as I read the instructions for assembling my nomination packet, which called for a daunting array of documents: multiple letters of support from both students and colleagues, a tabular summary of five years of course evaluations, a description of my teaching responsibilities, a CV—and a statement of teaching philosophy. That last requirement brought me up short. Had I ever written such a thing? I did not remember doing so but, rummaging around in my filing cabinet, I found a manila folder helpfully labeled PHILOSOPHY, which turned out to be crammed with notes I had forgotten I had written as a graduate student. They were a mashup of ideas and formats, some handwritten, others word-processed and then annotated extensively with highlighting and editorial comments, all of it from my years as a teaching assistant. Some of it was charmingly naïve. "I'm like a candle," I had written in one particularly sappy iteration, "bringing light to my students." Rereading the folder was a glimpse into earlier versions of my teaching self, and while in the moment I was anxious about the need to write something inventive and current, I was also strangely touched to encounter that new-teacher self again.

In the years since, I have worked on my statement of teaching philosophy in fits and starts, whenever a nomination or career advancement has called for an updated version of the document. It expands and contracts with the task at hand and with shifts in my teaching approach and perspective, but it has yet to coalesce into something that feels like me. One narrative-driven rendition foregrounded my childhood experience of playing strict schoolmarm to my younger sister's wayward student, pointing out that while those games indicated a nascent interest in becoming an educator on my part, they were no indication of the student-centered, active-learning pedagogical principles I would later come to hold. In a more recent version, I attempted to tell the story of a typical semester in my classrooms, regardless of course content or level. This version—which ended up being a part of a teaching award nomination packet the year I finally won—had me in tears of frustration by the end. It did the trick, in the sense that I was given the award, but it nonetheless felt to me like a still shot excerpted from a film: static, incomplete, and devoid of life and movement.

When grad students ask me if they can read my statement of teaching philosophy, I dodge the question.

* * *

We offer up our own confessions because we think it is time to come clean about something occluded within the teaching statement genre: the process of learning to teach. Our struggles with the teaching statement stemmed from our attempts to tidy up the messy affair of figuring out who we are as teachers. Though we are at two very different points in our careers—Megan a long-term non-tenure-track faculty member at a research university and Kate an early career scholar-teacher just now starting her first full-time position—we are both still experimenting with different techniques. We are both still trying on different teacherly personae, still learning how to teach—we confess it! No, we *embrace* it: we see adaptation, growth, and flexibility as fundamental parts of our pedagogies; in fact, these elements paradoxically constitute some of the most stable, unchanging principles of our philosophies.

So, we want to consider what it might mean to explicitly foreground this process in the statement of teaching philosophy—to intentionally integrate our own learning into statements of how we see ourselves as teachers. And this means taking seriously what was, for Kate, the most useful function of her first teaching statement draft: the opportunity to reflect and speculate on the teacher she wants to be and hopes she is in the process of becoming. In this chapter, we consider reframing the "philosophy of teaching" statement into a "learning to teach" statement. We offer an imagining of a teaching statement that foregrounds what we thought we had to hide: the evolutionary process of figuring out who we are and what we do when we teach.

BUNK OR BAD ASSIGNMENT?

Most of the recent writing on the teaching statement takes the form not of confessional, but of complaint. Publications like *The Chronicle of Higher Education* brim with protests—usually from faculty members who have sat on perhaps one too many hiring committees—against the pointlessness or banality of such documents. Leonard Cassuto (2013) refers to the statement as a "misbegotten genre" and a "bad prompt." Kevin Haggerty (2010) calls teaching statements "bunk." Rachel Narehood Austin (2006), a frequent search committee member in chemistry, is filled with "dread" at the prospect of reading "several hundred insipid teaching statements" whenever there is a new opening in her department.

In the *Chronicle*, suggestions abound for how to resolve this problem of the insufferable teaching statement. Mary Anne Lewis (2014), for example, recommends reframing the writing task as a self-portrait, while David Gooblar (2013) endorses composing the statement as a "blueprint for next semester's syllabi." Others propose replacing the teaching statement with a more illustrative document: Leonard Cassuto (2013), for instance, recommends an annotated syllabus in lieu of a statement. And a number of critics are in favor of ditching the requirement entirely. This at least seems to be the direction Jeremy Clay points toward in his *Chronicle* piece titled "Everything But the Teaching Statement" (2007), which paints the genre as an all-too-mysterious combination of a "screening form and Rorschach test."

Clearly there is a fairly broad consensus that the statement of teaching philosophy is torture to write and a misery to read. Grumpiness abounds. We get it. We are grumpy too. But we are hesitant to give up so quickly on the rare professional genre that calls on academics to reflect upon and articulate who we are as educators. After all, the statement of teaching philosophy has been, for us, a catalyst for some of the most compelling conversations about the classroom we have had, and a primary means and motivation for thinking intentionally about our pedagogical principles and practices.

In the institutional contexts in which the teaching statement circulates, the genre does indeed seem like a poorly conceived assignment: instructions are vague or contradictory, the audience endlessly variable and hard to identify, the purpose of the document often obscured. When that purpose is clear, the stakes are generally high: the statement of teaching philosophy is needed as part of a job application, or a teaching award nomination, or an advancement dossier.

There is also the question of whether statements of teaching philosophy actually demonstrate excellence or mastery of teaching. As Kevin Haggerty (2010) puts it, "Authors of impressive statements have demonstrated that they are good at the keyboard, not necessarily in the classroom." In short, neither the assignment nor its results seem to function well—especially not for new teachers in high-stakes contexts. Yet this is precisely the situation in which most of us find ourselves first tasked with crafting a teaching statement: as we apply for our first jobs after short stints as graduate instructors or teaching assistants. Accordingly, we wanted to think of a way to salvage what we see as valuable about the teaching statement, but also to reconfigure the assignment and how it operates in its institutional settings.

TRANSFORMING A GENRE

It may seem like we are advocating for a wholly new genre. Would the "learning to teach" statement still be a teaching statement? Could it still effectively operate in the same settings and with the same purpose as the statement does now? After all, there is a reason why we disguise the speculative nature of our philosophies. We write these documents with the intention of getting a job, an award, tenure—and we think that the selection committees that constitute our eventual audiences want to see a polished presentation of an intentional pedagogy. The teacher you want to become is of little interest to the document's intended readers; committees do not grant awards or offer jobs to candidates because of the teachers they hope to be. Perhaps those aspirations could or should be considered in the evaluation of teaching statements—but can we change how committees read teaching philosophies?

In the spirit of metamorphosis that this chapter champions, we want to argue for the "learning to teach" statement not as a new genre, but rather as a transformation of the existing one—a way of envisioning the teaching statement anew. This requires revising the way we write and, just as crucially, the way we read and evaluate these statements. We consider the teaching statement genre in the conditions that gave rise to it, as well as in its current institutional context—one that has occasioned a serious reckoning with how we hire and evaluate our faculty. Recent frustrations with the teaching statement, as well as the changing processes of hiring and retention in higher education more generally, indicate that the genre's readers may indeed be ready (if not already looking) for new ways of approaching the statement, new ways of considering what it might communicate about a particular candidate. We thus offer an analysis of the genre as it was, is, and could be, as we consider how and why we should advocate for new ways of approaching the teaching statement for both its writers and its readers.

MISBEGOTTEN? ORIGINS OF THE TEACHING STATEMENT IN HIGHER EDUCATION

In higher education, the genre of the statement of teaching philosophy was initially embedded in a larger movement to professionalize teaching. The rise of the genre at the university level corresponded with the publication of Ernest Boyer's pivotal 1990 report, *Scholarship Reconsidered*, which called for renewed attention to undergraduate education and a broadening of our conception of research to include teaching—what came to be called the scholarship of teaching and learning (1990, 24).

As interest in the scholarship of teaching and learning spread, so too did interest in the development of documents like the statement of teaching philosophy. Teaching portfolios—of which the statement was a key component—became an increasingly accepted means for faculty to articulate their teaching practices and to assess their teaching effectiveness. The portfolio, and the statement of teaching philosophy in particular, would seem to be an ideal vehicle for candid explorations of teaching problems not as obstacles but as natural elements of not only the processes of teaching and learning, but also the process of learning to teach.

Still, change would not happen overnight. In an educational environment that has long prioritized research over teaching, advocates of the scholarship of teaching and learning faced plenty of pushback. And the trends of dwindling educational funding and increasing corporate influence certainly did not help: In institutions increasingly subjugated to market forces, attempts to highlight and enhance teaching's centrality to the mission of institutions of higher education were at times obstructed. Instead of providing an opportunity for teachers to reflect on their practice and grow pedagogically through process, documents like the statement of teaching philosophy are all too often written—and read—under duress, reduced to job market products in which the performance of mastery is the primary goal.

Still, by the end of the twentieth century, the scholarship of teaching and learning in general and the teaching statement in particular had clearly established a firm footing in higher education hiring practices, as evidenced by the outpouring of thought pieces, writing guides, and academic articles on the topic. More recently, however, commentary on the teaching statement has become increasingly critical of the genre, just as the document itself has become an increasingly common staple of the academic dossier. The rhetorical quandary that arises from these conflicting impulses is at the heart of our proposed revisions to the genre.

REVISING OUR FOCUS: FROM REFLECTING BACK TO LOOKING FORWARD

The teaching statement, as it now stands, is what we would call a "me" document. Like its rhetorical kin, the personal statement and the statement of purpose, the genre requires an elision of rhetor and subject. When guides and advice sheets say that the teaching statement should allow its readers to see you in the classroom, to understand how you teach and why you teach that way, they are, in essence, saying that they want to know you as a teacher. Helen Grundman (2006) says as much in her instructions for composing the document: "[Y]our teaching statement is about you, not some abstract concept" (1331). And when jaded academics complain about the predictability and inauthenticity of these statements, they are, in essence, saying that its writers do not accurately or genuinely communicate themselves. Given that the personal statement and statement of purpose join the teaching philosophy as some of the most loathed genres of academic writing, we think it is safe to say that people are often quite bad at making arguments about themselves—especially when writers know that their articulations of self are going to be evaluated against a set of unknown standards and expectations that they will likely only partially meet.

This is the well-kept secret of "me" documents: they are speculative genres disguised as descriptive ones. You are applying for graduate school, so you portray yourself as someone who is already a scholar. You are applying for tenure, so you portray yourself as someone who is already a luminary in your field. You are applying for a teaching job, so you portray yourself as an experienced and established teacher—even when, of course, you are not. As Karen Kelsky (2015) writes in her book on PhD professionalization, these documents require writers to think of themselves as finished scholars and teachers—as a complete package "with a bow on top" (62). But what if the teaching statement's purpose were to speculate as well as describe? What if the statement was framed as one part of the process of developing a pedagogy, and approached as a document that is both anchored in the past and looking toward the future?

We are certainly not the first to embrace self-reflection as one of the teaching statement's most important offerings. Stephen Neaderhiser (2016), for example, describes the teaching statement as a "two-way mirror," one that allows others to view us, but also—and just as importantly—allows us to look at and reflect on ourselves (415). Gail Goodyear and Douglas Allchin (1998) say that statements "function both personally and publicly"—as opportunities to "clarify or reflect on practice . . . or to articulate a view of teaching for administrative decision-making" (103). Even Nancy Van Note Chism's now-classic 1998 piece on developing a philosophy of teaching calls for a section on one's "personal growth plan"—a reflective component illustrating how "one has grown in teaching over the years" (2). This directive is of limited value to new teachers, of course. One's teaching cannot have grown much if one's career is only months along. For us, though, the growth plan is not just a section; we see a future-facing approach as integral to the statement in its entirety.

The statement should be a flexible text that lets our growing edges show: the problems we are wrestling with, the new ideas we are testing out, our latest feats and face-plants, the fresh scholarship we are applying in our classrooms. It should be written—and read—more like a research statement, in that it would map not only where the teacher has been but also where they might be headed as an educator. Chism's question about future development is on the right track—this document should look to the future as much as it does to the past and present—but that component needs to be more than just an addendum about "keeping abreast of developments in the field."

CHANGING OUR LANGUAGE: FROM
METAPHOR TO METAMORPHOSIS

To revise the teaching statement as a genre requires rethinking what many consider the statement's most central feature: the metaphor. As Neaderhiser (2016) reminds us in his article on metaphor in teaching statements, metaphoric concepts structure so many of our teaching philosophies: the Burkean parlor; Mary Louise Pratt's contact zone; and models of the teacher as gardener, tour guide, and coach. Megan's most recent group of graduate instructors, for example, generated teaching-learning metaphors as diverse as a lighthouse, a circus lion tamer, a caravan, a message in a bottle, and a trampoline park.

Yet considering one's teaching through a singular conceptual metaphor can be more frustrating than it is generative. Ask Kristine Johnson, who published an article in *Pedagogy* (2006) about her struggle—and ultimate failure—to find a metaphor to ground her teaching identity. In her years as a young teacher, Johnson cycled through a number of figures: teacher as cultural critic, teacher as midwife, teacher as resource—none of which quite seemed to capture her teaching. Johnson ties her "inability to pull a ready-made teaching metaphor off the shelf" to the individuality of teaching practice and to her own identity as a millennial who is also teaching millennials (11). Yet Johnson's discomfort with the single conceptual metaphor points to a more general issue with the teaching statement: a unifying framework might enhance the elegance of a statement's composition, but it does not necessarily reflect—nor, for that matter, enhance—the changing and growing nature of someone's teaching.

Even though Johnson's case shows how it may not always make sense to force-fit one's teaching into the shape of a single metaphor, metaphoric devices can still be useful as a way for teachers to describe and articulate their teaching philosophies. The question, then, becomes: How can we employ metaphors that resist rather than reinforce the idea of our teaching philosophies as something monolithic and static? In his study, Neaderhiser works to show how metaphor can be used in less rigid ways—how, for example, writers can employ figurative language and allude to familiar metaphors of their discipline without structuring their statements around one controlling idea. Other scholars have adopted metamorphosis itself as a metaphor for teacherly identity, precisely because it offers a model of change and transformation. Ellen Riojas Clark and Belinda Bustos Flores (2014), for example, employ the caterpillar's metamorphosis as a conceptual framework for pedagogical identity development: teachers too, they argue, must go through stages of development and change in order to fully "explore and comprehend their own identity" and "appreciate the impact it will have on their teaching" (6). For Clark and Flores, this framework is a crucial part of their social justice pedagogy. A teacherly identity oriented around static principles, or for that matter a static identity, is one that fails to account for the importance of a flexible and mutable pedagogy that responds to the needs of a diverse student body and dynamic sociopolitical circumstances. In this way, Clark and Flores articulate what Neaderhiser and Johnson implicitly suggest: flexibility and change are essential to ethical and effective teaching. Yet statements of teacherly identity, in focusing on overarching teaching principles and philosophy, tend to cover up the ways in which a teacher has or will metamorphose.

One approach to the "learning to teach" statement, then, would be to incorporate structural metaphors—like metamorphosis—that imply change and mutability. By this we mean metaphors that indicate not how we change our students but, instead, how we change ourselves, how we change as teachers. The metaphors so commonly found in teaching statements—teachers as gardeners, as coaches, as tour guides—all focus on how the pedagogue transforms their students. But, as Clark and Flores suggest, we need a discursive space and we need discursive models for reflecting on how we ourselves, as teachers, can be and are in the process of transformation.

Another potential role for metaphors in teaching might be to function as what Kenneth Tobin (1990) calls a "master switch." His research showed that teachers' practices are often guided by the metaphors they have identified, and he argues that "significant changes in classroom practice are possible if teachers are assisted to understand their teaching role in terms of new metaphors" (123). Rather than settling on a single metaphor, or even a cluster of metaphors, to explain our teaching beliefs, we might identify the metaphorical constructions that intuitively underlie our practices and test them for soundness. In some cases, an operative metaphor may be the key to understanding why we teach the way we do. For example, a teacher who thinks of herself as a circus lion tamer might reevaluate her chosen metaphor, which imagines students as undomesticated animals who must be controlled with a whip or cane, and who could injure or kill her with a swipe of their claws. An unsound metaphor can be critically reconsidered and perhaps replaced. In fact, the statement could perhaps even be a place where we work through the consequences of such metaphors in order to distinguish whether, for example, it is possible to be both like and unlike the lion tamer. Metaphors can be useful both in pinpointing what we currently believe about teaching and learning and in facilitating the exploration of new possibilities that might help us reconceptualize our approach.

CHANGING OUR EXPECTATIONS: LEARNING
TO READ THE TEACHING STATEMENT

But reformulating the writer's task is not enough without a corresponding reconsideration of other rhetorical elements of this genre. We must also begin to rethink the spirit in which such documents, when they do become part of a dossier or teaching application, are read by their target audience—that looming panel of grumpy professors or that peevish promotion or teaching award committee. Beyond urging them to read more generously, what else is there to do?

Anis Bawarshi's (2001) concept of genres as "rhetorical ecosystems" (70) gives us a starting point. In this sense, the genre of the teaching statement—or the "learning to teach" statement—is a reinforcing phenomenon, "rhetorically shaping and reproducing our social environments, our practices, and our identities" (73). Within its rhetorical ecosystem, the statement both molds and is molded by its writers, its readers, its sites of reception. In short, Bawarshi's concept reminds us that, as we propose changes to the way the statement is conceived of and written, we must also turn a critical gaze toward its reception and consider changes there as well. Perhaps we must seek ways to shift, ever so slightly, the narrative built into the genre and its associated reading practices, to make way for something new.

We realize that we cannot dictate how hiring committees or university administrators evaluate these statements. We see this chapter as our contribution to an ongoing, and hopefully expanding, conversation about how to alter the rhetorical situation of a genre that needs some renovation—and innovation. We want to encourage all of the genre's participants—readers, writers, teachers—to think about how foregrounding learning, experimentation, and growth could serve the document as a tool for teachers to both reflect upon and promote themselves as educators. And the genre's intended readers may be more ready for this change than one might think. The sheer number of complaints—that candidates' expressions of mastery or passion ring inauthentic, or that their articulations of philosophical principles prove predictable or formulaic—suggests that perhaps the genre's readers do not necessarily want to see the kind of fixed and perfectly polished pedagogical expert that writers might think they do.

Perhaps, as we suggested earlier, we could read the "learning to teach" statement the way we read statements of research: as documents that foreground problems, are assumed to be in-progress, and ideally include speculative suggestions for future direction. In "The Scholarship of Teaching: What's the Problem?," Randy Bass (1999) points to a contradiction in the way we conceive of our scholarship versus our teaching: as he puts it, in one's research, "having a problem is at the heart of the investigative process; it is the compound of the generative questions about which all creative and productive activity revolves" (1). By contrast, he points out, having a problem in one's teaching is something to avoid at all costs and, barring that, something to ameliorate as quickly as possible. He proposes that we change "the status of the problem in teaching from terminal remediation to ongoing investigation" (1). This proposal, we would argue, is the key to reading the teaching statement differently—that is, as a document that poses questions, identifies challenges, and explores possibilities. In other words, we ask that readers prioritize their attention to teaching and learning as processes themselves.

We would ask that readers of these documents push back against the prevailing tendency to see the statement as a performance of mastery and instead see it as an ongoing narrative that tries to capture and describe a teacher's evolutionary stages. To put it in first-year-composition terms, the statement should be read not as a tidy five-paragraph theme but rather as an "I-search" à la Ken Macrorie (1988), a "living document" in which the traveler's tracks would not be erased or occluded but rather emphasized, demonstrating that the statement is meant to evolve rather than to encapsulate.

In this way, the "learning to teach" statement would be written—and read—as a journey or ongoing process rather than as a final statement or conclusive philosophy. The writer's anxiety of trying to present a polished expert-teacher self could give way, just a little, to the more flexible process of building an evolving document. We would like to propose that it be read as a document of inquiry—one that deliberately foregrounds teaching problems as opportunities for growth rather than simply as impediments. We would like to hope that a more process-oriented document might even make for more interesting (and less begrudging) reading.

* * *

The experience of becoming a teacher-learner should be lifelong. We better honor our students' incomplete learning when we position ourselves as learners too. We are always drafting—every semester is a new draft—and we build on what has come before. Why not build this same philosophical concept not only into our classroom practices but into our pedagogical compositions, too? An emphasis on learning about teaching can help us develop an identity on the page as a learner among fellow learners.

We see this approach as useful for new teachers, yes, but also for teachers at any stage of their careers. After all, we are all learning to teach—and this, we believe, is precisely the principle of good teaching too often covered up in statements of teaching philosophy. In this way, we see the teaching statement as an occluded and occluding genre. The teaching statement is occluded in that it is less visible than public or published genre; people often do not read or see a teaching statement until they are tasked with writing one. At the same time, the teaching statement occludes what we believe should be its most important feature: flexibility and change.

We have tried not to be too prescriptive, nor to provide fixed or static guidelines for the "learning to teach" statement. The ideas in this chapter, like such a statement, are in-process and speculative; we wanted to begin an exploration of what it might mean to transform the statement of teaching philosophy—to allow the genre to undergo its own metamorphosis. This is not a step-by-step how-to guide, nor is it meant to be; this is, as our title suggests, one step toward a statement that foregrounds what we are really all doing every time we step into the classroom: learning how to teach.

REFERENCES

Austin, Rachel Narehood. 2006. "Writing the Teaching Statement." *Science Magazine*. April 14, 2006. https://www.sciencemag.org/careers/2006/04/writing-teaching-statement.

Bass, Randy. 1999. "The Scholarship of Teaching: What's the Problem?" *Inventio: Creative Thinking about Learning and Teaching* 1 (1): 1–10.

Bawarshi, Anis. 2001. "The Ecology of Genre." In *Ecocomposition: Theoretical and Pedagogical Approaches*, edited by Christian R. Weisser and Sidney I. Dobrin, 69–80. Albany: State University of New York Press.

Boyer, Ernest L. 1990. *Scholarship Reconsidered: Priorities of the Professoriate*. Princeton, NJ: The Carnegie Foundation for the Advancement of Teaching.

Cassuto, Leonard. 2013. "What's Your Teaching Philosophy?" *The Chronicle of Higher Education*, December 2, 2013. https://www.chronicle.com/article/Whats-Your-Teaching/143315.

Chism, Nancy Van Note. 1998. "Developing a Philosophy of Teaching Statement." *Essays on Teaching Excellence: Toward the Best in the Academy* 9 (3): 1–2.

Clark, Ellen Riojas, and Belinda Bustos Flores. 2014. "The Metamorphosis of Teacher Identity: An Intersection of Ethnic Consciousness, Self-Conceptualization, and Belief Systems." In *Teacher Identity and the Struggle for Recognition: Meeting the Challenges of a Diverse Society*, edited by Patrick M. Jenlink, 3–14. New York: Rowman & Littlefield.

Clay, Jeremy S. 2007. "Everything but the Teaching Statement." *The Chronicle of Higher Education*, February 7, 2007. http://chronicle.com/article/Everything-But-the-Teaching/46672.

Gooblar, David. 2013. "Pedagogy Unbound: Two Birds, One Teaching Statement." Chroni-cleVitae, November 27, 2013. https://chroniclevitae.com/news/189-pedagogy-unbound -two-birds-one-teaching-statement.

Goodyear, Gail E., and Douglas Allchin. 1998. "Statements of Teaching Philosophy." In *To Improve the Academy: Resources for Faculty, Instructional, and Organizational Development*, edited by Matthew Kaplan, 17: 103–22. Stillwater, OK: New Forum Press.

Grundman, Helen G. 2006. "Writing a Teaching Philosophy Statement." *Notices of the American Mathematical Society* 53 (11): 1329–33.

Haggerty, Kevin D. 2010. "Teaching Statements Are Bunk." *The Chronicle of Higher Educa-tion*, February 19, 2010. http://chronicle.com/article/Teaching-Statements-Are-Bunk /64152.

Johnson, Kristine. 2006. "The Millennial Teacher: Metaphors for a New Generation." *Pedagogy* 6 (1): 7–24.

Kelsky, Karen. 2015. *The Professor Is in: The Essential Guide to Turning Your Ph.D. into a Job*. New York: Three Rivers Press.

Lewis, Mary Anne. 2014. "Teaching Statement as Self-Portrait." ChronicleVitae, October 3, 2014. https://chroniclevitae.com/news/734-teaching-statement-as-self-portrait.

Macrorie, Ken. 1988. "The I-Search Paper." In *The I-Search Paper: Revised Edition of Searching Writing*, by Ken Macrorie, 54–65. Portsmouth, NH: Boynton/Cook.

Neaderhiser, Stephen. 2016. "Conceiving of a Teacherly Identity: Metaphors of Composi-tion in Teaching Statements." *Pedagogy* 16 (3): 413–43.

Tobin, Kenneth. 1990. "Changing Metaphors and Beliefs: A Master Switch for Teaching?" *Theory into Practice* 29 (2): 122–27.

15

COGS IN THE PEDAGOGICAL MACHINE
The Structuration, Rhetorical Situations, and Perigenres Surrounding Classroom Observation Guidelines

Zack K. De Piero

TEACHING AT "UNIVERSITY B": A ROUND COG ON A SQUARE WHEEL

A curious exchange with a former colleague sparked my interest in taking a closer look at how classroom observations are conducted. Six weeks into my position as a full-time lecturer at this particular institution, my appointed mentor reached out to coordinate a day and time to hold my first observation. "I think I was supposed to ask you about a lesson plan," she casually noted, while acknowledging, "I don't usually have a visual lesson plan."

As a former junior high and high school English teacher in the Philadelphia School District, I was well-accustomed to making lesson plans. Lessons plans were, perhaps, the prized pedagogical genre of my teacher education program—as I imagine they are for many K–12 state certification programs—so, needless to say, I was happy to pass them along. I had two main goals for the class: (1) practice how to create logical outlines of texts—what could be considered this program's signature literacy practice, and (2) introduce the upcoming PowerPoint presentation assignment that required situating a scholarly journal article within a discourse community. I did not (and could not) put my imprint on this curriculum; at this stand-alone writing program, instructors were required to teach from one uniform set of materials, including the assigned readings, the assignment prompts, and the lone rubric that we used to grade all assignments—including students' midterm and final portfolios from other instructors' classes.

There were no guidelines for conducting classroom observations at this site—at least none that I had been made aware of—but I figured that I had showed my mentor enough to keep any red flags at bay. As

https://doi.org/10.7330/9781646422920.c015

I packed up my briefcase after class, she said, "I really liked the definition of *genre* you gave. What was it, again—a typical response to a social situation?" "Yeah, pretty much," I replied. I spelled out Miller's (1984) oft-cited definition that she offers in "Genre as Social Action": "Typified rhetorical actions based in recurrent [social] situations" (159)—a brief but potent description that has become a go-to definition for one of the most foundational concepts of the composition discipline. As a freshly minted PhD from a Language, Literacy, and Composition Studies program, I had Miller's definition on the tip of my tongue, ready to share with first-year writing students. Admittedly, it seemed strange that my new colleague was unfamiliar with such a seminal definition of the field.

In a follow-up email later that night, she asked a question that offered profound clues about the extent to which any given teaching observation was ultimately bound up in complexities and tensions that are inherently embedded in every program's organizational structures and cultures: "Did that definition of genre that you used come from the program materials?"

Soon thereafter, I ran into her on campus, and she offered generous compliments about my class. "Unfortunately," she winced, "I'm going to remove that genre stuff from my observation report—I don't want either of us to get into any trouble." My mentor-observer's decision to expunge parts of my lesson from her observation report—namely, my references to non-sanctioned curriculum—echoes Huckin's (2010) concept of *textual silence*. Huckin does not exclusively invoke the term to refer to inherently nefarious matters, but it *can* also be used to pinpoint instances of an "omission of some piece of information that is pertinent to the topic at hand" that, at times, can "be used for deception, to hide important information from the reader without good cause, to the advantage of special interests" (420). Walking away from that brief encounter, the thought creeped into my mind: *was I working at Nancy Welch's "University B"?*

Nancy Welch (1993) describes her experience as a doctoral student encountering similar struggles assimilating to a "radically different" pedagogical culture, which she calls "University B" (389). Her previous training foregrounded the writing process, from freewriting to workshopping, but what was equally noteworthy, she claims, was that institution's disposition toward cultivating novice instructors' pedagogical development: she felt supported as she navigated the liminal spaces of becoming a writing instructor. Conversely, at University B, she found that incoming instructors were expected to renounce previous identities, philosophies, and pedagogies that conflicted with the prevailing dominant culture: so much so that she observed numerous instances of "religious metaphors of testimony, confession, baptism, and conversion" at work (387). "That year," she recounts, "shed critical light on the language that constructs teachers as faithful or unfaithful, in the flock or out" (388). In that vein, my seemingly innocuous language (describing genre as social action) may have raised suspicions that I was an "unfaithful" member of the "out" flock.

I offer this anecdote to illuminate Giddens' (1984) theory of structuration, which posits that individual actors—from students to instructors to administrators—simultaneously shape and are shaped by the social structures surrounding them. This perpetually fluctuating reality embodies the rhetorical complexity of classroom observations, in effect, generating lines of inquiry about how and why they are conducted. To understand this unique pedagogical genre, the composition community must understand how they shape and are shaped by a myriad of factors. Curricular issues include the scope of course content, assignments, readings, and assessment. Logistical matters extend to scheduling, enrollment capacity, and available classroom technology. Contextual circumstances are illuminated by taking the student body into account: the extent (and range) of students' academic preparation, native language, culture, and familiarity with (and access to) technology. Arguably the most important variables that impact any given lesson, though, are those associated with the instructor: namely, their academic expertise, educational training, teaching philosophy, and teaching experiences. (These dynamics become doubly relevant when the observer's background is taken into account.) These latter variables, however, are not immediately visible within the confines of a fifty- to seventy-five-minute class. Giddens's theory of structuration foregrounds all of these factors together, creating a complex rhetorical equation that situates all literate activity within a particular place and time.

I also offer my "University B" experience because classroom observations are an undeniably personal experience, inextricably tied to an instructor's identity—and for some instructors, deeply so, particularly when past experiences have invalidated the principles that we bring to our daily trade. In light of this reality, any binding text used to conduct classroom observations at a given site—whether the document takes on the form of a questionnaire, a checklist, or a rubric—becomes an inextricably *personal* pedagogical genre.

By outlining the social conditions underlying the "typified rhetorical actions" that participants take "in recurrent situations" (Miller 1984, 159), we can begin to better understand how and why classroom observations are conducted in the ways that they are. In this chapter, I attempt to productively problematize classroom observation guidelines (COGs) as a unique pedagogical genre with considerable complexity by: (1) examining the fundamental tenets of the rhetorical situation underlying classroom observations—that is, of the exigence, writer, audience, goal, and context—and (2) identifying other pedagogical genres that circulate throughout a COG's activity system to account for this particular genre's tangential, tacit social functions.

Before highlighting relevant scholarship related to classroom observations, I'd also like to address my choice and usage of the term *COG*. In a literal sense, cogs are mechanical teeth that facilitate the connection and movement between parts. On a bike, for instance, each cog in the gear has a "bite" that grabs the chain, and once the chain becomes taut (around the rear and front derailleur), riders can put the wheels into motion by pedaling—all made possible by cogs. From this mechanical perspective, then, cogs are purely functional entities. However, cog can also carry a negative connotation in phrases like "cog in a wheel" and "cog in the machine." These phrases invoke an image of a cog being a small, interchangeable, and therefore inconsequential part of a greater whole. At the same time, though, each cog is required for the greater system to function.

Both of these meanings are present in my use of the acronym COG as a label for this pedagogy-oriented genre: (1) a detached functionalism, the facilitation of harmonious parts (albeit mindless, automated, and cookie-cutter parts) working together toward an overarching goal alongside (2) an unsettling feeling toward—and perhaps, principled resistance against—the perception of mercurial powers-that-be, an awareness of the tensions that lie at the intersection of professional hierarchy and positionality: of conformity and agency, of meeting expectations and making innovations, and of being a "boss [and/or] friend" (Jackson 2015, 45).

COMPETING VISIONS OF CLASSROOM OBSERVATIONS

A rhetorical genre analysis of COGs can be informed by scholarship on composition pedagogy (Tate et al. 2014), genre theory (Adler-Kassner and Wardle 2015; Bazerman 2004; Miller 1984), teacher education (Reid 2017), and assessment (Dryer 2013; Balester 2012; Anson et al. 2012; Gallagher 2010; Broad 2003, 2009; Huot 2002). Scholarly conversations about COGs in the postsecondary writing classroom specifically have been compiled in two sources: Chism's (2007) *Peer Review of Teaching: A*

Sourcebook and Dayton's (2015) edited collection, *Assessing the Teaching of Writing: New Trends, New Technologies.* For the ensuing overview, I largely focus my attention on this latter source.

DeCosta and Roen (2015) contend that the assessment of teaching should be considered scholarly work. They propose a heuristic that pairs Boyer's (1990) five categories of scholarship—discovery, application, integration, teaching and learning, and engagement—with Glassick et al.'s (1997) six criteria for evaluating scholarly activity: clear goals, adequate preparation, appropriate methods, significant results, effective presentation, and reflective critique. Their proposal suggests that enacting the COG genre—that is, observing other instructors' teaching practices—merits systematic inquiry. Observers, then, become participants in the pursuit of knowledge. In a similar vein, Anson (2015) advocates for integrating teaching portfolios into the evaluation process so that instructors can showcase their ongoing, data-driven self-reflection. Discussing his own mixed-methods approach, he analyzes students' end-of-semester perceptions of the class by pairing their quantitative Likert scale survey responses with their open-ended comments. He then attempts to make sense of the data so that it can be used as a feedback loop for enhancing teaching and learning (112). Such sentiments also echo Ed White's (2005) warning about the professional (and disciplinary) importance of creating academically responsible and rigorous assessment standards in the teaching of writing: "Assess thyself or assessment will be done unto thee" (33).

Other scholars appear to teeter toward the "done unto thee" camp, providing a vision in stark contrast to the aforementioned scholarship. "Observation as inquiry" and "teaching as self-reflection" are both largely absent from Jackson's (2015) accounts of how he conducts classroom observations. A self-described "thirty-something guy at the back of the class, wearing a tie and glasses, with a goldenrod observation sheet in front of me" (45), Jackson juxtaposes characterizations of the "best classes" and "worst classes" that he's observed: those in which he claims, "I can barely hold back my excitement" versus those where he admits, "I fight the urge to hustle the instructor out of the room so students will be safe from bad teaching's blast radius" (46). As the following excerpt illustrates, though, those two instances tend to be the outliers in Jackson's experiences as a writing program administrator-observer:

> Most often, though, I observe what could be called "generally competent teaching"—enthusiastic, well organized, and helpful. I have seen plenty of instructors who know their students' names and effectively deploy the tactics they've learned from more experienced instructors while swapping

ideas in the instructor carrels. They may not have a clue about what to do with the big football player in the back of the room crouching behind his newspaper fort; they may not make essential connections between one part of a lesson and another; they may assign activities that seem more like cognitive babysitting than learning; they may lead class discussions a bit woodenly, responding to each comment with little more than "good"; they may stare blankly at the bare walls while their students write or work in groups; they may not know much about how people learn to write, about rhetoric, or even about English grammar, punctuation, or usage. But beyond all expectation, they are doing a *pretty darn good job* teaching a college-level course they've (likely) never taken, whose content they have not yet mastered. (46)

The collateral damage from this excerpt leaves a "blast radius" of its own. Language matters—it plays an important role in shaping organizational culture—so I wonder what kinds of teaching, research, and even collegial cultures are being created by using this type of deficit model discourse. Paradoxically, though, Jackson sets a breathtakingly low bar for what he also characterizes as "generally competent teaching": a status that instructors achieve once they demonstrate their ability to (1) accurately pair students' names with faces and (2) recycle former instructors' methods.

Most troubling, however, are the epistemological assumptions embedded within that excerpt. From a methodological perspective, observation *can* be used as a knowledge-generating technique, but it is still—like all social science research methods—inherently limited. How could Jackson possibly *know* the extent of an instructor's "clue"-lessness in dealing with a particular student, particularly when this claim is based on one classroom observation?

Jackson and I, it seems, would conduct classroom observations in very dissimilar ways, likely yielding disparate observational outcomes. In some of his "best classes," I imagine that I would see instructors who succeed in enacting tried and true pedagogies but who might otherwise benefit from experimenting with new approaches and taking commendable risks. Conversely, I wonder what questions I would have before, during, or after I observed one of his "worst classes." For instance, I would want to ask: What other real-time, split-second decisions—tweaking a particular directive, providing a helpful analogy, asking a follow-up question—*might you* have made during that class, and how might they have impacted the trajectory of that particular class? In my mind, such reflective responses are arguably *more* telling about a colleague's "good teaching" practices than what we witness during the constraints of a given class.

Like a "best" teacher being swapped out for a "worst" teacher, the outcome of any given classroom observation could similarly change depending on whether Jackson, I, or somebody else conducted that same observation. So, how do these fluctuating circumstances complicate our understandings of the COG genre? For the remainder of this chapter, I examine this question by exploring the rhetorical situations underlying classroom observations.

DATA COLLECTION: BUILDING A CORPUS OF COGS

To examine sophisticated examples of the COG genre, I pinpointed a unique population: institutions that earned the Conference on College Composition and Communication (CCCC) Certificate of Excellence. During the summer of 2018, I emailed thirty-three individuals at seventeen institutions, explaining my interest in researching the COG genre. Although I had yet to settle on that particular term, I offered "teacher observation rubric" and "classroom observation criteria" as possibilities. In my outreach, I foregrounded the exploratory nature of my inquiry and explained my grounded theory approach to data collection; I also mentioned that I was interested in any relevant documents and materials related to how their particular program conducted classroom observations.

In their replies, respondents explicitly referenced a range of additional related pedagogical genres that informed their respective program's COG in some way. Some are discussed in this collection, such as syllabi (Albright; Stolley and Toth) and assignment prompts (Navickas). Others remain beyond the scope of this collection: lesson plans, observation notes (written *in situ* by the observer), post-observation narrative reflections (written by the instructor), student evaluations (of the instructor's teaching), and timelines for promotion and tenure. I refer to these materials as "perigenres."

Akin to words like *perimeter* or *periphery* that invoke a "just beyond" quality, a perigenre illuminates a principal genre of interest (in this case, an institution's COG) by indicating a relationship across those two genres. I introduce this new term because other terms do not precisely characterize this exact relationship across genres. While the notion of genre sets or systems emphasizes a focus on how various genres construct "their own micro-environments—their own social situations, practices, and relations" (Bawarshi 2001, 74), my conception of perigenres draws attention to how supplementary genres either inform or are used in conjunction with a primary genre of interest (e.g., a COG) and thereby add meaning to our understandings of that genre in some way, however tangentially connected each genre might be. In a word, perigenres point to intertextual relationships across genres to offer clues to how a particular genre—in this case, a COG—functions within a larger activity system.

Two different sets of data, then, inform my analysis: COGs, along with the perigenres that inform each program's COG. Altogether, my corpus includes data from fifteen institutions, and within those institutions, eighteen different programs. I do not use this data to offer generalizable claims about all writing programs that have awarded the designation of "excellence" by the CCCC organization. Instead, I use this data to examine the rhetorical dimensions of the COG genre. I begin by analyzing the names used to characterize COGs; each title brings unique rhetorical affordances and constraints for users of the genre. I then examine the implications of how writers' identities manifest within this genre. Finally, I turn to the wide range of perigenres that emerged from the data collection process as a way to examine COGs' audiences and purposes.

RHETORICAL IMPLICATIONS OF COG TITLES

Programs used a variety of titles to characterize their respective COGs. With each subtle fluctuation in terminology, the connotation of each COG may also shift, opening up rhetorical affordances and constraints for instructors and observers alike. Consider, for example, the connotative differences between the following two outcomes of a classroom observation: an observation "letter" compared to a "report." Letters typically invoke a direct audience—to the instructor who was just observed, for instance, and/or the WPA—and carry a modest degree of tonal informality. Reports, alternatively, take on a detached bureaucratic formalization, suggesting a document to be official when filed away into institutional memory. Such semantic differences yield subtle though consequential distinctions, particularly when conducting a rhetorical analysis on this genre.

The most common title in the corpus was "Form"; it was featured in six of the seventeen COGs. "Checklist" and "Report" appeared twice, and the following terms were used once: "Rubric," "Report," "Sheet," "Visit," and "Template." Many of these titles, interestingly, capture two distinct social purposes, referencing both the inscribed observation guidelines genre (the COG) as well as the COG's byproduct—the resulting document an observer creates during and/or after the observation.

"Checklist" offers the starkest example of this multifunctionality, albeit in a very reductive way—a tool that begets little else beyond checkmarks. Such a preset catalog of criteria imposes constraints on both instructors and observers, stripping both parties of some agency. From another perspective, though, such standardization heightens perceptions of fairness and transparency. Cataloging criteria in this way could also provide a means of working toward inter-rater reliability across observers.

The perception of such parity is also established by the term *peer* which was explicitly mentioned in two of seventeen COGs: "Peer Mentoring Observation Form" and "Peer Observation Checklist." Nevertheless, despite this distinction, it is likely that classroom observations are conducted by colleagues of similar rank at more than just these two institutions, especially when observations are conducted for more senior faculty. Still, "peer" is a somewhat misleading term because it implies a reflexivity. In the truest sense, peers would be afforded the ability to leverage an equivalent amount of power in each other's evaluation: to be observed and assessed, but also to observe and assess their peers (i.e., their observers).

UNKNOWN WRITERS AND INFORMED, ADOPTED, AND APPROPRIATED COGS

Based on textual analysis of the encoded features alone, it is difficult to determine the writer's identity for any given COG. Authors' names (e.g., that institution's WPA) were not explicitly mentioned in the COGs, likely because it is not a common convention of the genre. It is possible, however, to identify which COGs *were not* homegrown documents written entirely or exclusively within a particular writing program or English department: five of the COGs (roughly 30% of the corpus) were at least partially drawn from external sources.

University-affiliated teaching and learning institutes shaped three COGs, based on their acknowledgment within the header and/or footer of the documents. One writing program adopted a component of its COG, a checklist, from another university. Another site was considering adapting aspects from two different COGs, each developed through its on-campus teaching and learning institute as starting points for thinking through how they might conduct classroom observations. One of these was adapted from Chism's (1999) *Peer Review of Teaching*; the other drew from Harris and Cox's (2003) study on engineering classrooms. Another WPA acknowledged that Peter Elbow's work had considerably shaped their program's COG. Unfortunately, however, such findings cannot be extrapolated across the data set. Even if not explicitly mentioned within a program's COG, it is possible (even likely) that the document was tacitly shaped by external sources—that is, by other organizations, scholarship, or voices—in significant ways through pedagogical training, research, and/or participation in fieldwide events (e.g., conferences). Thus, notions of definitively determining authorship are problematic.

In one unusual instance, however, a COG under consideration in one writing program appears to have been appropriated from a K–12 public education site—the Ohio Teacher Evaluation System's Teacher Performance Observation Rubric—without any explicit attribution to its original source: a Google search yielded a duplicate document, albeit one without this writing program's name on it. This unique finding raises a red flag for the constructivist principles advocated by composition scholars who strongly encourage bottom-up processes that invite faculty input and remain responsive to programmatic particularities (e.g., Huot 2002; Broad 2003, 2009). If, in fact, this adopted and appropriated COG was entirely imported from a K–12 setting, then it falls far short of Huot's qualities for achieving validity by contemporary writing assessment standards: that is, that they are site-based, context-sensitive, and locally controlled.

PERIGENRES IN A COG'S ACTIVITY SYSTEM

Alongside COGs, additional pedagogical genres emerged from my exploratory inquiry, indicating how, to some extent, COGs take their cues from other genres. WPAs and writing faculty responded to my outreach with supplementary materials (perigenres) that contextualized their program's COG in some way, often illuminating the peripheral audiences and tertiary purposes associated with an instructor's teacher performance. These perigenres, conceptually, merely point to how two genres may hold mutually informed meaning. For example, at one site, the WPA included a one-page "Statement of Teaching Principles" that aligned with (and elaborated upon) one section of that program's COG. That perigenre, in turn, included a footnote that referenced the program's "Outcomes for First-Year Composition." In this particular example, the program's COG is explicitly informed by two perigenres: a "Statement of Teaching Principles" document as well as their "Outcomes for First-Year Composition," suggesting that—at this site—there is a relationship across COGs, teaching principles, and learning outcomes.

The notion of a perigenre functions differently than somewhat similar ideas like genre set or genre system. A genre set, defined by Bazerman (2004) as a "collection of types of texts someone in a particular role is likely to produce" (318), begins with examining the genres used by individuals in specific roles. The notion of a perigenre, in contrast, permeates individual roles and extends outward across a greater activity system. Alternatively, a genre system, or "the several genre sets of people working together in an organized way, plus the patterned relations in the production, flow, and use of these documents" (318), approximates the interconnected nature across genres by my use of "perigenres," but it remains restrictive in a more formal activity theory sense (i.e., tracing out the circulation of genres).

Eighteen total perigenres emerged from this exploratory inquiry into COGs. Those that most directly shape perceptions of an instructor's performance during a classroom observation included (1) pre-observation questionnaires to be completed by an instructor, (2) observation notes, (3) write-ups (i.e., review letter or report) of a classroom observation (or, in cases of online teaching, assessment of an instructor's use of an online course management system), and (4) post-observation narrative reflections written by instructors.

The data pointed to other pedagogical genres to be collected and/or taken into consideration before or during the observation that factor into the COG in some way, such as (5) syllabi, (6) assignment prompts, (7) lesson plans (including lesson objectives or goals), (8) handouts, and (9) a diagram of the classroom layout. (10) Programmatic learning outcomes are yet another pedagogical genre that aligns with the teaching and learning-oriented part of the genre set, though they remain somewhat distanced from those associated with the classroom observation itself. Other perigenres explicitly referenced in the data do not immediately address teaching and learning but nonetheless shape the classroom observation in some way. These genres included the (11) logistical procedures for conducting classroom observations (in the form of a letter or embedded within the COG) and (12) programmatic statements of pedagogical principles or values.

Six perigenres were associated with sustaining employment and achieving professional mobility: (13) student course evaluations, (14) summaries of previous course evaluations, (15) timelines for promotion and tenure that indicated the expected timeframe for when classroom observations should be conducted, and (16) reference letters or recommendations for awards and employment. Finally, respondents included two documents that facilitate a prospective faculty's recruitment process: (17) an "On-Campus Interview—Teaching Demonstration Evaluation" and (18) a "Form for Providing Feedback on a Classroom Teaching Observation or Microteaching Demonstration." These perigenres suggest on-campus interview questionnaires and mini-COGs for observing teaching demonstrations (for prospective job candidates) are two additional genres that factor into larger discussions of COGs.

Altogether, these eighteen perigenres function as a constellation of genres orbiting a given COG, albeit with different degrees of proximity. This spatial metaphor offers an insight into genre studies: in building onto and off of each other, pedagogical genres have complex intertextual relationships. However, those relationships not only support the other genres within that orbit; they also contribute to the context and purpose of the primary genre—the COG—as it is meant to be understood and taken up by its audience.

SHADOWY AUDIENCES, COMPETING PURPOSES, AND DEEPLY STRUCTURATED RHETORICAL SITUATIONS

The COG genre appears to be born from and perpetuated by a tacit assumption: simply, that postsecondary writing instructors ought to be observed. Though seemingly straightforward, this exigence leaves some questions unanswered that merit further inspection: what is the genre's intended uptake, who is responsible for that uptake, and for whom is it being generated? The emergence of the range of perigenres suggests that the answers to such questions are wide-ranging.

A COG's audience begins with the individuals who are present in the classroom during the observation: most obviously, the observer and instructor. Students, however, are another immediate audience; insofar as COGs might impact an instructor's teacherly decisions, students become the embodied recipients of those decisions. In this way, the phrase "being genred" (Schryer et al. 2003) is telling: for better or worse, the participants of any given genre—including its agent-less bystanders—are shaped by that particular genre. These implications become profound when participation in a given genre is perceived to place unnecessary constraints on users' activity. For example, similar to accusations levied at K–12 instructors who merely "teach to the test," postsecondary instructors might be more inclined to "teach to the COG"—a sobering reminder that assessment shapes instructional contexts, which could be seen as one of the more cautionary threshold concepts in the field of writing studies (Adler-Kassner and Wardle 2015).

The audiences of COGs and their byproducts (e.g., letters, recommendations, etc.) extend well beyond the classroom, toward the individuals who assume aspects of an institution's professional oversight such as the WPA and other senior administrators. In the event that the instructor being observed wishes to seek employment elsewhere, the hiring personnel at future institutions become a peripheral audience of this genre. Indeed, the stakes in classroom observations are high: a point underscored by the perigenres that emerged from data collection that are related to current and prospective employment such as recommendations, procedures for promotion, and on-campus interview questionnaires.

A given COG's audience is further complicated by the professional rank of each participant, namely, the instructor and observer. Should first-year composition (FYC) teaching assistants enrolled in non-composition graduate programs (like literature or creative writing programs, which comprise a sizable population of FYC instructors across the country) be held to the same standards as assistant professors? For such novices, the purpose of observation would likely become an occasion for fostering their still-emerging composition praxis. Anson (2015) echoes this distinction when he parses the different purposes of formative and summative evaluation, claiming that the "immediate purpose" of summative evaluation "is to judge, weigh, or rank the outcome of the teacher's ability at a particular career stage" (100). This "career stage" consideration is subtly consequential because it invites the idea that conducting classroom observations is a tacitly status-sensitive activity, suggesting that instructors could be held to different standards based on their seniority (which could, in turn, necessitate a modified COG).

Theoretically, such modifications make sense because audience and purpose are often intertwined: as a user's purpose changes, so too might their audience. Conversely, as a COG's audience shifts, so too might its purpose. Nevertheless, only scant traces of this duality can be detected within the data.

Alongside differences in status, the broader systems that detail explicit employment procedures further complicate understandings of the COG genre. For instance, it seems likely that institutions with faculty unions would use standardized COGs in an attempt to regularize observations. This regularization may, in turn, necessitate other pedagogical genres and procedures such as communication with union representatives to resolve disputes or complaints about a given observation. Undoubtedly, other institutional factors such as a university's overarching identity—for example, an "R1" research-intensive institution compared to a small, social justice-oriented liberal arts college—may also impact the construction of a particular COG.

At Jackson's (2015) program, the purpose of classroom observation sounds deceptively simple: "The purpose of observation," he writes, "is to improve student writing by improving the quality of the instruction they receive" (49). Foregrounding improvement might seem common-sensical (and it is certainly well-intentioned) but insofar as improvement requires analyzing a given phenomenon at multiple points in time—that is, conducting multiple observations of the same instructor—that goal isn't directly supported within the data set. According to the procedures and criteria explicitly encoded into the COGs within this data set, these fifteen programs only appear to draw inferences on instructors' teaching practicing based on a singular unit of time. Furthermore, as Jackson purports, if the ultimate goal of conducting classroom observations is, in fact, to "improve student writing," then it seems odd that any proce-dures for examining, analyzing, assessing, or otherwise considering stu-dents' writing are absent from the corpus samples with one exception: one COG asked observers to gather five papers, describe the instructor's comments, and consider the extent to which students' grades reflect "programmatic assessment criteria."

Also absent was any mention of an adjudication process; should an instructor wish to dispute the outcome of their classroom observation, these procedures—based on the corpus—remain unknown. Another noteworthy textual silence was the omission of any reference to previ-ous classroom observations and their byproducts. This finding is par-ticularly problematic for administrative philosophies that contend that classroom observations are primarily meant to illuminate pedagogical development: Without any comparative basis, to what extent can a given classroom observation adequately gauge an instructor's progress in the classroom?

Irrespective of whether a given classroom observation is intended to be formative, summative, or some combination, the activity of conduct-ing a classroom observation is used to fulfill a greater social purpose: to evaluate an instructor's teaching. Altogether, this array of human variables and institutional factors positions the writer, audience, and purpose of the COG genre in a state of continuous flux. Underlying every COG, then, is a highly structurated rhetorical situation.

TOWARD A COMPLETE PORTRAIT OF COGS AS A SOCIALLY EMBEDDED RHETORICAL GENRE

The ever-changing rhetorical situation underlying each classroom observation illustrates how and why COGs are an enigmatic genre. As my introductory anecdote indicates, a range of issues complicate classroom observations as a static social activity. Those related to the observer and instructor's professional profile include disciplinary background, pedagogical training, educational philosophy, and status/ rank. Programmatic aspects extend to course content, scheduling, and the degree of formality associated with observations at that site. Of course, there are also other important matters taken up by composition researchers including but not limited to textual silences and the processes (or lack thereof) surrounding instrument construction.

The expansive range of eighteen perigenres that emerged from my data collection suggests just how deeply embedded COGs are within their respective institutions. Without considering their immediate context of usage, extracting meaning via textual analysis alone remains murky. To understand the social functions of the COG genre, then, perigenres need to be taken into account.

Countless other perigenres could inform our understanding of the COG genre. Although they did not organically emerge from my inquiry, fieldwide perigenres include policy statements (e.g., the WPA Outcomes Statement for First-Year Composition [2014]), conference materials, responses to calls (i.e., for papers or presentations), and job descriptions. Institutional perigenres could include more formal endeavors such as faculty activity reports and institutional merit sheets, to more casual matters like departmental participation and even faculty conversations. An instructor's individual repository of texts and literate activity also certainly inform their pedagogical practices, from curated resources and "homegrown" materials (e.g., handouts, rubrics, informal surveys to solicit formative student feedback on teaching), to the many written and spoken microgenres embedded within student communication (e.g., emails and related course announcements, marginal and/or end comments, chats before/after class or during office hours). Perigenres extend even further still, to the texts and experiences that have shaped our development as instructors. The preparation and training materials for FYC teaching practicums, for instance, contain an abundance of perigenres that likely inform what those teaching assistants do—and why—during a given classroom period. An instructor's grading distributions may even hold consequential clues as to how their praxis manifests within a given classroom observation.

Certainly, I am not suggesting that each of these pedagogical perigenres must be components of a COG—or, more generally, the criteria by which an instructor's teaching practices are evaluated—but it seems clear that they inform composition scholar-practitioners' understanding of what transpires during a classroom observation, along with the rhetorical groundwork that has been laid long before a given observation even begins.

REFERENCES

Adler-Kassner, Linda, and Elizabeth Wardle, eds. 2015. *Naming What We Know: Threshold Concepts of Writing Studies.* Logan: Utah State University Press.

Anson, Chris, Deanna P. Dannels, Pamela Flash, and Amy L. Housley Gaffney. 2012. "Big Rubrics and Weird Genres: The Futility of Using Generic Assessment Tools across Diverse Instructional Contexts." *Journal of Writing Assessment* 5 (1). http://www.journalofwritingassessment.org/article.php?article=57.

Anson, Chris M. 2015. "Technology and Transparency: Sharing and Reflecting on the Evaluation of Teaching." In *Assessing the Teaching of Writing: Twenty-First Century Trends and Technologies,* edited by Amy E. Dayton, 99–117. Logan: Utah State University Press.

Balester, Valerie. 2012. "How Writing Rubrics Fail: Toward a Multicultural Model." In *Race and Writing Assessment,* edited by Asao B. Inoue and Mya Poe, 63–77. New York: Peter Lang.

Bawarshi, Anis. 2001. "The Ecology of Genre." In *Ecocomposition: Theoretical and Pedagogical Approaches,* edited by Christian R. Weisser and Sidney I. Dobrin, 69–80. Albany: State University of New York Press.

Bazerman, Charles. 2004. "Speech Acts, Genres, and Activity Systems: How Texts Organize Activity and People." In *What Writing Does and How It Does It: An Introduction to Analyzing Texts and Textual Practices,* edited by Charles Bazerman and Paul Prior, 309–39. Mahwah, NJ: Lawrence Erlbaum.

Boyer, Ernest L. 1990. *Scholarship Reconsidered: Priorities of the Professoriate.* Princeton, NJ: The Carnegie Foundation for the Advancement of Teaching.

Broad, Bob. 2003. *What We Really Value: Beyond Rubrics in Teaching and Assessing Writing.* Logan: Utah State University Press.

Broad, Bob. 2009. "Organic Matters: In Praise of Locally Grown Writing Assessment." In *Organic Writing Assessment: Dynamic Criteria Mapping in Action,* by Bob Broad, Linda Adler-Kassner, Barry Alford, Jane Detweiler, Heidi Estrem, Susanmarie Harrington, Maureen McBride, Eric Stalions, and Scott Weeden, 1–13. Logan: Utah State University Press.

Chism, Nancy Van Note. 1999. *Peer Review of Teaching: A Sourcebook.* Bolton, MA: Anker Publishing.

Chism, Nancy Van Note. 2007. *Peer Review of Teaching: A Sourcebook.* 2nd ed. Bolton, MA: Anker Publishing.

Council of Writing Program Administrators. 2014. "WPA Outcomes Statement for First-Year Composition (3.0)." July 17, 2014. http://wpacouncil.org/positions/outcomes.html.

Dayton, Amy E., ed. 2015. *Assessing the Teaching of Writing: Twenty-First Century Trends and Technologies.* Logan: Utah State University Press.

DeCosta, Meredith, and Duane Roen. 2015. "Assessing the Teaching of Writing: A Scholarly Approach." In *Assessing the Teaching of Writing: Twenty-First Century Trends and Technologies,* edited by Amy E. Dayton, 13–30. Logan: Utah State University Press.

Dryer, Dylan B. 2013. "Scaling Writing Ability: A Corpus-Driven Inquiry." *Written Communication* 30 (1): 3–35.

Gallagher, Chris W. 2010. "Assess Locally, Validate Globally: Heuristics for Validating Local Writing Assessments." *WPA: Writing Program Administration* 34 (1): 10–32.

Giddens, Anthony. 1984. *The Constitution of Society: Outline of the Theory of Structuration.* Berkeley: University of California Press.

Glassick, Charles E., Mary Taylor Huber, and Gene I. Maeroff. 1997. *Scholarship Assessed: Evaluation of the Professoriate.* San Francisco: Jossey-Bass.

Harris, Alene H., and Monica Farmer Cox. 2003. "Developing an Observation System to Capture Instructional Differences in Engineering Classrooms." *Journal of Engineering Education* 92 (4): 329–36.

Huckin, Thomas. 2010. "On Textual Silences, Large and Small." In *Traditions of Writing Research*, edited by Charles Bazerman, Robert Krut, Karen J. Lunsford, Susan McLeod, Suzie Null, Paul Rogers, and Amanda Stansell, 419–31. New York: Routledge.

Huot, Brian. 2002. *(Re)Articulating Writing Assessment for Teaching and Learning*. Logan: Utah State University Press.

Jackson, Brian. 2015. "Watching Other People Teach: The Challenge of Classroom Observations." In *Assessing the Teaching of Writing: Twenty-First Century Trends and Technologies*, edited by Amy E. Dayton, 45–60. Logan: Utah State University Press.

Miller, Carolyn R. 1984. "Genre as Social Action." *Quarterly Journal of Speech* 70 (2): 151–67.

Reid, E. Shelley. 2017. "On Learning to Teach: Letter to a New TA." *WPA: Writing Program Administration* 40 (2): 129–45.

Schryer, Catherine F., Lorelei Lingard, Marlee Spafford, and Kim Garwood. 2003. "Structure and Agency in Medical Case Presentations." In *Writing Selves/Writing Societies: Research from Activity Perspectives*, edited by Charles Bazerman and David R. Russell, 62–96. Fort Collins, CO: WAC Clearinghouse.

Tate, Gary, Amy Rupiper-Taggart, Kurt Schick, and Brooke Hessler, eds. 2014. *A Guide to Composition Pedagogies*. 2nd ed. New York: Oxford University Press.

Welch, Nancy. 1993. "Resisting the Faith: Conversion, Resistance, and the Training of Teachers." *College English* 55 (4): 387–401.

White, Edward M. 2005. "The Misuse of Writing Assessment for Political Purposes." *Journal of Writing Assessment* 2 (1): 21–35.

16

OUTCOMES STATEMENTS AS META-GENRES
The (Transformative) Role of Outcomes Statements in Program Revision

Logan Bearden

Within discourse communities, genres constitute and reinforce the values that inform participants' actions. Anthony Paré (2014) states that "consistency in understanding and responding to conventional rhetorical situations ensures communities that their discourse practices will produce the desired social actions" (A88). In academic programs, those desired social actions are the kinds of learning in which we ask students to engage, informed by genres like assignment sheets, rubrics, syllabi, and/or grading contracts. Too often, these programmatic documents go unnoticed, undertheorized, or underutilized. One useful way of conceptualizing the potentialities of these occluded genres is through Janet Giltrow's (2002) concept of meta-genres, representing the "atmospheres of wordings and activities" in and around genres (195). As Michael Carter (2007) notes, Giltrow's concept augments the notion of genre as a rhetorical action, as initially asserted by Carolyn Miller in 1984: If a genre is "a typified response to a recurrent rhetorical situation [that] directs our attention to certain patterns in the social action of language, patterns of recurring situations . . . a meta-genre, then, directs our attention to broader patterns of language as social action" (393). These textual atmospheres, these "broader patterns," according to Laurie McNeill (2005), prescribe "how writing should be produced, what it should look or sound like," thus typifying the genres they describe in the process (4). For academic programs, these meta-genres help to create the cultures that foster, reflect, and showcase the intellectual work that takes place therein.

Outcomes statements, for example, do just this. As a genre, outcomes statements outline the kinds of practices and behaviors in which students will have engaged by the end of the semester or curricular sequence.

https://doi.org/10.7330/9781646422920.c016

However, these programmatic documents often go unnoticed, an unfortunate occurrence, because they perform important work, operating at the intersection of institutional requirements and disciplinary knowledge. According to Kathleen Blake Yancey (2005), they delineate the content of curricula and programmatic values, detailing "what we want students to know, to understand, and to do at the conclusion of a course, a program, a major" (21). In so doing, Chris Gallagher (2012) writes that outcomes can provide "focus, stability, clarity, and transparency" for both instructors and students (44). Thus, by delineating and clarifying the curricular parameters of a program, outcomes also provide opportunities for reflection, assessment, and revision. Yancey contends that seeing outcomes in this way allows us to "think not of what's barely doable, but of what's visionary for our students—and for ourselves" (2005, 23). These reflective and visionary capabilities are why I argue that the meta-genre of the outcomes statement can be a vehicle through which meaningful and transformative curricular revisions can be made.

Seeing the outcomes statement as a meta-genre is to reclaim its utility, its possibilities, and its transformative potential. I argue that those of us who work within composition programs can harness this potential. To demonstrate this, in this chapter I examine how one composition program revised its outcomes and thus transformed its programmatic culture. Specifically, I pay attention to how the program's revised outcomes statement re-centers rhetoric as part of the curriculum and therefore makes space for multimodal composition, an approach that is altogether different from the more traditional focus on alphabetic writing skills alone. These revisions, made possible by and manifested in the meta-genre of the outcomes statement, had ripple-like effects on the culture of the program in terms of the assignments offered and the venues in which those assignments circulated, similar to the ecological shift Schoen, Nugent, Moody, and Ostergaard trace in their chapter in this collection. This chapter, like that one, offers an illustration of that transformative process.

OUTCOMES STATEMENT AS A TRANSFORMATIVE META-GENRE

In the last twenty years, writing studies has paid attention to the generative potential of outcomes statements for composition programs, evidenced by the Outcomes Statement endorsed and circulated by the Council of Writing Program Administrators (WPA OS). The WPA OS, originally released in 2000 and now in its third iteration, constitutes an attempt to "represent and regularize" what it is that we do in first-year composition (Council of Writing Program Administrators 2014). As a reflection of disciplinary best practices, Kimberly Harrison (2013) suggests the WPA OS "lends authority . . . to the individual WPAs and writing program faculty involved in program and curricular development" (32). The document thus has two interrelated functions: (1) it articulates shared, discipline-informed values for composition and composition programs and (2) it provides a prism through which local programs might reexamine their own program's values. In short, it constitutes an exigence for rhetorical action: to revisit, re-see, and revise local programs.

Anis Bawarshi and Mary Jo Reiff (2010) further elaborate on the potentials of outcomes, arguing that outcomes statements provide "the shared vocabulary for assigning, producing, reflecting on, and assessing student writing" (94). By viewing the WPA OS and outcomes statements in general as meta-genres, we see that these documents can create an environment that both fosters and constrains curricular content. That content is animated through other programmatic genres like assignment sheets, assessment materials, and teachers' guides, because those documents include, reference, and/or emerge in response to those outcomes. Additionally, that content is perceived by students, instructors, and administrators. This environment is inflected by outcomes, accumulating into a cultural perception of the curriculum, both inside the program and outside of it.

Viewing outcomes statements through the lens of (meta-)genre theory, however, requires that we conceive of outcomes as more than tools of assessment. Scholars in writing studies have taken issue with outcomes of late as a result of the general push toward reductive assessment practices. Gallagher (2012), for example, is particularly opposed to outcomes-based assessment because outcomes "represent the hoped-for conclusion of the educational experiences they reference: they are framed as termini of (rather than terminals in) those experiences" (44). By situating outcomes as endpoints or final results, the assessment might focus only on the outcomes themselves, ignoring what emerges from student work. Additionally, those studying the transfer of writing knowledge and advocating for threshold concepts in writing have called into question the effects outcomes have on the academy and on learning. For example, despite initially advocating for the pedagogical potential of outcomes statements, Yancey (2015) writes that "outcomes, which have offered both promise and help to writing programs, have become rigid and standardized" (xxviii). Heidi Estrem (2015) elaborates on this tendency toward rigidity, stating that "generalized, outcomes-based depictions of student learning about writing hold two immediate challenges: (1) they locate evidence of learning at the end of key experiences . . . and (2) they often depict writing as only a skill" (89–90). By locating writing knowledge at the *end* of the course, rather than within messy, troublesome learning processes, writing knowledge can be seen as something to be achieved rather than a sustained practice and area of academic study. Instead of prioritizing outcomes, these scholars argue that emphasizing threshold concepts would allow for a very different approach to learning. J. Blake Scott and Elizabeth Wardle (2015) write that "the nature of threshold concepts—not goals, not learning outcomes, but foundational assumptions that inform learning across time—makes them flexible tools for imagining a progression across student learning" (123). To summarize these two arguments: (1) outcomes (can) automatically assume ends whereas threshold concepts focus on the messy process of learning itself, on students being and becoming practitioners, and (2) outcomes can, if rigidly focused only on endpoints, lead to narrow assessment practices that obscure real learning. Either of these can lead to a reductive treatment of the program's content.

However, I contend if we view outcomes as a meta-genre, they point our attention to the cultures they create in which certain practices thrive. Giltrow (2002) writes that meta-genres "are widely recognized frames for the writing they direct, shared by readers and writers, collating their perceptions" (199). She uses these observations to think through the traces that meta-genres leave on institutions—the ways in which they influence the work that takes place therein. Bawarshi and Reiff (2010) agree, claiming that function of meta-genres generally "is to provide shared background knowledge and guidance in how to produce and negotiate genres within systems and sets of genres" (94). This theoretical approach to outcomes pays less attention to textual rules of form and more attention to interactions invited and made possible by these documents. In outlining a program's goals and articulating the values of a program (i.e., what we want students to learn), outcomes provide the motives that inform interactions between students and teachers, teachers and administrators. Outcomes, of course, do not completely control a curriculum, but they do possess a certain amount of influence over what takes place within programs. They validate certain assignments, and they inflect other genres (like teachers' guides, syllabi, or grading rubrics) and programmatic activities (like classroom activities, assessment practices, or professional development opportunities). Thus, it is important to view outcomes statements not just as documents or tools of assessment, but as meta-genres, forming and informed by motives, creating and constraining identities and actions, manifesting shared frames for those involved. This perspective has transformative potential, because if we understand that meta-genres influence and constrain the rhetorical work of textual genres and cultural contexts, then we can tap into that potential.

REVISION AND TRANSFORMATION IN A PROGRAM'S CULTURE

The transformative potential of the outcomes statement can be seen in the specific example I detail in this chapter, a writing program where the revision of their local outcomes statement served as a catalyst not only for curricular change but also for cultural transformation. I selected this particular program because of the ways in which it is very similar to many other writing programs around the country. The program is housed within an English Department at a comprehensive public university in the Midwest, best defined as a commuter campus, with a student population around 23,000. When I interviewed the former director of the First-Year Writing Program in May 2015, he described the university as "an opportunity-granting institution" that routinely "enrolls at-risk students who have not had an especially robust kind of high school track record." Additionally, the students who move through the program are both traditional and nontraditional students, unlike at other institutions where the population might be more homogenous. To deliver composition to this student population, the program employs a fairly diverse teaching faculty that includes full- and part-time lecturers, graduate teaching assistants (in linguistics, creative writing, rhetoric and composition, and literature), and tenure-track faculty (mostly trained in rhetoric and composition but some in literature). This demographic information demonstrates the ordinariness of the program: it does not possess inexhaustible financial resources or unique technological infra-structures to support transformative, innovative curriculum. However, this program managed to undergo curricular transformation through the act of revising the meta-genre of the outcomes statement.

According to Stephanie G. Hein and Carl D. Riegel (2011), curricu-lar transformation "extends beyond mere revision and involves radical changes in structure, content, outcomes, and at times, even culture" (3). What I recount in this chapter constitutes curricular transformation because the revisions to the outcomes statement made a cultural shift possible regarding the (perception of the) work that takes place in the program. The substantive revisions to the meta-genre included: crafting simpler, clarifying outcomes based on five guiding principles; centering those outcomes on rhetoric; and following the lead of the WPA OS by redefining the work of the program as *composition*, rather than exclusively (alphabetic) writing. These revised outcomes made it necessary to create new assignments, inviting students to compose new texts that are showcased in a semiannual event celebrating multimodal composition. In so doing, the program radically transformed the work of composition, beginning with the revision of its outcomes statement.

The program's outcomes were revised in the 2014–2015 academic year. According to the director, the previous outcomes were "felt to be kind of sprawling," because there were only "outcomes for the second course, and there were two sets of outcomes . . . composing process outcomes and learning process outcomes. And there were about thirteen bullets between the two lists." As programmatic documents, outcomes statements can and should help provide curricular clarity and stability, and as a meta-genre, such statements can typify the kinds of rhetorical interactions and experiences that take place within a program. Thus, this "sprawling" nature meant that the director felt that the program might have been perceived as correspondingly sprawling or inconsistent to faculty or to students, who are the ultimate recipients of the curriculum. Per conversations the director had with faculty, the complexities of the previous outcomes statement obfuscated more than clarified. To remedy this, the director said that he wanted "to devise a simple, elegant, no-nonsense set of principles" that would first cohere and then transform the program.

To begin this process, the director made use of the WPA OS. That document is itself an influential example of outcomes functioning as a meta-genre because of the discipline-specific ethos it lends to local programs that want to revise their curricula. In the contexts of this program, the director was particularly interested in invoking the WPA OS as a way to position the program within a network of other programs. The director stated that "by identifying our program with that organization what we've done is say that we're attuned to something bigger." That "something bigger" is the disciplinary authority and knowledge manifested by the document. This is a strategy that several other composition program directors have utilized, with the WPA OS providing exigence, model, and ethos for local curricular change. Kimberly Harrison (2013) argues that "the ethos of the WPA OS itself lends authority to the discipline of rhetoric and composition as it does to individual WPAs and writing program faculty involved in program and curricular development" (32). The WPA OS manifests curricular values that can be flexibly adapted to local contexts with the assistance of disciplinary authority. Debra Dew

(2013) describes this as the WPA OS functioning as a "generative heuristic," providing "inventional grounds" for curricular revisions (4). It does so by delineating vocabulary and concepts integral to the study of composition: rhetoric; process; conventions; and critical thinking. These concepts can formulate the guiding principles—the shared frames of reference that Giltrow mentions—for local programmatic outcomes, something that the director utilized by refocusing the program on rhetoric.

Additionally, the third iteration of the WPA OS, released in the summer of 2014, constituted a kairotic moment for the program to revise its outcomes statement. The revisions and additions to WPA OS 3.0 redefined the focus of the statement not on writing but on composition, in which student-writers "also attend to elements of design, incorporating images and graphical elements into texts intended for screens as well as printed pages" (Council of Writing Program Administrators 2014). The director of the program saw these changes as an opportunity to include multimodal composition within the program's curriculum. He stated that he used WPA OS 3.0 to make the argument that "we're tuned in to what good, exciting writing program directors are doing elsewhere . . . and if we are going to be better, we are going to have to do things differently here." Thus, the director made use of the WPA OS in three ways: invoking disciplinary authority to justify the revisions; drawing on the disciplinary expertise and vocabulary in the statement as inventional material for generating the frames guiding the new statement; and using the recent revisions to the WPA OS to justify making space for multimodality within the program's curriculum.

The old outcomes required that students write and use writing for learning. The five categories of composing process outcomes were: Critical Reading and Analysis; Research Practices and Processes; Writing Processes and Representation; Use of Evidence; and Syntax and Mechanics. The new statement is also based on five guiding principles, but the new principles are: Rhetoric, Process, Conventions, Multimodality, and Reflection, which then break down into ten total outcomes. Selecting these principles as the guiding structure for the meta-genre of the outcomes statement helped transform the culture of the program. Specifically, this statement re-focused the program on rhetoric, which I argue allowed for the inclusion of multimodality. By typifying the kinds of appropriate genres and texts supported by the program, the outcomes statement acted as a meta-genre that enabled the program to develop new kinds of assignments, craft new pedagogical connections, and use existing institutional structures to share this new work, thereby simultaneously shifting the culture of the program.

Rhetoric as a Programmatic Value

Read as a meta-genre, the collective outcomes of this program articulate values that define what constitutes "composition," and these values radiate out from the statement, influencing the culture and practices of the program. For example, rhetoric is one of the guiding principles of the program, as established in this new iteration of the outcomes statement. The director considers it to be the foundation of the curriculum. In the process of revising the statement, he and the associate director asked themselves what they wanted the program to value. As a result of that conversation, they decided they wanted "students to come through this space and encounter a rhetorical vocabulary . . . to approach their projects with a sense of how rhetorical considerations operate in projects." In short, the director and associate director saw value in rhetoric, because it provides a framework—a heuristic—for the composing process. Rhetoric was not absent from the previous version of this program's outcomes, but it certainly was not foregrounded. There was no category of outcomes dedicated to rhetoric in the previous statement. The closest was Writing Processes and Representation, which included four outcomes emphasizing the student's ability to:

1. recognize and follow genre conventions appropriate for a chosen type of writing;

2. choose and employ composing strategies appropriate for a given writing task;

3. make appropriate rhetorical choices so that his/her writing accomplishes its purposes and meets its audience's expectations; and

4. choose and employ strategies appropriate for adapting research material to different genres/audiences.

While the outcomes only invoked a variation of the term *rhetoric* once, they fall under the purview of rhetoric because they ask students to consider audience and purpose. However, the outcomes prescribed that the students' rhetorical choices would be made exclusively through the act of writing. The listed outcomes regularly utilize the term *writing* to describe the work that students complete; none of them acknowledge the possibility that students might engage in different kinds of composing, for example through visual or audio media. This prescribed medium has meta-generic implications. For example, Jody Shipka (2011) argues that when students are allowed to choose the modes, media, and materials that they believe will be the most rhetorically effective, they learn more than when those choices are made for them. In essence, in the culture and values outlined by the previous version of this outcomes statement, there was little to no room for other kinds of curricular content, other kinds of composing, and other kinds of learning. In fact, the old statement also had a category for Syntax and Mechanics, which further prescribed the kinds of writing that students produce. In this category, the outcomes read that students should be able to:

1. follow the conventions of usage, punctuation, and spelling in his/her writing according to the expectations for the chosen genre;

2. distinguish in his/her writing between intentional and unintentional divergences from the mechanics and sentence patterns of Standard Edited English; as well as

3. choose and employ in her/his writing strategies for editing unintentional divergences in mechanics and sentence patterns so as to meet the expectations of Standard Edited English.

These outcomes insisted that students engage in a certain kind of writing, creating a programmatic culture that privileged Standard Edited English and its role in the academy.

The revised outcomes—under the guiding principle of Rhetoric—fundamentally transform the values and therefore the culture in and around the program, shifting from alphabetic writing alone to rhetorical knowledge and performance. Those new outcomes read:

1. **Rhetorical Knowledge:** You will have practiced using language consciously and identifying rhetorical qualities in composing situations.

2. **Rhetorical Performance:** You will have enacted rhetoric by consciously constructive persuasive texts.

The first new outcome draws on the language of the WPA OS, but uses the outcome to cultivate a rhetorical awareness, a metalanguage that can be used to theorize the composing process. It helps to create a new programmatic environment in which students not only write, but also develop an awareness of what constitutes "rhetorical effectiveness" in different situations, moving away from prescribing the medium in which students work and expanding the forms of texts that students can create. The second outcome, in which students are enactors of rhetoric, builds on this, because the awareness cultivated in the first outcome gives students and composers a way to think through the process of crafting differently persuasive texts. These outcomes do not prescribe the kinds of texts that students make. They only require that the texts be persuasive, that students think consciously about the making of those texts. What is typified and sanctioned by these outcomes is not a kind of writing, but a way of thinking about meaning-making. This is more than just a textual revision. It is a cultural shift initiated by the revision of the meta-genre of the program's outcomes statement.

Multimodality as a Programmatic Value

In this cultural shift, this transition from a culture of "writing" to a culture of "composition," the program also included multimodal composition within the statement and the curriculum. There are now two outcomes specifically related to multimodality:

1. **Multimodal Transformation**: You will have adapted your writing to distinct rhetorical contexts, drawing attention to the way composition transforms across contexts and forms.
2. **Multimodal Design**: You will have composed using digital technologies, gaining an awareness of the possibilities and constraints of electronic environments.

The choice to include these outcomes is significant because, as a document, an outcomes statement can be shared both internally with instructors and students and externally on the program's website where it might function as the face of the program to administrators, prospective students, and interested researchers. The term *multimodal* is connected to contemporary scholarship specific to the discipline of writing studies. Using the term reinforces the new values added to the program with the inclusion of the rhetoric-based outcomes listed above. Those rhetoric-based outcomes invite multimodal composing by their capacious nature, expanding the definition of what it means to compose.

To reiterate, because outcomes are meta-genres, these textual revisions have cultural effects. When asked about the choice to include multimodality in the statement, the director of the program stated that he found the term "primes some focal kind of conspicuous attention to the affordances of composing, recognizing that composition manifests across media, creating space in the class for students to really get used to the different ways that materials can work together." This version of composition, presented in the program's outcomes, does not assume that students work with alphabetic writing only, which facilitated a cultural change in the perception of what students do and create in first-year writing. This is because collectively these outcomes sanction the parameters of the program, stipulating that it is appropriate and expected that students utilize digital technologies, theorize about the affordances of different composing materials, and consider the ways in which texts made from various materials can accomplish different tasks. This is a very different curriculum from the program crafted by the previous iteration of the outcomes, which did not reference the possibility of multimodal communication. Take, for example, the following two outcomes from the previous version of the program's outcomes statement:

1. **Critical Reading and Analysis**—The writer's ability to choose and employ reading strategies appropriate for a given writing task/assignment.

2. **Research Practices and Processes**—The writer's ability to choose and employ multiple modes of inquiry (field observation, interviews, etc.) relevant for a given writing task/assignment.

These outcomes require that the work students complete be writing, thereby constraining students' identities as composers. The meta-generic implication of these outcomes is a culture of alphabetic writing only. Such a culture does not align with contemporary scholarship in writing studies, which generally agrees that composition and literacy are and always have been multimodal (Kress 2009; Palmeri 2012; Prior 2005; Wysocki 2005).

The program's new outcomes no longer over-determine the media or materials in which students work. I contend that the wording of the revised statement achieves this shift. By changing the language in the outcomes, by choosing to include the term *multimodality*, the program changes the version of composition delivered to students. The textual combination of values—rhetoric and multimodality—within the meta-genre of the outcomes statement has cultural implications because, in this program, students do not just write; they compose. This changes the kinds of texts that students create, where students share those texts, and at the intersection of both, the perception of the program.

EVIDENCE OF META-GENERIC TRANSFORMATION

These meta-generic changes call into being new assignments and programmatic activities, demonstrating the ability of meta-genres like outcomes statements to cause significant cultural change. First, new assignments in the curriculum emerge from and reinforce the transformed definition of composition presented in the outcomes. For example, a common assignment in this program is a multimodal exploration of an academic article, a variation of the concept of a discourse community map. While the goal here is to help students cultivate a more nuanced awareness of academic sources and the ways in which those sources are utilized in writing, students achieve that awareness through the intersection of multimodality and rhetoric. The project asks students to visually map out important information they distill from interrogating the source. Typically, this information includes author background, sources influential to the text, key terms integral to the argument of the piece, and cultural events that may have taken place around the time of the article's composition. Students layer these on top of one another to make one cohesive visual. In making these choices—distilling only the parts most interesting to the student and choosing where and how to represent those parts on the maps—students use multimodal rhetoric to learn. The intersection of the visual and the alphabetic helps students accomplish several of the new outcomes from the revised outcomes statement simultaneously:

1. **Research Process**, in which students will "have practiced different research methods, which includes analyzing and using sources and developing primary research." In the mapping project, students cultivate an understanding of how academic articles can be resources for their writing by assembling their own multimodal versions of the key features of articles.

2. **Style Conventions**, in which students will "have developed awareness of conventions of academic research processes, including documentation systems and their purposes." Students broaden their awareness of these conventions by spending time reading the citations and references list, considering the texts that are influential to the source, and then representing those on their maps.

3. **Multimodal Transformation**, in which students will have drawn attention "to the way composition transforms across contexts and forms." Students build this understanding by using multiple modes (image, color, text, etc.) to demonstrate the ways in which they conceive of the source.

Thus, this is a very different assignment than the research paper, which according to Emily Isaacs (2018), "remains entrenched" in the curriculum of first-year composition programs (99). In a review of 105 state universities, she presents data that reveal "91.4 percent of courses included research instruction" and that the "research paper is alive and well at 80.2 percent" of institutions surveyed (99). In most programs, Isaacs illustrates, students learn research processes and skills by writing an academic research paper. In this program however, because the outcomes statement changes what counts as composition, students learn research skills and practices through multimodal rhetoric. New assignments, like this one, emerge from and respond to the new outcomes and simultaneously help students achieve the outcomes listed above and make an implicit argument about the values shared by the program.

Second, in addition to new assignments, new programmatic practices arise from and reinforce the cultural shift initiated by the outcomes statement, which is evident in the semiannual event that showcases the work of students within the program every year. For the curriculum transformed and the culture made possible by the revisions to the outcomes, the event provides a space to share multimodal texts internally and externally, thereby celebrating the role that multimodality plays within the program. The director described the showcase as "students' attempts to give different circulatory life to the work they've done." That circulation reminds students that the work they complete within the program "doesn't just land on the teacher's desk at the end of the semester." At the event, students present a multimodal adaptation of an inquiry-based research project to a public audience. For their presentations, students compose within a variety of genres, including posters, flyers, pamphlets, interactive games, and YouTube clips—whatever the students believe will be most rhetorically effective for the audience. Attendees are encouraged to interact with students, asking them questions about their research and the material choices they made in their composing processes. In this way, like the mapping project described above, the event invokes and animates the meta-genre of the outcomes statement in several different ways:

- **Rhetorical Knowledge**, in which students practice "using language consciously, identifying rhetoric qualities in composing situations." The event requires that students cultivate and utilize their knowledge of what makes a text rhetorically effective for different audiences.
- **Reflective Interaction**, in which students share their work with their "instructor, peers, and/or the university community and accounted for the impact of such interaction on composition." Here, students are actively sharing their work with others, and after the event, students in most sections compose a reflective piece about the experience and what it taught them about the composing process.
- **Multimodal Transformation**, in which students adapt their source work and findings to different situations and audiences. In circulating a multimodal version of a research project, students are able to consider how the act of composition changes across context and forms.

The resulting programmatic culture is one that encourages and celebrates multimodal rhetoric for audiences in and out of the program. For instance, various members of the university community circulate through the event—in addition to other students, the celebration has been attended in past years by the dean of the College of Arts and Sciences, the provost, and the president of the university. To these audiences, the event presents a specific vision of what counts as composition, a version that counters preconceived notions about first-year writing as only focusing on grammar, style, or argumentation.

With revised outcomes that now focus on rhetoric and include multimodal composition, this program has undergone a cultural shift. Whereas the previous outcomes emphasized alphabetic writing and the textual features of documents, like formatting structures or appropriate style, the new outcomes value composition as a multimodal, rhetorical practice. Through this event, that shift is evident to those within the program (student and teaching faculty) and those outside (faculty in other programs, deans, provosts), influencing and correcting perceptions about what takes place in the program. All of this was achieved through the transformative potential of seeing and utilizing the outcomes statement as a meta-genre.

CONCLUSION

The program detailed in this chapter used the meta-genre of the outcomes statement to shift the work of the program away from alphabetic writing and toward multimodal composition. It accomplished this by refocusing the statement on rhetoric, invoking the term, and using it consistently. This made space to include multimodal composition within the statement as well, because rhetoric does not prescribe the medium of alphabetic writing like the program's old outcomes did. The new multimodal outcomes changed the kinds of assignments that students complete, changed the venues in which students shared their work, and therefore created a culture that supports and encourages composition, not just writing. The semiannual celebration of student composing, for example, gives multimodal rhetoric a visible presence and home within the curriculum. And that event, by being public and inviting multiple kinds of stakeholders, helps to shift the perception of composition held by other members of the university.

The history of this textual-rhetorical transformation contains useful takeaways for those who study genre in the design and delivery of academic programs. If genres do the rhetorical work of sanctioning ways of (inter)acting and writing within discourse communities, then meta-genres inflect and inform the cultures that make that work possible, creating atmospheres in which certain actions and ways of being can thrive. Perceiving outcomes as a meta-genre points our attention to the role that such documents play in affecting and influencing the curricula and cultures of academic programs. From this perspective, they are not merely attempts toward standardization; they are, like Hannah and

Saidy argue in their chapter in this collection, on policy statements that facilitate and implement a programmatic or departmental vision, texts that can do the important work of transforming programs and shifting cultural perceptions about those programs.

Academic programs must continually reconcile updates to disciplinary knowledge, changes in student population, advances to composing technologies, differing demographics within the teaching faculty, and the ebb and flow of budgets. Viewing outcomes statements as a meta-genre is a place to start that process because they are a textual location in which we articulate our values and expectations. Others can and should take up this work, using their local outcomes statement to (re)examine and (re)define what it is that they care for in their programs. This can be an exercise in collaborative programmatic reflection. If a program already has an outcomes statement, the individuals who work therein can use that statement to initiate a conversation about values and about the ways in which those local values align with contemporary trends and best practices in disciplinary scholarship. If the program does not already have an outcomes statement, administration and teaching faculty could work together to consider and then detail what the values of the program are. In either situation, the meta-genre of the outcomes statement functions as an exigence and a starting point for curricular transformations through the creation and/or revision of the document. These textual revisions become meta-generic shifts, as those values and expectations radiate out into other documents (teachers' guides, syllabi, mission statements) and into programmatic practices (assessment, teaching evaluations, program events). The genre of the outcomes statement acts as a catalyst for the cultural (re)making of the curriculum and the way in which that curriculum is perceived. By harnessing the genre's transformative potential, those who work in academic programs can, as Yancey (2005) suggested, continue to do the work of articulating what is possible and visionary for our students and for ourselves.

REFERENCES

Bawarshi, Anis, and Mary Jo Reiff. 2010. *Genre: An Introduction to History, Theory, Research, and Pedagogy.* West Lafayette, IN: Parlor Press.

Carter, Michael. 2007. "Ways of Knowing, Doing, and Writing in the Disciplines." *College Composition and Communication* 58 (3): 385–418.

Council of Writing Program Administrators. 2014. "WPA Outcomes Statement for First-Year Composition (3.0)." July 17, 2014. http://wpacouncil.org/positions/outcomes.html.

Dew, Debra Frank. 2013. "CWPA Outcomes Statement as Heuristic for Inventing Writing-about-Writing Curricula." In *The WPA Outcomes Statement: A Decade Later,* edited by Nicholas N. Behm, Gregory R. Glau, Deborah H. Holdstein, Duane Roen, and Edward M. White, 3–17. Anderson, SC: Parlor Press.

Estrem, Heidi. 2015. "Threshold Concepts and Student Learning Outcomes." In *Naming What We Know: Threshold Concepts of Writing Studies*, edited by Linda Adler-Kassner and Elizabeth Wardle, 89–104. Logan: Utah State University Press.

Gallagher, Chris W. 2012. "The Trouble with Outcomes: Pragmatic Inquiry and Educational Aims." *College English* 75 (1): 42–60.

Giltrow, Janet. 2002. "Meta-Genre." In *The Rhetoric and Ideology of Genre: Strategies for Stability and Change*, edited by Richard M. Coe, Lorelei Lingard, and Tatiana Teslenko, 187–205. Cresskill, NJ: Hampton Press.

Harrison, Kimberly. 2013. "Building a Writing Program with WPA Outcomes: Authority, Ethos, and Professional Identity." In *The WPA Outcomes Statement: A Decade Later*, edited by Nicholas N. Behm, Gregory R. Glau, Deborah H. Holdstein, Duane Roen, and Edward M. White, 32–44. Anderson, SC: Parlor Press.

Hein, Stephanie G., and Carl D. Riegel. 2011. "A Systematic Model for Program Evaluation and Curricular Transformation: A Tale from the Trenches." *International CHRIE Conference-Refereed Track* 11. https://scholarworks.umass.edu/refereed/ICHRIE_2011/Friday/11.

Isaacs, Emily. 2018. *Writing at the State U: Instruction and Administration at 106 Comprehensive Universities*. Logan: Utah State University Press.

Kress, Gunther. 2009. *Multimodality: A Social Semiotic Approach to Contemporary Communication*. New York: Routledge.

McNeill, Laurie. 2005. "Genre under Construction: The Diary on the Internet." *Language@Internet* 2. http://www.languageatinternet.org/articles/2005/120.

Palmeri, Jason. 2012. *Remixing Composition: A History of Multimodal Writing Pedagogy*. Carbondale: Southern Illinois University Press.

Paré, Anthony. 2014. "Rhetorical Genre Theory and Academic Literacy." *Journal of Academic Language and Learning* 8 (1): A83–94.

Prior, Paul. 2005. "Moving Multimodality beyond the Binaries: A Response to Gunther Kress' 'Gains and Losses.'" *Computers and Composition* 22 (1): 23–30.

Scott, J. Blake, and Elizabeth Wardle. 2015. "Using Threshold Concepts to Inform Writing and Rhetoric Undergraduate Majors: The UCF Experiment." In *Naming What We Know: Threshold Concepts of Writing Studies*, edited by Linda Adler-Kassner and Elizabeth Wardle, 122–39. Logan: Utah State University Press.

Shipka, Jody. 2011. *Toward a Composition Made Whole*. Pittsburgh, PA: University of Pittsburgh Press.

Wysocki, Anne Frances. 2005. "awaywithwords: On the Possibilities in Unavailable Designs." *Computers and Composition* 22 (1): 55–62.

Yancey, Kathleen Blake. 2005. "Bowling Together: Developing, Distributing, and Using the WPA Outcomes Statement—and Making Cultural Change." In *The Outcomes Book: Debate and Consensus after the WPA Outcomes Statement*, edited by Susanmarie Harrington, Keith Rhodes, Ruth Overman Fischer, and Rita Malenczyk, 211–21. Logan: Utah State University Press.

Yancey, Kathleen Blake. 2015. "Coming to Terms: Composition/Rhetoric, Threshold Concepts, and a Disciplinary Core." In *Naming What We Know: Threshold Concepts of Writing Studies*, edited by Linda Adler-Kassner and Elizabeth Wardle, xvii–xxi. Logan: Utah State University Press.

INDEX

ABOUT THE AUTHORS

Stephen E. Neaderhiser is an assistant professor of English at Kent State University at Stark, where he coordinates the Professional Writing Studies program and teaches courses in composition, digital literacies, and popular culture. His research interests include the disciplinary historiography of composition studies, the occlusion of pedagogical genres, and the metaphoric language associated with teaching. His work has appeared in *Pedagogy*, *Composition Forum*, *Syllabus*, and *The Writing Center Journal*.

Michael Albright is an associate professor of English at Southwest Minnesota State University. He is involved in the Concurrent Enrollment program and supports multiple sections of composition and literature offered by high school partners. His research interests include literary representations of teachers and teaching, matters of professionalization, and issues in concurrent enrollment.

Lora Arduser is an associate professor of English at the University of Cincinnati, where she currently directs the Technical and Professional Writing program. Her primary research area is in the rhetoric of health and medicine. She is also co-editor of *Programmatic Perspectives* and the reviews editor for the journal *Rhetoric of Health and Medicine*.

Lesley Erin Bartlett is an assistant professor of English at Iowa State University, where she is the interim director of ISUComm Foundation Courses. Her scholarship focuses on composition theories and pedagogies, feminist rhetorics, and rhetorical performance. Her work has appeared in *English Leadership Quarterly*, *Feminist Teacher*, *Journal of the Assembly for Expanded Perspectives on Learning*, *Journal of Interactive Technology and Pedagogy*, and *Teaching/Writing*. She is co-editor of *Diverse Approaches to Teaching, Learning, and Writing Across the Curriculum: IWAC at 25* (2020).

Logan Bearden is an associate professor of written communication at Nova Southeastern University. His work focuses on multimodal composition, writing program administration, and the role of programmatic documents in curricular transformation. He has published in *WPA*, *JCLL*, and various edited collections. His book, *Making Progress: Programmatic and Administrative Strategies for Multimodal Curricular Transformation*, is forthcoming from USUP.

Lindsay Clark is an assistant professor of business administration at Sam Houston State University, where she teaches undergraduate and graduate business communication courses and co-chairs the University Writing in the Disciplines Committee, working with faculty to integrate and assess writing assignments in discipline-based courses. Her research includes visual and multimodal communication, genre theory and pedagogy, and teaching writing in the disciplines.

Dana Comi is an assistant professor of professional writing at Auburn University at Montgomery, where she teaches professional and technical communication. Her research interests include rhetorical genre studies, infrastructure studies, and public rhetorics. Her work has also appeared in *Present Tense*.

Zack K. De Piero is an assistant professor of English at Northampton Community College, where he teaches first-year writing, writing for the social sciences, and writing for the web. His research explores reading and writing pedagogies, and his work has been published in *Journal of College Literacy and Learning* and *Higher Education Research and Development.*

Matt Dowell is an assistant professor of English at Towson University, where he serves as director of First-Year Writing. His research interests include response to student writing and writing program administration as institutional space and place, including intersections with access and disability. He is the co-author of a forthcoming book chapter examining access and (in)access at academic conferences.

Amy Ferdinandt Stolley is an associate professor of writing and director of First-Year Writing at Grand Valley State University, where she teaches classes in first-year writing, style, and genre theory. Her scholarship focuses on the affective nature of writing program administration work and women's rhetorical history. She is the co-author of *GenAdmin: Theorizing WPA Identities in the Twenty-First Century* (2011), and her work has appeared in *WPA: Writing Program Administration, Peitho,* and numerous edited collections.

Mark A. Hannah is an associate professor of English at Arizona State University. His work examines intersections of law, rhetoric, and expertise in multidisciplinary problem-solving contexts, and his research has appeared in a range of edited collections and journals, including *College Composition and Communication, Nevada Law Journal, IEEE: Transactions on Professional Communication, Technical Communication, Technical Communication Quarterly, Journal of Technical Writing and Communication, Communication Design Quarterly,* and *Nature.*

Megan Knight is an associate professor of instruction in the Department of Rhetoric at University of Iowa, where, in addition to teaching undergraduate rhetoric, she offers graduate courses in pedagogy and scholarly writing, helps administer the Honors Writing Fellows peer writing tutor initiative, and regularly serves as leader in the department's teacher preparation program for graduate instructors. Her research interests include rhetoric and composition, andragogy, gender studies, and creative nonfiction.

Laura R. Micciche is a professor of English and director of the rhetoric and composition graduate program at University of Cincinnati. Her research focuses on composing processes, feminist pedagogies, and affect. Recent books include *Failure Pedagogies: Learning and Unlearning What It Means to Fail* (2020), co-edited with Allison D. Carr, and *Acknowledging Writing Partners* (2017). For six years, she served as editor of *Composition Studies,* an independent journal on rhetoric and composition.

Cindy Mooty is a special lecturer in the Department of Writing and Rhetoric at Oakland University, where she teaches courses in composition and business writing. Her research interests include genre studies, synchronous versus asynchronous pedagogy, and service-learning teaching practices.

Dustin Morris is an assistant professor of English at Wingate University. He teaches first-year writing and advanced writing courses, and his research interests include composition pedagogy, multimodal practices, and genre studies.

Kate Navickas is the director of the Cornell Writing Centers and teaches in the Knight Institute for Writing in the Disciplines at Cornell University. In addition to her research on feminist pedagogy and writing assignments, she is co-editor (with Courtney Adams Wooten, Jacob Babb, and Kristi Murray Costello) and contributor for *The Things We Carry:*

Strategies for Recognizing and Negotiating Emotional Labor in Writing Program Administration (2020). Her work has been published in *Pedagogy, Composition Forum,* and several edited collections.

Kate Nesbit is an assistant professor of English at Central College, where she teaches courses in British and global anglophone literature as well as writing and composition. Her researched focuses on the politics of listening and the voice, and her scholarship has appeared in *ELH, Victorian Poetry, European Romantic Review, Studies in the Novel,* and *Iowa Journal of Cultural Studies.*

Jim Nugent is a professor of writing and rhetoric at Oakland University. His research interests include text technologies, the pedagogy of code, and professional writing. He is editor of the journal *WPA: Writing Program Administration,* and his recent article " 'Other Stories to Tell': Scholarly Journal Editors as Archivists" (with Lori Ostergaard) appears in *College English.*

Lori Ostergaard is a professor and the former chair of the Department of Writing and Rhetoric, former director of First-Year Writing, and the current co-editor of *WPA: Writing Program Administration.* She has also co-edited the collections *Transforming English Studies: New Voices in an Emerging Genre* (2009), *Writing Majors: Eighteen Program Profiles* (2015), and *In the Archives of Composition: Writing and Rhetoric at High Schools and Normal Schools* (2015).

Cynthia Pengilly is an assistant professor of English at Central Washington University on ancestral Yakama Nation land. She serves as co-director of the Technical Writing Program and teaches courses in technical and professional communication, cultural rhetorics, medical/health rhetoric, and new media. Her research explores digital pedagogy, pedagogical genres, and embodied identities of multiply marginalized communities. She has several forthcoming articles and book chapters.

Jessica Rivera-Mueller is an assistant professor of English at Utah State University, where she directs the English concurrent enrollment program and teaches courses in English education and composition theory. Her scholarship focuses on facilitating teacher development for middle school, high school, and college English teachers. Her work has appeared in *Teaching/Writing: The Journal of Writing Teacher Education* and *Journal on Empowering Teaching Excellence.*

Christina Saidy is an associate professor of English at Arizona State University. Her research focuses on writing and writing transitions with secondary students, teachers in professional development groups, and students entering college. Her work has appeared in journals such as *English Journal, CCC, WPA, Teaching/Writing,* and *Teaching English in the Two-Year College.*

Megan Schoen is an associate professor in the Department of Writing and Rhetoric at Oakland University, where she serves as director of First-Year Writing. Her research interests include composition studies, writing program administration, writing across the curriculum, rhetorical theory, and comparative rhetorics. She has published in *Rhetoric Review, WPA, The WAC Journal,* and *Constellations.* She is a co-founder and co-editor of *Present Tense: A Journal of Rhetoric in Society.*

Virginia M. Schwarz is an assistant professor of English and affiliate faculty in the Metro College Success program at San Francisco State University. She teaches first-year writing along with graduate courses in composition, assessment, and education. Her research interests include classroom (un)grading practices, anti-oppressive approaches to teaching and learning, graduate student education, and community colleges. Her work has appeared in *CCC*, *Composition Studies*, and *Xchanges*.

Christopher Toth is a professor of writing at Grand Valley State University, where he serves as department chair. He teaches courses in business communication, professional writing, and document design. His research interests revolve around the intersections of visual rhetoric and professional communication.